Judicial Process in America

Judicial Process in America

FOURTH EDITION

Robert A. Carp, *University of Houston*

Ronald Stidham, *Appalachian State University*

 A Division of Congressional Quarterly Inc.

PRESS Washington, D.C.

Copyright © 1998 Congressional Quarterly Inc.
1414 22nd Street, N.W., Washington, D.C. 20037

Printed in the United States of America.

Third Printing.

Grateful acknowledgment is made to the following publishers for granting permission to reprint from copyrighted material: Princeton University Press, from J. Woodford Howard, Jr., *Courts of Appeals in the Federal Judicial System: A Study of the Second, Fifth, and District of Columbia Circuits*, copyright © 1981; University of Chicago Press, from Walter F. Murphy, *Elements of Judicial Strategy*, copyright © 1964; University of Tennessee Press, from Robert A. Carp and C.K. Rowland, *Policymaking and Politics in the Federal District Courts*, copyright © 1983.

Photo credits: 1 *Houston Chronicle*; 22 Scott J. Ferrell, Congressional Quarterly; 63, 132, 273 Reuters; 78 JoAnn Raker; 104 AP/Wide World Photos; 183 Providence Hospital; 209 *The Informer* (Houston, Texas); 260, 349 R. Michael Jenkins, Congressional Quarterly; 317, 377 Ken Heinen.

Cover art: Photodisc, Inc., copyright © 1998
Cover design: Debra Naylor
Text design: Kachergis Book Design, Pittsboro, North Carolina

LIBRARY OF CONGRESS CATALOGING-IN-PUBLICATION DATA

Carp, Robert A.
   Judicial process in America / Robert A. Carp, Ronald Stidham. —
4th ed.
      p.   cm.
   Includes bibliographical references and index.
      ISBN 1-56802-394-4
      1. Courts—United States.   2. Judges—United States.   3. Judicial process—
United States.   I. Stidham, Ronald, 1940–   .   II. Title.
   KF8700.C37   1998
   347.73'1—DC21   98–5039

To the memory of my longtime and much-cherished friends,
Arthur and Margaret Brunell

R.A.C.

To my sister Judy, with much love and affection

R.S.

Contents

Tables and Figures

Preface

In the time since the third edition of *Judicial Process in America* appeared in print, many changes have taken place in our federal and state judicial systems. The presence of judges appointed by President Bill Clinton is being felt at all tiers of the national-level judicial hierarchy. By the end of 1998 about a third of all U.S. trial and appellate judges will bear the Clinton label, and his appointees on the Supreme Court, Justices Ruth Bader Ginsburg and Stephen Gerald Breyer, now have well-established records of helping nudge the High Court in a more moderate ideological direction. Likewise, the president has made significant progress toward making his nominees "look like America"—that is, mirror its diversity of race and gender. Preliminary studies indicate that this more varied judiciary is, in fact, voting differently on some types of cases than had the virtually all-male, all-white judiciary of the past.

At the state level, the tort reform movement is in full throttle as more and more legislatures move to limit the size and nature of awards that civil litigants may win. Yet this is occurring at a time when civil damage awards against some wrongdoers are at all-time highs; the unprecedented state court rulings against the tobacco companies are good examples. Finally, evidence continues to mount that state courts are playing ever-increasing policy-making roles as more and more state programs and policies come under the scrutiny of state jurists.

One important change between this fourth and previous editions is that in this version we have separate chapters for our discussions of the history, organization, and day-to-day operations of the federal and state courts. This, we believe, will help students differentiate and keep clear the two judicial hierarchies. Also in this edition we have added new or expanded discussions of topics that have come under increasing attention either in the public eye or in scholarly research. For example, there is either new or more extensive coverage of the work of juvenile courts, the salaries of judicial professionals, tort law reform, the internal dynamics of jury deliberations, limits on peremptory challenges for race and gender, and philosophies underlying the sentencing of convicted criminals. As with all editions of this book, we have taken care to prepare a text that is highly readable for both academic and general audiences. The primary emphasis is on the federal courts, but we offer full coverage of state judicial systems, the role of the lawyer in American society, the nature of crime, and public policy concerns that color the entire judicial fabric. The book is designed as a primary text for courses in judicial process and behavior; it is also useful as a supplement in political science classes in constitutional law, American government, and law and society. Likewise it may serve as interesting reading in law-related courses in sociology, history, psychology, and criminology.

We have taken care to use minimal jargon and theoretical vocabulary of political science and the law without being condescending to the student. We believe it is possible to provide a keen and fundamental understanding of our court systems and their impacts on our daily lives without assuming that all readers are budding political scientists or lawyers. At times, of course, it is necessary and useful to employ technical terms and evoke theoretical concepts; still, we address the basic questions on a level that is meaningful to an educated layperson. For students who may desire more specialized explanations or who wish to explore more deeply some of the issues we discuss, the notes and suggested readings contain ample resources.

We have also tried to avoid stressing any one theoretical framework for the study of courts and legal questions, such as a systems model approach or a judicial realist perspective. Instructors partial to the tenets of modern behavioralism will find much here to gladden their hearts, but we have also tried to include some of the insights that more traditional scholarship has provided over the years. The book reflects the contributions not only of political scientists and legal scholars but also of historians, psychologists, court administrators, and journalists.

Throughout the text we are constantly mindful of the interrelation between the courts and public policy. We have worked from the premise that significant portions of our lives—as individuals and as a nation—are affected by what our federal and state judges choose to do and what they refrain from doing. We reject the common assumption that only liberals make public policy whereas conservatives practice restraint; rather, we believe that to some degree all judges engage in the inevitable activity of making policy. The question, as we see it, is not whether American judges make policy but, rather, which directions their policy decisions take. In the chapters that follow we will explain why this has come to be, how it happens, and what the consequences are for the United States today.

In Chapter 1 we set the theoretical stage. We note Americans' great respect for the law, but we also document their traditional willingness to violate the law when it is morally, economically, or politically expedient to do so. We also examine sources of law in the United States and several of the major philosophies concerning the role and function of law.

In Chapters 2 and 3 we examine respectively the organizational structure and workloads of the federal and state judicial systems from an historical perspective. As we shall see, the federal and state judiciaries are the products of two centuries of evolution, trial and error, and a pinch of serendipity. The distinction between routine norm enforcement and policy making by judges is first addressed in these two chapters.

In Chapter 4 we outline the jurisdiction of the several levels of U.S. courts and discuss the political and nonjusticiable realms of American life into which judges in principle are not supposed to enter. We believe that a full understanding of how judges affect citizens' lives also requires us to outline those many substantive areas into which federal and state jurists may not roam.

Chapter 5 is about the role of lawyers in American society—their training, values, and attitudes, and the public-policy goals of their professional associations. In this chapter we also provide data for the first time on the salaries of judicial professionals, including law clerks, district attorneys, defense attorneys, and so on. Finally, we explore the importance of judicial lobbying and the impact of interest groups on the judicial process.

In Chapter 6 we focus on the criminal court process at both the federal and state levels. We begin with a discussion of the nature and substance of crime; we then examine, step by step, the key stages of the criminal court process. At the end of the chapter we analyze sentencing options available to the judge, including the new forms of punishment called "alternative sentences."

In Chapter 7 we examine the civil court process. We begin with an analysis of the various types of civil cases and the options available to the complainant and the respondent. We then proceed through the pretrial hearing and jury selection. After a look at the trial and judgment we turn to the alternative methods available to resolve civil disputes, such as mediation and arbitration.

In Chapter 8, which focuses on the federal courts, we take a close look at the men and women who wear the black robe in the United States. What are their background characteristics and qualifications for office? How are they chosen? What are their values, and how do these values manifest themselves in their behavior as judges and justices? In a key section on the federal courts, we find a discernible policy link among the values of a majority of the voters in a presidential election, the values of the appointing president, and the subsequent policy content of decisions made by judges nominated by the chief executive.

In Chapter 9 we focus on state judicial tribunals and ask questions similar to those above about methods of choosing judges, the backgrounds of these jurists, and the public-policy consequences of selecting judges by one method or another—for example, electing judges versus having them appointed by the state governor.

Chapter 10 is the first of two on judicial decision making. Here we outline those aspects of the decision-making process that are common to all judges, in the context of the "legal subculture" (the traditional legal reasoning model for explaining judges' decisions) and the "democratic subculture" (a number of extralegal factors that appear to be associated with judges' policy decisions).

In Chapter 11 we examine the special case of decision making in collegial appellate courts. We explore the assumptions and contributions of small group theory, attitude and bloc analysis, and fact pattern approaches to understanding the behavior of multijudge tribunals.

In Chapter 12 we explore the policy impact of decisions made by federal and state courts and analyze the process by which judicial rulings are implemented—and why some are not implemented.

The last chapter has two general goals: to outline the primary factors that impel judges to engage in policy making, and to suggest the variables that determine the ideological direction of such policy making.

Many people contributed to the writing of this book, and to all of them we offer sincere thanks. At CQ Press, we would like to thank Brenda Carter, Tracy Villano, and Talia Greenberg. Several anonymous adopters of the previous edition offered helpful suggestions for updating and improving the text and we appreciate their assistance. For any errors that remain, we assume responsibility.

Robert A. Carp expresses his gratitude to three of his research assistants: John Dorris, Alex Garcia, and Mark McAdoo. Each was enormously helpful in coding the decisions of the federal district judges, which served as the basis for Figure 8-1 and Table 8-3. He is particularly indebted to McAdoo for his sophisticated suggestions for upgrading the procedures by which data from newly coded cases might be more simply incorporated into a larger database.

Ronald Stidham would like to express a debt of gratitude to his colleagues in the Political Science/Criminal Justice Department at Appalachian State University. Their friendship and support made the process of writing this new edition much easier. He also expresses thanks to his graduate research assistants, Paul Boyles and Amy Neese, for their help in finding information and checking sources in the library.

Judicial Process in America

CHAPTER 1

Foundations of Law in the United States

Dr. Stanislaw Burzynski's clash with the Food and Drug Administration illustrates how legal ambiguities can ignite fierce tension between those who enforce the law strictly and those who believe that they are being unfairly singled out for special legal prosecution.

DR. STANISLAW BURZYNSKI IS A licensed physician, but he is also a strong believer in what is termed "alternative medicine," that is, medical treatments lacking the approval of the Food and Drug Administration and the mainstream medical community. For the past fourteen years this Polish-born doctor has been waging a fierce battle against federal authorities who have sought to make a criminal case against him. Burzynski developed an experimental cancer treatment involving antineoplastons, synthesized versions of human peptides found in blood and urine. Since the late 1970s he is estimated to have prescribed the drug without government approval to around 2,500 people. Some, though not all, of his patients experienced remissions of their cancers, and for them Burzynski became a hero; but to the Food and Drug Administration, and eventually to federal prosecutors, he became a menace, a threat to the government's authority to determine what medications and treatments are safe for the American people.

The battle began in 1983 when the FDA sought to enjoin Dr. Burzynski from using his cancer drugs at all. Federal district judge Gabrielle McDonald ruled against the regulators. Exercising the great discretion which trial judges have, she ruled that the doctor could continue with his treatments—but only in his home state of Texas. If the drugs don't cross state lines, she ruled, the FDA could not intervene. But that was not the end of the matter. The FDA contended that the doctor had many out-of-state patients, and these individuals traveled to Houston for their initial treatment and then carried the drug across state lines for their personal long-term use. The FDA pressed the matter hard. After three unsuccessful grand jury investigations a fourth jury finally indicted Dr. Burzynski on forty counts of distributing an unapproved drug in interstate commerce, thirty-four counts of mail fraud, and one count of contempt for allegedly violating the 1983 court ruling. The trial jury could not agree on a verdict, and in March of 1997 a mistrial was declared. Sensing a lost cause, the U.S. attorneys decided to drop the first seventy-four charges against Burzynski, but as a sort of afterthought they re-tried him on the contempt of court charge. Prosecutors claimed that Burzynski knew that his patients would carry the drug across state lines; Burzynski countered that he was technically innocent because he did not personally "ship" the drug to other states.

The trial jury deliberated only three hours before acquitting Dr. Burzynski. Patients and their families who packed the courtroom cheered and wept when the jury verdict was read. Burzynski was joyful, and declared: "It's the end of 14 years of war. It's the beginning of the end of the war on cancer." But a spokesman from the National Council Against Health Fraud wasn't so sure, saying that the jury's decision "will confer legitimacy on Burzynski, embolden quacks into believing they can flout federal drug laws and divert patients from effective care."[1]

This factual account reveals much about the United States and the rule of law, and it suggests themes that we shall articulate not only in this chapter but throughout much of the rest of the text: How should the individual respond when law and morality are not seen as synonymous? How much discretion do district attorneys have in determining whether to prosecute the violators of a given law, and how do they exercise this discretion? What options are available to judges and juries in determining what evidence to consider at a trial? What legal and purely personal factors affect their final verdict and, if appropriate, the punishment assessed?

We begin our discussion of the "Foundations of Law in the United States" with a look at the law itself. This is appropriate because without law there would be no courts and no judges; there would be no political or judicial system through which disputes could be settled and decisions rendered. In this chapter we examine the sources of law in the United States, that is, the institutions and traditions that establish the rules of the legal game. We discuss the particular types of law that are used and define some of the basic legal terms. Likewise we shall explore the functions of law for society—what it enables us to avoid and accomplish as individuals and as a people that would be impossible without the existence of some commonly accepted rules. Finally we examine America's ambivalent tradition vis-à-vis the law, that is, how a nation founded on an *illegal* revolution and nurtured with a healthy tradition of civil disobedience can pride itself on being a land where respect for the law is ideally taught at every mother's knee. We also take note of the degree to which American society has become highly litigious and why this is significant for the study of the American judicial system.

Definition of Law

Before we address the sources of American law and discuss its variations and functions, we offer a working definition of the concept. A useful definition postulates that "law is a social norm the infraction of which is sanctioned in threat or in fact by the application of physical force by a party possessing the socially recognized privilege of so acting."[2] This definition suggests that law is comprised of three basic elements—force, official authority, and regularity—the combination of which differentiates law from mere custom or morals in society.

In an ideal society force would never have to be exercised; however, in the imperfect world the threat of its use is a foundation of any law-abiding society. Although substitutes for physical force may be used, such as confiscation of property or imposition of fines, the potential of physical punishment must nevertheless remain to deter a noncompliant lawbreaker. The right to apply this force constitutes the official element of our definition of law. The party that exercises this right of physical coercion represents a valid legal authority. Finally, the term regularity as used in the legal sense can be likened to its use by scientists. While the term does not reflect absolute certainty, it does suggest uniformity and consistency. The law calls for a degree of predictability, of regularity, in the way individuals are expected to behave or to be treated by the state. In our society this emphasis on regularity is manifested by adherence to prior court decisions and precedents (the common law doctrine of *stare decisis*) and also by the mandate of the Fourteenth Amendment to the U.S. Constitution that forbids the state to "deny to any person within its jurisdiction the *equal protection* of the law." [Emphasis added.]

Sources of Law in the United States

Where does law come from in the United States? At first the question seems a bit simpleminded. A typical response might be: "We get it from legislatures; that's what Congress and the state legislatures do." This answer is not wrong, but it is far from adequate—in fact, law comes from a large variety of sources in this country.

Constitutions

The U.S. Constitution is the primary source of law in the United States, as indeed it claims to be in Article VI: "This Constitution . . . shall be the supreme Law of the Land; and the Judges in every State shall be bound thereby, any Thing in the Constitution or Laws of any State to the Contrary notwithstanding." Thus none of the other types of law that we shall subsequently mention may stand if it is in conflict with the Constitution of the United States. Similarly, each state has its own separate constitution and all local laws must yield to its supremacy.

Acts of Legislative Bodies

Laws passed by Congress and by the various state legislatures constitute a sizable bulk of law in the United States. Statutes requiring us to pay income tax to Uncle Sam and state laws forbidding us from robbing a bank are both examples. But there are many other types of legislative bodies that also enact statutes and ordinances that regulate our lives as citizens. County commissioners (also known as county judges or boards of selectmen) act as legislative bodies for the various counties within the states.

Likewise city councils serve in a legislative capacity when they pass ordinances, fix property tax rates, establish building codes, and so on, at the municipal level. Then there are almost 50,000 "special districts" throughout the country, each of which is headed by an elected or appointed body that acts in a legislative capacity.

Examples of these would be school districts, fire prevention districts, water districts, and municipal utility districts.

Decisions of Quasi-Legislative and Quasi-Judicial Bodies

Sprinkled vertically and horizontally throughout the U.S. governmental structure are thousands of boards, agencies, commissions, departments, and so on, whose primary function is not to legislate or to adjudicate but that still may be called on to make rules or to render decisions that are semilegislative or semijudicial in character. The job of the U.S. Postal Service is obviously to deliver the mail, but sometimes it may be called on to act in a quasi-judicial capacity. For example, a local postmaster may refuse to deliver a piece of mail because he or she believes it to be pornographic in nature, for Congress has mandated that pornography may not be sent through the mail. The postmaster is acting in a semi- or quasi-judicial capacity in determining that a particular item is pornographic and hence not protected by the First Amendment.

The Securities and Exchange Commission is not basically a lawmaking body either, but when it determines that a particular company has run afoul of the securities laws or when it rules on a firm's qualification to be listed on the New York Stock Exchange, it becomes a source of law in the United States. In effect, it makes rules and decisions that affect a person's or a company's behavior and for which there are penalties for noncompliance. Although decisions of agencies such as this may be appealed to or reviewed by the courts, they are binding unless and until they are overturned by a judicial entity.

A university's board of regents may also be a source of law for the students, faculty, and staff members covered by its jurisdiction. These boards may set rules on such matters as which persons may lawfully enter the campus grounds, procedures to be followed before a staff member may be fired, or definitions of plagiarism. Violations of these rules or procedures carry with them penalties backed by the full force of the law.

Orders and Rulings of Political Executives

We learn in our school history classes that legislatures make the law and executives enforce the law. That is essentially true, but it is also a fact that political executives have some lawmaking capacity. This lawmaking occurs whenever presidents, governors, mayors, or others are called upon to fill in the details of legislation passed by legislative bodies, and sometimes when they promulgate orders purely in their executive capacity.

When Congress passes reciprocal trade agreement legislation, the goal is to encourage other countries to lower trade and tariff barriers to U.S.-produced goods, in exchange for which the United States will do the same. But there are so many thousands of goods, almost two hundred countries, and countless degrees of setting up or lowering trade barriers. What to do? The customary practice is for Congress to set basic guidelines for the reciprocal lowering of trade barriers but also to allow the president to make the actual decisions about how much to regulate a given tariff on any given commodity for a particular country. These "executive orders" of the president are published regularly in the *Federal Register* and carry the full force of law. Likewise at the state level, when a legislature delegates to the governor the right to "fill in the details of legislation," the state executive uses what is termed "ordinance making power," which also is a type of lawmaking capacity.

Political executives may promulgate orders that, within certain narrow but important realms, constitute the law of the land. For example, in the wake of a natural disaster such as a flood or tornado, a mayor may declare an official state of emergency that empowers him or her to issue binding rules of behavior for a limited period of time. A curfew ordering persons to be off the streets at a given hour is an example of a "law" made by a municipal chief executive. Though limited and usually temporary, such orders are indeed law and violations invoke penalties.

Judicial Decisions

When we learned in school that legislatures make the law and executives enforce the law, we were told that judges are supposed to *interpret* the law. So they do, but as we shall see again and again throughout this text, judges in fact make law as they interpret it. And we must note that judicial decisions themselves constitute a body of law in the United States. All the thousands upon thousands of court decisions that have been handed down by federal and state judges for the past two centuries are part of the *corpus juris*—the body of law—of the United States.

Judicial decisions may be grounded in or surround a variety of entities: any of the above-mentioned sources of law, past decisions of other judges, or legal principles that have evolved over the centuries. (For example, one cannot bring a lawsuit on behalf of another person unless that person is one's minor child or ward.) Judicial decisions may also be grounded in what is called "the common law," that is, those written (and sometimes unwritten) legal traditions and principles that have served as the basis of court decisions and accepted human behavior for many centuries. For instance, if a couple lives together as husband and wife for a specified period of years, the common law may be invoked to have their union recognized as a legal marriage.

Types of Law in the United States

Now that we have examined the wellsprings of American law, it is appropriate to take a brief look at the vessels wherein such laws are contained, that is, to examine the formal types of categories of law in the United States. What follows are definitions or explanations of the primary kinds of law that we shall make reference to subsequently in this text. (Note that types of law are not necessarily mutually exclusive.)

Statutory Law and Common Law

Statutory law is the type of law that is enacted by a legislative body such as Congress, a state legislature, or a city council although it could also include the written orders of various quasi-legislative bodies. The key here is that the enactments be in written form and be addressed to the needs of society as a whole. Examples of statutory law would be a congressional act increasing Social Security payments or a statute passed by a state legislature authorizing the death penalty for first-degree murder. Statutory law is often contrasted with the common law, which is a less orderly compilation of traditions, principles, and legal practices that have been handed down from one generation of lawyers and judges to the next. Because much of the common law is not systematically codified and delineated, as is statutory law, it is sometimes referred to as "the unwritten law." However, this is not entirely accurate. Much of the common law exists in the form of court decisions and legal precedents that are in fact in written form. The common law is known for its flexibility and capacity to change as it evolves in response to the changing needs and values of society.

Civil Law and Criminal Law

We shall have much more to say about these terms in Chapters 6 and 7, but suffice it to say here that civil law deals with disagreements between individuals— for example, a dispute over ownership of private property. It also deals with corporations, admiralty matters, and contracts. Criminal law, on the other hand, pertains to offenses against the state itself—actions that may be directed against a person but that are deemed to be offensive to society as a whole. Crimes such as drunken driving, armed robbery, and so on are punishable by fines or imprisonment.

Equity

Equity is best understood when contrasted with law; the primary difference between the two terms is, as we shall see, in the remedy involved. At *law* the only remedy is financial compensation, whereas in *equity* a judge is free to issue a remedy that will either prevent or cure the wrong that is about to happen. Because there are many circumstances when monetary settlements are inappropriate or inadequate, equity allows judges a degree of flexibility that they would not otherwise have. For example, let's say you were the owner of an old cabin located in the center of town and that this structure was the first built in the community. You wish to preserve it because of its historic value, but the city decides to expand the adjacent street and thereby destroy the cabin. Your remedy at law is to ask the city for monetary compensation, but to you this is totally inadequate. The cabin has little intrinsic value, although as a historic object it is priceless. Thus you may wish to ask a judge to issue a writ in equity that might order the city to move the cabin to another site or perhaps even to order the city to reconsider its plan to widen the street.

Private Law

Private law deals with the rights and obligations that private individuals and institutions have when they relate to one another. Much civil law is obviously in this category, for it covers subjects such as contracts between private persons and corporations and statutes pertaining to marriage and divorce.

Public Law

Public law addresses the relationship that individuals and institutions have with the state as a sovereign entity. The government makes laws in its capacity as the primary political unit to which all owe allegiance; in turn, the government is obliged to preserve and protect the citizens who live within its jurisdiction. Public law also deals with obligations that citizens have to the government, such as paying taxes or serving in the armed forces, or it may pertain to services or obligations that the state owes to its citizenry, such as laws providing for unemployment compensation or statutes protecting property rights. Criminal law also falls into this broad category as do laws that deal with such diverse subjects as defense, welfare, and taxation. Two subheadings in this category are administrative law and constitutional law.

Administrative Law. The decisions and regulations set forth by the various administrative agencies of our government are the substance of administrative law. Agencies, such as the Securities and Exchange Commission or a city health department, are empowered to oversee implementation or carry out specific mandates established by a legislative body. When one of these agencies promulgates rules or guidelines about how it intends to carry out its regulatory functions, the rules become part of administrative law.

Constitutional Law. Basically, constitutional law is the compilation of all court rulings on the meaning of the various words, phrases, and clauses in the U.S. Constitution. Although all courts have the authority to perform this function, it is the U.S. Supreme Court that has the final say about questions of constitutional law. For example, in 1952 the Supreme Court ruled that nothing inherent in Article II of the Constitution gave the president the right to seize and run the steel mills—even in time of emergency—without specific congressional authorization.[3]

State Law and Federal Law

Laws that are passed by one of the fifty state legislatures, ordinances promulgated by a state governor, and decisions handed down by a state court all constitute the *corpus juris* of a single state. They are compelling only for the citizens of that state and for outsiders who reside or do business there. State laws must not conflict either with federal law or with anything in the U.S. Constitution. Examples of state law are the income tax that Illinois has enacted for those who reside within its boundaries and New Mexico's criminal penalty for bank robbery. Federal law is made up of acts of Congress, presidential orders, U.S. court decisions, and so on. This body of law applies throughout the United States and usually pertains to topics that are relevant to persons in more than just one state. Examples include a congressional act forbidding the transportation of a stolen car across state lines and a U.S. Supreme Court decision outlawing prayer in the public schools. As with state law, federal law must be in harmony with the strictures of the U.S. Constitution.

Functions of Law

What is the function of law in the United States (or in any country, for that matter, because the function of law is more or less universal)? What dire things would occur were there no law or, conversely, what positive things can we do through law that would be impossible without it?

Throughout history some people have believed that there should be no government (and hence no laws) at all. Such individuals, called anarchists, have argued that governments by nature make rules and laws and that such restrictions impinge on personal freedom. In the past anarchists have used violence to overthrow governments and have assassinated heads of state. Such attempts to abolish law and authority have resulted in much destruction of life and property and temporary reigns of terror, but they have never brought about the elimination of law or government. Instead of increasing personal freedom, a state of anarchy virtually destroys personal freedom for all but the most powerful and savage of individuals. Few would deny that in today's world if people are to live together amicably, law must be an essential part of life. As our population expands and modern transportation and communication further link us together, every action that each of us takes affects another either directly or indirectly, possibly causing harm. When conflict results, it must be resolved peaceably using a rule of law. Otherwise disorder, death, and chaos reign. We must have some common set of rules that we agree to live by—a rule of law and order.

But what kind of law and order? There is truth to the anarchist's argument that laws restrict personal freedom. If there are too many rules, laws, and restrictions, totalitarianism results. That may be just about as bad as a state of anarchy. The trick is to strike a balance so that the positive things that law can do for us are not strangulated by the tyranny of the "law and order" offered by the totalitarian state.

Assuming, then, that we reject both anarchy and totalitarianism, what are the positive functions of law when it exists in a reasonable degree? Legal theorists tell us that there are several.

Providing Order and Predictability in Society

We live in a chaotic and uncertain world. People win lotteries while stock markets collapse; more and more persons are living to the age of a hundred yet babies die of AIDS; some ranchers manage to enlarge their herds just at the time of a beef shortage while corn farmers suffer from the worst drought in decades. Laws cannot avert most natural disasters, nor can they prevent random episodes of misfortune, but they can create an environment in which people can work and invest and pursue pleasure with a reasonable expectation that their activity is worth the effort. Without an orderly environment based on and backed by law the normal activities of life would be lacerated with chaos.

When we drive a car, for example, there must be rules to tell us which side of the road to drive on, how fast we can safely go, and when to slow down and stop. Without rules of the road there would be horrible traffic jams and terrible accidents because no driver would know what to expect from the others. Without a climate of law and order no parent would have the incentive to save for a child's college education. The knowledge that the bank will not simply close and that one's savings account will not be arbitrarily confiscated by the government or by some powerful party gives the parent an environment in which to save. Law and the predictability it provides cannot guarantee us a totally safe and predictable world, but it can create a climate in which people believe it is worthwhile to produce, to venture forth, and to live for the morrow.

Resolving Disputes

No matter how benign and loving people can be at times, altercations and disagreements are inevitable. How disputes are resolved between quarreling individuals, corporations, or governmental entities tells us much about the level and quality of the rule of law in a society. Without an orderly, peaceful process for dispute resolution there is either chaos or a climate in which the largest gang of thugs or those with the strongest fists prevail.

Let us say that a new fraternity house is built next to the home of Mr. Joe Six-Pack, a man who likes his peace-and-quiet. After Joe's sleep has been disrupted for the umpteenth time by loud music coming from the fraternity house, Joe decides it's time to get even. About sunrise one Sunday, after another sleepless night, Joe angrily runs over to his neighbor's parking lot and systematically begins to let air out of the students' tires—"just to teach those damn kids a lesson." He is caught in the act by several well-soused fraternity boys, just marking the end of a raucous night. Angry words are exchanged: "manhood" and "right-and-wrong" are at stake. A brawl ensues resulting in bloodshed and injury all around. How much better if Joe had turned this grievance over to the police, the courts, or campus authorities—all empowered by the law to peacefully resolve such matters.

Protecting Individuals and Property

Even libertarians, who take a very narrow view of the role of government, will readily acknowledge that the state must protect citizens from the outlaw who would inflict bodily harm or who would steal or destroy their worldly goods. Because of the importance to us of the safety of our persons and our property, many laws on the books deal with protection and security. Not only are laws in the criminal code intended to punish those who steal and do bodily harm, but civil statutes permit many crime victims to sue for monetary damages. The law has created police and sheriffs' departments, district attorneys' offices, courts, jails, and death chambers to deter and punish the criminal and to help people feel secure. This is not to say that there is no crime; everyone knows otherwise. But without a system of laws, crime would be much more prevalent and the fear of it would be much more paralyzing. Unless we could afford to hire our own bodyguards and security teams we would be in constant anxiety of loss of life and limb and property. However imperfect our system of law, prevention, and enforcement may be, it is certainly better than none.

Providing for the General Welfare

Laws and the institutions and programs they establish enable us to do corporately what would be impossible, or at least prohibitive, to do as individuals. Providing for the common defense, educating young people, putting out forest fires, controlling pollution, and caring for the sick and aged are all examples of activities that we could do only feebly, if at all, acting alone but that we can do efficiently and effectively as a society. As citizens we may disagree about which endeavors should be undertaken through the government by law. Some may believe, for example, that the aged should be cared for by family members or by private charity; others see such care as a corporate responsibility. But although we can disagree about the precise activities that the law should require of government, few would deny that there are many significant and beneficial results that are achieved through corporate endeavors. After all, the foundation of our legal system, the U.S. Constitution, was ordained to "establish Justice, insure domestic Tranquility, provide for the common defence, promote the general Welfare, and secure the Blessings of Liberty to ourselves and our Posterity."

Protecting Individual Liberties

Last, but surely not least, law should protect the individual's personal and civil rights against those forces which would curtail or restrict them. These basic freedoms might include those provided for in our nation's Bill of Rights, such as freedom of speech, of religion, and of the press, the right to a fair trial, and freedom from cruel and unusual punishment. They might also comprise some that are not stated in the Bill of Rights but that are implied, such as the right to personal privacy, or they might be rights that Congress has provided for with legislation, such as the right to be free from job discrimination based on gender or ethnic origin. Potential violators of these freedoms might be the government itself (e.g., a law unreasonably restricting freedom of assembly) or one's fellow citizens (e.g., a conspiracy among private individuals to discourage certain persons from voting). Although we may disagree about which freedoms are basic or about how extensively they should be provided for, it is fair to say that unless the law protects certain basic, immutable rights, then the nation's citizens are no more than cogs within a machine. It is the meaningful provision for these basic liberties that ensures the dignity and richness of the life of the individual.

The United States and the Rule of Law

We Americans pride ourselves on being a law-abiding people, and to the casual observer so we are. Few of us would question Abraham Lincoln's admonition that respect for the law should be taught the child at every mother's knee, and most of us are glad to proclaim that ours is a government of *law*, not of individuals. The fact that over 1.18 million of our fellow citizens reside in jail or prison on any given day is seen not as evidence that our society is lawless but rather as proof that in the United States respect for the law is paramount and disobedience to the law is punished.[4] A careful analysis of our history and traditions reveals, however, that our view of the law has in reality been ambivalent. A few examples from our history will illustrate our love-hate relationship with the rule of law.

An appropriate place to begin is the American Revolution. Few Americans can look back on that seven-year struggle and feel anything but pride when some images come to mind: the bold act of defiance of the Boston Tea Party, the shot fired at Concord that was "heard 'round the world," George Washington's daring attack on the Hessian troops at Trenton. But despite all the goosebumps raised in this patriotic reverie, we lose sight of one bothersome little fact—the Revolution was illegal! The wanton destruction of private property wrought by the Boston Tea Party and the killing of British troops sent to this land for the colonists' protection were illegal in every sense of the word. Indeed, the Founders were so keenly aware of this that they prepared a Declaration of Independence to justify to the rest of the world why a bloody and illegal revolt against the lawful government is sometimes permissible:

When in the Course of human events, it becomes necessary for one people to dissolve the political bands which have connected them with another, . . . a decent respect to the opinions of mankind requires that they should declare the causes which impel them to the separation. . . . [W]hen a long train of abuses and usurpations . . . evinces a design to reduce them under absolute Despotism, it is their right, it is their duty, to throw off such Government, and to provide new Guards for their future security.

The irony of our nation's birth is often overlooked: this citadel of law and order was born under the star of illegality and revolution.

Let us stroll a little further along our historical path and view John Brown's famous raid on the U.S. arsenal at Harpers Ferry in the fall of 1859. With thirteen white men and five black men, this militant opponent of slavery began his plan to lead a mass insurrection among the slaves and to create an Abolitionist republic on the ruins of the plantation South. After a small but bloody battle that lasted several days, Brown was captured, given a public trial, and duly hanged for murder and other assorted crimes. But were Brown's flagrantly violent and illegal actions justifiable, given the nobility of his vision? Many in the North believed so. Its moral and cultural elite took the line that Brown might have been insane, but his acts and intentions should be excused on the grounds that the compelling motive was divine. Horace Greeley wrote that the Harpers Ferry raid was "the work of a madman," but he had not "one reproachful word." Ralph Waldo Emerson described Brown as a "saint." Henry Thoreau, Theodore Parker, Henry Wadsworth Longfellow, William Cullen Bryant, and James Lowell—the whole Northern pantheon—took the position that Brown was an "angel of light," and not Brown but the society that hanged him was mad. It was also reported that "on the day Brown died, church bells tolled from New England to Chicago; Albany fired off one hundred guns in salute, and a governor of a large Northern state wrote in his diary that men were ready to march to Virginia."[5] Again the ambivalence: one ought always to obey the law—unless, of course, one hears a divine call that transcends the law.

Skipping over dozens of other keen illustrations of this truth, let us look at a couple of events from the middle part of this century. The civil rights movement that began in the 1950s caused many Americans to be torn between their natural desire to obey the law of the land and their call to change the system. As the Reverend Martin Luther King, Jr., sat in a Birmingham jail, he wrote a now famous letter to supporters who were disturbed by his having disobeyed the law during his civil rights protests:

You express a great deal of anxiety over our willingness to break laws. This is certainly a legitimate concern. Since we would diligently urge people to obey the Supreme Court's decision in 1954 outlawing segregation in the public schools, at first glance it may seem rather paradoxical for us consciously to break laws. One may well ask: "How can you advocate breaking some laws and obeying others?" The answer lies in the fact that there are two types of laws: just and unjust. I would be first to advocate obeying just laws. One has not only a legal but a moral responsibility to obey just laws. Conversely, one has a moral responsibility to disobey unjust laws. . . . Thus it is that I can urge men to obey the 1954 decision of the

Supreme Court, for it is morally right; and I can urge them to disobey segregation ordinances, for they are morally wrong.[6]

Even a member of the Supreme Court of the United States sanctioned civil disobedience during the heady days of the civil rights movement. Justice Abe Fortas said:

If I had been a Negro living in Birmingham or Little Rock or Plaquemines Parish, Louisiana, I hope I would have disobeyed the state laws that said that I might not enter the public waiting room in the bus station reserved for "Whites." I hope I would have insisted upon going into parks and swimming pools and schools which state or city law reserved for "Whites." I hope I would have had the courage to disobey, although the segregation ordinances were presumably law until they were declared unconstitutional.[7]

Those who opposed the civil rights movement and the Supreme Court decisions and congressional statutes that supported it likewise believed that their form of civil disobedience was in response to a higher calling. Quoting scripture as support of their belief that God created the white race separately from the colored races, segregationists argued that it was the divine will to keep the races apart. Thus defiance of integration orders was seen by many traditionalists as keeping in touch with the natural order of the universe as God had established it. That black and white should not mix with one another was believed to be "a self-evident truth," not to be overturned by the courts' desegregation orders.

The "pro-life offensive" conducted during the past two decades by opponents of abortion is a final example of how basically law-abiding persons may be ready and willing to break the law in response to what they believe is a higher calling. For example, after former preacher Paul Hill was sentenced to death for having murdered a doctor and his unarmed escort at an abortion clinic in Pensacola, Florida, he said: "I know for a fact that I'm going to go to heaven when I die. I am certainly guilty of no crimes. . . . My actions are honorable." Deeds less drastic than Hill's include "rescue actions" at abortion clinics all across the country conducted by protesters who have blocked access to these facilities and harassed doctors and nurses. Arrests of abortion protesters now number in the tens of thousands.[8]

Civil disobedience does not need a divine call. There are ample illustrations of the wholesale avoidance of laws that were thought to be economically harmful and unfair or that were seen as beyond the rightful authority of the state to enact.

American farmers are probably as law abiding a segment of the population as any, but they, too, can thwart the law when their economic livelihood is at stake. As early as George Washington's administration, state militias were activated and sent out to quash what came to be known as the Whiskey Rebellion, a series of lawless acts by the tillers of the soil who objected to the federal tax on their homemade elixirs. And during the terrible depression days of the 1930s, when, for example, one-third of the state of Iowa was being sold into bankruptcy, farmers often revolted. Thousands with shotguns held at bay local sheriffs who tried to serve papers on fellow farmers about to be dispossessed.

During the Prohibition era, from 1919 to 1933, many Americans refused to obey a law they thought to be unfair and in excess of the legitimate bounds of state authority. Not only did the laws prohibiting the production and sale of alcohol prove to be ineffective and unenforceable, but Americans actually seemed to relish flouting the law. The statistics on Prohibition enforcement reveal how the laws were honored in the breach: in 1921 the government seized a total of 95,933 illicit distilleries, stills, still worms, and fermenters; this number went to 172,537 by 1925 and jumped to 282,122 by 1930.[9] By 1932 President Herbert Hoover, who had originally supported Prohibition, began to talk about "the futility of the whole business."

One last example. In the vast majority of the states it is against the law to engage in a whole host of forbidden sexual activities—fornication, sodomy, adultery, homosexuality. The legislatures in most of the states have gone to great trouble to spell out for us which parts of our bodies may be touched by the parts of other people's bodies. That these laws are seldom obeyed or enforced is a secret to no one. Although most Americans still approve of forbidding sexual practices and acts that they find personally distasteful, few have much enthusiasm for putting police officers in every bedroom or for strictly enforcing laws that touch on very personal issues.

So, are we a law-abiding people or are we not? Is our respect for the law only superficial and our belief that everyone ought to obey the law mere cant? The truth, it would appear, is that Americans do honestly have great respect for the law and that our abhorrence of lawbreakers is genuine. But it is also fair to say that mixed with this tradition and orientation is a long-standing belief that sometimes people are called to respond to values higher than the ordinary law and thereby to engage in illegal behavior. Of course, one person's command to disobey the law and follow the dictates of conscience will appear to another as mere foolishness. Furthermore, Americans have a hefty pragmatic tradition vis-à-vis the law. Laws that drive us to the wall economically (such as farm foreclosures during the 1930s) and laws that are seen to needlessly impinge upon our personal pleasures (such as Prohibition and laws forbidding fornication) are just not taken as seriously as those that forbid bank robbery and rape.

Like the law, judges are viewed ambivalently by Americans. In general, judges are held in inordinately high esteem in the United States, and most Americans would be proud if a son or daughter grew up to become one. Yet Americans can be very quick to condemn judges whose rulings go against deeply held values or whose decisions are not in the best interests of their pocketbooks.[10] Whether this is hypocrisy or merely the complex and ambivalent nature of humankind is perhaps all in the eye of the beholder.

A Litigious Society

The raw statistics reveal that we Americans readily look to the courts to redress our grievances. The quarter of a million suits that are filed in the federal courts each year are dwarfed by the 100 million suits filed in the courts of the fifty states and the District of Columbia. That's about one for every two people in the United States; although many of these deal with relatively minor matters, about 12 million are filed in the *major* state and federal trial courts. As one contemporary expert has noted:

Ours is a law-drenched age. Because we are constantly inventing new and better ways of bumping into one another, we seek an orderly means of dulling the blows and repairing the damage. Of all the known methods of redressing grievances and settling disputes—pitched battle, rioting, dueling, mediating, flipping a coin, suing—only the latter has steadily won the day in these United States.

Though litigation has not routed all other forms of fight, it is gaining public favor as the legitimate and most effective means of seeking and winning one's just desserts.

So widespread is the impulse to sue that "litigation has become the nation's secular religion," and a growing array of procedural rules and substantive provisions is daily gaining its adherents.[11]

This virtual explosion of primarily civil litigation in the United States has led the courts to consider cases that in years past were settled privately among citizens or issues that often went unresolved. Some obviously deal with momentous subjects, such as the right of the states to curtail abortion and efforts by the Environmental Protection Agency to enjoin polluters of the environment. But many suits stagger the imagination by their audacity or triviality:

1. A Michigan resident has sued the state for $1 million because he says he caught "a cold and a hard cough" while visiting an art exhibit in the drafty capitol rotunda in Lansing. He is asking $1 million in damages.[12]

2. A 17-year-old Maryland high school student tried out for her school's football team. (Had school authorities prevented her from doing so, they could have been sued for sex discrimination.) The student was hurt during the first scrimmage, and she sued the school district for $1.5 million because no one had informed her "of the potential risks of serious injury inherent in the sport."[13]

3. A longtime employee of the Los Alamos Scientific Laboratory sued for occupational disability benefits, claiming that although he had never suffered any physical injury, he had become mentally disabled "by a neurotic fear that radiation would kill him."[14]

While such suits are frivolous, they still require the time and efforts of the jurists who must at least consider their merits within the 17,000 courthouses that dot the landscape. For example, a federal judge in West Virginia took several printed pages of the *Federal Supplement* to explain why the punishment of a state prisoner for his refusal to bury a dead skunk was not a violation of the prisoner's civil rights. A federal judge in Pennsylvania agonized at length in print as to whether the First Amendment protected from a tort action *Time* magazine, which had published a photograph of a man whose fly had become unzipped.[15]

Despite this plethora of less-than-monumental lawsuits, it must be noted that the judicial system appears to be fighting back against those who attempt to use the courts to advance totally frivolous causes. Rule 11 of the Federal Rules of Civil Procedure forbids the filing of worthless petitions, and this was made stronger in 1983 when U.S. trial judges were given the authority to impose sanctions for the filing of frivolous suits. (Critics of the rule have charged that it has had a chilling effect on civil rights suits, but law school studies have largely refuted that claim.[16]) And in 1991 the U.S. Supreme Court handed down two key decisions that reaffirmed the imposition of large fines on those filing specious lawsuits—thus sending out a strong message to the legal community that violations of Rule 11 will be taken seriously.[17] By the summer of 1997 twenty-nine states had laws on the books (many recently strengthened) to combat those who inundate their legal tribunals with worthless petitions.[18] But as with many things in the judiciary, the matter of human judgment is all important: what is frivolous to one person might be deadly serious to another.

Although there has in fact been a burst of litigation in the United States during the past several decades, we must not lose sight of the fact that Americans have always been litigious people. As early as 1835 the highly perceptive French observer Alexis de Tocqueville noted that "there is hardly a political question in the United States which does not sooner or later turn into a judicial one."[19] Indeed, as one contemporary scholar has said: "To express amazement at American litigiousness is akin to professing astonishment at learning that the roots of most Americans lie in other lands. We have been a litigious nation as we have been an immigrant one. Indeed, the two are related."[20] This scholar goes on to argue that our history was made by diverse groups who wanted to live according to their own customs but found themselves drawn haphazardly into a larger political community. As these groups bumped into one another and the edges became frayed, disputes resulted. But given a fairly strong common law legal tradition, such disputes were for the most part channeled into the courtroom rather than onto the battlefield. There are, of course, many reasons why Americans have been and continue to be a highly litigious people, and it is beyond the scope of this chapter to examine them all systematically. Suffice it to say that in the United States the courthouse has been and is the anvil on which a significant portion of our personal, societal, and political problems is hammered out.

America's judicial caseload is so enormous and far-ranging that to understand fully how our nation is governed and how its resources are allocated, we must study the courts that are such a vital part of this process. Given the significance of courts in formulating and implementing public policy in the United States, it is important that we know who the judges are, what their values are, and what powers and prerogatives they possess. And it is essential that we study how decisions are made and how they are implemented if we are to follow the judicial game.

Summary

In this chapter we looked briefly at law in the United States—the wells from which it springs, its basic types, and its functions in society. We also examined the ambivalent attitude that Americans have about the rule of law; this is a nation birthed in an illegal revolution, yet proud of its respect for law and order. Finally, we noted that our contentiousness as a people has been channeled largely through our legal and court systems. As a consequence, the high priests of our judicial temples, the judges, play a very significant role in our personal lives and in our evolution as a society and political entity.

NOTES

1. This account is based on material taken from Deborah Tedford, "Jury Acquits Burzynski of Last Remaining Charge," *Houston Chronicle,* May 28, 1997, A1; Todd Ackerman, "Alternative Medicine Gets a Boost," *Houston Chronicle,* June 1, 1997, A33; and Sue Blevins, "Fighting Cancer—and the FDA," *Wall Street Journal,* June 2, 1997, A22.

2. Stephen D. Ford, *The American Legal System: Its Dynamics and Limits* (St. Paul, Minn.: West, 1974), 13. Our elaborations on this definition of law are borrowed from Chapter 1 of Ford's text.

3. *Youngstown Sheet & Tube Co. v. Sawyer,* 343 U.S. 579 (1952).

4. In 1996 the nation added 55,876 inmates to its prison population, bringing the total number to just over 1.18 million. That means that there are about 615 inmates for every 100,000 U.S. residents. This rate puts the United States second only to Russia among all the countries in the world. (In Russia there are 690 inmates per 100,000 residents.) "Prison Population Surge Ebbs," *Houston Chronicle,* June 23, 1997, A3.

5. T. R. Fehrenbach, *Lone Star: A History of Texas and the Texans* (New York: American Legacy Press, 1968), 336.

6. Martin Luther King, Jr., "Letter from Birmingham Jail, April 16, 1963." The full text of the letter may be found in Martin Luther King, Jr., *Why We Can't Wait* (New York: Harper & Row, 1963).

7. Abe Fortas, *Concerning Dissent and Civil Disobedience* (New York: Signet, 1970), 18.

8. William Booth, "Abortion Doctor's Killer Receives Death Penalty," *Houston Chronicle,* December 7, 1994, A1.

9. Andrew Sinclair, "Prohibition: The Era of Excess," in Lawrence M. Friedman and Stewart Macaulay, eds., *Law and the Behavioral Sciences* (New York: Bobbs-Merrill, 1977), 353.

10. See, for example, Jack W. Peltason, *Fifty-Eight Lonely Men* (New York: Harcourt, Brace & World, 1961); and Jack Bass, *Unlikely Heroes* (New York: Simon & Schuster, 1981).

11. Jethro K. Lieberman, *The Litigious Society* (New York: Basic Books, 1983), viii.

12. *Houston Chronicle,* January 23, 1997, D2.

13. George F. Will, "Our Expanding Menu of Rights," *Newsweek,* December 14, 1992, 90.

14. Lieberman, *The Litigious Society,* 4.

15. Robert A. Carp and C. K. Rowland, *Policymaking and Politics in the Federal District Courts* (Knoxville: University of Tennessee Press, 1983), 18.

16. Stephen Wermiel, "High Court Agrees to Hear Case on Segregation at State Colleges," *Wall Street Journal,* April 16, 1991, B10.

17. *Chambers v. U.S. Department of the Army,* 499 U.S. 645 (1991); and *Kunstler v. Britt,* 499 U.S. 969 (1991).

18. This number was taken from the Web Page of the American Tort Reform Association (*http://www.atra.org/atra/default.html*) downloaded July 9, 1997. Note that the latest innovation that the states are beginning to adopt is the practice of requiring losing plaintiffs in civil suits to pay the attorney's fees of the defendant. This would supposedly make a potential plaintiff "think twice" before filing a frivolous lawsuit.

19. Alexis de Tocqueville, *Democracy in America,* ed. J. P. Mayer and Max Lerner, trans. George Lawrence (New York: Harper & Row, 1966), 248.

20. Lieberman, *The Litigious Society,* 13.

SUGGESTED READINGS

Calvi, James V., and Susan Coleman. *American Law and Legal Systems.* Englewood Cliffs, N.J.: Prentice-Hall, 1989. A systematic discussion of all the major types of law in the United States.

Friedman, Lawrence M. *A History of American Law,* 2d ed. New York: Simon & Schuster, 1985. Provides an in-depth chronology of the American legal system, including a discussion of the legal profession.

Hall, Kermit L. *The Magic Mirror: Law in American History.* New York: Oxford University Press, 1989. Discusses the historical interactions of law with events in the social and political realms.

Irons, Peter. *The Courage of Their Convictions: Sixteen Americans Who Fought Their Way to the Supreme Court.* New York: Penguin, 1990. Contains sixteen case studies of strong-minded individuals who fought their legal battles all the way to the Supreme Court.

Johnson, Conrad. *Philosophy of Law.* New York: Macmillan, 1993. A wide variety of selected readings about various philosophies of law, punishment, liberty, legal reasoning, and so on.

Lieberman, Jethro K. *The Litigious Society.* New York: Basic Books, 1983. Explains and documents the increasing tendency of Americans to file civil suits.

Macaulay, Stewart, Lawrence Friedman, and John Stookey, eds. *Law & Society: Readings on the Social Study of Law.* New York: W.W. Norton, 1995. A comprehensive and well-edited reader for the more advanced student interested in the interaction between the values of law and society.

Spiro, George W., and James L. Houghteling, Jr. *The Dynamics of Law,* 2d ed. New York: Harcourt Brace Jovanovich, 1981. A short, well-written discussion of the way in which the law interacts with social values, standards, and mores.

CHAPTER 2

History and Organization of the Federal Judicial System

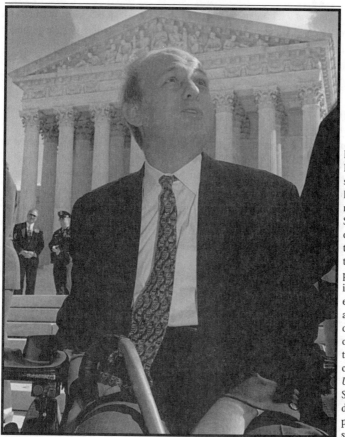

Former White House press secretary James Brady meets with reporters at the Supreme Court to discuss the constitutional challenge to the Brady Act's provision requiring local law enforcement agencies to conduct background checks of prospective handgun purchasers. In *Printz v. United States* the Supreme Court declared the provision unconstitutional.

ONE OF THE MOST IMPORTANT, most interesting, and most confusing features of the judiciary in the United States is what is known as the *dual court system*. This term simply means that each level of government (state and national) has its own set of courts. Thus, there are fifty-one separate court systems in the United States, one for each state and one for the federal government. As we shall see more clearly in the pages that follow, some legal problems are resolved entirely in the state courts, whereas others are handled entirely in the federal courts. Still others may receive attention from both sets of tribunals, a fact that sometimes causes friction between state and federal courts. This dissension is undoubtedly most evident when persons convicted of a crime by a state court seek relief in a federal court by means of a writ of habeas corpus—an order issued by a judge to determine whether a person has been lawfully imprisoned. The controversy over the use of this writ increased with the rise during the latter half of this century in the number of habeas corpus petitions filed in federal district courts by persons convicted in state courts. In 1941 there were 127 habeas petitions filed; in 1942, 130. The number began to rise sharply in 1962. By 1990 the number of habeas petitions filed had reached 11,000.[1]

Proponents of the use of the writ of habeas corpus point out that it is a right protected by the U.S. Constitution and thus argue that the federal courts should be widely accessible to state prisoners. Critics, on the other hand, feel that habeas corpus proceedings allow federal judges to interfere unduly in state legal matters.

Another complaint stems from the fact that state prisoners have traditionally been free to file a seemingly endless number of petitions in a variety of courts; consequently, death row inmates have been able to postpone their executions for years by a series of petitions filed in various courts.

The debate over habeas corpus relief led to calls for extensive study of the uses and abuses of the process. Both a special ad hoc committee of the Judicial Conference (chaired by former U.S. Supreme Court Justice Lewis F. Powell, Jr.) and the Federal Courts Study Committee looked at the problem. These efforts eventually bore fruit when in April 1996 President Bill Clinton signed into law the Antiterrorism and Effective Death Penalty Act. This law's habeas corpus provisions create one-year deadlines for filing habeas petitions, limit successive petitions, and restrict the review of state prisoner petitions if the claims were adjudicated on the merits in state courts. Furthermore, in capital cases the law establishes, among other things, a 180-day time frame for filing a habeas petition.[2]

To simplify matters as much as possible, we will discuss the federal courts in this chapter and the state courts in Chapter 3. Since knowledge of the historical events that helped shape the national court system can shed light on the present judicial structure, our study of the federal judiciary begins with a description of the court system as it has evolved over more than two centuries. We will first examine the three levels of the federal court system in the order in which they were established: the Supreme Court, the courts of appeals, and the district courts. The emphasis in our discussion of each level will be on historical development, policy-making roles, and decision-making procedures.

In a brief look at other federal courts we will focus on the distinction between constitutional and legislative courts, using the example of bankruptcy courts to illustrate a major difference in the two types. Next, we will discuss the individuals and organizations that provide staff support and administrative assistance in the daily operations of the courts. Our overview discussion will then conclude with a brief look at the workload of the federal courts.

The Historical Context

Prior to the adoption of the Constitution, the country was governed by the Articles of Confederation. Under the Articles, practically all functions of the national government were vested in a single-chamber legislature called a Congress. There was no separation of executive and legislative powers.

The absence of a national judiciary was considered a major weakness of the Articles of Confederation. Both James Madison and Alexander Hamilton, for example, saw a need for a separate judicial branch. Consequently, the delegates gathered at the Constitutional Convention in Philadelphia in 1787 expressed widespread agreement that a national judiciary should be established. There was a good deal of disagreement, however, on the specific form that the judicial branch should take.

The Constitutional Convention and Article III

The first proposal presented to the Constitutional Convention was the Randolph, or Virginia, Plan, which would have set up both a Supreme Court and inferior federal courts. Opponents of the Virginia Plan responded with the Paterson, or New Jersey, Plan, which called for the creation of a single federal supreme tribunal. Supporters of the New Jersey Plan were especially disturbed by the idea of lower federal courts. They argued that the state courts could hear all cases in the first instance and that a right of appeal to the Supreme Court would be sufficient to protect national rights and provide uniform judgments throughout the country.

The conflict between the states' rights advocates and the nationalists was resolved by one of the many compromises that characterized the Constitutional Convention. The compromise is found in Article III of the Constitution, which begins, "The judicial Power of the United States, shall be vested in one supreme Court, and in such inferior Courts as the Congress may from time to time ordain and establish." Thus the conflict would be postponed until the new government was in operation.

The Judiciary Act of 1789

Once the Constitution was ratified, action on the federal judiciary came quickly. When the new Congress convened in 1789, its first major concern was judicial organization. Discussions of Senate Bill 1 involved many of the same participants and arguments as were involved in the Constitutional Convention's debates on the judiciary. Once again, the question was whether lower federal courts should be created at all or whether federal claims should first be heard in state courts. Attempts to resolve this controversy split Congress into two distinct groups.

One group, which believed that federal law should be adjudicated in the state courts first and by the United States Supreme Court only on appeal, expressed the fear that the new government would destroy the rights of the states. Other legislators, suspicious of the parochial prejudice of state courts, feared that litigants from other states and other countries would be dealt with unjustly. This latter group naturally favored a judicial system that included lower federal courts. The law that emerged from this debate, the Judiciary Act of 1789, set up a judicial system composed of a Supreme Court, consisting of a chief justice and five associate justices; three circuit courts, each comprising two justices of the Supreme Court and a district judge; and thirteen district courts, each presided over by one district judge. The power to create inferior federal courts, then, was immediately exercised. In fact, Congress created not one but two sets of lower courts.

The U.S. Supreme Court

A First Look

A famous jurist once said, "The Supreme Court of the United States is distinctly American in conception and function, and owes little to prior judicial institutions."[3] To understand what the framers of the Constitution envisioned for the Court, we must consider another American concept: the federal form of government. The Founders provided for both a national government and state governments; the courts of the states were to be bound by federal laws. However, final interpretation of federal laws simply could not be left to a state court, and certainly not to several state tribunals, whose judgments might disagree. Thus, the Supreme Court must interpret federal legislation. Another of the Founders' intentions was for the federal government to act directly upon individual citizens as well as upon the states. The Supreme Court's function in the federal system may be summarized as follows:

In the most natural way, as the result of the creation of Federal law under a written constitution conferring limited powers, the Supreme Court of the United States came into being with its unique function. That court maintains the balance between State and Nation through the maintenance of the rights and duties of individuals.[4]

Given the High Court's importance to our system of government, it was perhaps inevitable that the Court would evoke great controversy. A leading student of the Supreme Court says:

Nothing in the Court's history is more striking than the fact that, while its significant and necessary place in the Federal form of Government has always been recognized by thoughtful and patriotic men, nevertheless, no branch of the Government and no institution under the Constitution has sustained more continuous attack or reached its present position after more vigorous opposition.[5]

The Court's First Decade

George Washington, in appointing the first Supreme Court justices, established two important traditions. First, he began the practice of naming to the Court those with whom he was politically compatible. Washington, the only president ever to have an opportunity to appoint the entire federal judiciary, did a good job of filling federal judgeships with party bedfellows. Without exception, the federal judgeships went to faithful Federalists.

The second tradition established by Washington was that of roughly equal geographic representation on the federal courts. His first six appointees to the Supreme Court included three Northerners and three Southerners. On the basis of ability and legal reputation, only three or four of Washington's original appointees actually merited their justiceships. Many able men were either passed over or declined to serve.

The chief justiceship was the most important appointment Washington made. The president felt that the man to head the first Supreme Court should be an eminent lawyer, statesman, executive, and leader. Many names were presented to Washington, and at least one person, James Wilson, formally applied for the position. Ultimately, Washington settled upon John Jay of New York. Although only forty-four years old, Jay had experience as a lawyer, a judge, and a diplomat. In addition, he was the main drafter of his state's first constitution. Concerning the selection of Jay as chief justice, it has been said:

That Washington picked Jay over his top two rivals for the post, James Wilson and John Rutledge, was either fortuitous or inspired—for it would scarcely have added to the fledgling Supreme Court's popular prestige to have its Chief Justice go insane, as Rutledge later did, or spend his last days jumping from one state to another to avoid being arrested for a debt, as did Wilson.[6]

Washington did, however, appoint both Wilson and Rutledge to the Court as associate justices. Neither man contributed significantly to the Court as a government institution; thus Washington became the first of many presidents to misjudge an appointee to the Court.

The remaining three associate justices who served on the original Supreme Court were William Cushing, John Blair, and James Iredell. Cushing remained on the Court for twenty years, more than twice as long as any of the other original justices, although senility affected his competency in later years. Blair was a close personal friend of Washington's, and Iredell was a strong Federalist from North Carolina who was instrumental in getting that state to join the Union. The appointments of Blair and Iredell, then, have been seen as sheer political reward. Despite the generally mediocre quality of the original six appointees, they were held in somewhat higher esteem by their contemporaries, according to studies of early letters and correspondence.[7]

The Supreme Court met for the first time on Monday, February 1, 1790, in the Royal Exchange, a building located in the Wall Street section of New York City. Compared with today's Supreme Court sessions, that first session was certainly unimpressive. Tongue in cheek, one Court historian noted: "The first President immediately on taking office settled down to the pressing business of being President. The first Congress enacted the first laws. The first Supreme Court adjourned."[8]

Only Jay, Wilson, and Cushing, the three Northern justices, were present on opening day. Justice Blair arrived from Virginia for the second day; Rutledge and Iredell, the other Southerners, did not appear at all during the opening session.

The Supreme Court's first session lasted just ten days. During this period the Court selected a clerk, chose a seal, and admitted several lawyers to practice before it in the future. There were, of course, no cases to be decided. In fact, the Court did not rule on a single case during its first three years. In spite of this insignificant and abbreviated beginning,

the New York and the Philadelphia newspapers described the proceedings of this first session of the Court more fully than any other event connected with the new Government; and their accounts were reproduced in the leading papers of all the States.[9]

The minor role the Supreme Court played continued throughout its first decade of existence. The period 1790–1799 saw several individuals decline their nomination to the Court and one, Robert H. Harrison, chose to accept a *state* position rather than a Supreme Court justiceship.

During its first decade the Court decided only about fifty cases. However, one of these, *Chisholm v. Georgia*, involved the Court in considerable controversy.[10] In *Chisholm* the justices held that a citizen of one state could sue another state in a federal court. That decision was vigorously attacked by states' rights forces and was ultimately overturned by ratification of the Eleventh Amendment in 1798.

Given the scarcity of Supreme Court business in the early days, Chief Justice Jay's contributions may be traced primarily to his circuit court decisions and his judicial conduct. In one circuit court opinion Jay and his colleagues, Justice Cushing and district judge Henry Marchant, unanimously held that Rhode Island could not permit a debtor to extend his obligations for three years and grant him immunity from arrest and penalties during that time.[11] Jay viewed such an action as a violation of the contract clause contained in Article I, Section 10. His view, a clear affirmation of national supremacy and federal judicial authority, may well have set the stage for John Marshall's later opinions along these lines.

In another circuit court case, Jay held that Congress had no authority to assign nonjudicial functions to the courts.[12] Congress had attempted to give the courts the duty of approving applications for military pensions, subject to suspension by the secretary of war and revision by Congress.

Perhaps the most important of Jay's contributions, however, was his insistence that the Supreme Court could not provide legal advice for the executive branch in the form of an advisory opinion. Jay was asked by Treasury Secretary Alexander Hamilton to issue an opinion on the constitutionality of a resolution passed by the Virginia House of Representatives that declared that a congressional bill for the assumption of the state debts was unconstitutional. President Washington also asked Jay for advice on questions relating to Washington's Neutrality Proclamation. In both instances, Jay's response was a firm no because Article III of the Constitution provides that the Court is to decide only cases pertaining to actual controversies. On balance, "despite his lack of judicial craftsmanship and the brief time in which he might display his personal talents, Jay was successful in establishing the dignity of the office and the independence of the Supreme Court."[13]

The Impact of Chief Justice Marshall

John Marshall served as chief justice from 1801 to 1835 and dominated the Court to a degree unmatched by any other justice. In effect, Marshall *was* the Court—perhaps because, in the words of one scholar, he "brought a first-class mind and a thoroughly engaging personality into second-class company."[14]

Marshall's dominance of the Court enabled him to initiate some major changes in the way opinions were presented. Prior to his tenure, the justices ordinarily wrote separate opinions (called *seriatim* opinions) in major cases. Under Marshall's stewardship, the Court adopted the practice of handing down a single opinion. As one might expect, the evidence shows that from 1801 to 1835 Marshall himself wrote almost half the opinions.[15]

It was Marshall's goal to keep dissension to a minimum. Arguing that dissent undermined the Court's authority, he tried to persuade the justices to settle their differences privately and then present a united front to the public. No doubt his first-class mind and engaging personality aided him in this endeavor. As strange as it may sound, so did the cozy living arrangements of the time. The justices lived in the same Washington, D.C., boardinghouse while the Court was in session. Thus, they were together before, during, and after work in a pleasant, comfortable routine that discouraged deep disagreements. Can you imagine having breakfast, lunch, and dinner every day with a fellow justice whom you have sharply criticized in a public opinion? Human nature, it would seem, was on Marshall's side in keeping dissension at a low level.

In addition to bringing about changes in opinion-writing practices, Marshall used his powers to involve the Court in the policy-making process. Early in his tenure as chief justice, the Court asserted its power to declare an act of Congress unconstitutional, in *Marbury v. Madison* (1803).[16]

This case had its beginnings in the presidential election of 1800, when Thomas Jefferson defeated John Adams in his bid for reelection. Before leaving office in March 1801, however, Adams and the lame-duck Federalist Congress combined efforts to create several new federal judgeships. To fill these new positions Adams nominated, and the Senate confirmed, loyal Federalists. In addition, Adams named his outgoing secretary of state, John Marshall, to be the new chief justice of the Supreme Court.

As secretary of state it had been Marshall's job to deliver the commissions of the newly appointed judges. Time ran out, however, and seventeen of the commissions were not delivered before Jefferson's inauguration. The new president ordered *his* secretary of state, James Madison, not to deliver the remaining commissions.

One of the disappointed nominees was William Marbury. He and three of his colleagues, all confirmed as justices of the peace for the District of Columbia, decided to ask the Supreme Court to force Madison to deliver their commissions. They relied upon Section 13 of the Judiciary Act of 1789, which granted the Supreme Court the authority to issue *writs of mandamus*—court orders commanding a public official to perform an official, nondiscretionary duty.

The case placed Marshall in an uncomfortable predicament. Some suggested that he disqualify himself because of his earlier involvement as secretary of state. There was also the question of the Court's power. If Marshall were to grant the writ, Madison (under Jefferson's orders) would be almost certain to refuse to deliver the commissions. The Supreme Court would then be powerless to enforce its order. On the other hand, if Marshall refused to grant the writ, Jefferson would win by default.

The decision Marshall fashioned from this seemingly impossible predicament was evidence of sheer genius. He declared Section 13 of the Judiciary Act of 1789 unconstitutional because it granted original jurisdiction to the Supreme Court in excess of that specified in Article III of the Constitution. Thus the Court's power to review and determine the constitutionality of acts of Congress was established. This decision is rightly seen as one of the single most important decisions the Supreme Court has ever handed down. A few years later the Court also claimed the right of judicial review over actions of state legislatures; during Marshall's tenure it overturned more than a dozen state laws on constitutional grounds.[17]

The Changing Issue Emphasis of the Supreme Court

We complete our brief historical review of the Supreme Court by looking at the major issue areas that have occupied the Court's attention. Until approximately 1865 the legal relationship between the national and state governments, or cases of federalism, dominated the Court's docket. John Marshall believed in a strong national government and was not hesitant to restrict state policies that interfered with its activities. A case in point is *Gibbons v. Ogden* (1824), in which the Court overturned a state monopoly over steamboat transportation on the ground that it interfered with national control over interstate commerce.[18] Another good example of Marshall's use of the Court to expand the federal government's powers came in *McCulloch v. Maryland* (1819), in which the chief justice held that the necessary-and-proper clause of the Constitution permitted Congress to establish a national bank.[19] The Court also ruled that the state could not tax a nationally chartered bank. The Court's insistence on a strong government in Washington did not significantly diminish after Marshall's death. Roger Taney, who succeeded Marshall as chief justice, served from 1836 to 1864. Although the Court's position during this period was not as uniformly favorable to the federal government, the Taney Court did not reverse the Marshall Court's direction.

During the period 1865–1937 issues of economic regulation dominated the Court's docket. The shift in emphasis from federalism to economic regulation was brought on by a growing number of national and state laws aimed at monitoring business activities. As such laws increased, so did the number of cases challenging their constitutionality. Early in this period the Court's position on regulation was mixed, but by the 1920s the bench had become quite hostile toward government regulatory policy. Federal regulations were generally overturned on the ground that they were unsupported by constitutional grants of power to Congress, whereas state laws were thrown out mainly as violations of economic rights protected by the Fourteenth Amendment.

Matters came to a head in the mid-1930s as a result of the Court's conflict with President Franklin D. Roosevelt, whose New Deal program to combat the effects of the Depression included broad measures to control the economy. "In the 16 months starting in January 1935, the Supreme Court heard cases involving ten major New Deal measures or actions; eight of them were declared unconstitutional by the Court."[20] Following his overwhelming reelection in 1936, Roosevelt fought back against the Court. On February 5, 1937, he proposed a plan whereby an additional justice could be added to the Court for each sitting justice over the age of seventy. The result of F.D.R.'s "Court-packing" plan would have been to increase the Court's size temporarily to fifteen justices.

While Roosevelt's proposal was being debated in Congress, the Court made an about-face and began to uphold New Deal legislation and similar state legislation.[21] This "switch in time that saved nine," as it has been called, came about because Chief Justice Charles Evans Hughes and Justice Owen Roberts changed their votes to establish majority support for the New Deal legislation. As a result, the Court-packing plan became a moot issue and quietly died in Congress.

Since 1937 the Supreme Court has focused on civil liberties concerns—in particular, the constitutional guarantees of freedom of expression and freedom of religion. In addition, an increasing number of cases have dealt with procedural rights of criminal defendants. Finally, the Court has decided a great number of cases concerning equal treatment by the government of racial minorities and other disadvantaged groups.

The Supreme Court's position on civil liberties and civil rights has varied a good deal over the years. Without doubt, it gave its strongest and most active support for civil liberties and civil rights during the period 1953–1969, when Earl Warren served as chief justice. Perhaps the best-known decision of the period was *Brown v. Board of Education* (1954), which ordered desegregation of the public schools.[22] Other notable decisions guaranteed the right to counsel in state trials, limited police search and seizure practices, required that police inform suspects of their rights, mandated legislatures to be apportioned according to population, and prohibited state-written and state-required prayer in public schools.[23] These and many other controversial decisions led to heavy criticism of the Warren Court.

Although the Court has dealt with a large number of civil rights and civil liberties claims since 1937, and still continues to do so, the term that ended in the summer of 1997 may be best remembered for decisions concerning federalism and separation of powers. As one observer put it,

The Court, proclaiming its primacy in deciding what the Constitution means, scolded Congress for infringing on state powers in the Brady handgun law, for enforcing religious freedom in ways that usurped the power of the courts and the states and for restricting the Internet in a law that violates the First Amendment.[24]

We next turn our attention to the various roles played by the Supreme Court, in particular, its policy-making function and its role as court of final appeal.

The Supreme Court as a Policy Maker

The Supreme Court's role as a policy maker derives from the fact that it interprets the law. Public policy issues come before the Court in the form of legal disputes that must be resolved.

Courts in any political system participate to some degree in the policymaking process because it is their job. Any judge faced with a choice between two or more interpretations and applications of a legislative act, executive order, or constitutional provision must choose among them because the controversy must be decided. And when the judge chooses, his or her interpretation becomes policy for the specific litigants. If the interpretation is accepted by the other judges, the judge has made policy for all jurisdictions in which that view prevails.[25]

An excellent example may be found in the area of racial equality. In the late 1880s many states enacted laws requiring the separation of blacks and whites in public facilities. In 1890, for instance, Louisiana enacted a law requiring separate but equal railroad accommodations for blacks and whites. A challenge came two years later. Homer Plessy, who was one-eighth black, protested against the Louisiana law by refusing to move from a seat in the white car of a train traveling from New Orleans to Covington, Louisiana. Arrested and charged with violating the statute, Plessy contended that the law was unconstitutional. The U.S. Supreme Court, in *Plessy v. Ferguson* (1896), upheld the Louisiana statute.[26] Thus the Court established the *separate-but-equal* policy that was to reign for about sixty years. During this period many states required that the races sit in different areas of buses, trains, terminals, and theaters; use different restrooms; and drink from different water fountains. Blacks were sometimes excluded from restaurants and public libraries. Perhaps most important, black students often had to attend inferior schools.

Separation of the races in public schools was contested in the famous *Brown v. Board of Education* case. Parents of black schoolchildren claimed that state laws requiring or permitting segregation deprived them of equal protection of the laws under the Fourteenth Amendment. The Supreme Court ruled that separate educational facilities are inherently unequal and, therefore, segregation constitutes a denial of equal protection. In the *Brown* decision the Court laid to rest the separate-but-equal doctrine and established a policy of desegregated public schools.

In an average year the Court decides, with signed opinions, between eighty and ninety cases. Thousands of other cases are disposed of with less than the full treatment. Thus the Court deals at length with a very select set of policy issues that, as noted, have varied throughout the Court's history.

In a democracy broad matters of public policy are, in theory at least, presumed to be left to the elected representatives of the people—not to judicial appointees with life terms. Thus, in principle, U.S. judges are not supposed to make policy. However, as we shall demonstrate when we discuss decision making in Chapters 10 and 11, in practice judges cannot help but make policy to some extent.

It should be noted that the Supreme Court differs from legislative and executive policy makers. Especially important is the fact that the Court has no self-starting device. The justices must wait for problems to be brought to them; there can be no judicial policy making if there is no litigation. The president and members of Congress have no such constraints. Moreover, even the most assertive Supreme Court is limited to some extent by the actions of other policy makers, such as lower-court judges, Congress, and the president. The Court depends upon others to implement or carry out its decisions. This process of implementation will be discussed in detail in Chapter 12.

The Supreme Court as Final Arbiter

The Supreme Court has both original and appellate jurisdiction. The two types of jurisdiction will be discussed in detail later, but a brief definition of each will be helpful at this point. *Original jurisdiction* means that a court has the power to hear a case for the first time. *Appellate jurisdiction* means that a higher court has the authority to review cases originally decided by a lower court.

The Supreme Court is overwhelmingly an appellate court since most of its time is devoted to reviewing decisions of lower courts. Regardless of whether its decisions are seen as correct, it is the highest appellate tribunal in the country. As such, it has the final word in the interpretation of the Constitution, acts of legislative bodies, and treaties—unless the Court's decision is altered by a constitutional amendment or, in some instances, by an act of Congress.

Since 1925 a device known as *certiorari* has allowed the High Court to exercise discretion in deciding which cases it should review. Under this method a person may *request* Supreme Court review of a lower-court decision; it is then up to the justices to determine whether the request should be granted. In the term concluded in June 1997, the Court handed down decisions with full opinions in eighty cases.[27] If review is granted, the Court issues a *writ of certiorari,* which is an order to the lower court to send up a complete record of the case. When certiorari is denied, the decision of the lower court stands.

The Supreme Court at Work

The formal session of the Supreme Court lasts from the first Monday in October until the business of the term is completed, usually in late June or July. Since 1935 the Supreme Court has had its own building in Washington. The imposing five-story marble building has the words "Equal Justice Under Law" carved above the entrance. It stands across from the Capitol. Formal sessions of the Court are held in a large courtroom that seats three hundred people. At the front of the courtroom is the bench where the justices are seated. When the Court is in session, the chief justice, followed by the eight associate justices in order of seniority (length of continuous service on the Court), enters through the purple draperies behind the bench and takes a seat. Seats are arranged according to seniority, with the chief justice in the center, the senior associate justice on the chief justice's right, the second-ranking associate justice on the left, and continuing alternately in declining order of seniority. Near the courtroom are the conference room, where the justices decide cases, and the chambers that contain offices for the justices and their staffs.

The Court's term is divided into *sittings*, of approximately two weeks each, during which it meets in open session and holds internal conferences, and *recesses*, during which the justices work behind closed doors as they consider cases and write opinions. The eighty to ninety cases per term that receive the Court's full treatment follow a fairly routine pattern, which is described below.

Oral Argument. Oral arguments are generally scheduled on Monday through Wednesday during the sittings. The sessions run from 10:00 a.m. until noon and from 1:00 until 3:00 p.m. Since the procedure is not a trial or the original hearing of a case, no jury is assembled and no witnesses are called. Instead, the two opposing attorneys present their arguments to the justices. The general practice is to allow thirty minutes for each side, although the Court may decide that additional time is necessary. The Court can normally hear four cases in one day. Attorneys presenting oral arguments are frequently interrupted with probing questions from the justices. The oral argument is considered very important by both attorneys and justices because it is the only stage in the process that allows such personal exchanges.

The Conference. On Fridays preceding the two-week sittings the Court holds conferences; during sittings it holds conferences on Wednesday afternoon and all day Friday. At the Wednesday meeting the justices discuss the cases argued on Monday. At the longer conference on Friday they discuss the cases that were argued on Tuesday and Wednesday, plus any other matters that need to be considered. The most important of these other matters are the certiorari petitions.

Prior to the Friday conference each justice is given a list of the cases that will be discussed. The conference begins at about 9:30 or 10:00 a.m. and runs until 5:30 or 6:00 p.m. As the justices enter the conference room they shake hands with each other and take their seats around a rectangular table. They meet behind locked doors, and no official record is kept of the discussions. The chief justice presides over the conference and offers an opinion first in each case. The other justices follow in descending order of seniority. At one time a formal vote was then taken in reverse order (with the junior justice voting first); however, today the justices usually indicate their view during the discussion, making a formal vote unnecessary.

A quorum for a decision on a case is six members, but there is seldom any difficulty in obtaining a quorum. Cases are sometimes decided by fewer than nine justices because of vacancies, illnesses, or nonparticipation because of possible conflicts of interest. Supreme Court decisions are made by a majority vote. In case of a tie the lower-court decision is upheld.

Opinion Writing. After a tentative decision has been reached in conference, the next step is to assign the Court's opinion to an individual justice. The chief justice, if voting with the majority, either writes the opinion or assigns it to another justice who voted with the majority. When the chief justice votes with the minority, then the most senior justice in the majority makes the assignment.

After the conference the justice who will write the Court's opinion begins work on an initial draft. Other justices may work on the case by writing alternative opinions. The completed opinion is circulated to justices in both the majority and the minority groups. The writer seeks to persuade justices originally in the minority to change their votes, and to keep his or her majority group intact. A bargaining process occurs and the wording of the opinion may be changed in order to satisfy other justices or obtain their support. A deep division in the Court makes it difficult to achieve a clear, coherent opinion and may even result in a shift in votes or in another justice's opinion becoming the Court's official ruling.

In most cases a single opinion does obtain majority support, although few rulings are unanimous. Those who disagree with the opinion of the Court are said to *dissent.* A dissent does not have to be accompanied by an opinion; in recent years, however, it usually has been. Whenever more than one justice dissents, each may write an opinion or all may join in a single opinion.

On occasion a justice will agree with the Court's decision but differ in his or her reason for reaching that conclusion. Such a justice may write what is called a *concurring opinion.* A good example may be found in Justice Potter Stewart's concurring opinion in *Stanley v. Georgia* (1969).[28] In that case an investigation of Stanley's alleged bookmaking activities led to the issuance of a search warrant for his home. Federal and state agents conducting the search found three reels of film, a projector, and a screen. After viewing the films, the state officers seized them as pornographic. Stanley was convicted of "knowingly having possession of obscene matter" in violation of Georgia law. The Supreme Court overturned the Georgia trial court's decision on the ground that mere private possession of lewd material could not constitutionally be made a crime. Justice Stewart agreed that the lower-court decision should be overturned, but he did so for quite a different reason; he felt that the films had been seized unlawfully in violation of the Fourth and Fourteenth Amendments.

An opinion labeled *concurring and dissenting* agrees with part of a Court ruling but disagrees with other parts. Finally, the Court occasionally issues a *per curiam opinion*—an unsigned opinion that is usually quite brief. Such opinions are often used when the Court accepts the case for review but gives it less than full treatment. For example, it may decide the case without benefit of oral argument and issue a *per curiam opinion* to explain the disposition of the case.

The U.S. Courts of Appeals

The courts of appeals have been described as "perhaps the least noticed of the regular constitutional courts."[29] They receive less media coverage than the Supreme Court, in part because their activities are simply not as dramatic. However, one should not assume that the courts of appeals are unimportant to the judicial system. Indeed, when we recall that in its 1996 term the Supreme Court handed down decisions with full opinions in only eighty cases, it becomes readily apparent that the courts of appeals are really the courts of last resort for most appeals in the federal court system.

Circuit Courts: 1789–1801

As noted earlier, the Judiciary Act of 1789 created three circuit courts—the southern, middle, and eastern circuits—each composed of two justices of the Supreme Court and a district judge. The circuit court was to hold two sessions each year in each district within the circuit.

It was the district judge who became primarily responsible for establishing the circuit court's workload. The two Supreme Court justices then came into the local area and participated in the cases. This practice tended to give a local rather than national focus to the circuit courts.

The circuit court system was regarded from the beginning as unsatisfactory, especially by Supreme Court justices, who objected to the traveling imposed upon them. As early as September 1790, Chief Justice Jay wrote to the president urging changes in the circuit-riding duties prescribed by the Judiciary Act of 1789. Justice Iredell, who resided in North Carolina, was particulary hard pressed; in addition to traveling some 1,000 miles between his home and Philadelphia (where Supreme Court sessions were held), he was required to tour the states of Georgia, North Carolina, and South Carolina twice annually. It is no wonder Iredell referred to his life as that of a "travelling postboy."[30]

Supreme Court justices were not the only ones who objected to the circuit-riding duties. Attorney General Edmund Randolph and President Washington also urged relief for the Supreme Court justices. Congress made a slight change in 1793 by altering the circuit court organization to include only one Supreme Court justice and one district judge. The Randolph proposal for separate circuit court judgeships to replace Supreme Court participation was not implemented, however. The circuit courts had become the center of a political controversy. The Federalists urged passage of Randolph's proposal for separate circuit judges; the Anti-Federalist leaders saw the Randolph proposal as an attempt to enlarge the federal judiciary and remove it from state surveillance.

Circuit Courts: 1801–1891

In the closing days of President Adams's administration in 1801, Congress passed the "midnight judges" act, which eliminated circuit riding by the Supreme Court justices, authorized the appointment of sixteen new circuit judges, and greatly extended the jurisdiction of the lower courts.

Some saw the Judiciary Act of 1801 as the Federalists' last-ditch effort to prolong their domination of government, whereas others viewed it as an extension of federal jurisdiction to suits that previously had been tried only in state courts. Certainly the Federalists were interested in federal judgeships, and they wanted to protect the judiciary from Anti-Federalists. The act of 1801, however, was not a last-minute effort. As we have seen, efforts to change the circuit courts had been continuing for more than ten years.

The new administration of Thomas Jefferson strongly opposed the "midnight judges" act, and Congress wasted little time in repealing it. The Circuit Court Act of 1802 restored circuit riding by Supreme Court justices and expanded the number of circuits. However, the 1802 legislation allowed the circuit court to be presided over by a single district judge. At first glance, such a change may seem slight, but it proved to be of great importance. Increasingly, the district judges began to assume responsibility for both district and circuit courts. In practice, then, original and appellate jurisdiction were both in the hands of the district judges.

The next major step in the development of the courts of appeals did not come until 1869, although there had been a growing recognition that some form of judicial reorganization was necessary. The pro-state and pronationalist interests disagreed on the exact form of judicial relief that should be enacted. The pronationalists did not want a plan that would transfer power from the national government to the states. They favored shifting many conflicts to the lower federal courts under the supervision of the Supreme Court. Thus, "reorganization of the circuit courts continued to be the key to the nationalists' strategy."[31]

Expansion of the circuit courts, allowing them greater control over appeals, would free the Supreme Court to concentrate on the key cases as well as to formulate policy. The pro-state interests also wanted to lessen the High Court's burden, but by reducing its power. Unable to do so, they were willing to accept only minor changes in the basic judicial structure established in 1789.

The political stalemate prevented any major reorganization between 1802 and 1869. Consequently, the courts simply were unable to handle the flood of litigation. Then, in 1869, Congress approved a measure that authorized the appointment of nine new circuit judges and reduced the Supreme Court justices' circuit court duty to one term every two years. Still, the High Court was flooded with cases because there were no limitations on the right of appeal to the Supreme Court. Six years later Congress broadened the jurisdiction of the circuit courts. The workload of the Supreme Court was not significantly decreased, however, since there was still an automatic right of appeal to the High Court. A more drastic revision of the federal judicial system was to come in 1891.

The Courts of Appeals: 1891 to the Present

On March 3, 1891, the Evarts Act was signed into law, creating new courts known as circuit courts of appeals. These new tribunals were to hear most of the appeals from district courts. The old circuit courts, which had existed since 1789, also remained—a situation surely confusing to all but the most serious students of the judicial system. The new circuit court of appeals was to consist of one circuit judge, one circuit court of appeals judge, one district judge, and a Supreme Court justice. Two judges constituted a quorum in these new courts.

Following passage of the Evarts Act, there were two trial tribunals in the federal judiciary: district courts and circuit courts. There were also two appellate tribunals: circuit courts of appeals and the Supreme Court. Most appeals of trial decisions were to go to the circuit court of appeals, although the act also allowed direct review in some instances by the Supreme Court. In short, creation of the circuit courts of appeals released the Supreme Court from many petty types of cases. There would still be appeals, but the High Court would now have much greater control over its own workload. Much of its former caseload was thus shifted to the two lower levels of the federal judiciary.

The next step in the evolution of the courts of appeals came in 1911. In that year Congress passed legislation abolishing the old circuit courts, which had no appellate jurisdiction and frequently duplicated the functions of district courts.

Today, as a result of a name change implemented in the 1948 Judicial Code, the intermediate appellate tribunals are officially known as courts of appeals. Despite their official name, they continue to be referred to colloquially as circuit courts. Although these intermediate appellate courts have been manned at one time or another by circuit judges, courts of appeals judges, district judges, and Supreme Court justices, they now are staffed by 179 authorized courts of appeals judges.

Nine regional courts of appeals, each covering several states, were created in 1891. Another, covering the District of Columbia, was absorbed into the system after 1893. Next came the Court of Appeals for the Tenth Circuit, which was carved from the Eighth Circuit in 1929. In 1981, following a long battle during which many civil rights activists expressed the fear that a split might negate gains they had made acting through the courts, the Court of Appeals for the Eleventh Circuit was carved from the Fifth Circuit.[32]

For several years the heavy caseload and geographical expanse of the Ninth Circuit have prompted discussions of a split in that circuit. A number of bills to accomplish that purpose have been introduced in Congress since 1990 but none have passed.

The courts of appeals in each of the twelve regional circuits are responsible for reviewing cases appealed from federal district courts (and in some cases from administrative agencies) within the boundaries of the circuit. Figure 2-1 shows the appellate and district court boundaries and indicates the states contained in each.

A specialized appellate court came into existence in 1982 when Congress established the Federal Circuit, a jurisdictional rather than a geographic circuit. The United States Court of Appeals for the Federal Circuit was created by consolidating the Court of Claims and the Court of Customs and Patent Appeals (types of courts that will be described later in this chapter).

The Review Function of the Courts of Appeals

As one modern-day student of our judiciary has noted:

The distribution of labor among the Supreme Court and the Courts of Appeals, implicit in the Judiciary Act of 1925, has matured into fully differentiated functions for federal appellate courts. Substantively, the Supreme Court has become more and more a constitutional tribunal. Courts of Appeals concentrate on statutory interpretation, administrative review, and error correction in masses of routine adjudications.[33]

Although the Supreme Court has had discretionary control of its docket since 1925, the courts of appeals still have no such luxury. Instead, their docket depends on how many and what types of cases are appealed to them.

FIGURE 2–1   District and Appellate Court Boundaries

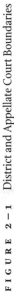

Puerto Rico [1]

Virgin Islands [3]

ME [1]
NH
VT
NY [2]
MA
RI
CT
NJ
PA [3]
DE
MD
DC
WV VA [4]
NC
SC
GA [11]
FL
OH [6]
MI
IN
KY
TN
AL
MS
LA
AR
MO
IA
WI [7]
MN
ND
SD
NE [8]
KS
OK
TX [5]
CO
WY
UT
NM [10]
MT
ID
WA
OR
NV
CA [9]
AZ

HI
Northern Mariana Islands [9]
Guam
AK

Federal Circuit
Washington, D.C.

D.C. Circuit
Washington, D.C.

———— District Boundaries

Number and composition of circuits set forth by 28 U.S.C. § 41

SOURCE: Administrative Office of the United States Courts.
NOTE: The large numerals indicate the Courts of Appeals.

Most of the cases reviewed by the courts of appeals originate in the federal district courts. Litigants disappointed with the lower-court decision may appeal the case to the court of appeals of the circuit in which the federal district court is located. The appellate courts have also been given authority to review the decisions of certain administrative agencies. This type of case enters the federal judicial system at the court of appeals level rather than at the federal district court level.

Since the courts of appeals have no control over which cases are brought to them, they deal with both highly important and routine matters. At one end of the spectrum are frivolous appeals or claims that have no substance and little or no chance for success. Such appeals are no doubt encouraged by the fact that the Supreme Court has ruled that assistance of counsel for first appeals should be granted to all indigents who have been convicted of a crime.[34] Occasionally a claim is successful, which then motivates other prisoners to appeal.

At the other end of the spectrum are the cases that raise major questions of public policy and evoke strong disagreement. Decisions by the courts of appeals in such cases are likely to establish policy for society as a whole, not just for the specific litigants. Civil liberties, reapportionment, religion, and education cases provide good examples of the kinds of disputes that may affect us all.

There are two purposes of review in the courts of appeals. The first is *error correction*. Judges in the various circuits are called upon to monitor the performance of federal district courts and federal agencies and to supervise their application and interpretation of national and state laws. In doing so, the courts of appeals do not seek out new factual evidence, but instead examine the record of the lower court for errors. In the process of correcting errors the courts of appeals also settle disputes and enforce national law.

The courts of appeals perform a second function: *sorting out and developing* those few cases worthy of Supreme Court review. The circuit judges tackle the legal issues earlier than the Supreme Court justices and may help shape what they consider review-worthy claims. Judicial scholars have found that appealed cases often differ in their second hearing from their first. An analysis of cases that raised civil liberties issues when taken from district courts to Court of Appeals for the Third, Fifth, and Eighth Circuits during the period 1956–1961 revealed that only about one-third had had a civil liberties content in the trial court.[35] In other words, the substance of the case shifted on appeal, and routine cases were given greater political significance. More recently, however, a study of Courts of Appeals in the Second, Fifth, and District of Columbia Circuits showed that in only 7 percent of the opinions had circuit judges reformulated the issues.[36]

The Courts of Appeals as Policy Makers

We noted earlier that the Supreme Court's role as a policy maker derives from the fact that it interprets the law; the same holds true for the courts of appeals. The scope of the courts of appeals' policy-making role takes on added importance when we recall that they are the courts of last resort in the vast majority of cases. A study of three circuits in 1986, for example, found that the U.S. Supreme Court reviewed only 19 of the nearly 4,000 decisions of those tribunals.[37]

As an illustration of the far-reaching impact of circuit court judges, consider the recent decision in a case involving the Fifth Circuit. For several years the University of Texas Law School (as well as many other law schools across the country) had been granting preference to black and Mexican-American applicants in order to increase the enrollment of these classes of minority students. This practice was challenged in a federal district court on the ground that it discriminated against white and nonpreferred minority applicants in violation of the Fourteenth Amendment. On March 18, 1996, a panel of Fifth Circuit judges ruled that the Fourteenth Amendment does not permit the school to discriminate in this way and that the law school may not use race as a factor in law school admissions.[38] The U.S. Supreme Court denied a petition for a writ of certiorari in the case,[39] thus leaving it the law of the land in Texas, Louisiana, and Mississippi, the states comprising the Fifth Circuit. Although it may technically be true that only schools in the Fifth Circuit are affected by the ruling, a recent editorial in *The National Law Journal* indicates otherwise, noting that

while cockeyed optimists might argue that *Hopwood*'s impact is limited to three states in the South . . . , the truth is that across the country law school (and other) deans, fearing similar litigation, are scrambling to come up with an alternative to affirmative action.[40]

A major difference in policy making by the Supreme Court and by the courts of appeals should be noted. Whereas there is one High Court for the entire country, each court of appeals covers only a specific region. Thus, the courts of appeals are more likely to make policy on a regional basis. Still, as evidenced by the *Hopwood* case, they are a part of the federal judicial system and "participate in both national and local policy networks, their decisions becoming regional law unless intolerable to the Justices."[41]

The Courts of Appeals at Work

As we noted earlier, the courts of appeals do not have the same degree of discretion as the Supreme Court to decide whether to accept a case for review. Still, as we shall see, circuit judges have developed methods for using their time as efficiently as possible.

Screening. During the screening stage the judges decide whether to give an appeal a full review or to dispose of it in some other way. The docket may be reduced to some extent by consolidating similar claims into single cases, a process that also results in a uniform decision. In deciding which cases can be disposed of without oral argument, the courts of appeals increasingly rely on law clerks or staff attorneys. These court personnel (discussed in greater detail below) read petitions and briefs and then submit recommendations to the judges. As a result, many cases are disposed of without reaching the oral argument stage. One recent study noted that prior to 1970 procedural terminations (terminations without a hearing) averaged 27 percent of the cases commenced in the courts of appeals. From 1970 through 1990 the average increased to 46 percent.[42]

Three-Judge Panels. Those cases given the full treatment are normally considered by panels of three judges rather than by all the judges in the circuit. This means that several cases can be heard at the same time by different three-judge panels, often sitting in different cities throughout the circuit.

As one might guess, in the past there has been some criticism of panel assignments, especially those made by a chief judge. An excellent example is offered by the Fifth Circuit in the early 1960s. Judge Ben F. Cameron claimed that Chief Judge Elbert F. Tuttle stacked the panels hearing civil rights cases so that they would be decided favorably to black claimants.[43]

Today panel assignments are typically made by the circuit executive or someone else and then a clerk assigns cases blindly to the panels. Since all the circuits now contain more than three judges, the panels change frequently so that the same three judges do not sit together permanently. Regardless of the method used to determine panel assignments, one fact remains clear: a decision reached by a majority of a three-judge panel does not necessarily reflect the views of a majority of the judges in the circuit.

En Banc Proceedings. Occasionally, different three-judge panels within the same circuit may reach conflicting decisions in similar cases. To resolve such conflicts and to promote circuit unanimity, federal statutes provide for an *en banc* procedure, in which all the circuit's judges sit together on a panel and decide a case. The exception to this general rule occurs in the large Ninth Circuit where assembling all the judges becomes too cumbersome. There, en banc panels normally consist of eleven judges. The en banc procedure may also be used when the case concerns an issue of extraordinary importance, as in the famous *Tinker* decision.[44] That case raised the question of whether high school students wearing black armbands in the classroom to protest the Vietnam War should be protected by the First Amendment. When the Court of Appeals for the Eighth Circuit heard that case in 1967, the en banc procedure was used.

The en banc procedure may be requested by the litigants or by the judges of the court. The circuits themselves have discretion to decide if and how the procedure will be used. Clearly, its use is the exception rather than the rule.

Oral Argument. Cases that have survived the screening process and have not been settled by the litigants are scheduled for oral argument. Attorneys for each side are given a short amount of time (in some cases no more than ten minutes) to discuss the points made in their written briefs and to answer questions from the judges.

The Decision. Following the oral argument the judges may confer briefly and, if they are in agreement, may announce their decision immediately. Otherwise, a decision will be announced only after the judges confer at greater length. Following the conference some decisions will be announced with a brief order or *per curiam opinion* of the court. A small portion of decisions will be accompanied by a longer, signed opinion and perhaps even dissenting and concurring opinions. Recent years have seen a general decrease in the number of published opinions, although circuits vary in their practices.

U.S. District Courts

The U.S. district courts represent the basic point of input for the federal judicial system. Although some cases are later taken to a court of appeals or perhaps even to the Supreme Court, most federal cases never move beyond the U.S. trial courts. In terms of sheer numbers of cases handled, the district courts are the workhorses of the federal judiciary. As we shall see, however, their importance extends beyond simply disposing of a large number of cases.

The First District Courts

Congress made the decision to create a national network of federal trial courts when it passed the Judiciary Act of 1789. Section 2 of the act established thirteen district courts by (1) making each of the eleven states then in the union a district, and (2) making the parts of Massachusetts and Virginia that were to become Maine and Kentucky into separate districts. That organizational scheme established the practice, which still exists, of honoring state boundary lines in drawing districts. Thus, from the very beginning "the federal judiciary was state-contained, with the administrative and political structure of the states becoming the organizational structure of the federal courts."[45]

The First District Judges

Each federal district court was to be presided over by a single judge who resided in the district. As soon as this became known, President Washington began receiving letters from individuals desiring appointment to the various judgeships. Many asked members of Congress or Vice President Adams to recommend them to President Washington. Personal applications were not necessarily successful and were not the only way in which names came to the president's attention. Harry Innes, for example, was not an applicant for the Kentucky judgeship but received it after being recommended by a member of Congress from his state.[46]

Not everyone nominated was willing to serve as a district judge, however. Three of the thirteen whose names were originally submitted to the Senate for confirmation declined the appointment—perhaps because the nominating process "did not permit consultation either with the individuals concerned or representatives of the 'neighborhood' who might know if the office would be accepted."[47] The rejections were somewhat embarrassing, and Washington resorted to careful preliminary screening of future appointments and relied more heavily on his secretary of state for recommendations.

In our discussion of early Supreme Court nominations we noted that many prospective nominees preferred state-level appointments. The same held true for district court appointments. Some declined federal district judgeships in order to pursue other federal or state positions. Still others simply held both a district judgeship and a state office simultaneously.[48] Eventually, states began to pass laws prohibiting state officeholders from accepting federal positions.

As new states came into the Union, additional district courts were created. The additions, along with resignations, gave Washington an opportunity to offer judgeships to thirty-three people, twenty-eight of whom accepted. A student of the early courts offers a profile of the judges Washington appointed. Their average age at appointment was forty-six. All but three were born in the United States, and sixteen had received college educations. All were members of the bar, and all but seven had state or local legal experience as judges, prosecutors, or attorneys general.[49] As we shall see in Chapter 8, presidents have continued to appoint lawyers with public service backgrounds to the federal bench.

Present Organization of the District Courts

The practice of respecting state boundaries in establishing district court jurisdictions began in 1789 and has been periodically reaffirmed by statutes ever since. As the country grew, new district courts were created. Eventually, Congress began to divide some states into more than one district. California, New York, and Texas have the most, with four each. Figure 2-1 shows the number of districts and their boundaries in each state. Other than consistently honoring state lines, the organization of district constituencies appears to follow no rational plan. Size and population vary widely from district to district. Over the years, a court was added for the District of Columbia, and several territories have been served by district courts. There are now U.S. district courts serving the fifty states, the District of Columbia, Guam, Puerto Rico, the Virgin Islands, and the Northern Mariana Islands.

Congress often provides further organizational detail by creating divisions within a district. In doing this, the national legislature precisely lists the counties included in a particular division as well as the cities in which court will be held.

As indicated, the original district courts were each assigned one judge. With the growth in population and litigation, Congress has periodically had to add judges to most of the districts. The Federal Judgeship Act of 1990 created 74 new district judgeships, bringing the current total to 649. Today all districts have more than one judge; the Southern District of New York, which includes Manhattan and the Bronx, currently has 28 judges and is thus the largest. Since each federal district court is normally presided over by a single judge, several trials may be in session at various cities within the district at any given time. The judges fulfill several functions, which we examine next.

The District Courts as Trial Courts

Congress established the district courts as the trial courts of the federal judicial system and gave them original jurisdiction over virtually all cases. They are the only federal courts in which attorneys examine and cross-examine witnesses. The factual record is thus established at this level; subsequent appeals of the trial court decision will focus on correcting errors rather than on reconstructing the facts. The task of determining the facts in a case often falls to a jury, a group of citizens from the community who serve as impartial arbiters of the facts and apply the law to the facts.

The Constitution guarantees the right to a jury trial in criminal cases in the Sixth Amendment and the same right in civil cases in the Seventh Amendment. The right can be waived, however, in which case the judge becomes the arbiter both of questions of fact and of matters of law. Such trials are referred to as *bench trials*. Two types of juries are associated with federal district courts. The *grand jury* is a group of men and women convened to determine whether there is probable cause to believe that a person has committed the federal crime of which he or she has been accused. Grand jurors meet periodically to hear charges brought by the U.S. attorney. *Petit jurors* are chosen at random from the community to hear evidence and determine whether a defendant in a civil trial has liability, or whether a defendant in a criminal trial is guilty or not guilty. Federal rules call for twelve jurors in criminal cases but permit fewer in civil cases. The federal district courts generally use six-person juries in civil cases.

Norm Enforcement by the District Courts

Some students of the judiciary make a distinction between norm enforcement and policy making by the courts.[50] Trial courts are viewed as engaging primarily in norm enforcement, whereas appellate courts are seen as having greater opportunity to make policy.

Norm enforcement is closely tied to the administration of justice, since all nations develop standards considered essential to a just and orderly society. Societal norms are embodied in statutes, administrative regulations, prior court decisions, and community traditions. Criminal statutes, for example, incorporate concepts of acceptable and unacceptable behavior into law. A judge deciding a case concerning an alleged violation of that law is basically practicing norm enforcement. Because cases of this type rarely allow the judge to escape the strict restraints of legal and procedural requirements, he or she has little chance to make new law or develop new policy. In civil cases, too, judges are often confined to norm enforcement; opportunities for policy making are infrequent. Rather, such litigation generally arises from a private dispute whose outcome is of interest only to the parties in the suit.

Policy Making by the District Courts

The district courts also play a policy-making role. One leading judicial scholar explains how this function differs from norm enforcement:

When they make policy, the courts do not exercise more discretion than when they enforce community norms. The difference lies in the intended impact of the decision. Policy decisions are intended to be guideposts for future actions; norm-enforcement decisions are aimed at the particular case at hand.[51]

The discretion that a federal trial judge exercises should not be overlooked, however. As Americans have become more litigation-conscious, disputes that were once resolved informally are now more likely to be decided in a court of law. The courts find themselves increasingly involved in domains once considered private. What does this mean for the federal district courts? According to one study, "These new areas of judicial involvement tend to be relatively free of clear, precise appellate court and legislative guidelines; and as a consequence the opportunity for trial court jurists to write on a clean slate, that is, to make policy, is formidable."[52] In other words, when the guidelines are not well established, district judges have a great deal of discretion to set policy. In fact, some district judges have gained considerable notoriety because of their policy-making activities. One well-known example is Judge William Wayne Justice of the Eastern District of Texas. For over two decades his orders dealing with the standards to be maintained in the state's prison system to comply with the Eighth Amendment's prohibition against cruel and unusual punishment have impacted state appropriations. Justice's far-reaching criminal justice, public education, and legislative redistricting decisions prompted the suggestion that if he were "in the legislature he would never be able to legislate as effectively as he does from the bench."[53]

Three-Judge District Courts

In 1903, Congress passed legislation providing for the use of special three-judge district courts in certain types of cases. Such courts are created on an ad hoc basis; the panels are disbanded when a case has been decided. Each panel must include at least one judge from the federal district court and at least one judge from the court of appeals. Normally, two district judges and one appellate judge constitute the panel. Appeals of decisions of three-judge district courts go directly to the Supreme Court.

The earliest types of cases to be heard by three-judge district courts were suits filed by the attorney general under the Sherman Antitrust Act or the Interstate Commerce Act. Congress later provided that these special courts could decide suits brought by private citizens challenging the constitutionality of state or federal statutes and seeking injunctions to prevent enforcement of the challenged statutes.

An example of the use of a three-judge district court is provided by the abortion case of *Roe v. Wade*.[54] Jane Roe (a pseudonym), a single, pregnant woman, challenged the constitutionality of the Texas antiabortion statute and sought an injunction to prohibit further enforcement of the law. The case was initially heard by a three-judge court consisting of district judges Sarah T. Hughes and W. N. Taylor and Fifth Circuit Court of Appeals Judge Irving L. Goldberg. The three-judge district court held the Texas abortion statute invalid but declined to issue an injunction against its enforcement on the ground that a federal intrusion into the state's affairs was not warranted. Roe then appealed the denial of the injunction directly to the Supreme Court.

Over the years congressional statutes, such as the Civil Rights Act of 1964, the Voting Rights Act of 1965, and the Presidential Election Campaign Fund Act of 1974, have specified the use of three-judge district courts. However, increases in the number of cases decided by such courts led to complaints about caseload problems, since appeals from the three-judge panels go directly to the Supreme Court. Thus, in 1976 Congress virtually eliminated three-judge district courts except in cases concerning reapportionment of state legislatures and congressional redistricting, and in some cases under the Civil Rights Acts.

Constitutional Courts and Legislative Courts

The Judiciary Act of 1789 established the three levels of the federal court system in existence today. Periodically, however, Congress has exercised its power, based on Article III and Article I of the Constitution, to create other federal courts. Courts established under Article III are known as *constitutional courts,* and those created under Article I are called *legislative courts.* The former handle the bulk of litigation in the system and, for this reason, will remain our focus. The Supreme Court, courts of appeals, and federal district courts are, of course, constitutional courts. The U.S. Court of Military Appeals is one example of a legislative court. It was created in 1950 under authority found in Article I, Section 8 of the Constitution, "To constitute Tribunals inferior to the supreme Court," and "To make Rules for the Government and Regulation of the land and naval Forces." Another important legislative court currently in existence is the United States Tax Court (formerly an administrative agency called the Tax Court of the United States, its name was changed by a 1969 statute). Another Article I court is the Court of Veterans Appeals, which was established by legislation signed by President Ronald Reagan on November 18, 1988. This court has exclusive jurisdiction to review decisions of the Board of Veterans Appeals. Judges on this court serve fifteen-year terms of office.

The two types of courts may be further distinguished by their functions. Legislative courts, unlike their constitutional counterparts, often have administrative and quasi-legislative as well as judicial duties. Another difference is that legislative courts are often created for the express purpose of helping to administer a specific congressional statute. Constitutional courts, on the other hand, are tribunals established to handle litigation.

Finally, the constitutional and legislative courts vary in their degree of independence from the other two branches of government. Article III (constitutional court) judges serve during a period of good behavior, or what amounts to life tenure. Since Article I (legislative court) judges have no constitutional guarantee of "good behavior" tenure, Congress may set specific terms of office for them. Judges of Article III courts are also constitutionally protected against salary reductions while in office. Those who serve as judges of legislative courts have no such protection. In sum, the constitutional courts have a greater degree of independence from the other two branches of government than the legislative courts. How important is such independence? Events surrounding the fate of federal bankruptcy courts reveal independence to be a major consideration.

On November 6, 1978, President Jimmy Carter signed into law the Bankruptcy Reform Act. That legislation (1) required that bankruptcy cases be filed in bankruptcy courts rather than in district courts; (2) extended the terms of current bankruptcy judges through March 1984; (3) provided that after March 3, 1984, bankruptcy judges were to be appointed by the president, with Senate confirmation, for fourteen-year terms; (4) simplified existing bankruptcy law; and (5) expanded the jurisdiction of bankruptcy judges. A system of bankruptcy courts was seemingly in place.

Trouble began, however, less than three years later. In a brief order issued on April 23, 1981, and a supplemental memorandum issued on July 24, 1981, U.S. District Judge Miles W. Lord of Minnesota held that the Bankruptcy Reform Act's delegation of Article III authority to bankruptcy judges was unconstitutional.[55] Judge Lord argued that Congress had exceeded its constitutional power when it authorized bankruptcy judges to exercise the jurisdiction and duties of district judges without at the same time vesting them with the tenure and salary protections given Article III judges. The independence question was at the heart of Judge Lord's decision.

The case was appealed to the Supreme Court, which, in a June 1982 decision, agreed that portions of the Bankruptcy Reform Act were unconstitutional. The Court held that certain powers granted by the act to bankruptcy judges could be exercised only by Article III judges, who are insulated from political pressures by life tenure and protection from pay cuts.[56] The Supreme Court asked Congress to pass remedial legislation aimed at handling the bankruptcy problem. After several failures on Congress's part, the federal district courts put into operation a contingency plan recommended by the Judicial Conference of the United States in September 1982.[57] Among other things, the Judicial Conference's emergency rule removed contested matters from bankruptcy judges to district court judges.

After several unsuccessful attempts Congress passed a law in July 1984 to correct the problem. The new legislation provided for the creation of bankruptcy courts as units of the district courts. Bankruptcy judges are now appointed for fourteen-year terms by the court of appeals for the circuit in which the district is located. Most bankruptcy cases can be handled entirely by the bankruptcy judge. However, in certain types of cases, such as personal injury or wrongful death, the bankruptcy judge may only submit proposed findings of fact and the district judge then enters the final order or judgment.

Administrative and Staff Support in the Federal Judiciary

In this section we focus on the daily operation of federal courts, a function that requires a myriad of personnel. Although judges are the most visible actors in the judicial system, a large supporting cast is also at work. Their efforts are necessary to perform the tasks for which judges are unskilled or unsuited, or for which they simply do not have adequate time. Some members of the support team, such as law clerks, may work specifically for one judge. Others—for example, U.S. magistrate judges—are assigned to a particular court. Still others may be employees of an agency, such as the Administrative Office of the United States Courts, that serves the entire judicial system. We begin with a look at U.S. magistrate judges and law clerks.

United States Magistrate Judges

In an effort to help federal district judges deal with increased workloads, Congress passed the Federal Magistrates Act in 1968. This legislation created the office of U.S. magistrate to replace the U.S. commissioners, who had performed limited duties for the federal trial courts for a number of years. In 1990, with passage of the Judicial Improvements Act, their title was changed to U.S. magistrate judge. Magistrate judges are formally appointed by the judges of the district court for eight-year terms of office, although they can be removed before the expiration of the term for "good cause." Currently, these officials are paid $122,912 per year.[58]

The magistrate judge system constitutes a structure that responds to each district court's specific needs and circumstances. Within guidelines set by the Federal Magistrates Acts of 1968, 1976, and 1979, the judges in each district court establish the duties and responsibilities of their magistrate judges. Most significantly, the 1979 legislation permits a magistrate judge, with the consent of the involved parties, to conduct all proceedings in a jury or nonjury civil matter and enter a judgment in the case, and to conduct a trial of persons accused of misdemeanors (less serious offenses than felonies) committed within the district, provided the defendants consent.

In other words, Congress has given federal district judges the authority to expand the scope of magistrate judges' participation in the judicial process. However, because each district has its own particular needs, a magistrate judge's specific duties may vary from one district to the next and from one judge to another. Because the decision to delegate responsibilities to a magistrate judge is still made by the district judge, a magistrate judge's participation in the processing of cases may be more narrow than that permitted by statute.

How has the role of the magistrate judge changed over the years? On the occasion of the twenty-fifth anniversary of the magistrate judge system, *The Third Branch* summed it up this way:

In the early years, magistrate judges spent a high percentage of their time on misdemeanor and petty offense cases, felony preliminary proceedings, prisoner petitions, and social security appeals. Today magistrate judges handle more civil case duties, with increasing focus on pretrial case management, including settlement, and the disposition of cases with the consent of the parties.[59]

Law Clerks

The first use of law clerks by an American judge is generally traced to Horace Gray of Massachusetts. In the summer of 1875, while serving as chief justice of the Massachusetts Supreme Court, he employed, at his own expense, a highly ranked new graduate of the Harvard Law School.[60] Each year, he would employ a new clerk from Harvard. When Gray was appointed to the U.S. Supreme Court in 1882, he brought a law clerk with him to the nation's highest court.

Justice Gray's successor on the High Court was Oliver Wendell Holmes, like Gray a former chief justice of the Massachusetts Supreme Court. Holmes also adopted the practice of annually hiring honor graduates of Harvard Law School as his clerks. At first, Holmes's clerks were selected by Professor John Chipman Gray. Upon Gray's death in 1915, Holmes asked a young Harvard Law School professor named Felix Frankfurter (later a Supreme Court justice himself) to serve as procurer of law clerks. When he joined the Court in 1916, Louis Brandeis made the same request of Frankfurter. Professor Frankfurter, whose proteges were known as the "happy hot dogs," thus supplied clerks for Holmes, Brandeis, and Holmes's successor, Benjamin Cardozo.

When William Howard Taft, a former law professor at Yale, became chief justice, he secured a new law clerk annually from the dean of the Yale Law School. Harlan Fiske Stone, former dean of the Columbia Law School, joined the Court in 1925 and made it his practice to hire a Columbia graduate each year. Over time, then, the short-term law professor protege became the typical Supreme Court law clerk.

Since these early beginnings there has been a steady growth in the use of law clerks by all federal courts. There are now more than 2,000 law clerks working for federal judges and over 600 more serving bankruptcy judges and U.S. magistrate judges.[61] In addition to the law clerks hired by individual judges, all appellate courts and some district courts hire staff law clerks who serve the entire court.

A law clerk's duties vary according to the preferences of the judge for whom he or she works. They also vary according to the type of court. Law clerks for federal district judges often serve primarily as research assistants. They spend a good deal of time examining the various motions filed in civil and criminal cases. They review each motion, noting the issues and the positions of the parties involved, then research important points raised in the motions and prepare written memorandums for the judges. Since their work is devoted to the earliest stages of the litigation process, they may have a substantial amount of contact with attorneys and witnesses. Law clerks at this level may also be involved in the initial drafting of opinions. In fact, one federal district judge said, "I even allow my law clerks to write memorandum opinions. I first tell him what I want and then he writes it up. Sometimes I sign it without changing a word."[62]

At the appellate level, the law clerk becomes involved in a case first by researching the issues of law and fact presented by an appeal. Saving the judge's time is important. Consider the courts of appeals. As we saw earlier, these courts do not have the same discretion to accept or reject a case that the Supreme Court has. Nevertheless, the courts of appeals now use certain screening devices to differentiate between cases that can be handled quickly and those that require more time and effort. Law clerks are an integral part of this screening process.

Beginning around 1960 some courts of appeals began to utilize a new concept: the staff law clerk. The staff clerk, who works for the entire court as opposed to a particular justice, began to be used primarily because of the rapid increase in the number of *pro se* matters (generally speaking, those involving indigents) coming before the courts of appeals. Today, some district courts also have *pro se* law clerks for handling prisoner petitions. In some circuits the staff law clerks deal only with *pro se* matters; in others they review nearly all cases on the court's docket. As a result of their review, a truncated process may be followed—that is, there is no oral argument or full briefing.

A number of cases are scheduled for oral argument, and the clerk may be called upon to assist the judge in preparing for it. Intensive analysis of the record by judges prior to oral argument is not always possible. They seldom have time to do more than scan pertinent portions of the record called to their attention by law clerks. As one judicial scholar aptly noted, "To prepare for oral argument, all but a handful of circuit judges rely upon bench memoranda prepared by their law clerks, plus their own notes from reading briefs." [63]

Once a decision has been reached by an appellate court, the law clerk frequently participates in writing the order that accompanies the decision. The clerk's participation generally consists of drafting a preliminary opinion or order pursuant to the judge's directions. A law clerk may also be asked to edit or check citations in an opinion written by the judge.

Since the work of the law clerk for a Supreme Court justice roughly parallels that of a clerk in the other appellate courts, all aspects of their responsibility do not need to be restated here. However, a few important points about Supreme Court law clerks deserve mention. First, it should be noted that clerks play an indispensable role in helping justices decide which cases should be heard. At the suggestion of Justice Lewis Powell in 1972, a majority of the Court's members began to participate in a "certpool"; the justices pool their clerks, divide up all filings, and circulate a single clerk's certiorari memo to all those participating in the pool.[64] The memo summarizes the facts of the case, the questions of law presented, and the recommended course of action—that is, whether the case should be granted a full hearing, denied, or dismissed. Justice John Paul Stevens, who does not participate in the certpool, nonetheless finds this initial reading of certiorari petitions by the law clerks invaluable. "They examine them all and select a small minority that they believe I should read myself. As a result, I do not even look at the papers in over 80 percent of the cases that are filed." [65]

Once the justices have voted to hear a case, the law clerks, like their counterparts in the courts of appeals, prepare bench memoranda that the justices may use during oral argument. Finally, law clerks for Supreme Court justices, like those who serve courts of appeals judges, help to draft opinions.

Administrative Office of the U.S. Courts

The administration of the federal judicial system as a whole is managed by the Administrative Office of the U.S. Courts, which essentially functions as "the judiciary's housekeeping agency."[66] Since its creation in 1939 it has handled everything from distributing supplies to negotiating with other government agencies for court accommodations in federal buildings to maintaining judicial personnel records to collecting data on cases in the federal courts.

The Administrative Office also serves a staff function for the Judicial Conference of the United States, the central administrative policy-making organization of the federal judicial system. In addition to providing statistical information to the conference's many committees, the Administrative Office acts as a reception center and clearinghouse for information and proposals directed to the Judicial Conference.

Closely related to this staff function is the Administrative Office's role as liaison for both the federal judicial system and the Judicial Conference. The Administrative Office serves as advocate for the judiciary in its dealings with Congress, the executive branch, professional groups, and the general public. Especially important is its representative role before Congress where, along with concerned judges, it presents the judiciary's budget proposals, requests for additional judgeships, suggestions for changes in court rules, and other key measures.

The Federal Judicial Center

The Federal Judicial Center, created in 1967, is the federal courts' agency for continuing education and research. Its duties fall generally into three categories: (1) conducting research on the federal courts, (2) making recommendations to improve the administration and management of the federal courts, and (3) developing educational and training programs for personnel of the judicial branch.

Since its inception, judges have benefitted from orientation sessions and other educational programs put on by the Federal Judicial Center. In recent years, magistrate judges, bankruptcy judges, and administrative personnel have also been the recipients of educational programs. The Federal Judicial Center's extensive use of videos and satellite technology allows it to reach large numbers of people. Chief Justice William Rehnquist noted that a videoseminar on new developments in federal habeas corpus law broadcast from the Center's studio in Washington reached approximately 1,700 judges, judicial staff members, and others.[67] It is estimated that the Federal Judicial Center's educational programs reached over 30,000 judges and judicial branch staff in 1996.[68]

Federal Court Workload

We conclude this chapter with a look at the workload of the federal courts. Our discussion will be rather brief since jurisdiction, or the authority of the courts to deal with specific issues, will be discussed in more detail in Chapter 4. The three levels of the federal judiciary are discussed in turn, beginning with the trial court level.

U.S. District Courts

For the twelve-month period ending June 30, 1995, slightly over 283,000 cases were commenced in the federal district courts. As Table 2-1 indicates, this figure has fluctuated somewhat over the past ten years, ranging from a high of 312,200 cases in 1985 to a low of 264,400 cases in 1990.

Criminal cases accounted for 16 percent of the district courts' docket in 1995. As with the total docket, the number of criminal cases has fluctuated somewhat over the past ten years, declining slightly from 46,500 cases in 1990 to 44,200 cases in 1995. Criminal cases, while fewer in number than civil cases, are generally more time consuming for the courts. Drug cases, which abound in some of the federal district courts in states bordering international boundaries, are especially complex and often involve multiple defendants.

Civil cases far outnumber criminal cases in the federal trial courts, making up 84 percent of the docket in 1995. Civil case filings have also fluctuated over the years. From a high of 273,700 in 1985, they declined to a low of 217,900 in 1990 before increasing to 239,000 in 1995.

U.S. Courts of Appeals

As Table 2-2 reveals, 31,739 cases found their way into one of the regional circuit courts in 1985. By 1990, this figure had climbed to 39,187. Between 1990 and 1995 the figure increased again to 47,269 cases. Criminal case appeals almost doubled

TABLE 2-1 Cases Commenced in U.S. District Courts, 1985, 1990, and 1995

	1985	1990	1995
Civil cases	273,700	217,900	239,000
Criminal cases	38,500	46,500	44,200
Total	312,200	264,400	283,200

SOURCE: Bureau of the Census, *The American Almanac 1996–1997* (Austin, Texas: Hoover's, Inc., 1996), 215.
NOTE: The figures are for fiscal years ending June 30.

TABLE 2-2   Cases Commenced in U.S. Courts of Appeals, 1985, 1990, and 1995

	1985	1990	1995
Criminal	4,989	9,493	10,171
U.S. civil	6,744	6,626	7,761
Private civil	16,827	20,490	25,992
Administrative appeals	3,179	2,578	3,345
Total	31,739	39,187	47,269

SOURCE: Based on figures found in Bureau of the Census, *The American Almanac 1996–1997* (Austin, Texas: Hoover's, Inc., 1996), 215.

NOTE: The figures are for fiscal years ending June 30.

between 1985 and 1990, a fact many attribute to passage in 1987 of Sentencing Guidelines that provided for appeals of sentences imposed by district judges and also to anti-crime legislation carrying mandatory minimum sentences for drug crimes. Defendants facing lengthy prison terms had great incentive to appeal. Between 1990 and 1995, the number of criminal cases filed in the courts of appeals increased at a much slower pace.

Private civil cases have increased steadily between 1985 and 1995. This may be attributed in large part to increases in prisoner petitions, many of which are *pro se* cases. Employment civil rights cases have also been on the rise.

U.S. Supreme Court

The overall caseload of the Supreme Court is large by historical standards, and the rate of increase appears to be on the upswing (see Table 2-3). Between 1985 and 1990 the total number of paid cases, pauper cases, and original jurisdiction cases on the High Court's docket increased from 5,158 to 6,316. By 1994, the total figure had increased to 8,100 cases.

Perhaps the key point to remember about the workload of the Supreme Court is that it has discretion to decide which cases merit its full attention. As a result, the number of cases actually argued before the Court has declined rather dramatically over the years. In the 1994 term only 94 cases were argued. Three were decided by per curiam opinions and the remaining 91 were decided by signed opinion.

Summary

In this chapter we offered a brief historical review of the development of the federal judiciary. Since preconstitutional times there has been a perennial concern for independent court systems.

TABLE 2-3 Cases Commenced and Decided by Signed Opinion in the U.S. Supreme Court, 1985, 1990, and 1994

	1985	1990	1994
Appellate cases on docket	2,571	2,351	2,515
Pauper cases on docket	2,577	3,951	5,574
Original cases on docket	10	14	11
Total cases on docket	5,158	6,316	8,100
Cases argued	171	125	94
Cases decided by signed opinion	161	121	91

SOURCE: Based on figures found in Bureau of the Census, *The American Almanac 1996–1997* (Austin, Texas: Hoover's, Inc., 1996), 214.

NOTE: Statutory term of the U.S. Supreme Court begins the first Monday in October.

We focused on the three basic levels created by the Judiciary Act of 1789, noting, however, that Congress has periodically created both constitutional and legislative courts. The bulk of federal litigation is handled by U.S. district courts, courts of appeals, and the Supreme Court. We also briefly examined the role of bankruptcy judges, magistrate judges, and law clerks associated with the federal judiciary.

In terms of administrative assistance for the federal courts, our discussion centered on the Administrative Office of the U.S. Courts and the Federal Judicial Center. A brief look at the workload of each of the three levels of the federal judiciary concluded the chapter.

NOTES

1. See Victor E. Flango, *Habeas Corpus in State and Federal Courts* (Williamsburg, Va.: National Center for State Courts and State Justice Institute, 1994), 9–10.

2. This summary is drawn from *The Third Branch* 28 (November 1996): 1–2.

3. Charles Evans Hughes, *The Supreme Court of the United States* (New York: Columbia University Press, 1966), 1.

4. Ibid., 2.

5. Charles Warren, *The Supreme Court in United States History*, vol. 1 (Boston: Little, Brown, 1924), 4.

6. Fred Rodell, *Nine Men* (New York: Random House, 1955), 47.

7. See Warren, *The Supreme Court in United States History*, vol. 1, 44.

8. John P. Frank, *Marble Palace* (New York: Knopf, 1958), 9.

9. Warren, *The Supreme Court in United States History*, vol. 1, 51.

10. *Chisholm v. Georgia*, 2 Dallas 419 (1793).

11. *Champion and Dickason v. Casey*, U.S. District Court for the District of Rhode Island, June 2, 1792.

12. *Hayburn's Case*, 2 Dallas 409 (1792).

13. Robert J. Steamer, *Chief Justice: Leadership and the Supreme Court* (Columbia: University of South Carolina Press, 1986), 232.

14. Frank, *Marble Palace,* 79.

15. See Sheldon Goldman, *Constitutional Law and Supreme Court Decision-Making* (New York: Harper & Row, 1982), 41.

16. *Marbury v. Madison,* 1 Cranch 137 (1803).

17. See Lawrence Baum, *The Supreme Court,* 5th ed. (Washington, D.C.: CQ Press, 1995), 22.

18. *Gibbons v. Ogden,* 9 Wheaton 1 (1824).

19. *McCulloch v. Maryland,* 4 Wheaton 316 (1819).

20. Goldman, *Constitutional Law and Supreme Court Decision-Making,* 249.

21. See *National Labor Relations Board v. Jones and Laughlin Steel Corp.,* 301 U.S. 1 (1937); *Steward Machine Co. v. Davis,* 301 U.S. 548 (1937); and *West Coast Hotel Co. v. Parrish,* 300 U.S. 379 (1937).

22. *Brown v. Board of Education,* 347 U.S. 483 (1954).

23. See *Gideon v. Wainwright,* 372 U.S. 335 (1963); *Mapp v. Ohio,* 367 U.S. 643 (1961); *Miranda v. Arizona,* 384 U.S. 436 (1966); *Baker v. Carr,* 369 U.S. 186 (1962); and *Engel v. Vitale,* 370 U.S. 421 (1962), respectively.

24. Tony Mauro, "Supreme Court Term: A Showcase of Power," *USA Today,* June 30, 1997, 3A. Two other interesting accounts of the Court's term may be found in Harvey Berkman, "Court Declares 'No Trespass,' " *The National Law Journal,* July 14, 1997, A1, A26; and Steven G. Calabresi, "A Constitutional Revolution," *Wall Street Journal,* July 10, 1997, A14. The cases are *Printz v. United States,* 95-1478 (June 27, 1997); *City of Boerne v. Flores,* 95-2074 (June 25, 1997); and *Reno v. ACLU,* 96-511 (June 26, 1997), respectively.

25. Robert H. Birkby, *The Court and Public Policy* (Washington, D.C.: CQ Press, 1983), 1.

26. *Plessy v. Ferguson,* 163 U.S. 537 (1896).

27. Legal Information Institute, "Important Decisions of the Supreme Court's 1996–97 Term," *http://supct.law.cornell.edu/supct/supct96 –97.html.*

28. *Stanley v. Georgia,* 394 U.S. 557 (1969).

29. Stephen T. Early, Jr., *Constitutional Courts of the United States* (Totowa, N.J.: Littlefield, Adams, 1977), 100.

30. See Warren, *The Supreme Court in United States History,* vol. 1, 85, 86.

31. Richard J. Richardson and Kenneth N. Vines, *The Politics of Federal Courts* (Boston: Little, Brown, 1970), 27.

32. For a thorough account of the Fifth Circuit split, see Deborah J. Barrow and Thomas G. Walker, *A Court Divided: The Fifth Circuit Court of Appeals and the Politics of Judicial Reform* (New Haven, Conn.: Yale University Press, 1988).

33. J. Woodford Howard, Jr., *Courts of Appeals in the Federal Judicial System: A Study of the Second, Fifth, and District of Columbia Circuits* (Princeton, N.J.: Princeton University Press, 1981), 75–76.

34. See *Douglas v. California,* 372 U.S. 353 (1963).

35. See Richard J. Richardson and Kenneth N. Vines, "Review, Dissent and the Appellate Process: A Political Interpretation," *Journal of Politics* 29 (August 1967): 597–616.

36. See Howard, *Courts of Appeals in the Federal Judicial System,* 42.

37. See Donald R. Songer, "The Circuit Courts of Appeals," in *The American Courts: A Critical Assessment,* ed. John B. Gates and Charles A. Johnson (Washington, D.C.: CQ Press, 1991), 47.

38. *Hopwood v. Texas,* No. 94-50664, Fifth Circuit, March 18, 1996.

39. *Hopwood v. Texas,* 116 S.Ct. 2581 (1996).

40. "Hopwood's Shadow," *The National Law Journal,* January 27, 1997, A22.

41. Howard, *Courts of Appeals in the Federal Judicial System,* 79.

42. Christine B. Harrington and Daniel S. Ward, "Patterns of Appellate Litigation, 1945–1990," in *Contemplating Courts,* ed. Lee Epstein (Washington, D.C.: CQ Press, 1995), 211.

43. See Early, *Constitutional Courts of the United States*, 112–113, for the specifics of Judge Cameron's charges.

44. *Tinker v. Des Moines Independent Community School District*, 393 U.S. 503 (1969).

45. Richardson and Vines, *The Politics of Federal Courts*, 21.

46. Dwight F. Henderson, *Courts for a New Nation* (Washington, D.C.: Public Affairs Press, 1971), 27.

47. Ibid., 28.

48. Ibid., 29–30.

49. Ibid., 30–31.

50. See Herbert Jacob, *Justice in America*, 4th ed. (Boston: Little, Brown, 1984), chap. 2.

51. Ibid., 37.

52. Robert A. Carp and C. K. Rowland, *Policymaking and Politics in the Federal District Courts* (Knoxville: University of Tennessee Press, 1983), 3.

53. Quoted in C. K. Rowland and Robert A. Carp, *Politics and Judgment in Federal District Courts* (Lawrence: University Press of Kansas, 1996), 2.

54. The decision of the three-judge district court may be found in *Roe v. Wade*, 314 F. Supp. 1217 (1970), and the Supreme Court decision in *Roe v. Wade*, 410 U.S. 113 (1973).

55. See *Northern Pipeline Construction Co. v. Marathon Pipe Line Company*, 6 B.R. 928 (1981) and 12 B.R. 946 (1981).

56. *Northern Pipeline Construction Co. v. Marathon Pipe Line Company*, 458 U.S. 50 (1982).

57. See *The Third Branch* 15 (January 1983): 1 and 8, for a chronology of events in this matter.

58. "What Lawyers Earn," *The National Law Journal*, June 2, 1997, B16.

59. *The Third Branch* 25 (October 1993): 6.

60. Our discussion of the historical evolution of law clerks is drawn from John Bilyeu Oakley and Robert S. Thompson, *Law Clerks and the Judicial Process* (Berkeley: University of California Press, 1980), 10–22.

61. Frank M. Coffin, *On Appeal: Courts, Lawyering, and Judging* (New York: W. W. Norton, 1994), 72.

62. Quoted in Robert A. Carp and Russell R. Wheeler, "Sink or Swim: The Socialization of a Federal District Judge," *Journal of Public Law* 21 (1972): 379.

63. Howard, *Courts of Appeals in the Federal Judicial System*, 198.

64. See David M. O'Brien, *Storm Center: The Supreme Court in American Politics*, 2d ed. (New York: W. W. Norton, 1990), 165.

65. J. P. Stevens, "Some Thoughts on Judicial Restraint," *Judicature* 66 (1982): 179.

66. Peter G. Fish, *The Politics of Federal Judicial Administration* (Princeton, N.J.: Princeton University Press, 1973), 124, 166.

67. William Rehnquist, "1996 Year-End Report on the Federal Judiciary," *The Third Branch* 29 (January 1997): 1–8.

68. Ibid.

SUGGESTED READINGS

Barrow, Deborah J., and Thomas G. Walker. *A Court Divided: The Fifth Circuit Court of Appeals and the Politics of Judicial Reform.* New Haven, Conn.: Yale University Press, 1988. An excellent study of the politics involved in the splitting of the Fifth Circuit Court of Appeals.

Baum, Lawrence. *The Supreme Court*, 6th ed. Washington, D.C.: CQ Press, 1998. A brief look at all aspects of the U.S. Supreme Court.

Carp, Robert A., and C. K. Rowland. *Policymaking and Politics in the Federal District Courts.* Knoxville: University of Tennessee Press, 1983. A thorough study of the various factors that influence the decisions of federal district judges.

Gates, John B., and Charles A. Johnson, eds. *The American Courts: A Critical Assessment.* Washington, D.C.: CQ Press, 1991. A collection of readings about state and federal trial and appellate courts, judicial selection, and judicial decision making.

Howard, J. Woodford, Jr. *Courts of Appeals in the Federal Judicial System.* Princeton, N.J.: Princeton University Press, 1981. A good study of federal courts of appeals in the Second, Fifth, and District of Columbia circuits.

Richardson, Richard J., and Kenneth N. Vines. *The Politics of Federal Courts.* Boston: Little, Brown, 1970. An excellent study of the politics involved in the creation of the federal judicial system.

Steamer, Robert J. *Chief Justice: Leadership and the Supreme Court.* Columbia: University of South Carolina Press, 1986. A thorough study of the leadership styles of the men who have served as chief justice.

CHAPTER 3

History and Organization of State Judicial Systems

With the denial of constitutional protection to same-sex marriages in Congress's Defense of Marriage Act of 1996, the arena now shifts back to the states, where laws on the subject are unclear or nonexistent.

AS WE NOTED IN CHAPTER 2, even prior to the Articles of Confederation and the writing of the U.S. Constitution in 1787, the colonies, as sovereign entities, already had written constitutions. Thus, the development of state court systems can be traced from the colonial period to the present in terms of organization and procedures.

Historical Development of State Courts

We should note at the outset that no two states are exactly alike when it comes to the organization of courts. Each state is entirely free to adopt any organizational scheme it chooses, create as many courts as it wishes, name those courts whatever it pleases, and establish their jurisdiction as it sees fit. Thus, the organization of state courts does not necessarily resemble the clear-cut three-tier system found at the federal level. For instance, we have seen that in the federal system the trial courts are called district courts and the appellate tribunals are known as circuit courts. However, in well over a dozen states the circuit courts are trial courts. Several other states use the term "superior court" for their major trial courts. Perhaps the most bewildering situation is found in New York, where the major trial courts are known as supreme courts.

Although there is a great deal of confusion surrounding the organization of state courts, there is no doubt about their importance. Because statutory law is more extensive in the states than at the federal level, covering everything from the most basic personal relationships to the state's most important public policies, the state courts handle a wide variety of cases. One study of state supreme courts says that the main categories of cases include:

appeals in major felonies; state regulation of business and professions; a wide range of private economic disputes, including business contracts and real estate; wills, trusts, and estates; divorce, child custody, and child support; and personal injury suits involving automobile accidents, medical malpractice, job-related injuries, and the like.[1]

Not surprisingly, then, the number of cases litigated annually in the state courts far exceeds those decided in the federal tribunals.

We begin our discussion of the historical evolution of the state court systems by noting that as colonists moved from England to settle in this country they naturally brought with them the various customs and traditions with which they were familiar. For this reason, American law borrowed heavily from English common law. Likewise, common law traditions became important factors in shaping the state court systems. Ohio and Pennsylvania, for example, still call their major trial courts the courts of common pleas, a title whose origin may be traced to England. Some traditions die hard; nonetheless, state courts have undergone major changes over the years.

The Colonial Period

During the colonial period political power was concentrated in the hands of the governor, who was appointed by the king of England. Since the governors performed executive, legislative, and judicial functions, there was no need for an elaborate court system. Thus, the courts of this period were rather simple institutions that borrowed their form from the English judiciary. However, the colonists greatly simplified the English procedures to suit their own needs.

The lowest level of the colonial judiciary consisted of local judges called justices of the peace or magistrates. They were appointed by the colony's governor. At the next level in the system were the county courts, the general trial courts for the colonies. These courts "were at the heart of colonial government."[2] In addition to deciding cases, they performed some administrative functions. Appeals from all courts were taken to the highest level—the governor and his council. Grand and petit juries were also introduced during this period and remain prominent features of the state judicial systems.

By the early eighteenth century the legal profession had begun to change. Lawyers trained in the English Inns of Court became more numerous, and as a consequence colonial court procedures were slowly replaced by more sophisticated English common law. In addition, common commercial needs and a common language helped to make colonial and English legal practices more similar. As one judicial scholar notes, "In a relatively short time—between 1760 and 1820—a rather backward colonial legal framework was transformed into a very English common law system."[3]

Early State Courts

Following the Revolution, the powers of the government were not only taken over by legislative bodies, but also greatly reduced. The former colonists were not eager to see the development of a large, independent judiciary since many of them harbored a distrust of lawyers and the common law. The state legislatures carefully watched the courts and in some instances removed judges or abolished specific courts because of unpopular decisions. However, the basic structure of the state judiciaries was not greatly altered.

Increasingly, a distrust of the judiciary developed as courts declared legislative actions unconstitutional. Conflicts between legislatures and judges, often stemming from opposing interests, became more prominent. Legislators seemed more responsive to policies that favored debtors, whereas courts generally reflected the views of creditors. These differences were important, however, because "out of this conflict over legislative and judicial power . . . the courts gradually emerged as an independent political institution."[4]

Modern State Courts

Moving from the Civil War to the early twentieth century, we find the state courts beset by still other problems. Increasing industrialization and the rapid growth of urban areas created new types of legal disputes and resulted in longer and more complex court cases. The state court systems, largely fashioned to handle the problems of a rural, agrarian society, were now faced with a crisis of backlogs as they struggled to adjust.

One typical response was to create new courts to handle the increased volume of cases. Often, courts were simply piled on top of each other. Another strategy was the addition of new courts coupled with a careful specification of their jurisdiction in terms of a specific geographic area. Still another response was to create specialized courts to handle one particular type of case. Small claims courts, juvenile courts, and domestic relations courts, for example, became increasingly prominent.

The result of all this activity was a confusing array of courts, especially in the major urban areas. Additional problems were created as well. One observer noted that

each court was a separate entity; each had a judge and a staff. Such an organizational structure meant there was no way to shift cases from an overloaded court to one with little to do. In addition, each court produced political patronage jobs for the city political machines.[5]

Chicago provides an appropriate example of such problems. By the early 1930s there were over 550 independent courts in the city, primarily justice of the peace courts, which handled minor cases.[6]

The largely unplanned expansion of state and local courts to meet specific needs led to a situation many have referred to as fragmentation. A multiplicity of trial courts was only one aspect of fragmentation, however. Many of these courts had very narrow jurisdiction. Furthermore, the jurisdictions of the various courts often overlapped. This meant that a case could be tried in a number of courts depending on the advantages each one offered. Court costs, court procedures, court delays, and last but certainly not least, the reputation of the judge all entered into the decision. For example, a strict, law-and-order district attorney prosecuting a criminal case might choose a court that had a reputation for handing out stiff sentences. An attorney filing a civil suit in behalf of a client might seek a court known for its complex procedures in order to draw the other side into a confusing web of legal technicalities. Political considerations were also involved in the choice of a court. The justice of the peace courts were especially political since many of them operated on a fee basis. Justices of the peace (J. P.'s) were often willing to trade favorable decisions for court business. In fact, the initials J. P. were often said to stand for "Justice for the Plaintiff."[7]

Early in the twentieth century, people began to speak out against the fragmenta-tion in the state court systems. The program of reforms that emerged in response is generally known as the court unification movement. The first well-known legal scholar to speak out in favor of court unification was Roscoe Pound, dean of the Harvard Law School.[8] Pound and others called for the consolidation of trial courts into a single set of courts or two sets of courts, one to hear major cases and one to hear minor cases.

There has, of course, been a good deal of opposition to court unification. Many trial lawyers who are in court almost daily become accustomed to existing court or-ganizations and therefore are opposed to change. Knowledge of the local courts is the key to their success, so they naturally are not eager to try cases in strange new courts.

Also, judges and other personnel associated with the courts are sometimes op-posed to reform. Their opposition often grows out of fear—of being transferred to new courts, or of having to learn new procedures, or of having to decide cases out-side their area of specialization. Nonlawyer judges, such as justices of the peace, of-ten oppose court reform because they view it as a threat to their jobs.

The court unification movement, then, has not been as successful as many would like. On the other hand, proponents of court reform have secured victories in some states. With this battle over court unification in mind, we next examine the basic organization of the state courts in a contemporary setting.

State Court Organization

Some states have moved in the direction of a unified court system, whereas oth-ers still operate with a bewildering complex of courts with overlapping jurisdiction. The state courts may be divided into four general categories or levels: trial courts of limited jurisdiction, trial courts of general jurisdiction, intermediate appellate courts, and courts of last resort.

Trial Courts of Limited Jurisdiction

Trial courts of limited jurisdiction handle the bulk of litigation in this country each year and constitute about 90 percent of all courts in the United States.[9] They have a variety of names: justice of the peace courts, magistrate courts, municipal courts, city courts, county courts, juvenile courts, domestic relations courts, and metropolitan courts, to name the more common ones.

The jurisdiction of these courts is limited to minor cases. In criminal matters, for example, it is commonly recognized that state courts deal with three levels of violations (each of which will be discussed more extensively in Chapter 6): infractions (the least serious), misdemeanors (more serious), and felonies (the most serious). Trial courts of limited jurisdiction handle infractions and misdemeanors. They may impose only limited fines (usually no more than $1,000) and jail sentences (generally no more than one year). In civil cases these courts are usually limited to disputes under a certain amount, such as $500. In addition, these types of courts are often limited to certain kinds of matters: traffic violations, domestic relations matters, or cases involving juveniles, for example. Another difference from trial courts of general jurisdiction is that in many instances these limited courts are not courts of record. Since their proceedings are not recorded, appeals of their decisions usually go to a trial court of general jurisdiction for what is known as a *trial de novo* (new trial).

Yet another distinguishing characteristic of trial courts of limited jurisdiction is that the presiding judges of such courts are often not required to have any formal legal training. Many, in fact, are only part-time judges who are sometimes unfamiliar with basic legal concepts.[10]

Many of these courts suffer from a lack of resources. Often, they have no permanent courtroom, meeting instead in grocery stores, restaurants, or private homes. Clerks are frequently not available to keep adequate records. The results are informal proceedings and the processing of cases on a mass basis. Full-fledged trials are rare and cases are disposed of quickly.

Finally, we should note that trial courts of limited jurisdiction are used in some states to handle preliminary matters in felony criminal cases. They often hold arraignments, set bail, appoint attorneys for indigent defendants, and conduct preliminary examinations. The case is then transferred to a trial court of general jurisdiction for such matters as hearing pleas, holding trials, and sentencing.

Trial Courts of General Jurisdiction

Most states have one set of major trial courts that handle the more serious criminal and civil cases. In addition, in many states special categories, such as juvenile criminal offenses, domestic relations cases, and probate cases, are under the jurisdiction of the general trial courts.

In the majority of states these courts also have an appellate function. They hear appeals in certain types of cases that originate in trial courts of limited jurisdiction. As we noted above, these appeals are often heard in a trial de novo, or tried again in the court of general jurisdiction.

General trial courts are usually divided into judicial districts or circuits. Although the practice varies by state, the general rule is to use existing political boundaries such as a county or a group of counties in establishing the district or circuit. In rural areas the judge may literally ride circuit and hold court in different parts of the territory according to a fixed schedule. In urban areas, on the other hand, judges hold court in a prescribed place throughout the year. In larger counties the group of judges may be divided into specializations. Some may hear only civil cases; others try criminal cases exclusively.

The courts at this level have a variety of names. The most common are district, circuit, and superior. As Table 3-1 indicates, Ohio and Pennsylvania still cling to the title "court of common pleas." New York is undoubtedly the most confusing of all: it calls its trial court of general jurisdiction the supreme court. The judges at this level are required by law in all states to have law degrees. These courts also maintain clerical help because they are courts of record. In other words, there is a degree of professionalism at this level that is often lacking in the trial courts of limited jurisdiction.

Intermediate Appellate Courts

The intermediate appellate courts are relative newcomers to the state judicial scene. Only thirteen such courts existed in 1911, whereas thirty-nine states had created them by 1995. Their basic purpose is to relieve the workload of the state's highest court.

In most instances these courts are called courts of appeals, although other names are occasionally used. Most states have one court of appeals with statewide jurisdiction. Other states, such as Ohio and Texas, have created regional appellate courts to hear appeals from trial courts in a specific area. Alabama and Tennessee have separate intermediate appellate courts for civil and criminal cases.

The names of these intermediate appellate courts vary, as shown in Table 3-2. The size of intermediate courts also varies from state to state. The court of appeals in Alaska, for example, has only three judges. At the other extreme we find eighty courts of appeals judges in Texas.[11] In some states the intermediate appeals courts sit en banc, whereas in other states they sit in permanent or rotating panels.

Generally speaking, the jurisdiction of intermediate appellate courts is mandatory since Americans hold to the view that parties in a case are entitled to at least one appeal. In numerous instances, then, these are the courts of last resort for litigants in the state court system.

TABLE 3-1 General Trial Courts in the United States

Name of court	State(s)[a]
Chancery Court	Mississippi, Tennessee
Chancery/Probate Court	Arkansas
Circuit Court	Alabama, Arkansas, Florida, Hawaii, Illinois, Indiana, Kentucky, Maryland, Michigan, Mississippi, Missouri, Oregon, South Carolina, South Dakota, Tennessee, Virginia, West Virginia, Wisconsin
County Court	New York
Court of Chancery	Delaware
Court of Common Pleas	Ohio, Pennsylvania
District Court	Colorado, Idaho, Iowa, Kansas, Louisiana, Minnesota, Montana, Nebraska, Nevada, New Mexico, North Dakota, Oklahoma, Texas, Utah, Vermont, Wyoming
Probate Court	Indiana
Superior Court	Alaska, Arizona, California, Connecticut, Delaware, Georgia, Indiana, Maine, New Hampshire, New Jersey, North Carolina, Rhode Island, Vermont, Washington
Supreme Court	New York
Tax Court	Oregon
Trial Court	Massachusetts

SOURCE: Council of State Governments, *The Book of the States, 1996–97* (Lexington, Ky.: Council of State Governments, 1996), 129–130. Copyright 1996. Reprinted with permission from *The Book of the States.*

[a] Some states have more than one general trial court.

Courts of Last Resort

Every state has a court of last resort. In fact, the states of Oklahoma and Texas have two highest courts. Both states have a supreme court with jurisdiction limited to appeals in civil cases and a court of criminal appeals for criminal cases. According to Table 3-3, most states call their highest courts supreme courts; other designations are the court of appeals (Maryland and New York), the supreme judicial court (Maine and Massachusetts), and the supreme court of appeals (West Virginia).

The courts of last resort range in size from three to nine judges (or justices in some states). They typically sit en banc and usually, although not necessarily, in the state capital.

TABLE 3-2   Intermediate Courts of Appeals in the United States

Court	State(s)
Appeals Court	Massachusetts
Appellate Court	Connecticut, Illinois
Appellate Division of Superior Court	New Jersey
Appellate Terms of Supreme Court	New York
Commonwealth Court	Pennsylvania
Court of Appeals	Alaska, Arizona, Arkansas, California, Colorado, Georgia, Idaho, Indiana, Iowa, Kansas, Kentucky, Louisiana, Michigan, Minnesota, Missouri, Nebraska, New Mexico, North Carolina, North Dakota, Ohio, Oklahoma, Oregon, South Carolina, Tennessee, Texas, Utah, Virginia, Washington, Wisconsin
Court of Civil Appeals	Alabama
Court of Criminal Appeals	Alabama, Tennessee
Court of Special Appeals	Maryland
District Court	Florida
Intermediate Court of Appeals	Hawaii
Superior Court	Pennsylvania

SOURCE: Council of State Governments, *The Book of the States, 1996–97* (Lexington, Ky.: Council of State Governments, 1996), 129–130. Copyright 1996. Reprinted with permission from *The Book of the States.*

The highest courts have jurisdiction in matters pertaining to state law and are, of course, the final arbiters in such matters. In states that have intermediate appellate courts, the supreme court's cases come primarily from these mid-level courts. In this situation the high court typically is allowed to exercise discretion in deciding which cases to review. Thus, it is likely to devote more time to cases that deal with the important policy issues of the state. When there is no intermediate court of appeals, cases generally go to the state's highest court on a mandatory review basis. This, of course, is likely to create a role of error correction for the court of last resort in rather routine cases and to reduce its opportunities for policy making.[12]

In most instances, then, the state courts of last resort resemble the U.S. Supreme Court in that they have a good deal of discretion in determining which cases will occupy their attention. Most state supreme courts also follow procedures similar to those of the U.S. Supreme Court. That is, when a case is accepted for review, the op-

TABLE 3-3 Courts of Last Resort in the United States

Court	State(s)
Court of Appeals	Maryland, New York
Court of Criminal Appeals	Oklahoma, Texas
Supreme Court	Alabama, Alaska, Arizona, Arkansas, California, Colorado, Connecticut, Delaware, Florida, Georgia, Hawaii, Idaho, Illinois, Indiana, Iowa, Kansas, Kentucky, Louisiana, Michigan, Minnesota, Mississippi, Missouri, Montana, Nebraska, Nevada, New Hampshire, New Jersey, New Mexico, North Carolina, North Dakota, Ohio, Oklahoma, Oregon, Pennsylvania, Rhode Island, South Carolina, South Dakota, Tennessee, Texas, Utah, Vermont, Virginia, Washington, Wisconsin, Wyoming
Supreme Court of Appeals	West Virginia
Supreme Judicial Court	Maine, Massachusetts

SOURCE: Council of State Governments, *The Book of the States, 1996–97* (Lexington, Ky.: Council of State Governments, 1996), 127–128. Copyright 1996. Reprinted with permission from *The Book of the States.*

posing parties file written briefs and later present oral arguments. Then, upon reaching a decision, the judges issue written opinions explaining that decision.

Juvenile Courts

Even the most casual reading of a daily newspaper or viewing of a nightly news broadcast acquaints one with the fact that there is increasing concern in the United States about the handling of cases involving juveniles. Not surprisingly, states have responded to the problem in a variety of ways.[13] Some have established a statewide network of courts specifically to handle matters involving juveniles. They are commonly called juvenile courts or family courts. Georgia, for example, has 159 juvenile courts throughout the state. Rhode Island and South Carolina provide good examples of another approach. These two states have family courts, which handle domestic relations matters as well as those involving juveniles. Still other states have juvenile and/or family courts in limited areas. In Colorado, there is a juvenile court for Denver. Louisiana has created four juvenile courts for the state and one family court in East Baton Rouge.

The most common approach is to give one or more of the state's limited or general trial courts jurisdiction to handle situations involving juveniles. In Alabama, for example, the circuit courts (trial courts of general jurisdiction) have jurisdiction over juvenile matters. In Kentucky, on the other hand, exclusive juvenile jurisdiction is lodged in trial courts of limited jurisdiction—the district courts.

Finally, some states apportion juvenile jurisdiction among more than one court. Recall the juvenile court in Denver. No one would believe that problems among juveniles in Colorado are limited to the city of Denver. Instead, the state of Colorado has given jurisdiction over juveniles to district courts (general trial courts) in areas of the state other than Denver.

As might be expected, there is some variation among the states as to when jurisdiction belongs to an adult court. States set a standard age at which defendants are tried in an adult court. In addition, many states require that more youthful offenders be tried in an adult court if special circumstances are present. In Illinois, for instance, the standard age at which juvenile jurisdiction transfers to adult courts is seventeen. The age limit drops to fifteen, however, for first degree murder, aggravated criminal sexual assault, armed robbery, robbery with a firearm, and unlawful use of weapons on school grounds.

Administrative and Staff Support in the State Judiciary

As we noted in Chapter 2, the daily operation of the federal courts requires the efforts of many individuals and organizations. This is no less true for the state court systems. We begin our discussion with a look at some important judicial actors who serve a single court or a single judge.

Magistrates

State magistrates, who may also be known in some states as commissioners or referees, are often used to perform some of the work in the early stages of civil and criminal case processing. In this way they are similar to the U.S. magistrate judges described in Chapter 2. In some jurisdictions they hold bond hearings and conduct preliminary investigations in criminal cases. They are also authorized in some states to make decisions in minor cases. In North Carolina, for example, the 676 magistrates who lend support to the state's district courts may accept guilty pleas on certain traffic violations as well as exercise jurisdiction over worthless check violations under $800.

Law Clerks

In the state courts law clerks are likely to be found, if at all, in the intermediate appellate courts and courts of last resort. Most state trial courts do not utilize law clerks, and they are practically unheard of in local trial courts of limited jurisdiction. As we saw at the national level, some law clerks serve individual judges while others serve an entire court as a staff attorney.

The number of authorized law clerks varies by state. In 1993, each justice of the California Supreme Court was authorized to hire eight law clerks. Another twenty-nine were authorized for the central law staff. At the other extreme, justices on Maryland's court of appeals (the state's court of last resort) had two law clerks each but had no central law staff.[14]

Administrative Office of the Courts

Every state now has an administrative office of courts or a similarly titled agency that performs a variety of administrative tasks for that state's court system. The size of each state's administrative office and its operating budget varies and, as a result, some of these agencies perform more tasks than others. Among the tasks more commonly associated with administrative offices are budget preparation, data processing, facility management, judicial education, public information, research, and personnel management. Indeed, a number of administrative offices have total or partial responsibility for one or more of these tasks. In some states still other tasks are assigned to administrative offices. Juvenile and adult probation are the responsibility of administrative offices in a few states, as is alternative dispute resolution (discussed in more detail in Chapter 7).

Court Clerks and Court Administrators

The clerk of the court has traditionally handled the day-to-day routines of the court. This includes making courtroom arrangements, keeping records of case proceedings, preparing orders and judgments resulting from court actions, collecting court fines and fees, and disbursing judicial monies. In the majority of states these officials are elected and may be referred to by other titles.

The traditional clerks of court have been replaced in many areas by court administrators. In contrast to the court clerk, who traditionally managed the operations of a specific courtroom, the modern court administrator may assist a presiding judge in running the entire courthouse. Even more broadly, in some states the administrator may work for a statewide organization that oversees all the state court systems at the city or county level. In summary,

Court administrators have emerged as professionals whose expertise in management provides much needed assistance to the judicial leadership at all levels of government. They can help resolve not only the minor technical problems that can easily grow to stymie any court system but can also lend invaluable assistance in the important broader areas of long-term planning and improved public relations.[15]

State Court Workload

The lion's share of the nation's judicial business exists at the state rather than the national level. The fact that federal judges adjudicate several hundred thousand cases a year is impressive; the fact that state courts handle several million in a year is overwhelming, even if the most important cases are handled at the federal level. It is true that justice of the peace and magistrate courts at the state level handle relatively minor matters. However, some of the biggest judgments in civil cases are awarded by ordinary state trial court juries. In a study of the largest verdicts of 1996, *The National Law Journal* reported that the undisputed winner was one for $22 billion in a Hawaiian trial court.[16]

Table 3-4 presents figures compiled by the National Center for State Courts on the caseloads of state courts of last resort and intermediate appellate courts in 1995. In all, some 235,129 mandatory cases and discretionary petitions were filed in the state appellate courts.

Reliable data on cases filed in the state trial courts are a bit harder to come by. Record keeping is much better in some states than in others, and there is also great variation among some of the lower-level courts, which often are not courts of record. Likewise, comparability between states is a problem. For example, in one state the request by an attorney for lawyer's fees may be considered merely another motion in the case that is being litigated, while in another state such a motion may be recorded as a separate issue and hence as a separate case. Still, the National Center for State Courts does an excellent job of tracking the figures for the states' trial courts. Table 3-5 indicates that 14,598,787 cases were filed in the general jurisdiction and limited jurisdiction courts in 1995. As with the federal courts, the vast majority

TABLE 3-4   Number of Cases Filed in State Appellate Courts, 1995

Type of court	Mandatory cases[a]	Discretionary petitions[b]	Total
Court of last resort	22,874	55,156	78,030
Intermediate appellate court	130,711	26,388	157,099
Total	153,585	81,544	235,129

SOURCE: Based on data found in National Center for State Courts, *State Court Caseload Statistics, 1995* (Williamsburg, Va.: National Center for State Courts, 1996), 105.

[a] Not all states provide for mandatory review.

[b] Not all states provide for discretionary review.

TABLE 3-5 Number of Civil and Criminal Cases Filed in State Trial Courts, 1995

Type of court	Civil	Criminal	Total
General jurisdiction	5,480,608	1,516,005	6,996,613
Limited jurisdiction	4,414,143	3,188,031	7,602,174
Total	9,894,751	4,704,036	14,598,787

SOURCE: Based on data found in National Center for State Courts, *State Court Caseload Statistics, 1995* (Williamsburg, Va.: National Center for State Courts, 1996), 138.

of the cases are civil, although it is often the criminal cases that receive the most publicity.

Summary

In this chapter we offered a brief historical review of the development of state judicial systems. No two state court systems are alike. However, there are four basic levels within the states: trial courts of limited jurisdiction, trial courts of general jurisdiction, intermediate appellate courts, and courts of last resort. We examined the work done at each of these four levels. Our discussion also included a brief look at the handling of juvenile cases within the states.

In discussing administrative assistance for the state courts, our review centered around administrative offices of the courts, law clerks, court clerks and court administrators, and magistrates. We concluded with a brief look at the workload of the state trial and appellate courts.

NOTES

1. Henry R. Glick, "Policy Making and State Supreme Courts," in *The American Courts: A Critical Assessment*, ed. John B. Gates and Charles A. Johnson (Washington, D.C.: CQ Press, 1991), 88.

2. Lawrence M. Friedman, *A History of American Law*, 2d ed. (New York: Simon & Schuster, 1985), 43.

3. Harry P. Stumpf, *American Judicial Politics* (San Diego: Harcourt Brace Jovanovich, 1988), 73.

4. David W. Neubauer, *America's Courts and the Criminal Justice System*, 2d ed. (Monterey, Calif.: Brooks/Cole, 1984), 37.

5. Ibid., 38.

6. See Albert Lepawsky, *The Judicial System of Metropolitan Chicago* (Chicago: University of Chicago Press, 1932), 19–23.

7. Henry J. Abraham, *The Judicial Process*, 6th ed. (New York: Oxford University Press, 1993), 138.

8. See Roscoe Pound, "The Causes of Popular Dissatisfaction With the Administration of Justice," *Journal of the American Judicature Society* 20 (1937): 178–187.

9. Stumpf, *American Judicial Politics*, 75.

10. See Allan Ashman and Pat Chapin, "Is the Bell Tolling for Nonlawyer Judges?" *Judicature* 59 (1976): 417–421.

11. See National Center for State Courts, *State Court Caseload Statistics, 1995* (Williamsburg, Va.: National Center for State Courts, 1996), 52.

12. For a study of the roles of state courts of last resort in these structural settings, see Burton M. Atkins and Henry R. Glick, "Environmental and Structural Variables as Determinants of Issues in State Courts of Last Resort," *American Journal of Political Science* 20 (February 1976): 97–115.

13. Our discussion of the various approaches to handling juvenile matters in the states is based on material found in National Center for State Courts, *State Court Caseload Statistics, 1995*, 84–88, 171–174.

14. The figures for California and Maryland are from National Center for State Courts, *State Court Organization 1993* (Williamsburg, Va.: National Center for State Courts, 1995), 187–188.

15. David J. Saari, Michael D. Planet, and Marcus W. Reinkensmeyer, "The Modern Court Managers: Who They Are and What They Do in the United States," in *Handbook of Court Administration and Management*, ed. Steven W. Hays and Cole Blease Graham, Jr. (New York: Marcel Dekker, 1993), 234.

16. See "Verdicts," *The National Law Journal*, February 10, 1997, C1–C16. The case is *Roxas v. Marcos*, 88-0522-02 (Circuit Court, Honolulu).

SUGGESTED READINGS

Hays, Steven W., and Cole Blease Graham, Jr. eds. *Handbook of Court Administration and Management.* New York: Marcel Dekker, 1993. A collection of readings that covers various aspects of management techniques in today's courts.

National Center for State Courts. *State Court Caseload Statistics, 1995.* Williamsburg, Va.: National Center for State Courts, 1996. An excellent source of statistics on state court case filings and dispositions.

National Center for State Courts. *State Court Organization 1993.* Williamsburg, Va.: National Center for State Courts, 1995. This resource presents detailed tables and figures pertaining to the organization and management of state courts.

Stumpf, Harry P., and John H. Culver. *The Politics of State Courts.* New York: Longman, 1992. A short textbook on the judicial process at the state level.

Tarr, G. Alan, and Mary Cornelia Aldis Porter. *State Supreme Courts in State and Nation.* New Haven, Conn.: Yale University Press, 1988. A general discussion of state supreme courts, with a focus on the high courts in Alabama, Ohio, and New Jersey.

CHAPTER 4

Jurisdiction and Policy-Making Boundaries

New York governor Mario Cuomo expresses his concern for the Hasidic Jewish community in the Village of Kiryas Joel. In 1989 the state of New York created a special school district solely for the benefit of this religious group, but five years later the Supreme Court determined that New York had in effect violated the First Amendment's ban on governmental "establishment of religion."

IN SETTING THE JURISDICTIONS OF COURTS, Congress and the U.S. Constitution—and their state counterparts—mandate the types of cases each court can hear. Because the role of legislative bodies in setting courts' jurisdictions is an ongoing one, we will consider how Congress in particular can influence judicial behavior by redefining the types of cases judges can hear. We will also provide a detailed discussion of judicial self-restraint, examining ten principles, derived from legal tradition and constitutional and statutory law, that govern a judge's decision about whether to review a case.

Federal Courts

U.S. District Courts

In the United States Code Congress has set forth the jurisdiction of the federal district courts. These tribunals have *original jurisdiction* in federal criminal and civil cases—that is, by law, the cases must be first heard in these courts, no matter who the parties are or how significant the issues.

Criminal Cases. These cases commence when the local U.S. attorneys have reason to believe that a violation of the U.S. Penal Code has occurred. After first obtaining an indictment from a federal grand jury, the U.S. attorney files charges against the accused in the district court in which he or she serves. Criminal activity as defined by Congress covers a wide range of behavior, including interstate theft of an automobile, illegal importation of narcotics, assassination of a president, conspiracy to deprive persons of their civil rights, and even the killing of a migratory bird out of season. For the past decade or so the most numerous types of criminal code violations have been embezzlement and fraud, larceny and theft, drunk driving and other traffic offenses, drug-related offenses, and forgery and counterfeiting. Some federal crimes, such as robbery, are comparatively uniform in occurrence in each of the ninety-four U.S. judicial districts, whereas others are endemic to certain geographic areas. For example, those districts next to the U.S. borders get an inordinate number of immigration cases, and districts in the Southern states have had the largest share of criminal violations of the civil rights laws.

After charges are filed against an accused, and if there is no plea bargain, a trial is conducted by a U.S. district judge. In court the defendant enjoys all the privileges and immunities granted in the Bill of Rights (such as "the right to a speedy and public trial") or by congressional legislation or Supreme Court rulings (for instance, a twelve-person jury must render a unanimous verdict). As noted in Chapter 2, defendants may waive the right to a trial by a jury of their peers. A defendant who is found not guilty of the crime is set free and may never be tried again for the same offense (the Fifth Amendment's protection against double jeopardy). If the accused is found guilty, the district judge determines the appropriate sentence within a range set by Congress. The length of a sentence is not appealable so long as it is within the range prescribed by Congress. A verdict of not guilty may not be appealed by the government, but convicted defendants may appeal if they believe that the judge or jury made an improper legal determination.

A majority of the district court caseload is civil in nature—that is, suits between private parties or between the U.S. government, acting in its nonprosecutorial capacity, and a private party. Civil cases that originate in the U.S. district courts may be placed in several categories. The first is litigation concerning the interpretation or application of the Constitution, acts of Congress, or U.S. treaties. Examples of cases in this category include the following: a petitioner claims that one of his federally protected civil rights has been violated, a litigant alleges that she is being harmed by a congressional statute that is unconstitutional, and a plaintiff argues that he is suffering injury from a treaty that is improperly affecting him. The key point is that a *federal* question must be raised in order for the U.S. trial courts to have jurisdiction. It is not enough to say that the federal courts should hear a case "because this is an important issue" or "because an awful lot of money is at stake." Unless one is able to invoke the Constitution or a federal law or treaty, the case must be litigated elsewhere (probably in the state courts).

There have traditionally been some minimal dollar amounts that had to be in controversy in some types of cases before the trial courts would hear them, but such amounts have been waived if the case falls into one of several general categories. For example, an alleged violation of a civil rights law, such as the Voting Rights Act of 1965, must be heard by the federal rather than the state judiciary. Other types of cases in this category are patent and copyright claims, passport and naturalization proceedings, admiralty and maritime disputes, and violations of the U.S. postal laws.

Another broad category of cases over which the U.S. trial courts exercise general original jurisdiction includes what are known as diversity of citizenship disputes. These disputes involve parties from different states, or the dispute is between an American citizen and a foreign country or citizen. Thus if a citizen of New York were injured in an automobile accident in Chicago by a driver from Illinois, the New Yorker could sue in federal court, since the parties to the suit were of "diverse citizenship." The requirement that at least $75,000 be at stake in diversity cases does not appear to be much of a barrier to the gates of the federal judiciary: even if actual injuries come to less than $75,000, one can always ask for "psychological damages" to push the amount in controversy above the jurisdictional threshold.

Federal district courts also have jurisdiction over petitions from convicted prisoners who contend that their incarceration (or perhaps their denial of parole) is in violation of their federally protected rights. In the vast majority of these cases prisoners ask for what is termed a *writ of habeas corpus*—that is, an order issued by a judge to determine whether a person has been lawfully imprisoned or detained. The judge would demand that the prison authorities either justify the detention or release the petitioner. Prisoners convicted in a state court must take care to argue that a *federally protected* right was violated—for example, the right to be represented by counsel at trial. Otherwise the federal courts would have no jurisdiction. Federal prisoners have a somewhat wider range for their appeals, since all their rights and options are within the penumbra of the U.S. Constitution.

Finally, the district courts have the authority to hear any other cases that Congress may validly prescribe by law. For example, although the Constitution grants to the U.S. Supreme Court original jurisdiction to hear "Cases affecting Ambassadors, other public Ministers and Consuls," Congress has also authorized the district courts to have concurrent original jurisdiction over cases involving such parties.

U.S. Courts of Appeals

The U.S. appellate courts have no original jurisdiction whatsoever; every case or controversy that comes to one of these intermediate-level panels has been first argued in some other forum. As indicated in Chapter 2, these tribunals, like the district courts, are the creations of Congress, and their structure and functions have varied considerably over time. Basically there are two general categories of cases over which Congress has granted the circuit courts appellate jurisdiction. The first of these are ordinary civil and criminal appeals from the federal trial courts, including the U.S. territorial courts, the U.S. Tax Court, and some District of Columbia courts. In criminal cases the appellant is the defendant because the government is not free to appeal a verdict of "not guilty." (However, if the question in a criminal case is one of defining the legal right of the defendant, then the government may appeal an adverse trial court ruling.) In civil cases the party that lost in the trial court is usually the appellant, although it is not unheard of for the winning party to appeal if it is not satisfied with the lower-court judgment.

The second broad category of appellate jurisdiction includes appeals from certain federal administrative agencies and departments and also from the important independent regulatory commissions, such as the Securities and Exchange Commission and the National Labor Relations Board. In recent years about 10 percent of the civil docket has consisted of administrative appeals. Because so many of the administrative and regulatory bodies have their home base in Washington, D.C., the appeals court for that circuit gets an inordinate number of such cases.

U.S. Supreme Court

The U.S. Supreme Court is the only federal court mentioned by name in the Constitution, which spells out the general contours of the High Court's jurisdiction. Although we usually think of the Supreme Court as an appellate tribunal, it does have some general *original* jurisdiction. Probably the most important subject of such jurisdiction is a suit between two or more states. For example, every so often the states of Texas and Louisiana spar in the Supreme Court over the proper boundary between them. By law the Sabine River divides the two states, but with great regularity this effluent changes its snaking course, thus requiring the Supreme Court (with considerable help from the U.S. Army Corps of Engineers) to determine where Louisiana ends and the Lone Star State begins.

In addition the High Court shares original jurisdiction (with the U.S. district courts) in certain cases brought by or against foreign ambassadors or consuls, in cases between the United States and a state, and in cases commenced by a state against citizens of another state or against aliens. In situations such as these, where jurisdiction is shared, the courts are said to have *concurrent jurisdiction.* Cases over which the Supreme Court has original jurisdiction are often important, but they do not constitute a sizable proportion of the overall caseload. In recent years fewer than 1 percent of the High Court's docket consisted of cases heard on original jurisdiction (see Table 2-3, page 59).

The U.S. Constitution declares that the Supreme Court "shall have appellate Jurisdiction . . . under such Regulations as the Congress shall make." Over the years Congress has passed much legislation setting forth the "Regulations" determining which cases may appear before the nation's most august judicial body. In essence, there are two main avenues through which appeals may reach the Supreme Court. First, there may be appeals from all lower federal constitutional and territorial courts and also from most, but not all, federal legislative courts. Second, the Supreme Court may hear appeals from the highest court in a state—as long as there is a "substantial federal question."

Most of the High Court's docket consists of cases in which it has agreed to issue a writ of certiorari—a discretionary action. Such a writ (which must be supported by at least four justices) is an order from the Supreme Court to a lower court demanding that it send up a complete record of a case so that the Supreme Court can review it. Historically the Supreme Court has agreed to grant the petition for a writ of certiorari in only a tiny proportion of cases—usually less than 10 percent of the time.

There is another method by which the Supreme Court exercises its appellate jurisdiction: *certification.* This procedure is followed when one of the appeals courts asks the Supreme Court for instructions regarding a question of law. The justices may choose to give the appellate judges binding instructions, or they may ask that the entire record be forwarded to the Supreme Court for review and final judgment.

Jurisdiction and Policy Making of State Courts

The jurisdictions of the fifty separate state court systems in the United States are established in virtually the same manner as those within the national court system.

Each state has a constitution that sets forth the authority and decision-making powers of its trial and appellate judges. Likewise, each state legislature passes laws that further detail the specific powers and prerogatives of judges and the rights and obligations of those who bring suit in the state courts. Because no two state constitutions or legislative bodies are alike, it is no surprise that the jurisdictions of individual state courts vary from one state to another. For example, one state constitution may give its supreme court "original jurisdiction" over all cases in which a state is suing one of its counties while another state constitution may confer such jurisdiction only on the low-level circuit courts. Similarly, one state legislature might define "felony theft" as the stealing of $2,000 or more, sending the case automatically to a county criminal court, whereas a case involving less than $2,000 would go to a municipal court authorized to handle only minor crimes. In another state, on the other hand, the legislature might draw the line between "felony" and "petty" theft at $1,000. Thus, while court jurisdictions vary from one state to another and from the national model, they are all derived in part from a constitution and in part from enactments of legislative bodies.

While we are addressing the subject of state courts we need to underscore the substantive importance of these tribunals in terms of policy making in the United States. In Chapter 3 we showed that well over 99 percent of the judicial workload in the United States consists of *state* rather than federal cases, and we further noted that of all judges in the United States, fully 95 percent work at the state level.[1] Moreover, it is important to understand that the comparison is more than just one of numbers; the fact is that the decisions of state jurists frequently have a great impact on public policy. For example, during the 1970s a number of suits were brought into federal court challenging the constitutionality of a state's spending vastly unequal sums on the education of its schoolchildren. (This occurred because poorer school districts obviously could not raise the same amount of money as could wealthy school districts.) The litigants claimed that children in the poorer districts were victims of unlawful discrimination in violation of their equal protection rights under the U.S. Constitution. The Supreme Court said they were not, however, in a conservative-dominated five-to-four decision.[2] But the matter did not end there. Litigation was then instituted in many states arguing that unequal educational opportunities were in violation of various clauses in the state constitutions. During the past two and a half decades such suits have been brought twenty-eight times in some twenty-four states. In fourteen of these cases state supreme courts invalidated their state's method of financing education, involving the reallocation of billions of dollars. In some instances these decisions altered the entire structure of the state educational system.[3]

Indeed there is considerable evidence that in recent years many minority groups and supporters of liberal causes, unable to obtain relief in the face of conservative Burger and Rehnquist Court majorities, have turned their litigation efforts toward the state judiciaries. For the constitutional guarantees in most states are just as supportive of the rights of minorities as is the U.S. Constitution, and the judiciaries in many states are dominated by liberal and progressive judges who are every bit as much predisposed toward the claims of minorities and civil libertarians as any liberal justice who ever sat on the Warren Court of the 1950s and 1960s.

For instance, in 1991 an appeals court in Michigan struck down a voter-approved ban on state-funded abortions for poor women. (The case concerned a fifteen-year-old who became pregnant after a gang rape.) The court said the ban on Medicaid-funded abortions violated women's rights to privacy and equal protection under the state constitution. It further ruled that the state "constitutional rights are broader than those in the U.S. Constitution."[4] In May 1993 a majority of the Hawaii Supreme Court decided that the state's ban on same-sex marriages violated equal-protection rights guaranteed in the state's constitution—rights that the court said were "more elaborate" than those in the federal Bill of Rights.[5] And Pennsylvania's highest court determined in 1991 that evidence seized with a deficient search warrant cannot be used in court, even if the police acted in good faith when obtaining the warrant. Such a ruling flies directly in the face of U.S. Supreme Court decisions that permit the introduction of illegally obtained evidence if it could be determined that the police acted in good faith. In a not-too-subtle poke at the U.S. Supreme Court's federal guidelines, the justices in the Quaker State urged all Pennsylvania state judges to apply "independent analysis" when examining state constitutional questions.[6] An analysis of this decision noted, "The decision is limited to Pennsylvania, but it follows a recent trend in constitutional law. Increasingly, states are finding that their constitutions are more protective of civil liberties than the U.S. Supreme Court's interpretation of the federal constitution. As a result, many state supreme courts have become receptive forums for civil liberties arguments that the U.S. Supreme Court has rejected."[7]

Although all analysts seem to agree on the importance of state court policy making, not all concur that liberal causes are the sole beneficiaries of these activities. In fact a study of all constitutionally based criminal procedure decisions of the courts of last resort of all fifty states during the 1970s and 1980s "reveals that the *adoption* of Burger-Rehnquist Court doctrines for state law far outpaces their rejection. Indeed, for every state high court decision repudiating U.S. Supreme Court doctrine there are at least two cases endorsing it."[8] This phenomenon has surely existed in the state of California, where a conservative majority on its Supreme Court "has more narrowly construed the rights accorded defendants in criminal prosecutions"; moreover, "because of the California court system's size and influence, the weight of its decision extends far beyond the state's borders." Furthermore, in the economic arena California's conservative court

has taken the lead in a movement to greatly limit the liability of business people for misbehavior of various kinds. The court has eviscerated thousands of lawsuits by employees seeking punitive damages for wrongful discharge. It has disallowed big damage awards obtained by consumers against insurance companies. It has prevented drug companies from being held liable for damages caused consumers by certain products.[9]

The purpose of this discussion is not to document systematically all the policy-making thrusts of state judges, nor is it to predict the ideological direction of state court decision making. Rather it is to emphasize that what is happening at the state court level is of great importance to all of us—to our pocketbooks and to our personal rights and liberties. Gone are the days when many public law scholars believed that only *federal* court activity had any keen impact on our lives, because the state judicial tribunals only immersed themselves in judicial trivia. The work of state courts is worthy of our full interest and attention.

Jurisdiction and Legislative Politics

In any discussion of the jurisdiction of the federal and state courts, there is one political reality that cannot be overemphasized: for all intents and purposes it is the Congress and the fifty state legislatures that determine what sorts of issues and cases the courts in their separate realms will hear. And equally important, what the omnipotent legislative branches give, they may also take away. It is true that some judges and judicial scholars argue that the U.S. Constitution (in Article III) and the respective state documents confer a certain inherent jurisdiction upon the judiciaries in some key areas, independent of the legislative will. Nevertheless, it is abundantly clear that the jurisdictional boundaries of American courts are a product of legislative judgments—determinations often flavored with the bittersweet spice of politics. We shall look at a few examples of this at the national level.

As we shall see in subsequent chapters, Congress may advance a particular cause by giving courts the authority to hear cases in a public-policy realm that previously had been forbidden territory for the judiciary. For example, when Congress passed the Civil Rights Act of 1968, it gave judges the authority to penalize individuals who interfere with "any person because of his race, color, religion or national origin and because he is or has been . . . traveling in . . . interstate commerce" (18 U.S.C.A., Sec. 245). Prior to 1968 the courts had no jurisdiction over incidents that stemmed from interference by one person with another's right to travel. Likewise Congress may discourage a particular social movement by passing legislation to make it virtually impossible for its advocates to have any success in the courts. For example, when the Hawaiian Supreme Court approved same-sex marriages in 1993, a conservative and frightened Congress was determined to discourage judges in other states from rendering similar decisions. The result was the Defense of Marriage Act, which President Clinton signed into law on September 20, 1996. In part the law was designed to prevent judges—both state and federal—from reading any meaning into the Fourteenth Amendment to the U.S. Constitution that would condone same-sex marriages. Among other things, the law defined marriage as "only a legal union between one man and one woman," and it permitted state courts to ignore judgments from courts in other states "respecting" marriages between two persons of the same gender.

Perhaps the most vivid illustration of congressional power over federal court jurisdiction occurred just after the Civil War, and the awesome nature of this legislative prerogative haunts the judiciary to this day. On February 5, 1867, Congress empowered the federal courts to grant habeas corpus to individuals imprisoned in violation of their constitutional rights. The Supreme Court was authorized to hear appeals of such cases. William McCardle was incarcerated by the military government of Mississippi for being in alleged violation of the Reconstruction laws. McCardle was alleged to have published "incendiary and libelous" articles that attacked his "unlawful restraint by military force." He sought relief in the circuit court but it was denied. He then appealed to the Supreme Court, which agreed to take the case.

After the arguments had been made before the High Court (but prior to a decision), Congress got into the act. Its anti-Southern majority feared that the Court would use the *McCardle* case as a vehicle to strike down all or part of the Reconstruction Acts—something Congress had no intention of permitting. And so, over President Andrew Johnson's veto, the following statute was enacted: "That so much of the act approved February 5, 1867 [as] authorized an appeal from the judgment of the Circuit Court to the Supreme Court of the United States, or the exercise of any such jurisdiction by said Supreme Court, on appeals which have been, or may hereafter be taken, [is] hereby repealed." Thus, while the Court was in the very process of deciding the case, Congress removed the subject matter from the federal docket. And was all this strictly legal and constitutional? Yes, indeed. Stunned by Congress's action but obedient to the clear strictures of the Constitution, the Court limply ruled that McCardle's appeal must now "be dismissed for want of jurisdiction." [10]

In other words, while discussing what courts do or may do, we must not lose sight of the commanding reality that the jurisdiction of U.S. courts is established by "the United States of America in Congress assembled." Likewise the jurisdictions of the courts in the states are very much governed by—and the political product of— the will of the state legislatures.

Judicial Self-Restraint

We will now look at the other side of the coin—at the activities that judges are forbidden to engage in, or at least discouraged from engaging in. These forbidden activities deal not so much with technical matters of jurisdiction as with a broader term, what the courts call *justiciability*—that is, the question of whether judges in the system *ought* to hear or refrain from hearing certain types of disputes. It is only by exploring both sides of the demarcation line between prescribed and proscribed activity that we can acquire insight into the role and function of our federal and state courts. In the following sections we shall look at ten separate aspects of judicial self-restraint, ten principles that serve to check and contain the power of American judges.[11] These maxims originate in a variety of sources—the U.S. Constitution and state constitutions, acts of Congress and of state legislatures, the common law tradition—and whenever possible we shall indicate their roots and the nature of their evolution. Some apply more to appellate courts than to trial courts, as we shall note. Although the primary examples provided will be illustrative of the federal judiciary, most apply to state judicial systems as well.

A Definite Controversy Must Exist

The U.S. Constitution states that "the judicial Power shall extend to all Cases, in Law and Equity, arising under this Constitution, the Laws of the United States, and Treaties made . . . under their Authority" (Article III, Section 2). The key word here is *cases.* Since 1789 the federal courts have chosen to interpret the term in its most literal sense—that is, there must be an actual controversy between legitimate adversaries who have met all the technical legal standards to institute a suit. The dispute must concern the protection of a meaningful, nontrivial right or the prevention or redress of a wrong that directly affects the parties to the suit. There are three corollaries to this general principle that breathe a little life into its rather abstract-sounding admonitions.

The first is that the federal courts do not render advisory opinions—that is, rulings about situations that are hypothetical or that have not caused an actual clash between adversaries. A dispute must be real and current before a court will agree to accept it for adjudication. Let us look at an example in which the U.S. Supreme Court refused to involve itself in a dispute because the facts and would-be parties were not considered "real." In 1902 Congress passed a law allocating certain pieces of land to the Cherokee Indians. Because such disbursements often stimulate a good deal of question about property rights, Congress sought to head off any possible disputes over land by authorizing certain land recipients to bring suits against the U.S. government in the court of claims, with appeal to the Supreme Court. They were permitted to do so "on their own behalf and on behalf of all other Cherokee citizens" who received land "to determine the validity of any acts of Congress passed since the said act." Stripped of the legalese, the law thus said: "If you have any hypothetical questions about how the law might affect anyone, just sue the United States, and the courts will answer these questions for you." The Supreme Court politely but pointedly said, "We don't do that sort of thing; we settle only real, actual cases or controversies." The act of Congress was found to be nothing more

than an attempt to provide for judicial determination, final in this court, of the constitutional validity of an act of Congress. [It] is true the United States is made a defendant to this action, but *it has no interest adverse to the claimants.* The object is not to assert a property right as against the government, or to demand compensation for alleged wrongs because of action on its part. . . . In a legal sense the judgment [amounts] to no more than an expression of opinion upon the validity of the [1902 act]. If such actions as are here attempted [are] sustained, the result will be that this court, instead of keeping within the limits of judicial power, and deciding cases or controversies arising between opposing parties, [will] be required to give opinions in the nature of advice concerning legislative action—a function never conferred upon it by the Constitution. [Emphasis added.] [12]

A second corollary of the general principle is that the parties to the suit must have proper *standing.* This notion deals with the matter of *who* may bring litigation to court. Although there are many aspects of the term *standing,* the most prominent component is that the person bringing suit must have suffered (or be immediately about to suffer) a direct and significant injury. As a general rule, a litigant cannot bring a claim on behalf of others (except for parents of minor children, or in special types of suits called *class actions*). In addition, the alleged injury must be personalized and immediate—not part of some generalized complaint.

On January 1, 1997, a new law took effect granting the president a line-item veto. A line-item veto permits the chief executive to cancel individual spending and tax items contained in appropriations bills that he has already signed into law. Immediately after the law was passed, six members of Congress who opposed the line-item veto filed suit in federal court to challenge its validity. They claimed that the statute violated the constitutional separation of powers doctrine, which requires that the powers of the chief executive be kept distinct from the powers of Congress. On April 10 a federal district court judge agreed, ruling that the Line Item Veto Act gave the president the unprecedented and "revolutionary" power to repeal a part of a statute, a legislative function that no president can exercise and that Congress may not delegate.[13]

When the case reached the Supreme Court, the justices, by a 7–2 vote, overruled the lower-court judge.[14] Refusing to go into the merits of the case at all, the majority noted that as of the date of the Court's decision, President Clinton had not yet *used* his line-item veto power; therefore, no one could claim any immediate, direct, or personal injury from the statute. Chief Justice Rehnquist, speaking for the majority, said that "we have consistently stressed that a plaintiff's complaint must establish that he has a 'personal stake' in the alleged dispute. . . . The institutional injury [the plaintiffs] . . . allege is wholly abstract and widely dispersed, and their attempt to litigate this dispute at this time and in this form is contrary to historical experience."[15] End of the matter—at least until such time as the president does use his veto power and someone challenges it who is able to show that his injury is great enought to give him "standing" to sue.

In fact, on August 11, 1997, President Clinton used the item veto for the first time. He struck out three provisions from several budget and tax bills that he had signed the previous week, contending that his action "will save the American people hundreds of millions of dollars over the next 10 years."[16] Since that time the president has used this veto power on several more occasions. If some of the recipients of these vetoed programs can now show "legal injury," the Supreme Court may grant them "standing" to challenge the item veto in court.

The third corollary of this general principle is that courts ordinarily will not hear a case that has become *moot,* that is, when the basic facts or the status of the parties have significantly changed in the interim between when the suit was first filed and when it comes before the judge(s). The death of a litigant or the fact that the litigants have ceased to be warring parties would render a case moot in most tribunals.

For example, in 1974 the U.S. Supreme Court agreed to hear a petition from Marco DeFunis, who challenged the constitutionality of the admissions policy of the University of Washington Law School. The law school gave preferential treatment to certain minority racial groups, even though such applicants did not rate as high as other, nonminority applicants according to the school's evaluation procedures based on objective tests and grades. DeFunis, a nonminority applicant, charged reverse discrimination in violation of his Fourteenth Amendment rights. During the initial trial of this case at the state court level, DeFunis had been admitted to the law school (on a sort of conditional basis), and when the case eventually reached the Supreme Court, he was in his final quarter of law school. (The law school conceded at oral argument before the Supreme Court that it would permit DeFunis to graduate if he continued to fulfill all requirements.) When the Supreme Court learned of this, a majority determined that the case had become moot. "The controversy between the parties has thus ceased to be 'definite and concrete' and no longer 'touches the legal relations of parties having adverse legal interests,'" said the Court.[17]

We must add, however, that sometimes judges for their own reasons may decide that a case is still ripe for adjudication, even though the status of the facts and parties would seem to have radically altered. Examples include cases where someone has challenged a state's refusal to permit an abortion or to permit the life-support system of a terminally ill person to be switched off. (In such cases, by the time the suit reaches an appellate court, the woman may already have given birth or the moribund person may have died.) In these cases the judges believed that the issues were so important that they needed to be addressed by the court. To declare such cases moot would, practically speaking, prevent them from ever being heard in time by an appellate body.

As we have seen and shall continue to observe in this book, there is a great deal of flexibility and common sense built into our legal system—factors that allow for discretion in judges' decision making. The principle of judicial self-restraint offers a counterpoint, guiding judges to what they may *not* do. They may not decide an issue unless there is an actual case or controversy. From this it follows that they do not consider abstract, hypothetical questions; they do not take a case unless the would-be litigants can demonstrate direct and substantial personal injury; and they (usually) do not take cases that have become moot. This principle is an important one because it means that judges are not free to wander about the countryside like medieval knights slaying all the evil dragons they encounter. They may rule only on concrete issues brought by truly injured parties directly affected by the facts of a case.

Although federal judges do not rule on abstract, hypothetical issues, many state courts are permitted to do so in some form or other (such as those in Massachusetts, South Dakota, and Colorado).[18] Federal legislative courts (see Chapter 2) may give advisory opinions as well. Also, American judges are empowered to render what are termed *declaratory judgments*. Such judgments are made in actual controversies in which a court is called on to define the rights of various parties under a statute, a will, or a contract. The judgments do not entail any type of coercive relief. As Justice Rehnquist once put it, "A declaratory judgment is simply a statement of rights, not a binding order."[19] The federal courts were given the authority to act in this capacity in the Federal Declaratory Judgment Act of 1934, and about three-fourths of the states grant their courts this power. Although there is a real difference between an abstract dispute that the federal courts (at least) must avoid and a situation where a declaratory judgment is in order, in the real world the line between the two is often a difficult one for jurists to draw.

A Plea Must Be Specific

Another constraint upon the judiciary is that judges will hear no case on the merits unless the petitioner is first able to cite a specific part of the Constitution as the basis of the plea. For example, the First Amendment forbids government from making a law "respecting an establishment of religion." In 1989 the state of New York created a special school district in Orange County solely for the benefit of the Satmar Hasids, a group of Hasidic Jews with East European roots that strongly resists assimilation into modern society. Most of the children attended parochial schools in the Village of Kiryas Joel, but these private schools weren't able to handle retarded and disabled students, and the Satmars claimed that such children within their community would be traumatized if forced to attend a public school. Responding to this situation the state legislature created a special district encompassing a single school that served only handicapped children from the Hasidic Jewish community. This arrangement was challenged by the association representing New York state's school boards. In June 1994 the U.S. Supreme Court ruled that indeed the creation of the one-school district effectively delegated political power to the orthodox Jewish group and therefore violated the First Amendment's ban on governmental "establishment of religion."[20] Whether or not we agree that the New York law was constitutional, there is little doubt that the school board association met the specific criteria for securing judicial review: the Constitution clearly forbids the government from delegating political power to a specific religious entity. The government here readily acknowledged that it had passed a law for the unique benefit of a singular religious community.

However, if one went into court and contended that a particular law or official action "violated the spirit of the Bill of Rights" or "offended the values of the Founders," a judge would dismiss the proceeding on the spot. For if judges were free to give concrete, substantive meaning to vague generalities such as these, there would be little check on what they could do. Who is to say what is the "spirit of the Bill of Rights" or the collective motivation of those who hammered out the Constitution? Judges who were free to roam too far from the specific clauses and strictures of the constitutional document itself would soon become judicial despots.

Despite what we have just said, we must also concede that in the real world this principle is not as simple and clear-cut as it sounds, because the Constitution contains many clauses that are open to a wide variety of interpretations. For example, the Constitution forbids Congress from passing any law abridging "freedom of speech," but such a term has been virtually impossible for jurists to define with any degree of precision. The Eighth Amendment prohibits "excessive bail" for criminal defendants, but what is excessive? The states are forbidden, in the Fourteenth Amendment, Section 1, from abridging "the privileges and immunities of citizens of the United States," but who is to say what these privileges and immunities are? The Constitution gives hardly a clue. Our point is that although petitioners must cite a particular constitutional clause as the basis for their plea—as opposed to some totally ambiguous concept—there are nevertheless enough vague clauses in the Constitution itself to give federal judges plenty of room to maneuver and make policy.

Beneficiaries May Not Sue

A third aspect of judicial self-restraint is that a case will be rejected out of hand if it is apparent that the petitioner has been the beneficiary of a law or an official action that he or she has subsequently chosen to challenge. Let us suppose that Farmer Brown has long been a member of the Soil Bank Program (designed to cut back on grain surpluses); under the program he agreed to take part of his land out of production and periodically was paid a subsidy by the federal government. After years as a participant he learns that his lazy, ne'er-do-well neighbors, the Joneses, are also drawing regular payments for letting their farmland lie fallow. The idea that his neighbors are getting something for nothing starts to offend Farmer Brown, and he begins to harbor grave doubts about the constitutionality of the whole program. Armed with a host of reasons why Congress had acted illegally, Brown challenges the legality of the Soil Bank Act in the local federal district court. As soon as it is brought to the judge's attention that Farmer Brown had himself been a member of the program and had gained financially from it, the suit is dismissed: one may not benefit from a particular governmental endeavor or official action and subsequently attack it in court.

Appellate Courts Rule on Legal—Not Factual—Questions

In the real world it is often very difficult for appellate court justices to tell whether a particular legal dispute is a question of who did what to whom (the facts of the case), or whether they are being asked to weigh and assess a series of events (the legal interpretation of the facts). A working proposition of state and federal appellate court practice is that these courts will generally not hear cases if the grounds for appeal are that the trial judge or jury wrongly amassed and identified the basic factual elements of the case. It is not that trial judges and juries always do a perfect job of making factual determinations. Rather, there is the belief that they are closer, sensorially and temporally, to the actual parties and physical evidence of the case. The odds are, so the theory goes, that they will do a much better job of making factual assessments than would an appellate body reading only a stale transcript of the case some months or years after the trial.[21] On the other hand, legal matters—that is, which laws to apply to the facts of a case, or how to assess the facts in light of the prevailing law—are appropriate for appellate review. On such issues collegial, or multijudge, appellate bodies presumably have a legitimate and better capacity "to say what the law is," as Chief Justice John Marshall put it.

We must, nevertheless, offer some qualification of what we have just said. In most jurisdictions appellate courts will hear appeals under what is called "the clearly erroneous rule," that is, when the petitioner contends that the trial court's determination of the facts was obviously and utterly wrong. The issue would not be a minor quibble about what the facts were but rather a belief that the trial court had made a finding that *totally* flew in the face of common sense. Likewise appellate courts may be willing to review an administrative agency's factual determinations

that were allegedly made "without substantial evidence." Despite these qualifications, however, it is still fair to say that trial courts are the primary determiners
of the facts or evidence in cases even though such determinations are not always absolutely conclusive.

Let us clarify this general principle with a concrete example. If X were convicted
of a crime and the sole grounds for her appeal were that the judge and jury had mistakenly found her guilty (that is, incorrectly sifted and identified the facts), the appeals court would probably dismiss the case out of hand. However, let us assume
that X provided evidence that she had asked for and been refused counsel during
her FBI interrogation and that her confession was therefore illegal. At trial the district judge ruled that the Fifth Amendment's right against self-incrimination did
not apply to X's interrogation by the FBI. The defendant argued to the contrary.
Such a contention would be appealable because the issue is one of legal—not factual—interpretation.

The fact that U.S. appellate courts are generally restricted to interpreting the law
and not to identifying and assembling facts is one additional check on the scope of
their decision making.

The Supreme Court Is Not Bound (Technically) by Precedents

If the High Court is free to overturn or circumvent past and supposedly controlling precedents when it decides a case, this might appear to be an argument for judicial activism—not restraint. In fact, this practice must be placed in the restraint
column. If the Supreme Court were inescapably bound by the dictates of its prior
rulings, it would have very little flexibility. It would not be free to back off when
discretion advised a cautious approach to a problem; it would not have liberty to
withdraw from a confrontation in which it might not be in the nation's or the
Court's interest to engage. By occasionally allowing itself the freedom to overrule a
past decision or to ignore a precedent that would seem to be controlling, the
Supreme Court establishes a corner of safety to which it can retreat if need be.
When wisdom dictates that the Court change direction or at least keep an open
mind, this principle of self-restraint is readily plucked from the judicial kit bag.

Other Remedies Must Be Exhausted

There is another principle of self-restraint that often frustrates the anxious litigant but is essential to the orderly administration of justice: courts in the United
States will not accept a case until all other remedies, legal and administrative, have
been exhausted. Although this caveat is often associated with the U.S. Supreme

Court, it is in fact a working principle for virtually all American judicial tribunals. In its simplest form this doctrine means that one must work up the ladder with one's legal petitions. Federal cases must first be heard by the U.S. trial courts, then reviewed by one of the appellate tribunals, and finally heard by the U.S. Supreme Court. This orderly procedure of events must and will occur despite the "importance" of the case or of the petitioners who filed it. For instance, in 1952 President Harry Truman seized the American steel mills in order to prevent a pending strike that he believed would imperil the war effort in the Korean conflict; both labor and management were suddenly told they were now working for Uncle Sam. The mill owners were furious and immediately brought suit, charging that the president had abused the powers of his office. A national legal-political crisis erupted. One might think that the Supreme Court would immediately take a case of this magnitude. Not so. In the traditional and orderly fashion of American federal justice, the controversy first went to the local district court in Washington, D.C., just as if it were the most ordinary dispute. Not until after the district court had ruled did the nation's highest tribunal have the opportunity to sink its teeth into this hearty piece of judicial meat. (The Supreme Court did, however, concede the need for expeditious behavior by granting certiorari before the court of appeals could rule on the merits of the case—thereby shortening the normal appellate process.)

Exhaustion of remedies refers to possible administrative relief as well as to adherence to the principle of a three-tiered judicial hierarchy. Such relief might be in the form of an appeal to an administrative officer, a hearing before a board or committee, or formal consideration of a matter by a legislative body. Let us consider a hypothetical illustration. Professor Ben Wheatley is denied tenure at a staunchly conservative institution. He is told that tenure was not granted because of his poor teaching record and lack of scholarly publications. He contends that denial of tenure is in retaliation for his having founded the nearby Sunshine Socialist Society, a nudist colony for gay atheists. He has the option of a hearing before the university's Grievance Committee, but he declines it, saying, "It would do no good; it would just be a waste of time." Rather, he takes his case immediately to the local federal district court, claiming that his Fourteenth Amendment rights have been violated. When the case is brought before the trial court, the judge will say to Professor Wheatley: "Before I will even look at this matter, you must first take your case before the official, duly established Grievance Committee at your university. It doesn't matter whether you believe that you will win or lose your petition before the committee. You must establish your record there and avail yourself of all the administrative appeals and remedies that your institution has provided. If you are then still dissatisfied with the outcome, you may at that time invoke the power of the federal district courts."

Thus, judicial restraint means that judges do not jump immediately into every controversy that appears to be important or that strikes their fancy. The restrained and orderly administration of justice requires that before any court may hear a case, all administrative and inferior legal remedies must first be exhausted.

Courts Do Not Decide "Political Questions"

U.S. judges are often called upon to determine the winner of a contested election, to rule on the legality of a newly drawn electoral district, or to involve themselves in voting rights cases. How then can we say that political questions are out of bounds for the American judiciary? The answer lies in the narrow, singular use of the word *political.* To U.S. judges, the executive and the legislative branches of government are political in that they are elected by the people for the purpose of making public policy. The judiciary, in contrast, was not designed by the Founders to be an instrument manifesting the popular will and is therefore not political. According to this line of reasoning, then, a political question is one that ought properly to be resolved by one of the other two branches of government (even though it may appear before the courts wrapped in judicial clothing). When judges determine that something is a political question and therefore not appropriate for judicial review, what they are saying in effect is this: "You litigants may have couched your plea in judicial terminology, but under our form of government, issues such as this ought properly to be decided at the ballot box, in the legislative halls, or in the chambers of the executive."

For example, when the state of Oregon gave its citizens the right to vote on popular statewide referendums and initiatives around the turn of the century, the Pacific States Telephone and Telegraph Company objected.[22] (The company feared that voters would bypass the more business-oriented legislature and pass laws restricting its rates and profits.) The company claimed that by permitting citizens directly to enact legislation, the state has "been reduced to a democracy," whereas Article IV, Section 4, of the Constitution guarantees to each state "a Republican Form of Government"—a term that supposedly means that laws are to be made only by the elected representatives of the people—not by the citizens directly. Pacific States Telephone demanded that the Court take action. Opting for discretion rather than valor, the High Court refused to rule on the merits of the case, declaring the issue to be a political question. The Court reasoned that since Article IV primarily pre-scribes the duties of Congress, it follows that the Founders wanted Congress—not the courts—to oversee the forms of government in the several states. In other words, the Court was being asked to invade the decision-making domain of one of the other (political) branches of government. And this it refused to do.

In recent decades an important political/nonpolitical dispute has concerned the matter of reapportionment of legislative districts. Prior to 1962 a majority on the Supreme Court refused to rule on the constitutionality of legislative districts with unequal populations, saying that such matters were "nonjusticiable" and that the Court dared not enter what Justice Frankfurter called "the political thicket." Ac-cording to traditional Supreme Court thinking, the Founders wanted legislatures to redistrict themselves—perhaps with some gentle prodding from the electorate. However, with the Supreme Court's decision in *Baker v. Carr*, the majority made an about-face.[23] Since 1962 the Court has held in scores of cases that the equal-protection clause of the Fourteenth Amendment requires legislative districts to be of equal population size, and furthermore that the courts should see to it that this mandate is carried out.

The refusal of the Supreme Court in recent decades to involve itself in foreign re-lations has likewise exemplified its desire to ignore the siren call of the political realm. For example, during the Vietnam War the Court repeatedly declined many ardent pleas to rule on the constitutionality of U.S. involvement.[24] Also, when Presi-dent Carter acted on his own initiative to end the Mutual Defense Treaty between the United States and Taiwan, this action was challenged in the courts by a number of senators and representatives. The High Court, consistent with tradition, refused to involve itself in this political question.[25]

Although the line between a taboo political question and a proper justiciable is-sue is not always a clear one, this doctrine provides the courts with still another op-portunity and impetus to exercise restraint.

The Burden of Proof Is on the Petitioner

Another weighty principle of self-restraint is the general agreement among the nation's jurists that an individual who would challenge the constitutionality of a statute bears the burden of proof. This is just a different way of saying that laws and official deeds are all presumed to be legal unless and until proven other-wise by a preponderance of evidence. The question of who has the burden of proof is of keen interest to lawyers because, in effect, it means: Which side has the bigger job to perform in the courtroom? And which party must assume the lion's share of the burden of convincing the court—or lose the case entirely? Thus, if one were attacking a particular statute, one would have to do more than demonstrate that it was "questionable" or "of doubtful constitutionality"; one must persuade the court that the evidence against the law was clear-cut and overwhelming—not often an easy task. In giving the benefit of the doubt to a statute or an executive act, judges have yet another area in which to exercise restraint.

The only exception to this burden of proof principle is in the realm of civil rights and liberties. Some jurists who are strong civil libertarians have long contended that when government attempts to restrict basic human freedoms, the burden of proof should shift to the government. And in fact in several specific areas of civil rights jurisprudence that philosophy now prevails. For example, the U.S. Supreme Court has ruled in a variety of cases that laws that treat persons differently according to their race or gender are automatically subject to "special scrutiny." This means that the burden of proof shifts to the government to demonstrate a compelling or overriding need to differentiate persons according to their ethnic origins or sex. For instance, the government has long argued (successfully) that there can be some major restrictions for women in the armed forces that prevent them from being assigned to full combat duty.

Laws Are Overturned on the Narrowest Grounds Only

Sometimes it becomes clear to a judge during a trial that the strictures of the Constitution have indeed been offended by a legislative or executive act. Even here, however, there is ample opportunity to proceed with caution. There are two common ways in which judges may act in a restrained manner even when they must reach for the blue pencil.

First, a judge may have the option of invalidating an official action on what is called statutory rather than constitutional grounds. Statutory invalidation means that a judge overturns an official's action because the official acted beyond the authority delegated to him or her by the law. Such a ruling has the function of saving the law itself while still nullifying the official's misdeed.

Let us look at a hypothetical example. Suppose that Congress continues to authorize postal officials to seize all obscene nude photographs that are shipped through the mail. A photographer attempts to mail pictures taken at his "art studio," but the pictures are seized by postal officials. The photographer protests that the statute violates his First Amendment rights and the case is eventually taken to the federal courts. Assuming that the judges are generally sympathetic to the position of the photographer, they have two basic options. They may declare the statute to be in violation of the Constitution and thus null and void, or they may select another stance that permits them to have it both ways. They may decide that the law itself passed constitutional muster, but that the postal official in question mistakenly decided that the nude photos were obscene. Thus the statute is preserved and a direct confrontation between the courts and Congress is averted, but the courts are able to give the petitioner virtually all of what he wants. This is an example of deciding a case on statutory rather than constitutional grounds.

There is a second method whereby restraint may be exercised under this general principle: judges may, if possible, invalidate only that portion of a law they find constitutionally defective rather than overturn the entire statute. For instance, in 1963 Congress passed the Higher Education Facilities Act, which provided construction grants for college buildings. Part of the law declared that for a twenty-year period, no part of the newly built structures could be used for "sectarian instruction, religious worship, or the programs of a divinity school." Since church-related universities as well as public institutions benefited from the act, the entire law was challenged in court as being in violation of the establishment of religion clause of the First Amendment. The Supreme Court determined that the basic thrust of the law did not violate the Constitution, but it did find the "twenty-year clause" to be objectionable. After all, the Court reasoned, most buildings last a good deal longer than two decades, and a building constructed at public expense could thus house religious activities during most of its lifetime. Rather than strike down the entire act, however, the Court majority merely substituted the word *never* for the phrase *twenty years*.[26] Thus the baby was not thrown out with the bath water and judicial restraint was maintained.

No Rulings Are Made on the "Wisdom" of Legislation

This final aspect of judicial self-restraint is probably the least understood by the public, the most often violated by the courts, and yet potentially the greatest harness on judicial activism in existence. What this admonition means, if followed strictly, is that the only basis for declaring a law or an official action unconstitutional is that it literally violates the Constitution on its face. Statutes do not offend the Constitution merely because they are unfair, are fiscally wasteful, or constitute bad public policy. Official actions can be struck down only if they step across the boundaries clearly set forth by the Founders. If taken truly to heart, this means that judges and justices are not free to invoke their own personal notions of right and wrong or of good and bad public policy when they examine the constitutionality of legislation.

A keen expression of this phenomenon of judicial self-restraint is found in Justice Potter Stewart's dissenting opinion in the case of *Griswold v. Connecticut.* The Court majority had struck down the state's law that forbade the use of contraceptive devices or the dissemination of birth control information. Stewart said, in effect, that the law was bad, but that its weaknesses didn't make it unconstitutional.

Since 1897 Connecticut has had on its books a law which forbids the use of contraceptives by anyone. I think this is an uncommonly silly law. As a practical matter, the law is obviously unenforceable, except in the oblique context of the present case. . . . But we are not asked in this case to say whether we think this law is unwise, or even asinine. We are asked to hold that it violates the United States Constitution. And that I cannot do.[27]

Another spinoff of this principle is that a law may be passed that all agree is good and wise but that is nevertheless unconstitutional; conversely, a statute may legalize the commission of an official deed that all know to be bad and dangerous but that still does not offend the Constitution. Permitting the police to dispose of "known criminals" without benefit of trial would probably save taxpayers a good deal of money and also reduce the crime rate, but it would be a clear, prima facie violation of the Constitution. On the other hand, a congressional tax on every sex act might be constitutionally permissible but would be a very unwise piece of legislation—not to mention difficult to enforce. Thus when we are speaking of laws or official acts, the adjectives *goodness* and *constitutionality* are no more synonymous than are *badness* and *unconstitutionality.*

Although few legal scholars would disagree with what we have just said, virtually all would point out that the principle of not ruling on the "wisdom" of a law is difficult to follow in the real world and is often honored in the breach. This is so because the Constitution, a rather brief document, is silent on many areas of public life and contains a number of phrases and admonitions that are open to a variety of interpretations—a theme that we shall touch upon continually throughout this text. For instance, the Constitution says that Congress may regulate interstate commerce. But what exactly is commerce, and how extensive does it have to be before it is of an "interstate" character? As human beings, judges have differed in the way they have responded to this question. The Constitution guarantees a person accused of a crime the right to a defense attorney. But does this right continue if one appeals a guilty verdict and, if so, for how many appeals? Strict constructionists and loose constructionists have responded differently to these queries.

In all, despite the inevitable intrusion of judges' personal values into their interpretation of many portions of the Constitution, virtually every jurist subscribes to the general principle that laws can be invalidated only if they offend the Constitution—not the personal preferences of the judges.

Summary

In this chapter we have focused on what federal and state courts are supposed to do and on what they must refrain from doing. They adjudicate cases that come within their lawful original or appellate jurisdiction. Federal district courts hear criminal cases and civil suits that deal with federal questions, diversity of citizenship matters, prisoners' petitions, and any other issues authorized by Congress. The appellate courts, having no original jurisdiction whatever, take appeals from the district courts and from numerous administrative and regulatory agencies. The U.S. Supreme Court has original jurisdiction over suits between two or more states and in cases where ambassadors or public ministers are parties to a suit. Its appellate jurisdiction, regulated entirely by Congress, permits it to hear appeals from the circuit courts and from state courts of last resort. Since 1988 Congress has delegated to the High Court the right to control its own appellate caseload. As for state courts, the previous chapter summarized the primary contours of their jurisdictions, but in this chapter we emphasized the great importance of the issues that are adjudicated at the state level.

Under our legal system federal courts are not to adjudicate questions unless there is a real case or controversy at stake, although many state courts may render advisory opinions. All pleas to the courts must be based on a *specific* portion of the Constitution. Judges are also to dismiss suits in which a petitioner is challenging a law from which he or she has benefited. Federal and state appellate courts may rule only on matters of law—not on factual questions. Not being bound entirely by its precedents, the Supreme Court is free to exercise flexibility and restraint if it wishes to do so. All courts insist that litigants exhaust every legal and administrative remedy before a case will be decided. Courts in the United States are to eschew political questions and insist that the burden of proof rests on those who contend that a law or official action is unconstitutional. If judges must nullify an act of the legislature or the executive, they are to do so on the narrowest grounds possible. Finally, courts ought not rule on the wisdom or desirability of a law but are to strike down legislation only if it clearly violates the letter of the Constitution.

NOTES

1. Richard A. Posner, *The Federal Courts: Challenge and Reform* (Cambridge, Mass.: Harvard University Press, 1996), 37.

2. *San Antonio Independent School District v. Rodriguez*, 411 U.S. 1 (1973).

3. William Kinney Swinford, "Resolving the Dispute over Methods of Financing Elementary and Secondary Education" (Ph.D. dissertation, Ohio State University, 1993), 3–4.

4. "Michigan Appeals Court Rejects Ban on State-Funded Abortions," *Houston Chronicle*, February 21, 1991, 3A.

5. "Gay Marriage Ruling," *Wall Street Journal*, May 7, 1993, B2. The Hawaiian Supreme Court ruling may be overturned in 1998 if the state's voters approve the following amendment to their Constitution: "The legislature shall have the power to reserve marriage to opposite-sex couples." See David Orgon Coolidge, "At Last, Hawaiians Have Their Say on Gay Marriage," *Wall Street Journal*, April 23, 1997, A19.

6. Milo Geyelin and Ellen Joan Pollock, "Pennsylvania High Court Tightens Rules on Police Seizure of Evidence," *Wall Street Journal*, February 7, 1991, B4.

7. Ibid. For an excellent *empirical* analysis of the nature of state supreme court policy making, see Craig F. Emmert and Carol Ann Traut, "State Supreme Courts, State Constitutions, and Judicial Policy-making," *Justice System Journal* 16 (1992): 37–48.

8. Barry Latzer, "The Hidden Conservatism of the State Court 'Revolution,'" *Judicature* 74 (1991): 190.

9. Richard B. Schmitt, "Right Turn: California High Court Makes Mark on Law by Limiting Damages," *Wall Street Journal*, July 11, 1989, A1.

10. *Ex Parte McCardle*, 74 U.S. (7 Wall.) 506 (1869).

11. For our discussion of the many aspects of judicial self-restraint we acknowledge our debt to Henry J. Abraham, on whose classic analysis of the subject we largely relied. See *The Judicial Process*, 6th ed. (New York: Oxford University Press, 1993), chap. 9.

12. *Muskrat v. United States*, 219 U.S. 346 (1911).

13. *Raines v. Byrd*, U.S. Supreme Court (June 26, 1997), No. 96-1671.

14. Linda Greenhouse, "Supreme Court to Speed Process of Studying Line-Item Veto Power," *Houston Chronicle*, April 24, 1997, A16.

15. Edward Felsenthal, "Justices Clear Way for Line-Item Veto, Ruling Challengers Lack Legal Standing," *Wall Street Journal*, June 27, 1997, A16.

16. Robert A. Rankin, "Clinton Vetoes 3 Items," *Miami Herald International Edition*, August 12, 1997, A1.

17. *DeFunis v. Odegaard*, 416 U.S. 317 (1974).

18. Seven state constitutions expressly impose on their state supreme courts a duty to render advisory opinions (Colorado, Florida, Maine, Massachusetts, New Hampshire, Rhode Island, and South Dakota). In Alabama and Delaware, state courts have upheld laws authorizing advisory opinions even in the absence of a constitutional mandate. In North Carolina, the power to issue advisory opinions comes from a series of judicial decisions. For a general discussion of this topic, see "The State Advisory Opinion in Perspective," *Fordham Law Review* 44 (1975): 81–113.

19. *Steffel v. Thompson*, 415 U.S. 452 (1974) at 482.

20. *Board of Education of Kiryas Joel Village School District v. Grumet*, 512 U.S. 687 (1994).

21. One innovation in this realm is worth noting. At the present time in five federal courtrooms and in parts of six states, appeals judges are able to view *videotapes* of trials whose judgments are appealed to them. For an interesting discussion of this practice and conjecture about its future implications, see Junda Woo, "Videotapes Give Appeals Cases New Dimension," *Wall Street Journal*, April 14, 1992, B1.

22. *Pacific States Telephone & Telegraph v. Oregon*, 223 U.S. 118 (1912).

23. *Baker v. Carr*, 369 U.S. 186 (1962).

24. *Massachusetts v. Laird*, 400 U.S. 886 (1970).

25. *Goldwater v. Carter*, 444 U.S. 996 (1979).

26. *Tilton v. Richardson*, 403 U.S. 672 (1971).

27. *Griswold v. Connecticut*, 381 U.S. 479 (1965).

SUGGESTED READINGS

Abraham, Henry J. *The Judicial Process*, 6th ed. New York: Oxford University Press, 1993. A traditional but classic discussion of the judicial process—especially Chapter 9, which focuses on judicial self-restraint.

Halpern, Stephen C., and Charles M. Lamb, eds. *Supreme Court Activism and Restraint*. Lexington, Mass.: Lexington Books, 1982. An excellent series of individual essays about the history and the pros and cons of judicial activism and restraint.

Stumpf, Harry P., and John H. Culver. *The Politics of State Courts*. New York: Longman, 1992. A short, up-to-date textbook on the judicial process at the state level.

Tarr, G. Alan, and Mary Cornelia Aldis Porter. *State Supreme Courts in State and Nation*. New Haven, Conn.: Yale University Press, 1988. A general discussion of state supreme courts, with a focus on the high courts in Alabama, Ohio, and New Jersey.

The Third Branch: Newsletter of the Federal Courts. Printed monthly by the Administrative Office of the U.S. Courts. Washington, D.C.: Government Printing Office. A monthly report on activities, problems, and events related to day-to-day operations of the federal judiciary.

CHAPTER 5

Lawyers, Litigants, and Interest Groups in the Judicial Process

Linda Brown, plaintiff in *Brown v. Board of Education*, at age nine. Although the suit was filed by her parents, the NAACP supplied the legal help and money necessary to pursue the case all the way to the Supreme Court.

IN THIS CHAPTER WE LAY the foundation for a detailed examination of the courts in action by focusing on three crucial actors in the judicial process: lawyers, litigants, and interest groups. Judges in the United States make decisions only in the context of cases that are brought to the courts by individuals or groups who have some sort of disagreement or dispute with each other. These adversaries, commonly called litigants, sometimes argue their own cases in such minor forums as small claims courts, but they are almost always represented by lawyers in the more important judicial arenas.

Given the importance of lawyers in our system of justice, the first part of our discussion will be devoted to an examination of the legal profession. Following that we will turn our attention to the role of individual litigants and interest groups in the judicial process. Although our discussion applies generally to both the federal and state judicial systems, it will be necessary in some instances to distinguish between the two levels. These distinctions will become more clear in the pages that follow.

Lawyers and the Legal Profession

Our examination of lawyers focuses on the training and work of attorneys in the United States. In keeping with a basic theme of earlier chapters, we will first examine lawyers and the legal profession in a historical context.[1]

Development of the Legal Profession

The Colonial Period. Lawyers were not at all popular during the early colonial years; there were, in fact, very few lawyers to be found among the early settlers. Eventually, however, lawyers became necessary to a growing society facing problems that required their skills. Some who rendered legal services had been trained in England; others were laymen who had only a smattering of legal knowledge. In spite of constant complaints about those who practiced law, "there was a competent, professional bar, dominated by brilliant and successful lawyers . . . in all major communities by 1750."[2]

There were no law schools during this period to train those interested in the legal profession. Some young men, especially those who lived in the South, where there were no colleges, went to England for their education and attended the Inns of Court. The Inns were not formal law schools, but were part of the English legal culture and allowed students to become familiar with English law.

Americans who aspired to the law during this period generally went through some form of clerkship or apprenticeship with an established lawyer. In other words, the student paid a fee to the lawyer, who promised to train him in the law. As might be expected, some found this to be a fruitful experience, whereas others complained that it was of little or no value.

Each colony established its own standards for admission to the bar (the entire group of lawyers permitted to practice law in the courts of that colony). In some instances the colony's highest court was given control over licensing and admission to the bar. In Massachusetts each court admitted its own lawyers; in Rhode Island any court could admit lawyers, but admission by one court automatically meant admission to all the courts in the colony.

The impact of lawyers on the American political system was evident during this early period. Of the fifty-six signers of the Declaration of Independence, twenty-five were lawyers, and thirty-one of the fifty-five delegates to the Constitutional Convention were lawyers.[3] Among the leading Founders of the Republic who were lawyers, one finds John Marshall, John Adams, Thomas Jefferson, James Wilson, John Jay, and George Wythe, to name a few.

The Revolution to the Mid-Nineteenth Century. After the Revolution the number of lawyers increased rapidly, since neither legal education nor admission to the bar was very strict. During the first half of the nineteenth century there were no large law firms. However, some lawyers garnered wealth by representing rich clients and prosperous merchants. Other lawyers simply eked out a living by handling petty claims in minor courts.

It seems that the right social background was as important then as it is today. As one American legal historian says:

There is evidence, indeed, that the bar, after the first Revolutionary generation, drew even more heavily than before upon children of professionals, as compared to children of farmers or laborers. Between 1810 and 1840, it seems, more than half the lawyers, who were college graduates and were admitted to the bar in Massachusetts, were sons of lawyers and judges; before 1810 the figure was about 38 percent.[4]

The apprenticeship method continued to be the most popular way to receive legal training, but law schools were coming into existence. The first law schools grew out of law offices that had begun to specialize in training clerks or apprentices. The earliest such school was the Litchfield School, founded by Judge Tapping Reeve in 1784. This school, which taught by the lecture method, placed primary emphasis on commercial law.

Eventually, a few colleges began to teach law as part of their general curriculum. William and Mary College was the first to establish a chair of law, and George Wythe was appointed to the professorship. Professorships were also established at the University of Virginia, the University of Pennsylvania, and the University of Maryland during the late eighteenth and early nineteenth centuries.

A chair of law was established at Harvard in 1816, and the first professor, Isaac Parker, worked to bring about a professional, independent law school. A major gift from Nathan Dane in 1826 helped to realize this goal. He gave Harvard $10,000 to support a professorship and suggested that the first Dane professor be Joseph

Story. Story was an associate justice of the United States Supreme Court when he accepted the position in 1829.[5] Harvard awarded an LL.B. (Bachelor of Laws) degree to students who completed the law school course. Harvard was to become the model for all newer schools.

The Second Half of the Nineteenth Century. During the second half of the nineteenth century, the number of law schools increased dramatically. In 1850 only 15 law schools were operating, but by 1900 there were 102.[6]

There were two major differences between law schools of that time and those of today. First, law schools did not usually require any previous college work. Second, in 1850 the standard law school curriculum could be completed in one year. Later in the 1800s many law schools instituted two-year programs.

In 1870 major changes began at Harvard that were to have a lasting impact on legal training. In that year Christopher Columbus Langdell was appointed dean of the law school. As a start, Langdell instituted stiffer entrance requirements. A student who did not have a college degree was required to pass an entrance test. Langdell also made it more difficult to graduate. The law school course was increased to two years in 1871 and to three years in 1876. Another hurdle was the requirement that a student pass first-year final examinations before proceeding to the second-year courses.

Without doubt, however, the most lasting change attributed to Langdell was the introduction of the case method of teaching. This method replaced lectures and textbooks with casebooks. The casebooks (collections of actual case reports) were designed to explain the principles of law, what they meant, and how they developed. Teachers then used the Socratic method to guide the students to a discovery of legal concepts found in the cases. Students initially resisted this new method of teaching law, but other schools eventually adopted the Harvard approach. In fact, it remains the accepted method in many law schools today.

As the demand for lawyers increased during the late 1800s, there was a corresponding acceleration in the creation of new law schools. It was not really expensive to open a law school, and a number of night schools, using lawyers and judges as part-time faculty members, sprang into existence. Standards were often lax and the curriculum tended to emphasize local practice. These schools' major contribution lay in making legal training more readily available to poor, immigrant, and working-class students.

Naturally, then, the legal profession itself changed dramatically during this time. Lawyers no longer came solely from the upper rungs of society. Bar associations became interested in legal education as a way of controlling entry into the profession. Around the turn of the century, the Association of American Law Schools was created and, along with the American Bar Association (ABA), became involved in the accreditation of law schools.

The Twentieth Century. This century has seen some major changes in the legal profession. For one thing, there has been a dramatic increase in the number of people wanting to study law. By the 1960s the number of applicants to law schools had grown so large that nearly all schools became more selective. The more prestigious schools in particular accepted only the best students. In response to social pressure and litigation, many law schools began actively recruiting female and minority applicants.

During the first half of the twentieth century, the case method of instruction continued to dominate the legal education process. By the 1920s, however, the legal realist movement (discussed more completely in Chapter 10) began to have an impact on the law school curriculum. Two new courses, administrative law and taxation, started to find their way into the schedule. Some schools also began to add clinical training to the curriculum.

By the 1960s the curriculum in some law schools had been expanded to include social concerns such as civil rights law and law-and-poverty issues. Foreign law courses were also available. In spite of these alterations and additions, however, the core law school curriculum has been highly resistant to radical changes.

The twentieth century has been an active period for the organized bar. The ABA adopted in 1908 a canon of ethics to guide the conduct of lawyers. Most states followed suit by adopting the ABA canon or one of their own.

Another twentieth-century development is the integrated bar. This simply means that all lawyers in the state belong to a single bar association, pay dues to it, and are disciplined by it. The move toward an integrated bar began about the middle of the century.

Finally, we should note that the increasing use of advertising by lawyers has had a profound impact on the legal profession. In a 1977 decision the U.S. Supreme Court struck down Arizona's ban on such advertising.[7] Today, on television stations across the country one can see lawyers making appeals to attract new clients. Furthermore, legal "clinics," established to handle the business generated by the increased use of advertising, have spread rapidly.

Growth and Stratification

The number of lawyers has risen sharply over the past forty years. In 1951 the number of attorneys in the United States stood at 221,605. By December 1991 that figure had risen to 777,119, and estimates are that it could hit one million by the year 2000.[8] The number of attorneys has been increasing faster than the general population in this country.

Where do all these new attorneys find employment? A study of the class of 1995, surveyed six months after receiving their J.D. degrees, provides some answers. Initial employment was overwhelmingly in one of three broad categories: private practice, public service, or business and industry. A majority (56.1 percent) went into private practice with a law firm. A little over one fourth (26.6 percent) of the newly employed graduates opted for some type of public service. Some of this group (12.8 percent) went to work for the government, others (11.8 percent) accepted judicial clerkships, and still others (2 percent) went into some sort of public interest practice. The business and industry category accounted for 13.4 percent of the jobs.[9] It is apparent, then, that America's lawyers choose to apply their professional training in a variety of settings. As one might expect, some environments are more profitable and prestigious than others. This situation has led to what is known as professional stratification. Because of the increasing numbers of women and blacks entering the legal field and the increased specialization within the profession, America's lawyers have become a less homogeneous group. The result is a profession stratified into "two hemispheres divided by backgrounds, clients, functions, structures, rewards, and associations." [10]

One of the major factors influencing the prestige rating is the type of legal specialty and the type of clientele served. Lawyers with specialties who serve big business and large institutions occupy the top hemisphere; those who represent individual interests find themselves in the bottom hemisphere.

At the top of the prestige ladder are the elite law firms. These are the Wall Street firms—the venerable firms originally (or still) situated on New York City's Wall Street—and other large national firms.

The basic pattern followed by the large national firms was established early in the twentieth century by Paul D. Cravath, the head of a Wall Street law firm. The ideal candidate for Cravath, Swaine & Moore was a member of Phi Beta Kappa and editor of the law review at Harvard, Yale, or Columbia. Those recruited served a kind of internship during which they performed general work for a number of the firm's partners.[11] Later they moved into an area of specialization and by the tenth year were evaluated for a partnership with the firm. Some lawyers were rewarded with partnerships; others left for another job.

The Cravath approach was used by many other New York firms; collectively the attorneys working for such firms came to be known as the Wall Street lawyers.

These attorneys are totally dedicated to the interests of their clients and work long, hard hours on their behalf. The Wall Street lawyers have traditionally been known less for court appearances than for the counseling they provide their clients. The clients must be able to pay for this high-powered legal talent, and thus tend to be major corporations rather than individuals. It should be noted, however, that many of these large national firms often provide *pro bono* (free) legal services to further civil rights, civil liberties, consumer interests, and environmental causes.

The large national firms consist of partners and associates. The associates are paid salaries and in essence work for the partners. According to a *National Law Journal* survey, partners who share in the profits of a large law firm currently earn between $211,000 and $738,000 per year.[12] These large firms compete for the best graduates from the nation's law schools, tempting first-year associates with large beginning salaries, annual salary increases, and, in some instances, opportunities for bonuses. Recent figures indicate that the median base salary in a firm of over 250 lawyers is $70,000 for a first-year associate and $100,000 for a seventh-year associate.[13] The most prestigious firms have 250 or more lawyers and also employ hundreds of other people as paralegals, administrators, librarians, and secretaries. In addition to New York City, prestigious firms are found in other major cities, such as Chicago, Houston, Los Angeles, San Francisco, and Washington, D.C. Many of these firms have branches in several U.S. cities and even abroad.

A notch below those working in large national firms are those employed as attorneys by large corporations. As noted above, many corporations use national law firms as outside counsel. Increasingly, however, corporations are hiring their own salaried attorneys as in-house counsel. In fact, the legal staffs of some corporations rival those of private firms in size. Further, these corporations compete with the major law firms for the best law school graduates.

The legal division of a typical large corporation is headed by a senior-level official known as the general counsel. This individual often carries a title such as vice-president or secretary as well. Rather than representing the corporation in court (this is usually handled by outside counsel when necessary), the legal division handles the multitude of legal problems faced by the modern corporation. For example, the legal division monitors the company's personnel practices to ensure compliance with federal and state regulations concerning hiring and removal procedures. The corporation's attorneys may offer assistance in strategic planning by advising the board of directors about such things as contractual agreements, mergers, stock sales, and other business practices. The company lawyers may also help educate other employees about the laws that apply to their specific jobs and make sure that they are in compliance with them. The legal division of a large company also serves as a liaison with outside counsel.

Given the wide range of duties and responsibilities of a corporation's general counsel, it is not surprising that these individuals are among the nation's highest paid professionals. In fiscal 1996 the median cash compensation (salary and bonuses) for the chief legal officers in corporations was $260,000, up from $225,000 in 1995.[14]

Most of the nation's lawyers toil in the bottom hemisphere, the lowest level of the legal profession in terms of prestige. One study aptly noted that "the Manhattan megafirm with scores of highly paid associates may command headlines for the moment, but the truth is that most lawyers . . . work in firms of fewer than 20 lawyers. . . ."[15]

Generally speaking, the lawyers in this hemisphere do not command the high salaries associated with large national law firms and major corporations. According to a recent study, the average starting salary for graduates in the class of 1995 was $45,590.[16] Furthermore, the same study notes that "nearly half of all salaries were in the $25,001–40,000 range, and salaries of $30,000 and $35,000 were the most frequently reported."[17]

Whereas the attorneys in the upper hemisphere are primarily involved in representing corporate clients, the lawyers who work in the lower hemisphere are engaged in a wide range of activities. They are much more likely to be found, day in and day out, in the courtrooms of the United States. These are the attorneys who represent clients in personal injury suits, who prosecute and defend persons accused of crimes, who represent husbands and wives in divorce proceedings, who help people conduct real estate transactions, and who help people prepare wills, to name just a few activities.

As might be expected, many attorneys, especially those in a solo practice, handle many types of cases, rather than specialize in one or two areas. Some charge a flat hourly rate for their activities; those representing plaintiffs in a personal injury suit often work under a contingency fee arrangement. Under this arrangement the attorney receives no compensation in advance. Instead, if the suit is successful and the plaintiff is awarded monetary damages, the lawyer receives a certain percentage for his or her services.

As noted earlier, attorneys who work for the government are generally included in the lower hemisphere. Some, such as the U.S. attorney general and the solicitor general of the United States, occupy quite prestigious positions, but many toil in rather obscure and poorly paid positions. A number of attorneys opt for careers as judges at the federal or state level. The judges will be dealt with more extensively at various points throughout the remainder of this book.

Another common distinction in terms of specialization in the legal profession is that between plaintiffs and defense attorneys. The former group initiates lawsuits, whereas the latter group defends those accused of wrongdoing in civil and criminal cases. Only rarely do they cross the line to assume the opposing role.

Since the remainder of this book focuses on the work of the courts, it seems appropriate to look more extensively at the lawyers who handle cases in these courts. In some instances the litigants are private individuals and are thus represented by attorneys who are engaged in private practice. In other cases one of the parties involved in the suit may be the state or federal government. When that occurs a government attorney as well as a private lawyer may be involved in the case.

Government Attorneys in the Judicial Process

Government attorneys work at all levels of the judicial process, from trial courts to the highest state and federal appellate courts. Since the bulk of the cases never move beyond the trial courts, our discussion will begin with the government lawyers most commonly associated with this level of the judicial system.

Federal Prosecutors. Although the exact origins of the public prosecutor are uncertain, the prosecution of criminal cases in colonial America became the responsibility of a district attorney (or a person with an equivalent title) who was appointed by the governor and assigned to a specific region. The practice persisted, and by the end of the American Revolution every state had passed legislation creating a public prosecutor. In most instances he was an elected county official. The Judiciary Act of 1789 also provided for a United States attorney to be appointed by the president for each federal district court. Since these beginnings, "the prosecutor has become the most powerful figure in the criminal justice system." [18]

Today, each federal judicial district has a U.S. attorney and one or more assistant U.S. attorneys. The U.S. attorney is paid $115,700 per year while the salary for assistants ranges from $29,700 to $109,400, depending upon such factors as locale, experience, and supervisory responsibilities. [19] The number of assistant U.S. attorneys varies from district to district, with larger urban areas having over a hundred.

U.S. attorneys are appointed by the president and confirmed by the Senate. Nominees must reside in the district to which they are appointed and must be attorneys. They serve a formal term of four years but can be reappointed indefinitely or removed at the president's discretion.[20] The appointment of a U.S. attorney is often a political reward.[21] Overwhelmingly, only lawyers who belong to the president's party are considered; it has become customary for U.S. attorneys to resign their positions when the opposition party wins the presidency. Since each nominee must be confirmed by the Senate, the senator or senators of the president's party in the state where the vacancy exists become important actors in the appointment process. The assistant U.S. attorneys are formally appointed by the U.S. attorney general, although in practice they are chosen by the U.S. attorney, who forwards the selection to the attorney general for ratification. Assistant U.S. attorneys may be fired by the attorney general.

The basic tasks handled by U.S. attorneys and their assistants are to prosecute defendants in the federal district courts and to defend the United States when it is sued in a federal trial court. Primarily, then, they function as prosecutors for the federal government, with considerable discretion in deciding which criminal cases to prosecute. The U.S. attorneys have the authority to determine which civil cases to try to settle out of court and which ones to take to trial. The U.S. attorney is in a very good position to influence the federal district court's docket.

Since U.S. attorneys and judges within a district must work together on an ongoing basis, their relationship is extremely important. In some districts the relationship may be close and informal, whereas in other districts the atmosphere may be more businesslike. Although many factors play a role, one leading study notes that a close rapport between the judge and the U.S. attorney is most likely in a small district because of the close physical proximity of their offices. At the other extreme, "large districts must institutionalize procedures for scheduling cases and arranging the docket, cutting the occasions for informal contact." [22] Regardless of the working arrangement, U.S. attorneys engage in more litigation in the federal district courts than anyone else. Therefore, they and their staffs are vital participants in policy making in the federal trial courts.

Prosecutors at the State Level. Those who prosecute persons accused of violating state criminal statutes are commonly known as *district attorneys.* In most states they are elected county officials; however, in a few states they are appointed. The district attorney's office usually employs a number of assistants who do most of the actual trial work. The salary range for prosecutors at this level is quite varied and depends upon such factors as rank, experience, and responsibilities. A recent study, for example, noted that in Montgomery County, Alabama, an entry-level prosecutor earns $35,000 while the district attorney earns $109,200 annually.[23] Most of these assistant district attorneys are recent graduates of law school and are using the position to gain trial experience. Many will later enter private practice, often as criminal defense attorneys. Others will seek to become district attorneys or perhaps judges after a few years.

The district attorney's office has a great deal of discretion in the handling of cases. Given budget and personnel constraints, not all cases can be afforded the same amount of time and attention. Therefore, some cases are dismissed, others are not prosecuted, and still others are prosecuted vigorously in court. Most cases, however, are subject to plea bargaining. This means that the district attorney's office agrees to accept the defendant's plea of guilty to a reduced charge or to drop other charges against the defendant. (Plea bargaining will be discussed at greater length in Chapter 6.)

District attorney's offices are organized in different ways. Some use what is known as the horizontal, or zone, model. This model, often found in heavily populated areas, assigns assistants to different steps in the judicial process. Some will screen cases that enter the prosecutor's office. Others will be assigned to courts to deal with bond hearings, probable-cause hearings, misdemeanor cases, or felony cases. Still others will specialize in presenting cases to the grand jury. Those assigned to a particular courtroom become a part of the courtroom work group and interact more with other courtroom work group members than with the assistant prosecutors who have other assignments.[24]

A second organizational model, found frequently in smaller jurisdictions, is the vertical prosecution model. In this scheme each assistant is fully responsible for an assigned caseload. This means that one person receives the case when it is filed and follows it through to a final disposition.

Finally, some jurisdictions use a mixed model, which attempts to combine the best features of the other two models. Routine cases are likely to be handled in a horizontal model, and certain types of cases call for the vertical model. For instance, the district attorney's office may establish bureaus to deal with organized crime, repeat offenders, drug trafficking, or other special problems. Such bureaus are staffed with persons having special training or experience in the particular areas.

Public Defenders. Quite often the person charged with violating a state or federal criminal statute is unable to pay for the services of a defense attorney. In some areas a government official known as a *public defender* bears the responsibility for representing indigent defendants. Thus, the public defender is a counterpart of the prosecutor. Unlike the district attorney, however, the public defender is usually appointed rather than elected.

At the federal level public defender salaries are set by the circuit courts of appeals; however, they cannot exceed the salary of the U.S. attorney for the district where representation is provided. Salaries for assistant public defenders are established by the federal public defender. Once again, they are limited by what assistant U.S. attorneys in the district are paid. Recent figures indicate a national salary range of $29,700 to $115,700.[25]

In some parts of the country there are statewide public defender systems; in other regions the public defender is a local official, usually associated with a county government. In New York City an independent organization known as the Legal Aid Society represents all indigent criminal defendants except those charged with murder.[26] New York's Legal Aid Society also has a civil division. As one would expect, salaries for public defenders and assistant public defenders at the state and local levels vary widely. Salaries in the small city of Frankfort, Kentucky, and the large urban area of Los Angeles, California, illustrate the contrast. In Frankfort, the range is from $23,388 to $62,000; in Los Angeles the range is $42,461 to $135,000.[27]

Like the district attorney, the public defender employs assistants and investigative personnel. Furthermore, there is a great deal of similarity to the prosecutor's office in the organizational scheme used by public defenders. Some are organized horizontally, some vertically, and some in a mixed model.

Other Government Lawyers. At both the state and federal levels there are government attorneys who are better known for their work in appellate courts than in trial courts. For example, each state has an attorney general who supervises a staff of attorneys who are charged with the responsibility of handling the legal affairs of the state. At the federal level the Department of Justice has similar responsibilities on behalf of the United States.

The U.S. Department of Justice. Although the Justice Department is an agency of the executive branch of the government, it has a natural association with the judicial branch. Many of the cases heard in the federal courts involve the national government in one capacity or another. Sometimes the government is sued; in other instances the government initiates the lawsuit. In either case, an attorney must represent the government. Most of the litigation involving the federal government is handled by the Justice Department, although a number of other government agencies have attorneys on their payrolls.

The Justice Department has several key divisions. The Office of Solicitor General is extremely important in cases argued before the Supreme Court. There are also seven legal divisions within the Justice Department: Antitrust, Civil, Civil Rights, Criminal, Internal Security, Land and Natural Resources, and Tax; each has a staff of specialized lawyers and is headed by an assistant attorney general. The seven legal divisions supervise the handling of litigation by the U.S. attorneys, take cases to the courts of appeals, and aid the solicitor general's office in cases argued before the Supreme Court.

U.S. Solicitor General. The solicitor general of the United States, the third-ranking official in the Justice Department, is assisted by five deputies and about twenty assistant solicitors general. The solicitor general's primary function is to decide, on behalf of the United States, which cases will and will not be presented to the Supreme Court for review. Whenever an executive branch department or agency loses a case in one of the courts of appeals and wishes a Supreme Court review, that department or agency will formally request that the Justice Department seek certiorari. The solicitor general will determine whether to appeal the lower-court decision.

Naturally, there are many factors to be taken into account when making such a decision. Perhaps the most important consideration is the fact that there is a limit to the number of cases the Supreme Court can hear in a given term. Thus, the solicitor general must determine whether a particular case is one of the ninety or so cases that deserve extensive consideration by the Court during that term. How successful have solicitors general been in this assessment? The most extensive study to date tells us that

the advantage that the solicitor general enjoys in his capacity as a petitioner is clear. The solicitor general sought certiorari in 1,294 cases between 1959 and 1989, and was successful in obtaining the Court's review 69.78 percent of the time. Certiorari requests were granted in only 4.9 percent of the private litigation.[28]

In addition to deciding whether to seek Supreme Court review of a particular lower-court decision, the solicitor general personally argues most of the government's cases heard by the High Court. However, there are some kinds of cases that the solicitor general may feel are more appropriately argued by a person who holds a particular office in government. Former solicitor general Rex E. Lee pointed out that the "tradition has been that the hardest cases—the most important cases—usually are argued by the Solicitor General."[29]

Although the solicitor general works for the attorney general and serves at the pleasure of the president, it has traditionally been argued that this official "must have the independence to exercise his craft as a lawyer on behalf of the institution of government without being a mouthpiece for the President."[30] In recent years, however, some have suggested that the solicitor general's office has become more politicized and thus more likely to press for adoption of the president's agenda.[31]

State Attorneys General. Each state has an attorney general who serves as its chief legal official. Salaries vary widely for this position. For example, Montana's attorney general earns $54,330 per year while the New York attorney general is paid $110,000 annually.[32] In most states this official is elected on a partisan statewide ballot. The attorney general oversees a staff of attorneys who primarily handle the civil cases involving the state. Although the prosecution of criminal defendants is generally handled by the local district attorneys, the attorney general's office often plays an important role in investigating statewide criminal activities. Thus, the attorney general and his or her staff may work closely with the local district attorney in preparing a case against a particular defendant.

The state attorney general does not usually control appeals in the state courts as the solicitor general does in the federal courts. Furthermore, the state attorney general normally argues cases before the state supreme court only when a state agency is involved in the case.

The state attorneys general also perform the important function of issuing advisory opinions to state and local agencies; many of these agencies simply cannot afford their own legal staff. Quite often, the attorney general's opinion will interpret an aspect of state law not yet ruled on by the courts. Although the advisory opinion might eventually be overruled in a case brought before the courts, the attorney general's opinion is important in determining the behavior of state and local agencies.

Private Lawyers in the Judicial Process

In criminal cases in the United States the defendant has a constitutional right to be represented by an attorney. As we noted above, some jurisdictions have established public defender's offices to represent indigent defendants. In other areas, there is some method of assigning a private attorney to represent a defendant who cannot afford to hire one. Those defendants who can afford to hire their own lawyers will of course do so.

In civil cases neither the plaintiff nor the defendant is constitutionally entitled to the services of an attorney. However, in the civil arena the legal issues are often so complex as to demand the services of an attorney. Various forms of legal assistance are usually available to those who need help.

Assigned Defense Counsel. In many jurisdictions throughout the country, especially rural areas, some method of appointing a private lawyer to represent an indigent defendant is the standard procedure. Usually the assignment is made by an individual judge on an ad hoc basis. Local bar associations or lawyers themselves often provide the courts with a list of attorneys who are willing to provide such services. Compensation for providing representation for an indigent defendant is generally based on a flat rate for hours spent in and out of court. The fee varies from area to area, and often according to the case's complexity. At any rate, it is usually a good deal less than an attorney would earn for providing services to a private client.

Private Defense Counsel. Some attorneys in private practice specialize in criminal defense work. Such lawyers are more often found in solo practices or in small firms than in the large law firms. Although the personal and private lives of criminal defense attorneys are depicted as rather glamorous on television, the average real-life criminal defense lawyer works long hours for low pay and low prestige.[33]

One of the major worries of the criminal defense attorney is getting paid. The clients are usually poor and often not very trustworthy; therefore, the criminal defense lawyer generally requires payment of a part of the fee in advance. Often, this is all the lawyer will collect. So the average criminal defense attorney must handle a large number of cases in order to survive. The large volume of cases in turn means that the attorney must spend a great deal of time in court and in the office juggling cases. All told, the lawyer who specializes in criminal defense work typically leads a rather hectic life.

The Courtroom Workgroup

We noted earlier that assistant district attorneys assigned to a specific courtroom become a part of the *courtroom workgroup*. Simply put, rather than functioning as an occasional gathering of strangers who resolve a particular conflict and then go their separate ways, "courts are permanent organizations."[34]

The most visible members of the courtroom workgroup—judges, prosecutors, and defense attorneys—are commonly associated with specific functions: prosecutors push for convictions of those accused of criminal offenses against the government, defense attorneys seek acquittals for their clients, and judges serve as neutral arbiters to guarantee a fair trial. In reality, members of the courtroom workgroup share certain values and goals and are not the fierce adversaries that many Americans imagine. In fact, cooperation between judges, prosecutors, and defense attorneys is the norm.

The most important goal of the courtroom workgroup is to handle cases expeditiously. Judges and prosecutors are interested in disposing of cases quickly to present a picture of accomplishment and efficiency. Because private defense attorneys need to handle a large volume of cases to survive, resolving cases quickly works to their advantage. And public defenders seek quick dispositions simply because they lack adequate resources to handle their caseloads.

A second important goal of the courtroom workgroup is to maintain group cohesion. Naturally, conflict between the members makes work more difficult and interferes with the expeditious handling of cases. Therefore, the workgroup stresses cooperation and censures those who violate this norm.

Finally, the courtroom workgroup is interested in reducing or controlling uncertainty. In practice this means that all members of the workgroup work to avoid trials. Trials, especially jury trials, produce a great deal of uncertainty since they require substantial investments of time and effort without any reasonable guarantee of a desirable outcome.

To attain the goals of handling cases expeditiously, maintaining group cohesion, and reducing uncertainty, workgroup members employ several techniques. Although unilateral decisions and adversarial proceedings occur, negotiation is the most commonly used technique in criminal courtrooms. The members negotiate over a variety of issues—continuances, hearing dates, and exchange of information, to mention just a few. Without doubt, however, plea bargaining is the most heavily publicized subject of negotiation among courtroom workgroup members. Plea bargaining and its ramifications will be discussed more fully in Chapter 6.

Legal Services for the Poor

Although criminal defendants are constitutionally entitled to be represented by a lawyer, those who are defendants in a civil case or who wish to initiate a civil case do not have the right to representation. That means, then, that those who do not have the funds to hire a lawyer may find it difficult to obtain justice.

In order to deal with this problem, legal aid services of one sort or another are now found in many areas. Legal aid societies were established in New York and Chicago as early as the late 1880s, and many other major cities followed suit in the twentieth century. Although some legal aid societies are sponsored by bar associations, most are supported by private contributions. There are also legal aid bureaus associated with charitable organizations in some areas. In addition, many law schools operate legal aid clinics to provide both legal assistance for the poor and valuable training for law students.

In 1974 Congress created the Legal Services Corporation (LSC), which distributes money to a number of legal services agencies throughout the country. By 1995 it had a total of 1,200 offices dealing with such matters as family, consumer, housing, landlord-tenant, and welfare problems.[35]

Since the early 1980s the LSC has been unpopular among many conservatives, and "there are renewed efforts in Congress to phase it out over five years to save $1.6 billion."[36] Critics contend that there are other agencies available to provide legal aid to the needy. The National Service Legal Corps, for example, is setting up interdisciplinary teams of attorneys, paralegals, social workers, health providers, and educators throughout the country to work on a number of issues that affect the poor.[37]

One other source of legal help for indigents deserves mention. Many lawyers provide legal services *pro bono publico* ("for the public good") because they see it as a professional obligation.

What about people who are not indigent but are still too poor to hire a competent private attorney? Two relatively low cost methods are available: legal clinics and prepaid legal plans.[38]

A legal clinic is a high-volume, high-efficiency law firm. These clinics depend upon advertising and publicity to generate clients and keep costs down by relying on standard forms and delegating most of the routine work to paralegals (non-lawyers who are specifically trained to handle many of the routine aspects of legal work). The legal clinics concentrate on such fairly common legal problems as divorces, traffic offenses, personal bankruptcies, and wills.

Prepaid legal plans, also referred to as legal insurance plans, may be financed in two ways. One method is to enroll a group of people such as a labor union. A second method is simply to sign up individuals. Some plans make available a designated lawyer or group of lawyers from whom the client may choose. Other plans allow the client to choose any lawyer; however, there is usually a limit on how much of the attorney's fee will be covered.

Labor unions have been active in organizing prepaid legal plans. A plan established by the United Auto Workers, for example, covers over 150,000 Chrysler employees, retired employees, and their families.

Litigants

In this section we take a brief look at the parties who are involved in the cases taken before the courts. In some instances the litigants are individuals, whereas in other cases one or more of the litigants may be a government agency, a corporation, a union, an interest group, or a university. In short, almost any individual or group has the potential to become a litigant in the courts.

What motivates a person or group to take a grievance to court? In criminal cases the answer to this question is relatively simple. A state or federal criminal statute has allegedly been violated and the government prosecutes the party charged with violating the statute. In civil cases the answer is not quite so easy, however. Although some persons readily take their grievances to court, many others avoid this route because of the time and expense involved. Still, enough cases are filed annually to cause concern about how the federal and state courts can manage their dockets.

In his study of the U.S. Supreme Court, Lawrence Baum concludes that the motives of litigants before that tribunal take two general forms: "ordinary" litigation and "political" litigation.[39] Baum's conclusions apply to other courts as well.

Political scientist Phillip Cooper points out that judges are called upon to resolve two kinds of disputes: private law cases and public law controversies. Private law disputes are those in which one private citizen or organization sues another. Public law controversies involve the government more directly. In these situations a citizen or organization contends that a government agency or official has violated a right established by a constitution or statute. Cooper goes on to state that "legal actions, whether public law or private law contests, may either be policy oriented or compensatory."[40]

A classic example of private, or ordinary, compensation-oriented litigation is when a person injured in an automobile accident sues the driver of the other car in an effort to win monetary damages to compensate him for the medical bills he had to pay. Quite obviously, this type of litigation is personal and is not aimed at changing governmental or business policies.

Some private law cases, however, are policy oriented or political in nature. Personal injury suits and product liability suits may appear on the surface to be simply compensatory in nature, but in reality may also be used to change the manufacturing or business practices of the private firms being sued. A good example may be found in *Greenman v. Yuba Power Products, Inc.*, a case decided by the California Supreme Court.[41] In that case, the plaintiff was injured while using a Shopsmith (a combination power tool that can be used as a saw, a drill, or a wood lathe) that his wife had given him as a Christmas present. He had used the lathe several times without difficulty, when a piece of wood suddenly flew out of the machine and struck him on the forehead, causing serious injuries. Substantial evidence was introduced at the trial to indicate that the plaintiff's injuries were caused by defective design and construction of the Shopsmith. The plaintiff was awarded damages in the amount of $65,000, and the verdict was upheld on appeal. In short, not only was the plaintiff compensated for his injuries, but the manufacturer was also forced to reconsider the design and construction of the product.

Most political or policy-oriented lawsuits, however, are public law controversies. That is, they are suits brought against the government primarily to stop allegedly illegal policies or practices. They may, of course, also seek damages or some other specific form of relief. A case decided by the Oregon Supreme Court, *Thornburg v. Port of Portland,* provides a good example.[42] The plaintiffs, who lived close to the Portland International Airport, complained that the noise from jet aircraft made their land unusable. They contended that since their land was no longer usable it had in effect been taken by the government agency and they should be compensated for their loss. The Oregon Supreme Court agreed with this contention.

Political or policy-oriented litigation is more prevalent in the appellate courts than in the trial courts and is most common in the U.S. Supreme Court. Ordinary compensatory litigation is often terminated early in the judicial process because the litigants find it more profitable to settle their dispute or accept the verdict of a trial court. On the other hand, litigants in political cases generally do little to advance their policy goals by gaining victories at the lower levels of the judiciary. Instead, they prefer the more widespread publicity that is attached to a decision by an appellate tribunal. Pursuing cases in the appellate courts is expensive; therefore, many lawsuits that reach this level are supported in one way or another by interest groups.

Interest Groups in the Judicial Process

Although interest groups are probably better known for their attempts to influence legislative and executive decisions, they also pursue their policy goals in the courts. In fact, some groups have found the judicial branch to be far more receptive to their efforts than either of the other two branches of government. Interest groups that do not have the economic resources to mount an intensive lobbying effort in Congress or a state legislature may find it much easier to hire a lawyer and find some constitutional or statutory provision upon which to base a court case. Likewise, a small group with few registered voters among its members may lack the political clout to exert much influence on legislators and executives. Large memberships and political clout are not prerequisites for filing suits in the courts, however.

Interest groups may also turn to the courts because they find the judicial branch more sympathetic to their policy goals than the other two branches. The National Association for the Advancement of Colored People (NAACP) provides an excellent example. This group, which dates from the early twentieth century, soon realized that Congress and the executive branch were not very sympathetic to the struggle for civil rights of black citizens. Seeing the courts as potentially more sympathetic, the NAACP started to focus its efforts on litigation as a means of achieving its goals. As the Supreme Court became more favorable to civil rights after 1937, the NAACP began to realize the value of the judiciary as a forum for its activities and eventually established the Legal Defense Fund, a separate organization composed of lawyers who represented them in litigation.

Following the pattern established by the NAACP, other minority group organizations began to use the courts. Cases dealing with the rights of Hispanics and women came to be pursued vigorously by groups such as the Mexican-American Legal Defense and Education Fund and the National Organization for Women.

Throughout the 1960s interest groups with liberal policy goals fared especially well in the federal courts. In addition, the public interest law firm concept, attributed to Ralph Nader, gained prominence during this period. The public interest law firms pursue cases that serve the public interest in general—including cases in the areas of consumer rights, employment discrimination, occupational safety, civil liberties, and environmental concerns.

In the 1970s, with the increasing conservatism of the federal courts stemming from President Nixon's appointment strategy, some major changes began to take place in the interaction between interest groups and the judiciary. For one thing, conservative interest groups began to resort to the federal courts more frequently than they had in the 1950s and 1960s, thus resuming the trend of the late nineteenth and early twentieth centuries.[43] This is in part a reaction to the successes of liberal interest groups. It is also due, of course, to the increasingly favorable forum that the federal courts have provided for conservative viewpoints. This latter trend persisted throughout the 1980s because of President Reagan's success in placing judges on the federal bench who shared his conservative policy views.

The 1970s, 1980s, and into the 1990s also saw predominantly liberal interest groups seeking forums other than the federal courts in which to pursue their policy goals. Some took their battles to the legislative branch, whereas others preferred to file their suits in state courts rather than in the federal courts.

Interest group involvement in the judicial process may take several different forms depending upon the goals of the particular group. However, two principal tactics stand out: involvement in test cases and presentation of information before the courts through *amicus curiae* briefs.

Test Cases

Since the judiciary engages in policy making only by rendering decisions in specific cases, one favorite tactic of interest groups is to make sure that a case appropriate for obtaining its policy goals is brought before the court. In some instances this means that the interest group will initiate and totally sponsor the case by providing all the necessary resources. Undoubtedly, the best-known example of this type of sponsorship is to be found in the *Brown v. Board of Education* case.[44] In that case, although the suit against the Board of Education of Topeka, Kansas, was filed by the parents of Linda Brown, the NAACP supplied the legal help and money necessary to pursue the case all the way to the Supreme Court, where Thurgood Marshall (who later became a U.S. Supreme Court justice) argued the case on behalf of the plaintiff and the NAACP. As a result, the NAACP gained a victory through the Supreme Court's decision that segregation in the public schools violates the equal protection clause of the Fourteenth Amendment.

Interest groups may also provide assistance in a case initiated by someone else, but which nonetheless raises issues of importance to the group. A good example of this situation may be found in a freedom of religion case, *Wisconsin v. Yoder.*[45] That case was initiated by the state of Wisconsin when it filed criminal complaints charging Jonas Yoder and others with failure to send their children to school until the age of sixteen as required by state law. Yoder and the others, members of the Amish faith, believed that education beyond the eighth grade led to the breakdown of the values they cherished and to "worldly" influences on their children.

An organization known as the National Committee for Amish Religious Freedom (NCARF), which had been formed in 1965 by non-Amish ministers, bankers, lawyers, and professors to defend the right of the Amish to pursue their way of life, came to the defense of Yoder and the others. The NCARF provided William R. Ball as defense attorney, as well as a number of expert witnesses who testified on behalf of the Amish.

Following a decision against the Amish in the trial court, the NCARF appealed to a Wisconsin circuit court, which upheld the trial court's decision. An appeal was made to the Wisconsin Supreme Court, which ruled in favor of the Amish, saying that the compulsory school attendance law violated the free exercise of religion clause of the First Amendment. Wisconsin then appealed to the U.S. Supreme Court, which on May 15, 1972, sustained the religious objection that the NCARF had raised to the compulsory school attendance laws.

Thus, even though the NCARF did not initiate the litigation, it found its test case and pursued it through four courts to obtain its objective. Without the actions of the NCARF the religious freedom interests of the Amish might not have been adequately presented, especially at the appellate level, since the Amish generally refused to defend themselves in litigation.

How extensive is interest group sponsorship of cases? A recent study of Supreme Court records and briefs found that in the 1987 term, "organized interests represented appellants in 38.2 percent of the cases and appellees in 44.2 percent. Overall, they participated as sponsors in 65.4 (n = 89) of the 136 cases decided with full opinion."[46] The author found that commercial interests (such as a chamber of commerce or a major airline company) and legal groups (such as the American Bar Association or the Pacific Legal Foundation) dominated interest group sponsorship of cases in the 1987 term.[47]

The American Civil Liberties Union (ACLU), an organization dedicated to defending the Bill of Rights, is probably the interest group best known for sponsorship of cases in the nation's courts.[48] On the occasion of its seventieth anniversary in 1990, it was noted that "the ACLU had been involved in 80 percent of the post-1920 'landmark' cases regularly cited in constitutional law texts."[49] Although the ACLU has obviously participated in a wide range of cases over the years, its involvement in the controversial issue of church-state relations is perhaps most marked. The following account from a history of the ACLU summarizes the organization's involvement in this area of constitutional law from 1951 to 1971.

Between 1951 and 1957 the ACLU's national office handled all four of the major church-state cases reaching the Supreme Court in which there was any ACLU involvement; between 1958 and 1964, the [local] affiliates initiated six of the seven cases with ACLU involvement; and between 1965 and 1971, the affiliates initiated eighteen out of nineteen.[50]

Three religion cases in which the ACLU participated stand out. In 1961 the Supreme Court struck down a Maryland requirement that all public officials swear an oath that they believe in God.[51] A year later, in *Engel v. Vitale,* the Court ruled against the required recitation in the public schools of a prayer written by state officials.[52] Then, in 1963, when the Philadelphia ACLU challenged the Pennsylvania Bible-reading law, the Court declared that the required reading of Bible verses in the public schools was unconstitutional.[53]

As the above examples illustrate, the bulk of the literature on interest group involvement in litigation has focused on cases concerning major constitutional issues that have reached the Supreme Court. Since only a small percentage of cases ever reaches the nation's highest court, however, most of the work of interest group lawyers deals with more routine work at the lower levels of the judiciary. Rather than fashioning major test cases for the appellate courts, these attorneys may simply be required to deal with the legal problems of their groups' clientele.

A 1983 study of the routine activities of three litigation-oriented civil rights groups active in Mississippi in the mid-1960s provides some interesting insights.[54] For one thing, the authors of this study found that although the lawyers associated with the Lawyers Committee for Civil Rights under Law, the Lawyers Constitutional Defense Committee, and the NAACP Legal Defense Fund evidently preferred to litigate in the federal courts, most of their work was done in the state and local tribunals. However, most of the cases concerning issues at the heart of the civil rights movement, such as demonstrations, school desegregation, voting rights, and public accommodations, were litigated in the federal courts. The activities of these attorneys covered a wide variety of needs. In addition to litigating major civil rights questions, they also defended blacks and civil rights workers who ran into difficulties with the local authorities. These interest group attorneys, then, performed many of the functions of a specialized legal aid society: they provided legal representation to those involved in an important movement for social change. Furthermore, they performed the all-important function of drawing attention to the plight of black citizens by keeping cases before the courts.

Amicus Curiae Briefs

Submission of *amicus curiae* ("friend of the court") briefs is the easiest method by which interest groups can become involved in cases. Consequently, it is also the most common form of group involvement. This method allows a group to get its message before the court even though it does not control the case. Provided it has the permission of the parties to the case or the permission of the court, an interest group may submit an amicus brief to supplement the arguments of the parties.

The frequency of amicus curiae participation has increased over the years. Recently, two Supreme Court scholars noted that "on average, 84.4 percent of all full opinion cases decided between 1986 and 1991 contained at least one amicus curiae brief, and the average amicus case contained 4.4 briefs."[55]

Sometimes these briefs are aimed at strengthening the position of one of the parties in the case. When the *Wisconsin v. Yoder* case was argued before the U.S. Supreme Court, the cause of the Amish was supported by amicus curiae briefs filed by the General Conference of Seventh Day Adventists, the National Council of Churches of Christ in the United States, the Synagogue Council of America, the American Jewish Congress, the National Jewish Commission on Law and Public Affairs, and the Mennonite Central Committee.[56] All supported exemption of the Amish from the compulsory school attendance laws.

As might be expected, some cases attract amicus briefs supporting both parties in the case. For example, when the abortion cases were argued before the Supreme Court in 1973, there were forty-seven amicus curiae briefs filed, some of which could be classified as pro-choice and others as antiabortion.[57]

Sometimes "friend of the court" briefs are used not to strengthen the arguments of one of the parties but to suggest to the court the group's own view of how the case should be resolved. A classic example of this occurred in *Mapp v. Ohio.*[58] When that case was presented to the Supreme Court the argument by the parties focused (1) on the issue of whether someone should be convicted for "mere possession" of obscene material, and (2) on the "shocking" nature of the search that led to the discovery of the material. However, the defendant's lawyer did not urge a change in the ruling that improperly seized evidence could still be used in the trial. Instead, the exclusionary issue was raised in the amicus curiae brief filed by the American Civil Liberties Union and the Ohio Civil Liberties Union.[59] The Supreme Court, without dealing with the obscenity issue, handed down a landmark constitutional decision excluding illegally seized evidence from trials in state courts (the exclusionary rule). Thus, it was the interest group's argument that provided the policy view adopted by the Supreme Court.

Scholars have recently begun to pay more attention to the fact that amicus curiae briefs are often filed in an attempt to persuade an appellate court to either grant or deny review of a lower-court decision. A recent study of the U.S. Supreme Court found, for instance, that the presence of amicus briefs significantly increased the chances that the Court would give full treatment to the case and concluded that "interested parties can have a significant and positive impact on the Court's agenda by participating as amici curiae prior to the Court's decision on certiorari or jurisdiction."[60]

We also need to pay special attention to the role of the government as a "friend of the court." Unlike private interest groups, all levels of the government can submit such briefs without obtaining permission. The solicitor general of the United States is especially important in this regard. One study of the solicitor general reports that this official was involved in 518 amicus cases decided by a full Supreme

Court opinion between 1959 and 1986.[61] In some instances the Supreme Court may invite the solicitor general to present an amicus brief. It seems clear, then, that the Supreme Court values the input of the solicitor general's office.

As we noted earlier, the solicitor general is far more successful than private litigants in getting acceptance for certiorari petitions. In addition, the solicitor general's amicus briefs in support of others' appeals or petitions are quite successful. One study noted that

when the government filed an amicus brief on behalf of the appellant or petitioner, the Court granted review in 87.6 percent of the cases. Surprisingly, this success is even greater than when the government sought the Court's review of its own cases.[62]

We should note in closing our discussion of amicus curiae briefs that the filing of such briefs is a tactic used in appellate rather than trial courts. Furthermore, the literature on "friend of the court" participation deals almost exclusively with the federal courts although amicus briefs may be filed in state appellate courts as well.

Summary

In this chapter we have laid the groundwork for later chapters, which deal more extensively with the steps in the judicial process. Here, our focus has been on three important actors in the judicial process: lawyers, litigants, and interest groups.

We traced the development of the legal profession from its beginnings in colonial days to the contemporary practice of law. Our discussion focused on the stratification of the legal profession and the various types of lawyers who practice in the United States. Singled out for special emphasis were the government lawyers who are primarily involved in handling cases in the state and federal trial and appellate courts.

We next turned our attention to those who become litigants in our nation's courts. In some cases the adversaries are ordinary litigants who are primarily concerned with being compensated for their losses. At other times, the combatants are involved in political litigation and have as their major goal influencing public policy. Still other cases feature litigants who are interested in both personal compensation and exerting some influence over public policy.

We concluded with an examination of the role of interest groups in the judicial process. Following a brief look at the reasons groups become involved in litigation, we turned our attention to the major strategies and tactics used by interest groups in the judicial arena: involvement in test cases and the use of amicus curiae briefs.

NOTES

1. Our discussion draws heavily upon Lawrence M. Friedman, *A History of American Law*, 2d ed. (New York: Simon & Schuster, 1985).

2. Ibid., 97.

3. Ibid., 101.

4. Ibid., 306.

5. Ibid., 321.

6. Ibid., 607.

7. *Bates v. State Bar*, 433 U.S. 350 (1977).

8. See *CQ Researcher*, May 22, 1992, 442, and *Business Week*, April 13, 1992, 61.

9. See Law School Admission Council, *The Official Guide to U.S. Law Schools 1998* (New York: Broadway Books, 1997), 33.

10. Richard Abel, "The Transformation of the American Legal Profession," *Law and Society Review* 20 (1986): 6.

11. See Erwin O. Smigel, *The Wall Street Lawyer: Professional Organization Man* (Glencoe, Ill.: Free Press, 1964).

12. "What Lawyers Earn," *The National Law Journal*, June 2, 1997, B10.

13. Ibid., B8 and B12.

14. Ibid., B8.

15. "Law Poll," *ABA Journal*, September 1, 1986, 44.

16. Law School Admission Council, *The Official Guide*, 35.

17. Ibid.

18. Howard Abadinsky, *Law and Justice*, 2d ed. (Chicago: Nelson-Hall, 1991), 187.

19. "What Lawyers Earn," B16.

20. For a good case study of the firing of a U.S. attorney, see Howard Ball, *Courts and Politics: The Federal Judicial System* (Englewood Cliffs, N.J.: Prentice-Hall, 1980), 202–206.

21. For an in-depth analysis of the appointment process for U.S. attorneys, see James Eisenstein, *Counsel for the United States: U.S. Attorneys in the Political and Legal Systems* (Baltimore: Johns Hopkins University Press, 1978), chap. 3.

22. A detailed study of the relationship between U.S. attorneys and federal district judges may be found in ibid., chap. 7.

23. "What Lawyers Earn," B16.

24. See James Eisenstein and Herbert Jacob, *Felony Justice* (Boston: Little, Brown, 1977).

25. "What Lawyers Earn," B9.

26. Abadinsky, *Law and Justice*, 201.

27. "What Lawyers Earn," B9.

28. Rebecca Mae Salokar, *The Solicitor General: The Politics of Law* (Philadelphia: Temple University Press, 1992), 25.

29. For a fuller discussion of this matter, see "Interview with Solicitor General Rex E. Lee," *The Third Branch* 14 (May 1982): 5.

30. Lincoln Caplan, "The Tenth Justice," pt. 1, *New Yorker*, August 10, 1987, 40.

31. See Caplan, "The Tenth Justice," pt. 1, 41–58; and pt. 2, *New Yorker*, August 17, 1987, 30–62. Also see Stephen L. Wasby, *The Supreme Court in the Federal Judicial System*, 3d ed. (Chicago: Nelson-Hall, 1988), 146–147 and Salokar, *The Solicitor General*, 172–173.

32. "What Lawyers Earn," B16.

33. See Paul Wice, *Criminal Lawyers: An Endangered Species* (Beverly Hills, Calif.: Sage, 1978).

34. Eisenstein and Jacob, *Felony Justice,* 20. Our discussion of the concept of the courtroom work-group relies heavily on Eisenstein and Jacob's discussion.

35. Steven Vago, *Law and Society,* 5th ed. (Saddle River, N.J.: Prentice-Hall, 1997), 347.

36. Ibid., 348.

37. Ibid.

38. Our discussion of legal clinics and prepaid legal plans is drawn from ibid., 348–349.

39. Lawrence Baum, *The Supreme Court,* 6th ed. (Washington, D.C.: CQ Press, 1998), 84–87.

40. Phillip J. Cooper, *Hard Judicial Choices* (New York: Oxford University Press, 1988), 13.

41. 59 Cal. 2d 57 (1963).

42. 233 Or. 178 (1962).

43. See Karen O'Connor and Lee Epstein, "The Rise of Conservative Interest Group Litigation," *Journal of Politics* 45 (May 1983): 479–489; and Lee Epstein, *Conservatives in Court* (Knoxville: University of Tennessee Press, 1985).

44. 347 U.S. 483 (1954).

45. 406 U.S. 205 (1972). Also see the excellent discussion of this case in Richard C. Cortner, *The Supreme Court and Civil Liberties Policy* (Palo Alto, Calif.: Mayfield, 1975), 153–182. Our discussion is based on this study.

46. Lee Epstein, "Courts and Interest Groups," in *The American Courts: A Critical Assessment,* ed. John B. Gates and Charles A. Johnson (Washington, D.C.: CQ Press, 1991), 350.

47. Ibid., 354.

48. For a complete history of the American Civil Liberties Union, see Samuel Walker, *In Defense of American Liberties: A History of the ACLU* (New York: Oxford University Press, 1990).

49. Ibid., 371.

50. Ibid., 224.

51. *Torcaso v. Watkins,* 367 U.S. 488 (1961).

52. 370 U.S. 421 (1962).

53. *Abington School District v. Schempp,* 374 U.S. 203 (1963).

54. See Joseph Stewart, Jr., and Edward V. Heck, "The Day-to-Day Activities of Interest Group Lawyers," *Social Science Quarterly* 64 (March 1983): 173–182.

55. Lee Epstein and Thomas G. Walker, *Constitutional Law for a Changing America: Rights, Liberties, and Justice,* 2d ed. (Washington, D.C.: CQ Press, 1995), 37.

56. See Cortner, *The Supreme Court and Civil Liberties Policy,* 169–170.

57. Ibid., 53–54.

58. 367 U.S. 643 (1961).

59. See Wasby, *The Supreme Court in the Federal Judicial System,* 151–152.

60. Gregory A. Caldeira and John R. Wright, "Organized Interests and Agenda Setting in the U.S. Supreme Court," *American Political Science Review* 82 (December 1988): 1122.

61. Salokar, *The Solicitor General,* 145.

62. Ibid., 27.

SUGGESTED READINGS

Cortner, Richard C. *The Supreme Court and Civil Liberties Policy.* Palo Alto, Calif.: Mayfield, 1975. Case studies of several major Supreme Court decisions and how they evolved through the judicial system.

Eisenstein, James. *Counsel for the United States: U.S. Attorneys in the Political and Legal Systems.* Baltimore: Johns Hopkins University Press, 1978. A study of the selection, roles, and functions of U.S. attorneys.

Eisenstein, James, and Herbert Jacob. *Felony Justice.* Boston: Little, Brown, 1977. The authors describe the courtroom workgroup and its role in the processing of felony criminal cases.

Epstein, Lee. *Conservatives in Court.* Knoxville: University of Tennessee Press, 1985. A study of the tactics used by conservative interest groups to influence decisions of the U.S. Supreme Court.

Epstein, Lee, and Joseph F. Kobylka. *The Supreme Court and Legal Change: Abortion and the Death Penalty.* Chapel Hill: University of North Carolina Press, 1992. A study of the nature and tactics of interest groups involved in trying to influence decisions of the U.S. Supreme Court in abortion and death penalty cases.

Friedman, Lawrence M. *A History of American Law,* 2d ed. New York: Simon & Schuster, 1985. An excellent summary of the development of law in the United States.

Salokar, Rebecca Mae. *The Solicitor General: The Politics of Law.* Philadelphia: Temple University Press, 1992. An examination of the roles, functions, legal duties, and political activities of the U.S. Solicitor General.

Walker, Samuel E. *In Defense of American Liberties: A History of the ACLU.* New York: Oxford University Press, 1991. A detailed historical analysis of one of the interest groups most frequently involved in the American judicial system.

CHAPTER 6

The Criminal Court Process

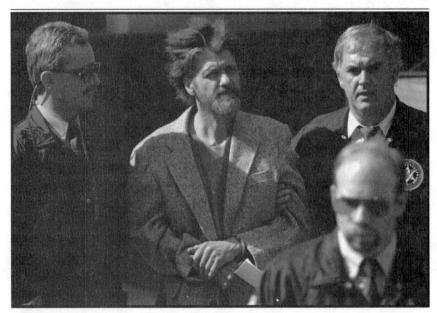

Theodore Kaczynski, the suspected Unabomber, is led into federal court prior to being charged with a weapons violation April 4, 1996. In well-known cases such as this it is often difficult to obtain an unbiased jury panel because of extensive pre-trial publicity.

THIS IS THE FIRST OF TWO CHAPTERS that examine our courts from a judicial process perspective. This chapter analyzes the *criminal* process—from the stage when a law is first broken to subsequent stages such as arrest, indictment, trial, and appeal. Chapter 7 examines the *civil* process in the same manner to provide the reader with a sense of how the system looks and feels to a litigant or observer. In both chapters readers must be mindful that there is no such thing as a single criminal or civil court process in the United States. Rather, in our federal system there is a court process at the national level, and each state and territory has its own set of rules and regulations that affect the judicial process. There are, of course, norms and similarities among all of these governmental entities, and our discussion will focus primarily on them, but we wish to emphasize that no two states have identical judicial process systems, nor are they identical to that of the national government.

The Nature and Substance of Crime

"The way you treat me is a crime," a mother scolds her headstrong teenager, who has been rude to her for the umpteenth time that day. We hear comments such as this with some frequency in today's world; although we know what the mother is getting at, we also realize that in the literal sense there has been no crime committed. Being discourteous to one's parents may be wrong and immoral, but in the United States, at least, it is not a crime because it does not violate any specific law. And in realizing this we get a handle on the nature of criminality. An act is not automatically a crime because it is hurtful or sinful; after all, only about half of the Ten Commandments are enforced by criminal law. An action constitutes a true crime only if it specifically violates a criminal statute duly enacted by Congress, a state legislature, or some other public authority.

A good working definition of a *crime*, then, is that it is an offense against the state punishable by fine, imprisonment, or death. A crime is a violation of obligations due the community as a whole and can be punished only by the state. The sanctions of imprisonment and death cannot be imposed by a civil court or in a civil action (although a fine may be either a civil or a criminal penalty).

In the United States crimes come in great variety. Most constitute sins of commission, such as aggravated assault and embezzlement; a few consist of sins of omission—failure to stop and render aid after a traffic accident or failure to file an income tax return. Some the state considers serious (such as murder and treason), and this seriousness is reflected in the corresponding punishments such as life imprisonment or the death penalty. Others the state considers only mildly reprehensible (such as double parking or disturbing the peace), and punishments of a light fine or a night in the local jail reflect the seriousness of the official slap on the wrist.

Some crimes constitute actions that virtually all the citizens consider outside the sphere of acceptable human conduct (such as kidnapping or rape), whereas other crimes constitute actions about which opinion would be divided. Relevant laws include a Nebraska statute that would forbid bingo games at church suppers and the North Carolina sodomy law that instructs couples (even married straight couples) about which parts of the human body may be touched and how. Other criminal statutes are plain silly. In Wisconsin it is illegal to sing in a bar, and in Louisiana it is forbidden to appear drunk at a meeting of a literary society.

The most serious crimes in the United States are called *felonies*. In a majority of the states a felony is any offense for which the penalty may be death or imprisonment in the penitentiary (a jail is not a penitentiary); all other offenses are misdemeanors or infractions. In other states (and under the U.S. Criminal Code) a felony is an offense for which the penalty may be death or imprisonment for a year or more. Thus, felonies are distinguished in some states according to the *place* where the punishment occurs; in some states and according to the federal government the *length* of the sentence is the key factor. Examples of common felonies include murder, forcible rape, and armed robbery.

Misdemeanors are regarded as petty crimes by the state, and their punishment usually consists of confinement in a city or county jail for less than a year. Public drunkenness, small-time gambling, and vagrancy are common examples of misdemeanor offenses. Some states have a third category of offense known as infractions. Often they include minor traffic offenses (such as parking violations), and the penalty is usually a small fine. Fines may also be part of the penalty for misdemeanors and felonies.

Categories of Crime

In thinking about various types of crime it is useful to sort them according to their public policy implications.[1] We shall look at five broad categories that comprise the primary offenses against the state in the United States today: conventional, economic, syndicated, political, and consensual.

Conventional Crimes

Property crimes make up the lion's share of the 38.4 million "conventional" crimes committed annually in the United States. In 1995 the U.S. Justice Department determined that 74 percent of all offenses (28 million) were crimes against personal property while 1 percent involved personal theft.[2] Property crimes such as these are distinguished by the government from crimes of violence, although in reality the two often go hand in glove. The thief who breaks into a house and who inadvertently confronts a resistant owner is likely to be involved in more than just the property crime of burglary.

The less numerous, but more feared, conventional crimes are those against the person. These crimes of violence include murder and nonnegligent manslaughter, forcible rape, robbery, and aggravated assault. In 1995, for every one thousand persons age twelve or older, there occurred two rapes or sexual assaults, two assaults with serious injury, and five robberies. Murders were the least frequent violent victimization—about eight victims per 100,000 persons.[3]

Despite these sobering statistics, and contrary to the popular myth about "soaring" crime rates, serious conventional crime has been declining over the past decade and a half, and even crimes of violence have now started to recede. According to the Federal Bureau of Investigation, in 1995 the overall crime index rate fell for the fourth straight year, down 11 percent from the rate of 1991. Property crimes continued a sixteen-year decline, and crimes of violence declined 12 percent after remaining essentially unchanged since 1992.[4]

Economic Crimes

Most of our thoughts about crime turn toward one of the above-mentioned types of conventional criminal activity. We fear having someone break into our homes and hope that the kid who steals our hubcaps is "sent up for a long time." It is to combating these conventional, headline-making crimes that we want most of the nation's police resources devoted. Yet in dollars-and-cents terms, conventional crimes are not where the money is; it is the cost of *economic* crimes that robs the nation blind. No two scholars can agree on the annual cost of such crimes, since the vast majority go undiscovered and unreported, but a conservative estimate would put the price tag at well over $150 billion.

What are economic crimes? It would be too narrow to call them merely white-collar crimes because such a definition does not take into consideration the fact that many such crimes are committed by persons *outside* their occupations—for example, a person filing a grossly inflated insurance claim. Harold J. Vetter and Leonard Territo list four broad categories of economic crimes that plague the nation.

1. *Personal crimes* consist of nonviolent criminal activity that one person inflicts on another with the hope of monetary gain. Examples include intentionally writing a bad check, cheating on one's income tax, and committing welfare frauds.

2. *Abuse of trust* occurs when business or government employees violate their fidelity to their employer or clients and engage in practices such as commercial bribery, theft and embezzlement from the workplace, and filling out false expense accounts.

3. *Business crimes* are crimes that are not actually part of the central purpose of the business enterprise but are rather incidental to (or in furtherance of) it. Misleading advertising, violations of the antitrust laws, and false depreciation figures computed for corporate income tax purposes are all business crimes. For example, in recent years the tobacco companies have been accused by government agencies at both state and national levels of false and misleading advertising that over the decades have led many smokers and potential smokers to believe that tobacco products were safe to ingest. The resulting illnesses and deaths among tobacco

users have costs these victims (and the insurance companies and governments underwriting their health care expenses) hundreds of billions of dollars.

4. *Con games* are white-collar criminal activities committed under the guise of a business. The "magic electric belt" that you can send away for to improve your sex life, or the Ph.D. diploma that you will receive for only $100 and an essay on your life experiences both fall into this category.[5]

Not only are economic crimes extremely costly to the American people, but they have two other characteristics that make them relevant to some of the broader themes of this chapter. First, economic crimes are harder to detect and prove in court than the other conventional crimes. Convicting a thief who is caught red-handed running out of a jewelry store with a bag of watches and diamonds is a relatively easy and routine endeavor. Not so with most economic crimes. For example, in 1987 a Harris County (Houston), Texas, commissioner was accused of accepting an illegal gift from a contractor. The contractor, out of the goodness of his heart, had paved a mile-long driveway from the commissioner's home to a nearby highway. "It was just an anniversary gift to me and my wife," said the commissioner. It took two juries (one of them was hung), enduring weeks of testimony and deliberation, before the court could finally determine that a crime had in fact been committed.

Because most citizens do not regard economic crimes as serious as burglary or assault, fewer law enforcement resources are earmarked for these illegalities. Also, sentencing judges and juries look much more kindly on the stockbroker whose "misjudgment" caused her to engage in a little illegal insider trading (after all she didn't hurt anyone, did she?) than on the young pickpocket who was caught separating someone from his wallet.

Syndicated, or Organized, Crimes

Syndicated crime differs from others addressed here in that it is engaged in by groups of people and is often directed on some type of hierarchical basis. It represents an ongoing activity that is inexorably entwined with fear and corruption. Organized crime may manifest itself in a variety of ways, but it tends to focus on several areas that are particularly lucrative, namely, trafficking in illegal drugs (such as cocaine or marijuana), gambling, prostitution, and loansharking. The latter is moneylending at exorbitant interest rates and high repayment rates. (Failure to pay may net the borrower a broken thumb or worse.) Figures are not readily available on the cost of organized crime, but no one doubts that it totals many billions of dollars.

Political Crimes

The usual meaning of "political crime" has been that it constitutes an offense against the government: treason, armed rebellion, assassination of public officials, and sedition. However, in recent decades legal scholars have come to use the term to include as well crimes committed *by the government* against individual citizens, dissident groups, and foreign governments or nationals. Examples of this murky definition of political crime might include illegal wiretaps and bugging by the FBI of politically dissident groups or the refusal of the military to investigate incidents of sexual harassment.

When we think of political crimes and of how judges and juries ought to, and actually do, respond to them, there are a couple of factors that complicate our analysis. One is that ordinary crimes can be committed to make a political point under the guise of what legal scholars call symbolic speech. When antiabortion activists are jailed for blocking the entrance to an abortion clinic, are they being punished for an ordinary act of criminal trespass or for their religious beliefs? When a soldier publicly acknowledges that he is homosexual and is promptly booted out of the service, is he guilty of violating the code of military justice or is he merely being singled out for punishment for drawing attention to the military's discrimination against gays and lesbians? It is questions such as these that often bedevil the judges and juries who must address the would-be political criminal.

In this same vein, the demarcation between the political crime and its conventional counterpart is often blurred when the government singles out unpopular persons or dissidents for meticulous application of a law that would not be enforced against ordinary folk. An unpopular group of protesters may suddenly find themselves under arrest for parading without a permit or for disorderly conduct, whereas a loud and drunken band of revelers had passed by an hour before without action by the authorities. A minority youth may be arrested for vagrancy or trespassing if he is found walking at night in an all-white neighborhood "where he clearly doesn't belong." The values and attitudes of American judges and juries are sorely tested when such cases appear before them in court.

Consensual Crimes

A final category is the so-called victimless crime, such as prostitution, gambling, illegal drug use, and unlawful sexual practices between consenting adults. Such crimes are called consensual because both perpetrator and client desire the forbidden activity, but to call them all "victimless" sticks in the throats of many. The children whose parents spend their money and time on drugs rather than on properly caring for them may well regard themselves as victims. And tidy homeowners whose streets suddenly become part of a prostitution circuit and whose shrubbery begins to serve as both bedroom and bathroom clearly would not agree that this activity is victimless. Nevertheless, because a great number of Americans question whether many of these consensual activities should in fact be proscribed by the criminal code, difficult problems are created for law enforcement officials, judges, and juries.

One of our primary themes is that a significant amount of discretion exists at all levels of the judicial process. We also demonstrate that the way in which decision makers exercise this discretion is a function of their values and attitudes. Because attitudes about consensual, or victimless, crimes vary significantly among police officers, the public at large (and the potential jurors they represent), and judges, it is not surprising that studies reveal large differences in the way our judicial system treats participants in consensual criminal activity.

Elements of a Crime

In theory, at least, every crime has several distinct elements. Furthermore, unless the state is able to demonstrate in court the existence of these essential elements there can be no conviction. Although the judicial process in the courtroom may not focus separately and distinctly on each of these elements, they are at least implicit throughout the entire process of duly convicting someone of a criminal offense.

A Law Defining the Crime and the Punishment

As we have previously indicated, if an act is to be prohibited or required by the law, a duly constituted authority (usually Congress or a state legislature) must properly spell out the matter so that the citizenry can know in advance what conduct is prohibited or required. The lawmakers must also set forth the penalties to be imposed upon the individual who engages in the harmful conduct. If there is no definition of the illegal act, and no penalty prescribed, there is no crime.

Several years ago one of the authors served on a state grand jury, and on several occasions a sheriff's deputy appeared before us to present evidence on a "pyramid club" scheme that he had been investigating. Persons, often elderly people living alone, were persuaded to buy membership shares in the club, and they were then asked to recruit other members. The original purchaser of the club membership would receive a percentage of the membership fees of all the new members, and so on. Obviously, some would make money from this scam, but ultimately most would be left holding the bag.

Before long a majority of the grand jurors were persuaded that an indictment was in order, and we so informed the district attorney. After a day or so of delay the D.A. appeared before us and said: "What this club is doing is wrong and shameful and people are being victimized, *but in this state there is no law against pyramid schemes*. You can do nothing." As the Latin maxim succinctly puts it, *nullum crimen sine lege—no crime without law.*

There are several corollaries to this general principle that also serve as grist for the criminal justice mill. One is that the U.S. Constitution forbids criminal laws that are *ex post facto*, that is, laws that declare certain conduct to be illegal *after* the conduct takes place. Past harmful or undesirable actions may not be declared criminal under our legal system. Likewise, the state may not pass what are termed bills of attainder. Those are laws that single out a particular person or group of persons and declare that something is criminal for them but legal for the rest of us. In the United States if an action (or inaction) is to be criminal, it must be so for all citizens.

A final corollary is that a law defining a crime must be precise so that the average person can determine in advance what conduct is prohibited or required. As the U.S. Supreme Court has put it, a statute defining a crime must be "sufficiently explicit to inform those who are subject to it what conduct on their part will render them liable to penalties."[6] Imagine the ease (and fun?) with which the Supreme Court struck down this Jacksonville, Florida, municipal vagrancy ordinance. Imagine, too, how many of us could go very many days without running afoul of at least some of its all-encompassing proscriptions. Criminal penalties were levied against

rogues and vagabonds; dissolute persons who go about begging; common gamblers; persons who use juggling or unlawful games or plays; common drunkards; common night walkers, thieves, pilferers, or pickpockets; traders in stolen property, lewd, wanton, and lascivious persons; keepers of gambling places; common railers and brawlers; persons wandering or strolling around from place to place without any lawful purpose or object; habitual loafers; disorderly persons; persons neglecting all lawful business and habitually spending their time by frequenting houses of ill fame, gaming houses, or places where alcoholic beverages are sold or served; and persons able to work but habitually living on their wives or minor children.[7]

In addition to the law defining the crime, there must be a formal penalty attached to it. Traditional jurisprudence has always held that the punishment is an integral part of the crime. A number of years ago the state of Wyoming sought to convict a man for practicing medicine without a license. There was no question that the accused was actively prescribing medicines and even performing operations. During his trial it was noticed that the law forbidding unlicensed medical practice said not a word about what would happen to someone who did it! The judge was forced to instruct the jury to bring in a verdict for the accused. (The "doctor" promptly decided to leave town, and the Wyoming legislature soon added a penalty clause to the statute.)

The Actus Reus

Actus reus is the traditional Latin phrase meaning the criminal action committed by the accused that gives rise to the legal prosecution. The *actus reus* is the material element of the crime and will obviously vary from one offense to another. This element may be the commission of an action that is forbidden (for instance, assault and battery), or it may be the failure to perform an action that is required (for instance, a person's refusal to stop and render aid to a motor vehicle accident victim).

The Mens Rea

The *mens rea* is the essential mental element of the crime. An old legal axiom holds that "an act does not make the doer of it guilty, unless the mind be guilty; that is, unless the intention be criminal." Our legal system has always made a distinction between harm that was caused intentionally and harm that was caused by simple negligence or accident. "Even a dog," said Justice Oliver Wendell Holmes, "distinguishes between being stumbled over and being kicked."[8] Thus, if one person takes the life of another, the state does not always call it murder. If the killing was done with malice aforethought by a sane individual, it will likely be termed "murder in the first degree." But if the killing occurred in the passion of a barroom brawl, it would more likely be called "second degree murder"; that carries a lesser penalty. Reckless driving on the highway that results in the death of another would correspondingly be considered "negligent homicide"—a wrong, to be sure; but not as serious in the eyes of the state as the *intentional* killing of another.

Sometimes the judge or jury's determination of the *mens rea* actually defines the crime itself. Suppose that Police Officer Nelson comes upon Wino Willie lying inside a television warehouse on a cold winter's night. An arrest is made, but what is to be the charge and the crime for eventual conviction: burglary or simple criminal trespass? Burglary is defined as "entering a building without the consent of the owner with the intent to commit theft," whereas trespass means "to enter a building or habitation without the effective consent of the owner." Did Willie break into that warehouse to steal televisions or merely to keep warm while he drank? The determination of the *mens rea* here will influence whether Willie's time away from society is several years or only a few months.

An Injury or Result

Except for regulatory crimes where a definition of the injury is rather abstract (for example, an illegal merger of two large airlines), a crime consists of a specific injury or a wrong perpetrated by one person against another. The crime may harm society at large, such as selling military secrets to a foreign government, or the injury may be inflicted upon an individual, and because of its nature is considered to offend society as a whole. In fact the nature of the injury, as with the *mens rea*, often determines the nature of the crime itself. For example, consider two hotheads who have been cutting each other off in traffic. Finally they both stop their cars and come out fighting. Suppose one of them actually hits the other so hard he dies; the crime may be "murder" (of some degree). If the man does not die but suffers serious bodily harm, the crime is "aggravated assault." If the injury is minor, the charge may be only "simple assault." Because the nature of the injury often determines the offense, it is frequently asserted that the nature of the injury is the key legal element of the crime.

It should be noted that some actions may be criminal even though no injury is actually inflicted. Most crimes of criminal conspiracy fall into this category. For instance, if several persons were to plan to assassinate a judge or to bribe jurors in an attempt to keep a criminal from being convicted, the crime would be "conspiracy to obstruct justice"; this would be a crime even if the judge went unharmed and no money was ever passed to the jurors. All that is required is that the crime be planned and intended and that some specific, overt act be taken by one of the conspirators in furtherance of their plan (such as the purchase of a weapon or possession of a map of the route that the judge takes between his home and the courtroom).

A Causal Relationship Between the Action and the Resultant Injury

Before there can be a conviction for a criminal offense the state must prove that the accused's conduct constituted the "proximate cause" of the injury or result. This means that the defendant, acting in a natural and continuous sequence, produced the harmful situation. In other words, it must be clear that without the defendant's conduct, there would have been no harm or injury. Usually proving a causal relationship is not difficult. If A stabs B with a knife and inflicts a minor wound, there is no doubt that A is guilty of "assault with a deadly weapon." But what if B does not obtain proper medical care for the wound, develops an infection, and subsequently dies? Is A now guilty of manslaughter or murder? Or what if after being stabbed, B stumbles across a third party and causes injury to her? Is A to blame for this, too?

Resolution of questions such as these are often difficult for judges and juries. The law requires that all circumstances be taken into account. The accused can be convicted only if the state can prove that his or her conduct is the direct, immediate, or determining cause of the resultant harm to the victim. If other circumstances have come into play, the question becomes: Was the injury inflicted by the defendant sufficient to cause the result had the intervening factor(s) not occurred? Only if the harmful consequences were beyond the control of the accused or were not a natural or probable consequence of his or her actions is the defendant free from criminal liability.

Procedures Before a Criminal Trial

Before there can be a criminal trial, federal and state laws require a whole series of procedures and events. Some of these stages are mandated by the U.S. Constitution and state constitutions, some by court decisions, and others by legislative enactments; custom and tradition often account for the rest. Although the exact nature of these several procedural events varies from federal to state practice—and from one state to another—there are still some basic similarities throughout the country. We shall concentrate on the common patterns and indicate whenever possible where differences exist. We shall also provide further evidence for our thesis that these several procedures are not as automatic or routine as they might appear; rather, the decision makers exercise at all stages ample discretion according to their values, attitudes, and views of the world.

The Arrest

There are about 700,000 law enforcement officers in the United States today—about one for every other person in our jails and prisons. Each year these officers make over 11 million arrests (not counting traffic offenses).[9] The arrest is significant for our purposes here because it represents the first substantial contact between the state and the accused. The U.S. legal system provides for two basic types of arrest—those with a warrant and those without. A *warrant* is issued after a complaint, filed by one person against another, has been presented and reviewed by a magistrate who has found "probable cause" for the arrest. Arrests without a warrant occur when a crime is committed in the presence of a police officer or when an officer has probable cause to believe that someone has committed (or is about to commit) a crime. Such a belief must later be established in a sworn statement or testimony. In the United States up to 95 percent of all arrests are made without a warrant.

An officer's decision whether to make an arrest is far from simple or automatic. To be sure, the officer who witnesses a murder will make an arrest on the spot if possible. But most lawbreaking incidents are not that simple or clear-cut, and police officials possess—and exercise—wide discretion about whether to take someone into custody. There are simply not sufficient resources available to the police for them to proceed against all activities that Congress and the legislatures have forbidden. Consequently, discretion must be exercised in determining how to allocate the time and resources that do exist. To deny police discretion at the point of arrest, said political scientist Thurman Arnold, would be "like directing a general to attack the enemy on all fronts at once."

Criminal justice scholars have identified several areas in which police discretion is at a maximum: (1) minor or trivial offenses; (2) situations in which the victim will not seek prosecution; (3) cases in which the victim is also involved in misconduct; and (4) criminal conduct thought to reflect the mores of a community subgroup.

Trivial Offenses. Many police manuals advise their officers that when minor violations of the law are concerned, a warning is a more appropriate response than a formal arrest. Not only does this make common sense for borderline, trivial offenses, but it also has the effect of conserving law enforcement resources for more serious conduct. Traffic violations, misconduct by juveniles, drunkenness, gambling, vagrancy, and use of the services of a prostitute all constitute less serious crimes and entail a lot of close judgment calls by police. Let's look at a few illustrations.

The use of a warning rather than making an arrest or issuing a ticket is common in cases concerning minor traffic violations. In fact, the officer's discretion in such situations is so well known to the motoring public that almost all of us have heard an errant driver plead, "Couldn't you just give me a warning this time, officer?" The following interview with former state director of the Texas Department of Public Safety Adrian Speir is instructive not only about discretion vis-à-vis traffic violations but about the allocation of police resources in general:

"We just don't have enough manpower to have as much law enforcement as it takes to bring about voluntary compliance [with the speed limit laws] on a statewide level," Speir said. "On a typical day, 578 highway patrol units are on duty, or an average of one for every 122 miles. Troopers have other things to do besides clock speeders—chase drunk drivers, appear in court, enforce criminal laws, answer accident calls, and the like. So, choices must be made, limits drawn," says Speir.

"Our people are instructed to enforce the law and to file a case in speeding when they are convinced there is a substantial violation of the law," he said. What is a "substantial violation?" "We mean a degree that would get a person above the arguments of nominal speedometer error, tire slippage, human error in reading the radar. We do not encourage our people to be too technical. We are trying to get above the argumentative stage," he said. So when do you pass the argumentative stage?

"I am not going to tell you that they have got a three mile . . . tolerance or a five-mile tolerance. If I . . . [did], then people out in the state could drive that much above the limit," Speir said. He added that other factors might enter into a trooper's decision whether to write a speeding ticket, such as whether a driver was weaving in and out of traffic or using a car with defective equipment. Then, he said, "some counties are stricter about prosecution than others. If the county attorney feels five or six miles over the limit is not substantial, then that would indicate he would be batting his head against a brick wall if he filed cases under that limit." [10]

Another illustration of police discretion in the minor crime realm deals with gambling offenses. Although an arrest might well be made for someone conducting a big-time, syndicated gambling operation, the "friendly little neighborhood poker game" is often ignored by police officials. The former head of the Houston, Texas, vice squad once told a group of prospective grand jurors that "if respectable groups are engaged in gambling, such as church groups, only a warning is issued—and even then only after a complaint had been received. . . . If Sister Rosita is running a church bingo game, I'm sure not going to arrest her. I just wasn't raised that way."

Whether to arrest the "John" who procures the intimate favors of a prostitute is also subject to police discretion and frequently officers are under pressure to turn a blind eye. Again, Houston's former vice squad head tells it like it is: "It is not the policy of the police department to enforce the law which makes it illegal for a man to be in the company of a prostitute. Why, the man might be someone with a family or a bank president! Also, we have a lot of big conventions here in town, and when the men come here . . . they like to have a little fun. If you start arresting these people, they wouldn't hold their conventions here any more, and then we'd have the mayor and all the restaurant and hotel owners on our backs." (Conventions in Houston bring in almost one-half billion dollars annually.)

Finally, there is evidence that the demeanor of the accused may well influence the decision of the officer. The following quotation from an interview between one of the authors and an anonymous police officer is insightful, and its portrayal of reality is supported by much empirical evidence:

Q: In these minor sorts of cases how do you determine whether to make an arrest?

A: Well, lots of times it depends on whether the guy's got an attitude problem.

Q: A what?

A: An attitude problem. I mean if he's a smart ass and starts arguing with you and gets real lippy, we'll probably take him in. But if he's decent and admits he's wrong, we'll probably let him go. I mean, nobody enjoys filling out forms for hours on end that you got to do after you make an arrest.

Victim Will Not Seek Prosecution. Nonenforcement of the law is also the rule in situations where the victim of a crime will not expend his or her own time to help the state in a successful prosecution of a case. The reasons why a crime victim would not cooperate with the police in making an arrest are varied. In the instance of minor property crimes, the victim is often interested only in restitution; if that occurs, the victim may be satisfied. For example, when people are caught shoplifting, merchants frequently are unwilling to prosecute, asserting that they cannot afford the time away from the store to testify in court or that they do not want to risk a loss of goodwill. Unless the police have already expended considerable resources in investigating a particular property crime, they are generally obliged to abide by the victim's wishes.

When the victim of a crime is in a "continuing relationship" with the criminal, the police often decline to make an arrest. Such relationships include landlord and tenant, one neighbor and another (did X have a right to chop down Y's tree because its leaves continued to fall on X's yard?), and, until recently, husband and wife. In this last case, however, heightened media coverage of domestic violence has had a significant impact on police procedures. In fact, an increasing number of studies by criminologists have indicated that arrests in domestic violence cases were effective in protecting the victim.[11] These and similar studies contributed to the passage of mandatory arrest laws that are now in effect in about a third of the states.[12]

Rape and child molestation constitute another major category of crimes for which there are often no arrests because the victims will not or cannot cooperate with the police. Oftentimes the victim is personally acquainted with, or related to, the criminal, and the fear of reprisals or of ugly publicity is sufficient to inhibit pressing a complaint. We know, for instance, that less than half of all rapes and considerably less than half of all cases of child molestation are ever reported to the police. And in many cases that are reported, victims (or their parents) have second thoughts about prosecution and the charges are subsequently dropped.

Victim Also Involved in Misconduct. When police officers perceive that the victim of a crime is also involved in some type of improper or questionable conduct, the officers frequently opt not to make an arrest. Let us say that a Mr. Macho engages and pays for the services of a lady of the evening, but she fails to show up at the appointed place. Mr. Macho knows his rights and complains to the local officer on the beat. In such circumstances the officer may possibly detain the prostitute long enough to obtain a return of the victim's money, or he may merely tease the complainant and suggest that he has learned his lesson. In any case, it is not likely that an arrest will be made in any situation where the victim does not have clean hands, and officers well know that even if they do make an arrest, such cases are usually dropped by the prosecution.

Criminal Conduct Thought to Reflect the Mores of a Community Subgroup. A final area of maximum police discretion regarding the matter of an arrest deals with lawbreaking that officers ignore because they regard it as normal and acceptable for members of racial minorities or members of the lower social classes. Studies have shown that police officers, usually white and from middle-class backgrounds, tend to regard the street violence, petty property crimes, and family altercations in minority and poor areas as just "normal for those kinds of people." On the other hand, such behavior in middle- and upper-middle-class neighborhoods is not seen as natural or acceptable, and the officer is more likely to make an arrest.

For example, if Officer Jones is summoned to a million-dollar condominium on Chicago's exclusive Lake Shore Drive upon learning that a man has stabbed his socialite wife, there will likely be an arrest for assault with a deadly weapon; after all, people like that just oughtn't to behave in such a fashion, and if they do an arrest is definitely in order. However, if Officer Jones had been called to a ghetto neighborhood across town for an identical incident, his diary of events would more likely read as follows: "Called to scene of family disturbance in minority area. Woman hurt. Took her to the emergency ward to get her sewed up. Everything quiet. No arrest."

A vivid real-life illustration of this phenomenon is contained in an excerpt from a computer transcript provided by the Los Angeles Police Department. A message transmitted from an officer's patrol car concerned a domestic dispute in a black household. One officer said it was "right out of 'Gorillas in the Mist.' " "Ha, ha, ha, ha," responded their unidentified correspondent, "Let me guess who be the parties."[13] One suspects that the officers' account of this domestic dispute would have had a vastly different tone had the incident occurred in an upper-class, nonminority neighborhood. In sum, we see that the decision whether to make an arrest when a crime has been committed is not always simple and automatic for the police officer. Although no one would seriously doubt that officers must be given leeway to exercise their common sense and good judgment in close-call situations, it is also clear that discretion may be arbitrary and subject to abuse. At the very least we know that to a substantial degree, the decision making of police officers is the product of their own attitudes and values, community pressures, the "attitude" of the accused, and organizational constraints—which, as we shall subsequently see, is true as well for prosecutors, judges, and other court personnel.

Appearance Before a Magistrate

After a suspect is arrested for a crime, he or she is "booked" at the police station—that is, the facts surrounding the arrest are recorded and the accused may be fingerprinted and photographed. The next major step is for the accused to appear before a lower-level judicial official whose title may be judge, magistrate, or commissioner. Such an appearance is supposed to occur "without unnecessary delay"; although the meaning of this phrase varies from state to state, twenty-four hours has traditionally been the maximum delay permitted by law. However, in 1991 the more conservative U.S. Supreme Court ruled in a five-to-four decision that police may now detain an individual arrested without a warrant for up to *forty-eight hours* without a court hearing on whether the arrest was justified.[14]

This appearance is the occasion of several important events in the criminal justice process. First, the accused must be informed of the precise charges and must be informed of all constitutional rights and guarantees. Among others, these rights include those of the now famous *Miranda* decision of the Warren Court handed down in 1966: that the accused "must be warned prior to any questioning that he has the right to remain silent, that anything he says can be used against him in a court of law, that he has the right to the presence of an attorney, and that if he cannot afford an attorney one will be appointed for him prior to any questioning."[15] (Such warnings must also be given by the arresting officer if the officer questions the suspect about the crime.) In some states the accused must be informed about other rights that are provided for in the state's Bill of Rights, such as the right to a speedy trial and the right to confront hostile witnesses.

Second, the magistrate will determine whether the accused is to be released on bail and, if so, what the amount of bail is to be. Constitutionally the only requirement for the amount is that it shall not be "excessive." If the magistrate believes that the accused will in fact appear for any future trial proceedings, no bail at all may be required and the accused may be released "on his own recognizance." Bail is considered to be a privilege—not a right—and it may be denied altogether in capital punishment cases for which the evidence of guilt is strong or if the magistrate believes that the accused will flee from prosecution no matter what the amount of bail.

The subject of bail has been riddled with controversy for a variety of reasons. One is that it is often used as a form of preventive detention when a judge intentionally sets bail at a level that is impossible for the defendant to make. A judge's decision to do this can be based on factors such as the defendant's prior criminal record, publicity the case may have generated, the recommendation of the prosecutor, and the defendant's previous conduct while out on bail. If a defendant cannot make bail (even $50 is prohibitive for those without means), he or she must remain in jail. This subjects legally innocent persons to punishment; it separates them from their family, friends, and jobs; it hinders their efforts to prepare for their defense in court; and it adds to the overcrowding that already bedevils most county jails.

An alternative to bail is to release the defendant "on recognizance" basically on a pledge by the defendant to return to court on the appointed date for trial. In some jurisdictions there are special programs designed to maximize the number of persons eligible for release on recognizance. Perhaps the best known and most often copied of these is the Manhattan Bail Project. Here defendants are interviewed by pretrial investigators according to a special point system that takes into consideration such factors as the defendant's prior record, ties to the local community, and employment.

In minor cases the accused may be asked to plead innocence or guilt. If the plea is guilty, a sentence may be pronounced on the spot. If the defendant pleads not guilty, a trial date is scheduled. However, in the typical serious (felony) case the next primary duty of the magistrate is to determine whether the defendant requires a preliminary hearing. If such a hearing is appropriate, the matter is adjourned by the prosecution and a subsequent stage of the criminal justice process begins.

The Grand Jury Process or the Preliminary Hearing

At the federal level all persons accused of a crime are guaranteed by the Fifth Amendment to have their cases considered by a grand jury. However, the Supreme

Court has refused to make this right binding on the states, and indeed today only about half of the states even use grand juries; in some of these, they are used for only special types of cases. Those states that do not use grand juries employ what is called a preliminary hearing or an examining trial. (A few states use both procedures.) Regardless of which method is used, the primary purpose of this stage in the criminal justice process is to determine whether there is "probable cause" for the accused to be subjected to a formal trial.

The Grand Jury. Grand juries consist of sixteen to twenty-three citizens, usually selected at random from the voter registration lists, who render decisions by a majority vote.[16] Their terms may last anywhere from one month to one year, and some may hear over a thousand cases during their term. The prosecutor alone presents evidence to the grand jury; not only are the accused and his or her attorney absent from the proceedings, but usually they have no idea which grand jury is hearing the case or when. If a majority believes there is a "probable cause," then an indictment, or "true bill," is brought. Otherwise the result is a "no bill."

Less than 5 percent of all grand jury decisions result in no bills, and contrary to popular belief, no bills do not necessarily serve as a measure of grand jury independence vis-à-vis the prosecutor. Oftentimes the district attorney will ask the grand jury to render a no bill for personal reasons. Here is a statement made by a prosecutor to a state grand jury on which one of the authors served:

Now here's a case where I'd like a little help from you all. There's a guy that's been after me every day for the past month because he says his brother-in-law borrowed his TV and some money and won't give 'em back. He wants me to file theft charges, but I keep telling him we're not a bill collection agency. I told him I would take the case to the grand jury, and I'm sure hoping you'll vote a no bill, and as soon as you do, I'm going to get on the phone and tell that guy that those "bleeding hearts" on the grand jury [laughs] wouldn't bring an indictment. That would sure get me off the hook.

Historically there have been two arguments in favor of grand juries. One is to serve as a check on a prosecutor who might be using the office to harass an innocent person for political or personal reasons. (Even though the innocent person might well eventually be found not guilty at trial, the cost and embarrassment of being tried for a crime is clearly a significant form of harassment.) Ideally an unbiased group of citizens would interpose themselves between an unethical prosecutor and the defendant.

A second justification for a grand jury is simply to make sure that the D.A. has done some homework and has in fact secured enough evidence to warrant the trouble and expense—for both the state and the accused—of a full-fledged trial. Sometimes in the haste and tedious routine of the criminal justice process, persons are brought to trial when in fact there is insufficient evidence to justify it. Here is a factual account of how a state grand jury served to prevent this from happening (albeit quite by accident):

We had one case where the prosecutor tells us that several witnesses claim they saw this guy driving a stolen vehicle. So we vote a true bill—no questions asked. Then later on in the day when we were eating our sandwiches during lunch, one lady [also on the grand jury] was leafing through the files just for something to do. She says to us: "Hey, you know that guy we indicted this morning for auto theft. He claims he was on National Guard duty at the time a thousand miles away."

Now we figured that that wasn't the sort of defense you'd lie about because it could be checked out so easily, so we called the D.A. back in. We asked him if he had called the guy's commanding officer on the WATS line to check out his story. The D.A. told us we weren't supposed to be trying this case and that there was probable cause because of the witnesses. But we made him call anyway, and sure enough there was a record that the guy was on guard duty the day the car was stolen. That day we did what a grand jury was supposed to be doing but, my God, it was only because that lady was bored with her baloney sandwich.

The evidence is pretty substantial that the prosecutor tends to dominate the grand jury process and that the jury's utility as a check on the motives and thoroughness of the district attorney is minimal.[17]

The Preliminary Hearing. In the majority of states that have abolished the grand jury system a preliminary hearing is used to determine whether there is probable cause for the accused to be bound over for trial. At this hearing the prosecution presents its case, and the accused has the right to cross-examine witnesses and to produce favorable evidence. Usually the defense elects not to fight at this stage of the criminal process; in fact, a preliminary hearing is waived by the defense in the vast majority of cases.

If the examining judge determines that there is probable cause for a trial or if the preliminary examination is waived, the prosecutor must file a "bill of information" with the court where the trial will be held. This serves to outline precisely the charges that will be adjudicated in the new legal setting. Usually about two weeks are allowed for the process.

The Arraignment

Arraignment refers to the process in which the defendant is brought before the judge in the court where he or she is to be tried in order to respond to the grand jury indictment or the prosecutor's bill of information. The prosecutor or a clerk usually reads in open court the charges that have been brought against the accused.

The defendant is informed that there is a constitutional right to be represented by an attorney and that a lawyer will be appointed without charge if necessary.

The defendant has several options about how to plead to the charges. The most common pleas, of course, are guilty and not guilty. But the accused may also plead not guilty by reason of insanity, former jeopardy (having been tried on the same charge at another time), or *nolo contendere* (no contest). *Nolo contendere* in effect means that the accused does not deny the facts of the case but claims that he or she has not committed any crime, or it may mean that the defendant does not understand the charges. The *nolo contendere* plea can be entered only with the consent of the judge (and sometimes the prosecutor as well). Such a plea has two advantages: it may help the accused save face vis-à-vis the public because he or she can later claim that technically there was no guilty verdict even though there may have been a sentence or a fine. Also, the plea may spare the defendant from certain civil penalties that might follow a guilty plea (for example, a civil suit that might follow from conviction for fraud or embezzlement).

If the accused pleads not guilty, the judge will schedule a date for a trial. If the plea is guilty, the defendant may be sentenced on the spot or at a later date set by the judge. Before the court will accept a guilty plea, the judge must certify that the plea was made voluntarily and that the defendant was aware of the implications of the plea. A guilty plea is to all intents and purposes the equivalent to a formal verdict of guilty.

The Possibility of a Plea Bargain

Before we begin to talk about the procedures of a formal criminal trial we must dwell on the important fact that at both the state and federal levels *at least 90 percent of all criminal cases never go to trial.* That is because before the trial date a bargain has been struck between the prosecutor and the defendant's attorney concerning the official charges to be brought and the nature of the sentence that the state will recommend to the court. In effect, some form of leniency is promised in exchange for a guilty plea.

Under plea bargaining the role of the judges in the criminal justice system is much smaller than most of us assume. Most people believe that the courts operate under a pure adversary system in which the judge's role is to make a disinterested sentencing after hearing full arguments from both sides. But because plea bargaining virtually seals the fate of the defendant *before* trial, the role of the judge is simply to ensure that the proper legal and constitutional procedures have been followed.

Judicial scholars are not unanimous on why plea bargaining has become the norm rather than the exception, and indeed some have argued that in some form plea bargaining has always been with us. (That is, the state has always been more lenient to those who admit their guilt, are repentant, and cooperate with the government.) Nevertheless, there is evidence that the average felony trial is longer now than it was several decades ago and that defendants are filing more pretrial pleas and postconviction motions now than in the past. No doubt the changes are due at least in part to the Warren Court's many decisions favoring the rights of criminal defendants. But for whatever reasons the ever-increasing caseloads of the past several decades have made the judicial system ever more dependent on the quick and simple plea bargain. There are three (not mutually exclusive) basic types of such bargains.

Reduction of Charges. The most common form of agreement between a prosecutor and a defendant is a reduction of the charge to one less serious than that supported by the evidence. The defendant is thereby subject to a lower maximum sentence and is likely to receive a lighter sentence than would have been the case under a guilty verdict on the original charge. For example, a common plea bargain in many states for an individual accused of theft is to plead guilty to burglary with the intent to commit theft. This exposes the criminal to a substantially reduced range of sentence possibilities.

A second reason for a defendant to plead guilty to a reduced charge is to avoid a record of conviction for an offense that carries a social stigma. The "good family man" and "pillar of the church" caught in the act of "indecency with a child" might be quite willing to plead guilty to the reduced charge of disorderly conduct.

Another possibility is that the defendant may wish to avoid a felony record altogether. A college student who hopes to be a lawyer or a public school teacher might be eager to plead guilty to almost any misdemeanor offered by the prosecutor rather than face a felony charge and risk being excluded from the legal and teaching professions.

Deletion of Tangent Charges. A second form of plea bargain is the agreement of the district attorney to drop other charges pending against an individual. There are two variations on this theme. One is an agreement not to prosecute "vertically," that is, not to prosecute more serious charges filed against the individual. For example, it is common in many jurisdictions for individuals using credit cards illegally to be charged simultaneously with forgery and possession of a stolen credit card. A bargain may be made to drop the forgery indictment in exchange for a plea of guilty on the lesser charge. The second type of agreement is to dismiss additional indictments for the same crime ("horizontal" charges) pending against the accused. It is not unusual for several counts of burglary to be dropped following a confession to one other burglary indictment. (For an indictment to be dropped, most jurisdictions require the prosecutor to file a motion of *nolle prosequi*—"I refuse to prosecute"—with the court, but such motions are usually granted as a matter of course.)

Another variation of the type of plea bargaining that is concerned with dropping charges is the agreement in which a "repeater" clause is dropped from an indictment. At the federal level and in many states a person is considered a "habitual criminal" upon the third conviction for a violent felony anywhere in the United States. The mandatory sentence for the habitual criminal is life imprisonment. It is rather common, at least in state courts, for the habitual violent criminal charge to be dropped in exchange for a plea of guilty. For example, in Texas an individual convicted of theft as a habitual criminal must be sentenced to life imprisonment and will not be eligible for parole for at least twenty years. On the other hand, an individual who is offered the chance to plead guilty to "theft—second offense" must be given a sentence of ten years in prison but will be eligible for parole after serving only one-third of that sentence. The difference between twenty years of working on the rock pile and three years and four months is a keen incentive for a "three-time loser" to admit to being a "two-time loser."

A final wrinkle of this type of plea bargaining is the agreement in which indictments in different courts are consolidated into one court in order that the sentences may run concurrently. As indictments or preliminary hearing rulings are handed down in many jurisdictions, they are placed on a trial docket on a rotation system. (The first charge is placed on a docket of court 1, the second on court 2, and so on.) This means that a defendant charged with four counts of forgery and one charge of possession of a forged instrument might find herself on the docket of five different courts. Generally it is common practice in such multicourt districts to transfer all of a person's indictments to the first court listed. This gives the presiding judge the discretion of allowing all of the defendant's sentences to run concurrently. Although it is not often done, it is possible that an individual who refuses to plead guilty to any charges will simply not have the other indictments transferred, creating the likelihood of "stacked" (consecutive) sentences.

Sentence Bargaining. A third form of plea bargaining concerns a plea of guilty from the defendant in exchange for a prosecutor's agreement to ask the judge for a lighter sentence.[18] At first blush it might seem that this type of plea negotiation is a weak substitute for either the reduction-of-charge or the dropping-of-charge form. After all, under sentence bargaining the state can make only a nonbinding recommendation to the court regarding the sentence, whereas under the other two types the state's concessions are concrete and not subject to doubt.

The strength of the sentence negotiation, however, is based upon the realities of the limited resources of the judicial system. At the state level, at least, prosecutors are able to promise the defendant a fairly specific sentence with confidence that the judge will accept the recommendation. If the judge were not to do so, the prosecutor's credibility would quickly begin to wane, and many of the defendants who had been pleading guilty would begin to plead not guilty and take their chances in court. The result would be a gigantic increase in court dockets that would literally overwhelm the judicial system and bring it to a complete standstill. Prosecutors and judges understand this reality, and so do the defense attorneys.

Constitutional and Statutory Restrictions on Plea Bargaining. At both the state and federal levels, the requirements of due process of law mean that plea bargains must be made voluntarily and with comprehension. This means that the defendant must be admonished by the court of the consequences of a guilty plea (for example, you waive all opportunities to change your mind at a later date), that the accused must be sane, and that, as one typical state puts it, "It must plainly appear that the defendant is uninfluenced by any consideration of fear, or by any persuasion, or delusive hope of pardon, prompting him to confess his guilt." It would appear from these requirements that the prosecutor's promise of a lighter sentence in exchange for a guilty plea would violate the letter, if not the spirit, of the due process clause. Not so, the courts have ruled. As long as judges tell the defendants that, at least in principle, they are subject to any sentence that is pronounced and the accused acknowledge this, the requirement of due process has been met. Thus when a state court certifies that a guilty plea was "knowingly and understandingly made," a form of legal fiction has often been in the works.

For the first two types of plea bargains there are some stricter standards that govern the federal courts. One is that the judge may not actually participate in the process of plea bargaining; at the state level judges may play an active role in this process. Likewise, if a plea bargain has been made between the U.S. attorney and the defendant, the government may not renege on the agreement. If the federal government does so, the federal district judge must withdraw the guilty plea. Finally, the Federal Rules of Criminal Procedure require that "the court shall not enter a judgment upon a plea of guilty unless it is satisfied that there is a factual basis for the plea." This means that before a guilty plea may be accepted, the prosecution must present a summary of the evidence against the accused, and the judge must agree that there is strong evidence of the defendant's guilt.

Arguments For and Against Plea Bargaining. For the defendant the obvious advantage of the bargain is that he or she is treated less harshly than would be the case if the accused were convicted and sentenced under maximum conditions. Also, the absence of a trial often lessens publicity on the case, and because of personal interests or simple social pressures, the accused may wish to avoid the length and publicity of a formal trial. Finally, some penologists (professionals in the field of punishment and rehabilitation) argue that the first step toward rehabilitation is for a criminal to admit guilt and to recognize his or her problem. The idea is that a guilty plea is at least nominally the first step toward a successful return to society.

There are also some distinct advantages for the state and for society as a whole. The most obvious is the certainty of conviction, because no matter how strong the evidence may appear, there is always the possibility of an acquittal as long as a trial is pending. (Evidence may be stolen or lost; important witnesses may die or drop out of sight; the prosecutor may make a key error in court that results in a mistrial.) Also, the district attorney's office and judges are saved an enormous amount of time and effort by their not having to prepare and preside over cases in which there is no real contention of innocence or that are not suited to the trial process. Finally, it is argued that when police officers are not required to be in court testifying in criminal trials, they have more time to devote to preventing and solving crimes.

Lest this all seem too good to be true, there is a negative side to plea bargains as well. The most frequent objection to plea bargaining is that the defendant's sentence may well be based upon nonpenological grounds. With the large volume of cases making plea bargaining the rule, the sentence often bears no relation at all to the specific facts of the case, to the correctional needs of the criminal, or to society's legitimate interest in vigorous prosecution of the case. A second defect is that if plea bargaining becomes the norm of a particular system, then undue pressure may be placed upon even innocent persons to plead guilty. Studies have shown that in some jurisdictions the less the chance for conviction, the harder the bargaining may be because the prosecutor wants to get at least some form of minimal confession out of the accused.

A third disadvantage of plea bargaining is the possibility of the abuse called *overcharging*—that is, the process whereby the prosecutor brings charges against the accused more severe than the evidence warrants, with the hope that this will strengthen his or her hand in subsequent negotiations with the defense attorney. One of us who served on a state grand jury had this exchange with a representative of the district attorney's office:

GRAND JUROR: In this case where one fellow killed another in that barroom fight, why do you want us to indict on a first-degree murder charge? There doesn't seem to be any premeditation here. You'll never get a conviction on that.

D.A.: Oh, I know. But it will strengthen our hand at the time when we talk with his attorney.

(The grand jury in question chose to indict on a lesser and more appropriate charge.)

Another flaw with the plea bargaining system is its very low level of visibility. This is really the flip side of flexibility. Bargains between prosecutor and defense attorney are not made in open court presided over by a neutral jurist and for all to observe; rather, they are more likely made over a cup of coffee in a basement courthouse cafeteria where the conscience of the two lawyers is the primary guide. When the defendant enters the guilty plea in open court and swears that no promise by the state has induced this plea, the prosecutor and defense counsel mutely corroborate the defendant's false statement. Meanwhile, the judge remains uninformed of the facts and is therefore unable to determine the fairness or validity of the agreement.

Finally, the system has the potential to circumvent key procedural and constitutional rules of evidence. Because the prosecutor need not present any evidence or witnesses in court, a bluff may result in a conviction even though the case might not be able to pass the muster of the due process clause. The defense may be at a disadvantage because the rules of discovery (the laws that allow the defense to know in detail the evidence the prosecution will present) in some states limit the defense counsel's case preparation to the period *after* the plea bargain has occurred. Thus the plea bargain may deprive the accused of basic constitutional rights.

The Adversarial Process

Before we begin to describe the format and substance of the criminal trial we must first outline the nature of the *adversarial process* as it exists in American courtrooms. While this chapter is about criminal courts, the principles of the adversarial process are largely true of civil trials as well (see Chapter 7). The adversarial model is based on the assumption that every case or controversy has two sides to it: in criminal cases the government claims a defendant is guilty while the defendant contends innocence; in civil cases the plaintiff asserts that the person he or she is suing has caused some injury while the respondent denies responsibility. In the courtroom each party vies against the other; each provides his or her side of the story as he or she sees it. The theory (or hope) underlying this model is that the truth will emerge if each party is given unbridled opportunity to present the full panoply of evidence, facts, and arguments before a neutral and attentive judge (and jury).

The lawyers representing each side are the major players in this courtroom drama. The judge acts more as a passive, disinterested referee whose primary role is to keep both sides within the accepted rules of legal procedure and courtroom decorum. The judge eventually determines which side has won in accordance with the rules of evidence, but only after both sides have had a full opportunity to "fight it out."

While the adversarial process is the norm in the United States, it is not in most other countries. Most use a version of what legal scholars call the "inquisitorial method," in which the judge is the primary actor in the courtroom and where the attorneys passively defend their client's interests. Under this method the judge actively and aggressively conducts an inquiry into the truth of the charges that the state or a plaintiff has lodged against a defendant. The inquisitorial process generally views the accused in criminal cases as guilty unless and until a judge's inquiry determines otherwise. On the other hand, under the adversarial model the accused is more likely to be presumed innocent; the state carries the heavy burden of convincing a judge and jury that the defendant is guilty *beyond a reasonable doubt.*

Procedures During a Criminal Trial

Assuming that there has been no plea bargain and the accused maintains his or her innocence, there will be a formal trial. This is a right guaranteed by the Sixth Amendment to all Americans charged with federal crimes and a right guaranteed by the various state constitutions and by the Fourteenth Amendment—to all persons charged with state offenses. There are many constitutional and statutory rights that the accused is provided during the trial. We shall not enumerate them all here, but the following are at least the primary rights that are binding on both the federal and state courts.

Basic Rights Guaranteed During the Trial Process

The Sixth Amendment says, "In all criminal prosecutions, the accused shall enjoy the right to a speedy and public trial." The Founders emphasized the word *speedy* so that an accused would not languish in prison for a long time prior to the trial or have the determination of his or her fate put off for an unduly long period of time. But how soon is "speedy"? Although this word has been defined in various ways by the Supreme Court,[19] Congress gave new meaning to the term when it passed the Speedy Trial Act of 1974. The act mandated time limits, ultimately reaching 100 days, within which criminal charges must either be brought to trial or dismissed. Most states have similar measures on the statute books, although the precise time period varies from one jurisdiction to another. By "public trial" the Founders meant to discourage the notion of secret proceedings whereby an accused could be tried without public knowledge and whisked off to some unknown detention camp—a state of affairs still typical of totalitarian regimes today.

The Sixth Amendment also guarantees us the right to an impartial jury. At the very least this has meant that the prospective jurors must not be prejudiced one way or the other before the trial begins. For example, a potential juror may not be a friend or relative of the prosecutor or the crime victim; nor may someone serve who believes that anyone of the defendant's race or ethnic ancestry is "probably the criminal type." (We shall have more to say about the selection of the jury in a moment.) What the concept of an "impartial jury of one's peers" has come to mean in practice is that jurors are to be selected randomly from the voter registration lists—supplemented in an increasing number of jurisdictions by lists based on automobile registrations, driver's licenses, telephone books, welfare rolls, and so on.[20] Although this does not provide a perfect cross-section of the community, since not all persons are registered to vote, the Supreme Court has said that this method is good enough. The High Court has also ruled that no class of persons (such as blacks or women) may be systematically excluded from jury service. This does not mean that a black defendant, for example, has a right to have other persons of the same racial background on a jury; it means only that no racial category may be intentionally kept from jury service.

Besides being guaranteed the right to be tried in the same locale where the crime was committed and to be informed of the charges against us, we have the right to be confronted with the witnesses against us. We have the right to know who our accusers are and what they are charging so that a proper defense may be formulated. The accused is also guaranteed the opportunity "to have the Assistance of Counsel for his defence." Prior to the 1960s this meant that one had this right (at the state level) only for serious crimes and only if one could pay for an attorney. However, because of a series of Supreme Court decisions, it is now the law of the land that one is guaranteed an attorney if tried for any crime that may result in a prison term, and the government must pick up the tab for the legal defense for an indigent defendant. This is the rule at both the national and state levels.

With defense attorneys, as with many things in life, you usually get what you pay for. If money is no object, then you can afford to hire an experienced and highly competent defense lawyer who will be a superb advocate on your behalf. This does not automatically mean that you will be acquitted if you are guilty, but it may mean that you will obtain a more advantageous plea bargain or a lighter sentence if convicted. If you are not wealthy or have no means at all, you may be forced to rely on the services of a public defender appointed on your behalf by the state. Most public defenders are relatively young and inexperienced, and although some have a reputation for putting on a vigorous defense (such as those in Cook County [Chicago], Illinois) most are not or will never be within the top ranks of the legal profession.

Defense attorneys, whether paid by the defendant or the state, are often the subject of considerable criticism. It is said that they give too little time and effort to their clients' cases because of the limited resources of most public defenders' offices and because it is financially advantageous for private attorneys to turn cases over as rapidly as possible. Also, in many jurisdictions a public defender is given a fixed amount per case regardless of how much time the case takes. This may well encourage a public defender to pressure a client to plead guilty so that the case will take less time.

The Fifth Amendment to the U.S. Constitution declares that no person shall "be subject for the same offence to be twice put in jeopardy of life and limb." This is the famous "double jeopardy" clause and means in effect that no one may be tried twice for the same crime by any state government or by the federal government. It does not mean, however, that a person may not be tried twice for the same action if that action has violated both national and state laws. For example, someone who robs a federally chartered bank in New Jersey runs afoul of both federal and state law. It is possible and quite legal that that person could be tried and acquitted for that offense in a New Jersey court and subsequently be tried for that same action in federal court. Again, this clause means that the same level of government may not try you twice for the same crime.

Sometimes the answer to the question of which level of the judiciary has jurisdiction for a particular type of offense is a bit muddled. For instance, the Racketeer Influenced and Corrupt Organizations (RICO) section of the Organized Crime Control Act of 1970 authorizes prosecution in federal court for violations of certain state laws if the actions come under a certain special definition of "racketeering." Thus, beginning in 1985, a number of Cook County (Chicago), Illinois, state judges were prosecuted under RICO for accepting bribes.

Another important right guaranteed to the accused at both the state and federal levels is not to "be compelled in any criminal case to be a witness against himself." This has been interpreted to mean that the fact that someone elects not to testify on his or her own behalf in court may not be used against the person by judge and jury. This guarantee serves to reinforce the principle that under our judicial system the burden of proof is on the state; the accused is presumed innocent until the government proves otherwise beyond a reasonable doubt.

Finally, the Supreme Court has interpreted the guarantee of due process of law to mean that evidence procured in an illegal search and seizure may not be used against the accused at trial. The source of this so-called exclusionary rule is the Fourth Amendment to the U.S. Constitution; the Supreme Court has made its strictures binding on the states as well. The Court's purpose was to eliminate any incentive the police might have to illegally obtain evidence against the accused. Many have argued that this right does not in fact discourage improper police behavior and that it serves only as a technical loophole to free the guilty. Thus the more conservative Burger and Rehnquist Courts have taken steps to narrow the effect of the exclusionary rule. Civil libertarians have countered that this rule is a key element in the basic concepts of due process and fair play.

Selection of Jurors

If the accused elects not to have a bench trial—that is, not to be tried and sentenced by a judge alone—his or her fate will be determined by a jury. At the federal level twelve persons must render a unanimous verdict. At the state level such criteria apply only to the most serious offenses. In many states a jury may consist of fewer than twelve persons and render verdicts by other than unanimous decisions. (Acceptable votes might be eleven to one, ten to two, or five to one.)

A group of veniremen (sometimes known as an array) is summoned from a panel of potential jurors to appear in a given courtroom.[21] The veniremen are then questioned in open court about their general qualifications for jury service in a process known as *voir dire*. The prosecutor and the defense attorney ask general and specific questions of the potential jurors. Are they citizens of the state? Can they comprehend the English language? Have they or anyone in their family ever been tried for a criminal offense? Have they read about or formed any opinions about the case at hand?

In conducting the voir dire the state and the defense have two general types of goals. The first is to eliminate all members of the panel who have an obvious reason why they might not render an impartial decision in the case. Common examples might be someone who is excluded by law from serving on a jury, a juror who is a friend or relative of a participant in the trial, someone who openly admits a strong bias in the case at hand. Objections to jurors in this category are known as challenges for cause, and the number of such challenges is unlimited. It is the judge who determines whether these challenges are valid.

There is a second goal that the opposing attorneys have in questioning the array of jurors: to eliminate those who they believe would be unfavorable to their side even though there is no overt reason for the potential bias. This can be done because each side is given a number of what are termed peremptory challenges—requests to the court to exclude a prospective juror with no reason given. It is customary in most states to give the defense more peremptory challenges than the prosecution. At the federal level one to three challenges per juror are usually permitted each side, depending on the nature of the offense; as many as twenty are allowed in capital cases. The use of peremptory challenges is more of an art than a science and is usually based on the hunch of the attorneys. For example, in a case where a poor person stole groceries from a supermarket, a prosecutor might use available challenges to exclude jurors of low economic status, thinking that they might be more sympathetic to the accused. Or in a case involving a sexual offender, a defense attorney might try to eliminate jurors who belong to fundamentalist religions, thinking that they would take a more judgmental stance in such matters than those of more "liberal" religious convictions.

In the past attorneys were able to exclude potential jurors via the peremptory challenge for virtually any reason whatsoever. However, in recent years the Supreme Court has begun to interpret the Fourteenth Amendment's Equal Protection Clause to restrict this unbridled discretion. In 1986 the High Court ruled in the case of *Batson v. Kentucky*[22] that prosecutors may not use their challenges to exclude blacks from serving on a criminal jury. Out of this case came what is known as "the *Batson* rule," which bars the discriminatory use of peremptory challenges. In 1994 the Court extended the prohibition to include women.[23] Since that time some courts have expanded the *Batson* rule to include other groups as well, for example, ethnic groups such as Italian-Americans and Jews[24] and even to exclusions based on sexual orientation.[25]

The process of questioning and challenging prospective jurors continues until all those duly challenged for cause are eliminated, the peremptory challenges are either used up or waived, and a jury of twelve (six in some states) has been created. In some states alternate jurors are also chosen. They attend the trial but participate in deliberations only if one of the original jurors is unable to continue in the proceedings. Once the panel has been selected they are sworn in by the judge or the clerk of the court.

Opening Statements

After the formal trial begins, both the prosecution and the defense make an opening statement (although in no state is the defense compelled to do so). Long and detailed statements are more likely to be made in jury trials than in bench trials. Their purpose is to provide members of the jury—who lack familiarity with the law and with procedures of criminal investigation—with an outline of the major objectives of each side's case, the evidence that is to be presented, the witnesses that are to be called, and what each side seeks to prove from the evidence of the witnesses. If the opening statements are well presented, the jurors will find it easier to grasp the meaning and significance of the evidence and testimony, and ideally they will be less likely to get confused and bogged down in the complexities and technicalities of the case. The usual procedure is for the state to make its opening statement first and for the defense to follow with a statement about how it will refute that case.

The Prosecution's Case

After the opening statements the prosecutor presents the evidence amassed by the state against the accused. Evidence is generally of two types—physical evidence and the testimony of witnesses. The physical evidence may include things such as bullets, ballistics tests, fingerprints, handwriting samples, blood and urine tests, and other documents or hard items that serve as physical aids. The defense may object to the admission of any of these tangible items and will if successful have the item excluded from consideration. If there is no successful defense objection, the physical evidence is labeled by one of the courtroom personnel and becomes part of the official record.

Most evidence at criminal trials takes the form of testimony of witnesses. The format is a question-and-answer procedure that may appear a bit stilted, but its purpose is to elicit very specific information in an orderly fashion. The goal is to present only evidence that is relevant to the immediate case at hand and not to give confusing or irrelevant information or illegal evidence that might result in a mistrial (for example, evidence that the accused had a prior conviction for an identical offense). The following hypothetical question and answer between a district attorney and a police officer is typical:

D.A.: Please state your name and occupation.

OFFICER: My name is Frank Benoit. I am employed as a police officer by the District of Columbia.

D.A.: Did you have reason to be at or near the corner of Massachusetts and Eighteenth about seven o'clock on the evening of March 5?

OFFICER: Yes, I was summoned to a liquor store at that address after a witness phoned the department and said she saw someone breaking into the building.

D.A.: What did you observe after you arrived on the scene?

OFFICER: I observed a white male with what appeared to be a crate of liquor under his arm.

D.A.: What was he doing at the time?

OFFICER: He was running away from the building.

D.A.: What did you do at that time?

OFFICER: I subdued the man and placed him under arrest.

D.A.: Is the person whom you saw running from the building and arrested sitting in this courtroom today?

OFFICER: Yes, sir.

D.A.: Would you point out that man?

OFFICER: He is sitting to the left of the defense attorney.

D.A.: Your Honor, may the record show that the officer pointed to the defendant in this case?

After each witness, the defense attorney has the right to cross-examine. The goal of the defense will be to impeach the testimony of the prosecution witness, that is, to discredit it. The attorney may attempt to confuse, fluster, or anger the witness, causing him or her to lose self-control and begin providing confusing or conflicting testimony. The prosecution's witness's testimony may also be impeached if defense witnesses who contradict the version of events suggested by the state are subsequently presented. Upon completion of the cross-examination, the prosecutor may conduct a "redirect examination," which serves to clarify or correct some telling point made during the cross-examination. After the state has presented all its evidence and witnesses, it rests its case.

The Case for the Defense

The presentation of the case for the defense is similar in style and format to that of the prosecution. Tangible evidence is less common in the defense's case, and most of the evidence will be that of witnesses who are prepared to rebut or contradict the prosecution's arguments. The witnesses are questioned by the defense attorney in the same style as those in the prosecution case. Each defense witness may in turn be cross-examined by the district attorney, and then a redirect examination is in order.

The real difference between the case for the prosecution and the case for the defense lies in their obligation before the law. The defense is not required by law to present any new or additional evidence or any witnesses at all. The defense may consist merely of challenging the credibility or the legality of the state's evidence and witnesses. And as we have already noted, the defense is not obligated to prove the innocence of the accused; it need show only that the state's case is not beyond a reasonable doubt. The defendant need not even take the stand. (However, if he or she elects to do so, the accused faces the same risks of cross-examination as any other witness.)

After the defense has rested its case, the prosecution has the right to go back on the attack and present rebuttal evidence. In turn, the defense may offer a rejoinder known as a surrebuttal. After that point each side is ready for the closing arguments. Oftentimes this is one of the more dramatic episodes in the trial because each side seeks to sum up its case, condense its strongest arguments, and make one last appeal to the jury. New evidence may not be presented at this stage, and the arguments of both sides tend to ring with emotion and appeals to values that transcend the immediate case. The prosecutor may talk about the crime problem in general, about the need for law and order, and about the need not to let compassion for the accused get in the way of empathy for the crime victim. The defense attorney, on the other hand, may remind the jurors "how we have all made mistakes in this life," or that in a free, democratic society any doubt they have should be resolved in favor of the accused. The prosecution probably avoids emotionalism more than the defense attorney, however, because it is well known that many jury verdicts have been reversed on appeal after the district attorney injected prejudicial statements into the closing statements.

Role of the Judge During the Trial

The judge's role in the trial, although very important, is a relatively passive one. He or she does not present any evidence or take an active part in the examination of the witnesses. The judge is called upon to rule on the many motions of the prosecu-tor and of the defense attorney regarding the types of evidence that may be present-ed and the kinds of questions that may be asked of the witnesses. In some jurisdic-tions the judge is permitted to ask substantive questions of the witnesses and also to comment to the jury about the credibility of the evidence that is presented; in other states the judge is constrained from such activity. Still, even within the Ameri-can legal tradition there is room for a variety of judicial styles that depend on the personality, training, and wisdom of individual judges. We saw this vividly in the O.J. Simpson trial presided over by California state judge Lance Ito, and the Timo-thy McVeigh trial, presided over by U.S. District Judge Richard Matsch. The com-paratively inexperienced Ito never appeared to be in control of the courtroom pro-ceedings, which lasted for eight long months. He allowed an inordinately large number of peremptory challenges, which greatly delayed jury selection; he permit-ted the attorneys to bicker endlessly, both in and outside of the courtroom; and he refused to restrict lengthy excursions on the witness stand (e.g., nine days of testi-mony by police criminalist Dennis Fung). Judge Matsch, by contrast, kept tight reins on the McVeigh trial, which lasted less than six weeks. He refused to grant the lawyers any additional peremptory jury challenges, permitted no grandstanding through use of his controversial gag order on participants, and insisted that the lawyers greatly streamline the presentation of their evidence.[26] While judicial styles then do vary from one courtroom to another, there are nevertheless some traits that all American jurists are expected to manifest.

First and foremost, the judge is expected to play the part of a disinterested party whose primary job is to see to it that both sides are allowed to present their cases as fully as possible within the confines of the law. If judges depart from the appear-ance or practice of being fair and neutral parties, they run counter to fundamental tenets of American jurisprudence and risk having their decisions overturned by an appellate court. This was demonstrated in 1991 when a federal appeals court threw out the forty-five-year prison sentence of television evangelist Jim Bakker. (Bakker had been convicted on twenty-four counts of wire fraud, mail fraud, and conspir-acy by which he had fleeced millions of dollars from his television viewers.) During the sentencing process, U.S. trial judge Robert Potter made several statements that suggested that his own personal feelings about religion impermissibly compro-mised his neutrality. Potter said in open court that Bakker "had no thought what-ever about his victims. And those of us who do have a religion are ridiculed as be-ing saps [of] money-grubbing preachers or priests." In its demand that Bakker be resentenced by another judge, the appellate court said that judges "cannot sanction sentencing procedures that create the perception of the bench as a pulpit from which judges announce their personal sense of religiosity and simultaneously punish defendants for offending it."[27] Thus American judges must be, or at least appear to be, objective, disinterested decision makers.

Although judges do for the most part play such a role, there is also evidence that the backgrounds and values of the jurists affect their decisions in the close calls, that is, when they are called upon to rule on a motion for which the arguments are about equally strong or on a point of law that is open to a variety of interpretations. Evidence for this discretion and the way it is influenced by the values of the judges comes from a variety of sources—a subject discussed in greater detail in Chapters 8 and 9.

Role of the Jury During the Trial

Passive is the word that characterizes the jurors' role during the trial. Their job is to listen attentively to the cases presented by the two opposing attorneys and then come to a decision based solely on the evidence that is set forth. They are ordinarily not permitted to ask questions either of the witnesses or of the judge, nor are they even allowed to take notes of the proceedings. This is not because of constitutional or statutory prohibitions but primarily because it has been the traditional practice of courts in America. Our "adversarial" form of justice requires our lawyers to play the primary role during the trial; the judge and jury are to behave as dispassionate observers.

Not all trial courts in the United States follow this norm, however, and in recent years many judges have allowed jurors to become more involved in the judicial arena. Chicago's chief U.S. district court judge John F. Grady has for over a decade permitted jurors in his courtroom to take notes. In an argument that should appeal to many readers of this text, Grady contends that asking juries to absorb passively all the testimony they hear "is like asking a college student to take a course without any notes and then take a final exam by memory." He notes further that "Judges who try cases without a jury sure don't sit there and do nothing—they take notes and ask questions." Many practicing attorneys and judicial scholars don't agree, however. Some lawyers fear that interruptions from the jury box will upset their carefully planned trial strategies, ride roughshod over time-honored rules of evidence, or change jurors from neutral observers to advocates of one side or the other. As one prominent Kansas City, Missouri, attorney put it, "When you're scoring a baseball game, you're prone to miss something on the field."

In some states a few trial judges have allowed jurors to take fairly active roles in the trial. For instance, Wisconsin circuit court judge Mark Frankel likes to recall a trial in which one of his jurors elicited "the smoking gun." The case concerned a stabbing in which the defendant claimed that he acted in self-defense. The district attorney held the victim's blood-stained jacket and sweater in front of the jurors and pointed to the slits where the knife had entered. Then one juror, acting on a re-markable hunch, passed Judge Frankel a note asking him to order the victim to put on the garments in question and to twist around in a variety of positions. Frankel agreed. To the astonishment of many in the courtroom, the slits in the garments lined up perfectly only when the victim curled up into a self-protective crouch—thus casting real doubt on the defendant's argument that he had stabbed the victim in self-defense. The jury subsequently convicted the defendant. Frankel concluded that the juror's suggestion "changed the whole picture of the case."[28]

Likewise, at the federal level there has been an increasing tendency in recent years to allow jurors greater participation in the questioning of witnesses. At least four U.S. appellate courts have given tacit approval to the practice so long as jurors are not permitted to blurt out queries in the midst of trial and attorneys are given a chance to object to specific questions before they are posed to witnesses.[29] Still, at both state and federal levels the role of the jury remains basically passive, and the "jury liberation" movement remains in the experimental stage.

Instructions to the Jury

An important function of the judge during the trial is to charge the jury after the prosecution and defense have rested their cases. Although the jury's job is to weigh and assess the facts of the case, it is the judge who must instruct the jurors about the meaning of the law and how the law is to be applied. The judge's instructions can be drafted in a way that favors one side or another. For example, if someone were accused of embezzlement and the judge favored acquittal, it might be possible to give the jury such a narrow legal definition of the word *embezzlement* that it would be difficult to bring in a guilty verdict. Likewise, if the judge were disposed toward conviction, a broader discussion of the laws on embezzlement might facili-tate a conviction.

Both the prosecutor and the defense attorney know well that the nature of the instructions can nudge the jury in one direction or another. Consequently, it is of-ten the practice for each side in the case to submit its own set of instructions to the judge asking that its version be the official one read to the jury. The judge may then select one of the two sets of instructions or, as often as not, develop one (perhaps based on selected parts of those offered or on a previously used set of instructions).

Because many cases are overturned on appeal as a result of faulty jury instructions, judges tend to take great care that the wording be technically and legally correct. The problem with this, however, is that although highly technical legal instructions may please an appellate court, they are often incomprehensible to individual jurors. Some studies indicate that jurors spend up to 25 percent of their deliberation time simply trying to decipher what the instructions mean.[30] A 1992 study of jurors in Cook County (Chicago), Illinois, revealed that as many as *75 percent* don't understand parts of the instructions given to them in death-penalty cases.[31] Judges tend to decline the jury's subsequent pleas to clarify instructions or to put them into everyday language because to do so would risk saying something that will move one side or the other to appeal the instructions.

Whatever the thrust or bias of the instructions, they must all have some basic elements. One is to define for the jurors the crime with which the accused is charged. This may involve giving the jurors a variety of options about what kind of verdict to bring. For example, if one person has taken the life of another, the state may be trying the accused for first-degree murder. Nevertheless, the judge may be obliged to acquaint the jury with the legal definition of second-degree murder or manslaughter if they should determine that the defendant was the killer but did not act with malice aforethought. Or if the accused is pleading not guilty for reason of insanity, the judge must offer in the instructions the proper legal definition of insanity.

It is also incumbent upon the judge to remind the jury that the burden of proof is on the state and that the accused is presumed to be innocent. If, after considering all the evidence, the jury still has a "reasonable doubt" as to the guilt of the accused, they must bring in a not guilty verdict. Jurors are often troubled by what this means. "How sure do we have to be," they often ask themselves, "75 percent, 90 percent, 99 percent?" What is "reasonable" and how strong may the "doubt" be? One judge defined the matter as follows:

It is such a doubt as would cause a juror, after careful and candid and impartial consideration of all the evidence, to be so undecided, that he cannot say that he has an abiding conviction of the defendant's guilt. It is such a doubt as would cause a reasonable person to hesitate or pause in the graver or more important transactions of life. However, it is not a fanciful doubt nor a whimsical doubt, nor a doubt based on conjecture.[32]

Despite this and other guidelines that the juror may be given to help determine reasonable doubt, in the final analysis each person has to decide alone at the moment when he or she votes to acquit or convict.

Finally, the judge usually acquaints the jurors with a variety of procedural matters: how to contact the judge if they have questions, the order in which they must consider the charges if there are more than one, who must sign the official documents that express the verdict of the jury. After the instructions are read to the jury (and the attorneys for each side have been given an opportunity to offer objections), the jurors retreat into a deliberation room to decide the fate of the accused.

The Jury's Decision

The jury deliberates in complete privacy; no outsiders observe or participate in its debate. During their deliberation jurors may request the clarification of legal questions from the judge, and they may look at items of evidence or selected segments of the case transcript, but they may consult nothing else—no law dictionaries, no legal writings, no opinions from experts. When it has reached a decision by a vote of its members, the jury returns to the courtroom to announce its verdict. If it has not reached a decision by nightfall, the jurors are sent home with firm instructions neither to discuss the case with others nor read about the case in the newspapers. In very important or notorious cases, the jury may be *sequestered* by the judge, which means that its members will spend the night in a local hotel away from the public eye.

If the jury becomes deadlocked and cannot reach a verdict, it may report that fact to the judge. In such an event the judge may insist that the jury continue its effort to reach a verdict, saying something like: "The state and the accused have spent a lot of time and money on this case, and if you can't agree, then another jury just like you folks is going to have to go through this whole thing again." (There's nothing like instilling a little guilt to motivate human behavior.) Or, if the judge is convinced that the jury is in fact hopelessly deadlocked, he or she may dismiss the jury and call for a new trial.

Research studies indicate that most juries dealing with criminal cases make their decisions fairly quickly. Almost all juries take a vote soon after they retire to their chambers ("just a nonbinding straw vote to see where we are"). In 30 percent of the cases it takes only one vote to reach a unanimous decision. (As the foreman of the jury that convicted Oklahoma City bomber Timothy McVeigh put it, "It was unanimous from the get-go.")[33] In 90 percent of the remainder, the majority on the first ballot eventually wins out. Hung juries—those in which *no* verdict can be reached—tend to occur only when a large minority existed on the first ballot.

Scholars have also learned that juries often reach the same verdict that the judge would have, had he or she been solely responsible for the decision. One large jury study asked judges to state how they would have decided jury cases over which they presided. It was found that judge and jury agreed in 81 percent of the criminal cases (about the same as in civil cases). In 19 percent of the criminal cases the judge and jury disagreed, with the judge showing a marked tendency to convict where the juries had acquitted. Most disagreement occurred over drunk-driving cases and rape cases.[34]

In drunk-driving cases many jurors apparently envisioned themselves in similar situations and had sympathy for the accused. In forcible rape cases the jury was likely to believe that the woman had encouraged the attack because of the way she was dressed or the place where the rape occurred—for instance, in the back room of a sleazy bar. This phenomenon was vividly called to the nation's attention when a state jury in Fort Lauderdale, Florida, acquitted the defendant in a rape case in which the evidence was clear and overwhelming that the assailant had sexually assaulted the victim. When juror Roy Diamond was asked by a reporter why his jury had opted for acquittal in the face of such clear-cut evidence, he replied: "She asked for it. The way she was dressed with that skirt you could see everything she had. She was advertising for sex." (The twenty-two-year-old victim had been wearing a tank top, lace skirt, and no undergarments at the time of the assault.)[35]

In recent years studies have documented another phenomenon characterizing jurors' behavior. As citizens, they may denounce crime and call for greater measures to curtail and punish it, but as jurors they seek to understand the criminal act and link punishment to their explanation of the behavior. In a 1995 study one scholar asked experimental jurors to sentence a man for writing a $100 check against an imaginary bank account. As the study continued, additional facts about the defendant were revealed to the jurors. When they were told that he had a long criminal record, the sentence jumped from ten months to thirty years. However, when the jurors heard a defense psychiatrist "explain" the defendant's behavior, the penalty dropped from thirty to five years. (When psychiatrists testified for both sides, the sentence evened out at fifteen years.)[36] In a parallel experimental study jurors decided a case about an abusive husband under three different situations: the husband's spouse was a good wife and mother; she was incompetent in those roles; and, finally, she was a bad wife and mother. As the battered woman went from the good- to the bad-wife end of the scale, the percentage of guilty verdicts rose dramatically—even though her quality as a wife and mother had, legally, nothing whatsoever to do with the probability of her husband's guilt.[37]

Jurors, like police officers, prosecutors, grand jurors, and judges, reflect their personal values and backgrounds in their decision-making process. Studies have shown that men talk more than women in the jury deliberation process and have more influence on the final outcome. Not surprisingly, well-educated people play a more significant role than those with weak educational backgrounds. There is also some evidence that ethnic or racial minorities carry some of their underdog values into the jury deliberation rooms and are more likely to favor the accused.

When the members of the jury do finally reach a decision, they return to the courtroom and their verdict is announced in open court, often by the jury foreman. It is commonplace at this time for either the prosecutor or the defense attorney to ask that the jury be polled, that is, that each juror be asked individually if the general verdict actually reflects his or her own opinion. The purpose of this is to determine whether each juror supports the overall verdict or whether he or she is just caving in to group pressure. If the polling procedure reveals that the jury is indeed not of one mind, it may be sent back to the jury room to continue deliberations; in some jurisdictions a mistrial may be declared. If a mistrial is declared, the case may be tried again before another jury. There is no double jeopardy because the original jury did not agree on a verdict. On the other hand, if the jury's verdict is not guilty, the defendant is discharged on the spot and is free to leave the courtroom (unless, of course, there are other charges pending).

Procedures After a Criminal Trial

At the close of the criminal trial there are generally two stages that remain for the defendant if he or she has been found guilty: sentencing and an appeal.

Sentencing

Sentencing is the court's formal pronouncement of judgment upon the defendant, at which time the punishment or penalty is set forth.

Penologists have traditionally given four justifications for punishing those who break the laws of society: retribution, incapacitation, deterrence, and rehabilitation. Each one contains separate, though not mutually exclusive, philosophies about why the state should punish offenders. Some emphasize past actions while others focus on the future behavior of the criminal. Some place their primary focus on the rights and needs of society while others are more oriented toward the criminal as a human being.

Retribution in its most basic sense stems from the ancient principle of revenge—the moral right of society to punish those who have inflicted harm on a member of that society, or as the book of Leviticus succinctly puts it: "An eye for an eye, a tooth for a tooth." While there is harshness in this principle, it carries with it the modulating notion that it is the state that should punish according to some form of due process of law—as opposed to private citizens carrying out a rampage of revenge. In addition, once the punishment is exacted, that is the end of the matter. The state and the victim do not have the right to commence a vendetta against the criminal or his family. Still, there are weaknesses underlying this philosophy of punishment. First, if taken literally it would force the state into untold acts of brutality. For example, if by intent or by accident Mr. X causes the blindness of another person, do we really want the state to put out both of Mr. X's eyes as retribution? Likewise, while the concept of inflicting injury for injury is comprehensible in terms of crimes of violence, it is not a very useful tool for crimes against property. For instance, if Ms. Y was found to have engaged in a willful and unlawful misuse of a computer software program, what would be the appropriate punishment in terms of "an eye for an eye"?

A second justification for punishment is *incapacitation.* Its underlying assumption is that if you remove offenders from society by putting them in prison (or by executing them), they will no longer be a threat to that society. There is clearly some truth to this proposition, however simplistic, especially since there is increasing evidence that a small number of criminals are responsible for a large number of crimes: "lock the crooks up and we'll all be better off for it." Nevertheless, there are some key questions that this philosophy does not address. For example, for how long should the criminal be put in prison? What about evidence that suggests that prison time makes criminals harder and meaner and thus even more of a threat to society when their incarceration ends? Finally, does the state have any responsibility to reform or rehabilitate the offender?

Deterrence is a third reason to justify the state's handing down a punishment. The focus here is not so much on punishing the wrongdoer (although it surely does that); rather the emphasis is on preventing others in society from breaking the law. If the state severely punishes a criminal, that punishment will serve as a warning to others that the same will happen to them if they break the law. This philosophy is based partially on the notion that people obey the law not just because they are good but also because they don't want to be caught and be punished; the more immediate and severe the punishment, the greater the likelihood that people will adhere to the law. While this argument is persuasive, we know that in the real world it doesn't always work this way. America is second only to Russia in the percentage of its population in prison, and yet the nation still has a huge amount of crime. Likewise, much crime, particularly crimes of violence, is committed on the spur of the moment, or under the influence of drugs or alcohol, when the wrongdoers are in no state of mind to calculate the odds of getting caught or the severity of their possible punishment.

Finally, *rehabilitation* is a more modern justification for punishing the law-breaker. Its thesis is that people commit crimes because society has failed to provide them with a proper home environment when they were young, a good education, or a job; it also accedes that a criminal may be ill physically or mentally, or possibly a victim of substance abuse. Thus the purpose of the sentence is not to punish but to treat the individual needs of the lawbreaker. ("Teach him a trade and get him off the bottle, and he won't have to steal for a living.") While rehabilitation surely does work in some cases, this philosophy has begun to sink under the weight of current evidence. In recent decades data have shown that whether criminals are treated harshly in prison or offered a gentle rehabilitating hand, the likelihood of their engaging in future criminal activity is about the same. Likewise there is evidence to show that often the reason why prisoners enroll in prison-offered counseling, education, and religious programs is not because they wish to change their behavior but because they wish to use this "good behavior" to gain an early release from prison.

In sum, while all four philosophies of sentencing contain some compelling elements, each contains some inconsistencies and shortcomings, and none seem to address all the complex aspects of this important but very complicated societal issue.[38]

At the federal level and in most states, sentences are imposed by the judge only.[39] However, in several states the defendant may elect to be sentenced by either a judge or a jury, and in capital cases states generally require that no death sentence shall be imposed unless it is the determination of twelve unanimous jurors. Some states have a bifurcated procedure for determining innocence or guilt and then imposing a sentence for the guilty: after a jury finds someone guilty, the jury deliberates a second time to determine the sentence. In fact, in several states a new jury is empaneled expressly for sentencing. At this time the rules of evidence are more relaxed, and the jury may be permitted to hear evidence that was excluded during the actual trial (for example, the previous criminal record of the accused).

After the judge pronounces the sentence, it is customary for several weeks to elapse between the time the defendant is found guilty and the time when the penalty is imposed. This interval permits the judge to hear and consider any posttrial motions that the defense attorney might make (such as a motion for a new trial) and to allow a probation officer to conduct a presentence investigation. The probation officer is a professional with a background in criminology, psychology, or social work who makes a recommendation to the judge about the length of the sentence to be imposed. It is customary for the probation officer to examine factors such as the background of the criminal, the seriousness of the crime committed, and the likelihood that the criminal will continue to engage in illegal activity. Judges are not required to follow the probation officer's recommendation, but it is still a major factor in the judge's calculus as to what the sentence shall be. Judges are presented with a variety of alternatives and a range of sentences when it comes to punishment for the criminal. Many of these alternatives involve the concept of rehabilitation and call for the assistance of professionals in the fields of criminology and social science.

The lightest punishment that a judge can hand down is that of probation. This is often the penalty if the crime is regarded as minor or if the judge believes that the guilty person is not likely to engage in additional criminal activity. (For example, a woman with no prior criminal record who kills her husband after being beaten and maltreated for twenty years is unlikely to go on a rampage of bank robberies or additional killings.) If a probated sentence is handed down, the criminal may not spend any time in prison as long as the conditions of the probation are maintained. Such conditions might include staying away from bars or convicted criminals, not committing other crimes, or with increasing frequency, performing some type of community service. For example, figure skater Tonya Harding was ordered to serve food to senior citizens as her community service for her part in the attack on Olympic rival Nancy Kerrigan. These "alternative sentencing programs" have been prompted by tight budgets and overcrowded prisons and have been on the rise in recent years. (Ten years ago there were about 20 formal alternative sentencing programs nationwide; in 1994 there were more than 300.)[40] If a criminal serves out his or her probation or "alternative sentence" without incident, the criminal record is usually wiped clean, and in the eyes of the law it is as if no crime had ever been committed.

If the judge is not disposed toward probation and feels that "hard time" is in order, he or she must impose a prison sentence that is within a range prescribed by law.

For example, in a certain state the penalty for aggravated assault may be a prison term of "no less than five but no more than fifteen years in the state penitentiary." The reason for a range of years rather than an automatically assigned number is that the law recognizes that not all crimes and criminals are alike and that in principle the punishment should fit the crime. Thus a criminal with a prior record who held up a liquor store might be given a longer sentence than the person with no record who embezzled some money in order to pay for his child's life-or-death surgery.

Flexibility in the sentencing process thus has its advantages, but there is another side to this coin: sentencing disparities among judges are often great and frequently result in sentences that vary significantly for essentially the same crime and set of circumstances. That is, there is much empirical evidence that judges do not view similar sets of facts and come to the same determinations with regard to sentences. A former official of the Federal Bureau of Prisons anonymously provided us with an example of the injustice that can result:

The first man has been convicted of cashing a check for $58.40. He was out of work at the time of his offense, and when his wife became ill and he needed money for rent, food, and doctor bills, he became a victim of temptation. He had no prior criminal record. The other man cashed a check for $35.20. He was also out of work, and his wife had just left him for another man. His prior record consisted of a drunk charge and a nonsupport charge. Our examination of these two cases indicates no significant difference for sentencing purposes. But they appeared before different judges, and the first man received fifteen years in prison and the second man received thirty days.

In an effort to eliminate gross disparities in sentencing for basically the same set of circumstances, the federal government and many states have attempted to develop sets of precise guidelines to create greater consistency among judges. At the national level this effort was manifested by the enactment of the Sentencing Reform Act of 1987, but congressional concern for this problem goes back many years. In October 1984 Congress passed the Comprehensive Crime Control Act, which among other things created a Sentencing Commission. This commission was authorized to study the problem of sentencing disparities among federal jurists and to develop a set of guidelines for sentences. It began its determination of guideline ranges "by estimating the average sentences now being served," and thus it expected that its suggested guidelines would "in many instances . . . approximate existing practice."

The guidelines contain a Sentencing Table with 43 offense levels on the vertical axis and six categories of criminal history on the horizontal axis. Offenders in criminal history category

1 would likely have little or no criminal record, while those in category 6 would likely have extensive criminal histories.

The judge would find the applicable guideline sentencing range, which the table expresses in months of imprisonment, by determining the offense level and then reading across the axis to the proper criminal history category. Offense level 4, for example, which could apply to an offender convicted of theft of $100 or less, prescribes a sentencing range of 0 to 4 months for an offender in criminal history category 1, and 6 to 12 months for an offender in criminal history category 6. Offense level 38, which could apply to an offender convicted of aircraft hijacking, prescribes a sentencing range of 235–293 months for offenders in criminal history category 1, and 360 months to life for offenders in both the 5th and 6th criminal history categories.[41]

Congress provided that judges may depart from the guidelines only if they find "an aggravating or mitigating circumstance" that the commission did not adequately consider. Although the congressional guidelines do not specify the kinds of factors that could constitute grounds for departure from the sentencing guidelines, Congress did state that such grounds could not include race, sex, national origin, creed, religion, socioeconomic status, drug dependence, or alcohol abuse.[42]

What have been the effects of the Sentencing Reform Act? Besides stirring up a storm of controversy among U.S. judges who resent restrictions on their traditionally wide sentencing authority, two observations now appear warranted. First, the majority of federal judges do seem to be adhering to the sentencing guidelines, and thus aggregate disparities among judges have declined. Second, there is mounting evidence that "many judges are devising ways to get around the rules in their own cases." A number of recent studies have found that judges, prosecutors, and defense lawyers may cooperate to circumvent the guidelines when they believe the projected sentence is too harsh. They do this by fudging the actual facts of a crime. Examples include classifying guns found on drug dealers as being for "sport" and therefore not covered by the guidelines, or reducing the weight of marijuana for the "drying" that would occur between the arrest and trial dates. In fact, one recent study found that "judges in districts that were below the average in lengths of sentences before the guidelines went into effect are continuing to find ways to be lenient."[43] Thus the federal guidelines are having a measurable effect but not without major rear guard action by those jurists who either resent them or who believe them to be too harsh for certain defendants.

The states, too, have a variety of programs for avoiding vast disparities in judges' sentences. By 1995 twenty-two states had created commissions to establish sentencing guidelines for their judges, and as of late 1997 such guidelines were in effect in seventeen states.[44] Likewise, almost all of the states have now enacted *mandatory sentencing laws* that require an automatic, specific sentence upon conviction of certain crimes—particularly violent crimes, crimes in which a gun was used, or crimes perpetrated by habitual offenders. How successful have these reforms been now that we have had a decade or so to evaluate their effectiveness? One recent study concluded that "state guidelines reforms have clearly succeeded in their goal of encouraging more informed and rational sentencing policy decisions. Published evaluations also suggest that state guidelines have generally succeeded in achieving their goals of reducing sentencing disparity, lessening the impact of short-term political pressures on sentencing policy, and linking sentencing severity to available correctional resources."[45]

Despite the enormous impact that judges have on the sentence, they do not necessarily have the final say on the matter. Whenever a prison term is set by the judge, it is still subject to the parole laws of the federal government and of the states. Thus parole boards (and sometimes the president and governors who may grant pardons or commute sentences) have the final say about how long an inmate actually stays in prison. Evidence collected by the Justice Department for the state level suggests that parole boards and governors have not been hesitant about exercising their prerogatives. In fact, the average prisoner serves less than half the court-ordered maximum sentence. In a survey of thirty-three states, the Justice Department's Bureau of Justice Statistics found that the average prisoner released from confinement had been sentenced to three years but the median time served was seventeen months—only 45 percent of that sentence! [46] This median time period should begin to rapidly increase, however, because of the numerous mandatory minimum-time sentence laws that have been enacted in recent years by Congress and the various state legislatures.

An Appeal

At both the state and federal levels everyone has the right to at least one appeal upon conviction of a felony. About a third of all criminals avail themselves of this privilege. An appeal is based on the contention that an error of law was made during the trial process. Such an error must be "reversible" as opposed to "harmless." (An error is considered harmless if its occurrence had no effect on the outcome of the trial.) A reversible error, however, is a serious one that might have affected the verdict of the judge or jury. For example, a successful appeal might be based on the argument that evidence was improperly admitted at trial, that the judge's instructions to the jury were flawed, or that a guilty plea was not voluntarily made. As we stressed in Chapter 4, however, appeals must be based on questions of procedure and legal interpretations, not on factual determinations of the defendant's guilt or innocence as such. Furthermore, under most circumstances one cannot appeal the length of one's sentence in the United States (as long as it was in the range prescribed by law). This is unlike the practice of most other Western democracies, which routinely permit criminals to contest in the appeals courts the length of their prison terms.

If an appeal is successful, the defendant does not usually just go free. The usual practice is for the appellate court to remand the case (send it back down) to the lower court for a new trial. At that point the prosecution must determine whether the procedural errors in the original trial can be overcome in a second trial and whether it is worth the time and effort to do so. A second trial is not considered double jeopardy, since the defendant has chosen to appeal the original conviction.

In 1991 the Supreme Court made it harder for convicted criminals, especially those on death row, to repeatedly challenge the constitutionality of their convictions. The High Court ruled that when a prisoner files a second habeas corpus petition in federal court,[47] the prosecutor must specify which claims are being made for the very first time. The prisoner is then obliged to provide compelling reasons why these new issues, such as the unavailability of factual or legal information, weren't raised in the initial petition. The prisoner must now demonstrate that his or her case was actually prejudiced by the alleged constitutional violations.[48]

The Supreme Court's tightening of the screw for death penalty appeals has not been without effect. To illustrate, at the state level in 1976 fewer than 500 persons were awaiting execution, but by the fall of 1997 more than 3,200 persons were on death row. Texas, for example, had executed some thirty prisoners by the summer of 1997—easily surpassing its record of twenty executions set in 1935. At the federal level, only thirty-four persons have been executed during this entire century, but at the current time some thirteen inmates have a date with the lethal-injection chamber located at the correctional facility in Terre Haute, Indiana.[49]

The media and champions of "law and order" often make much of appellate courts that turn loose obviously guilty criminals and of convictions reversed on technicalities. Surely this does happen, and indeed one might argue that this is inevitable in a democratic country whose legal system is based on fair play and the presumption of the innocence of the accused. But we need to keep in mind a few basic facts and figures. First, about 90 percent of all defendants plead guilty, and this plea virtually excludes the possibility of an appeal. Of the remaining group, two-thirds are found guilty at trial, and only about a third of these actually appeal. Of those who do appeal, only about 20 percent have their convictions reversed. Of those whose convictions are reversed, many are found guilty at a subsequent trial. (For example, in the famous case of *Miranda v. Arizona*,[50] which spearheaded the criminal rights emphasis of the Warren Court, Miranda's conviction was overturned by the High Court because tainted evidence had been used to convict him. Nevertheless at a subsequent trial—minus the tainted evidence—he was again convicted for the same crime.) Thus when we talk of the number of persons convicted of crimes who are subsequently freed because of reversible court errors, we are talking about a small fraction of 1 percent. Most of us would consider that an acceptable risk in a free society.

Summary

We began this chapter by talking about the nature and substance of crime—at least as it is understood in twentieth-century America. We then walked through the myriad procedures that constitute the judicial process at the federal and state levels. We analyzed the various aspects of crime that lead to an arrest, the subsequent appearance before a magistrate, and the activity of the grand jury or the preliminary hearing. We also observed how plea bargaining enormously tempers the criminal court process. We outlined the basic rights of the accused in a criminal trial and looked at the vagaries of the jury selection process. We then examined the key players at the trial—the prosecutor, the defense attorney, and the judge. After discussing the work of the jury, we discussed the posttrial procedures of sentencing and appeal. Throughout the chapter we stressed a theme that we shall develop throughout the text, namely, that the backgrounds and attitudes of the criminal justice participants have as much to do with the nature and quality of justice as do the formal rules of the game. Whether we are talking about police officers, prosecutors, judges, or juries, the criminal justice system is greatly influenced by the role perceptions, mores, and values of the men and women who dispense justice in America.

NOTES

1. We wish to express our debt to the following, from whom we borrowed this categorization: Harold J. Vetter and Leonard Territo, *Crime and Justice in America* (St. Paul, Minn.: West, 1984), chap. 1.

2. U.S. Department of Justice, Bureau of Justice Statistics (*http://www.ojp.usdoj.gov/bjs/cvictgen.htm*), 1.

3. Ibid.

4. U.S. Department of Justice, Bureau of Justice Statistics (*http://www.ojp.usdoj.gov/bjs/cvict.htm#ncvs*), 1.

5. Vetter and Territo, *Crime and Justice in America*, 11.

6. *Whitney v. California*, 274 U.S. 357 (1927).

7. Ordinance unanimously declared invalid in *Patachristou v. City of Jacksonville*, 405 U.S. 156 (1972).

8. Quotation in David W. Neubauer, *America's Courts and the Criminal Justice System*, 2d ed. (Monterey, Calif.: Brooks/Cole, 1984), 64.

9. "Arresting Statistics," *Newsweek*, May 26, 1997, 72.

10. "Trying to Enforce Unpopular Law Is Plaguing the Highway Patrol," *Houston Chronicle*, September 25, 1977, 1:18.

11. L. W. Sherman and R. A. Berk, "The Specific Deterrent Effects of Arrest for Domestic Assault," *American Sociological Review* 49 (1984): 261–272; and R. A. Berk and L. W. Sherman, "Police Responses to Domestic Violence Incidents: An Analysis of an Experimental Design with Incomplete Randomization," *Journal of the American Statistical Association* 83 (1988): 70–76.

12. For a more extensive discussion of this subject, see Gennaro F. Vito and Ronald M. Holmes, *Criminology* (Belmont, Calif.: Wadsworth, 1994), 83–85.

13. "Los Angeles Aftershocks," *Newsweek*, April 1, 1991, 18–19. (The exchange occurred the same night in March of 1991 that a group of Los Angeles police officers beat up a black motorist, Rodney King. The incident was videotaped by a neighbor and was later shown extensively on national television.)

14. *County of Riverside v. McLaughlin*, 500 U.S. 44 (1991).

15. *Miranda v. Arizona*, 384 U.S. 436 (1966). This decision was undermined somewhat in 1991 when the U.S. Supreme Court ruled that under some circumstances confessions that are coerced from defendants by police can be used as evidence. *Arizona v. Fulminante*, 499 U.S. 279 (1991).

16. There are variations of this, however. In Texas, for example, grand juries consist of twelve persons chosen because they are friends or neighbors of judge-appointed jury commissioners. A vote of nine members is required for a decision.

17. See Robert A. Carp, "The Behavior of Grand Juries: Acquiescence or Justice?" *Social Science Quarterly* 55 (1975): 853–870.

18. Bargains on the sentence are primarily conducted at the state rather than the federal level because federal sentences are largely within the bailiwick of the judge with advice from the probation officer—with both acting under congressional sentencing guidelines that took effect November 1, 1987.

19. In the case of *Barker v. Wingo*, 407 U.S. 514 (1972), the Supreme Court permitted a delay of as much as five years because it felt the various trial date postponements were justified.

20. Also, in many jurisdictions laws exempt persons in specific occupations (for example, doctors, members of the clergy, police officers) and in specific situations (for example, full-time students, persons over sixty-five years of age, mothers with young children at home).

21. We have very little systematic evidence of how many potential jurors actually show up when called for jury duty, but fragmentary data are rather alarming. For example, in Harris County (Houston), Texas, of nearly 600,000 residents who were summoned for possible jury service between November 1994 and November 1995, only 57 percent showed up! Joe Stinebaker, "Many Called, Few Serve," *Houston Chronicle*, July 22, 1996, A14.

22. *Batson v. Kentucky*, 476 U.S. 79 (1986).

23. *J.E.B. v. Alabama*, 511 U.S. 127 (1994).

24. Daniel Wise, " '*Batson*' Protection Extended to Jews," *The National Law Journal*, April 28, 1997, A10.

25. Victoria Slind-Flor, "Illegal to Exclude Gays From Jury," *The National Law Journal*, August 26, 1996, A11.

26. For a more extensive discussion of the contrast between these two judges, see Paul M. Barrett and Margaret A. Jacobs, "How McVeigh's Trial, for All Its Complexity, Proceeded So Rapidly," *Wall Street Journal*, June 3, 1997, A1.

27. Milo Geyelin and Arthur S. Hayes, "Bakker's 45-Year Sentence Is Thrown Out," *Wall Street Journal*, February 13, 1991, B2.

28. Tamar Jacoby with Tim Padgett, "Waking Up the Jury Box," *Newsweek*, August 7, 1989, 51.

29. "Jurors May Question Witnesses during Trial, Appeals Court Rules," *Wall Street Journal*, August 6, 1992, B3. For an excellent study of this general subject matter, see Larry Heuer and Steven Penrod, "Juror Notetaking and Question Asking During Trials," *Law and Human Behavior* 18 (1994): 121–150; and Heuer and Penrod, "Increasing Juror Participation in Trials Through Note Taking and Question Asking," *Judicature* 79 (1996): 256–263.

30. See Shari Seidman Diamond and Judith N. Levi, "Improving Decisions on Death by Revising and Testing Jury Instructions," *Judicature* 79 (1996): 224–233; and Peter Annin and Tom Morganthau, "The Verdict: Death," Newsweek, June 23, 1997, 41.

31. Helene Cooper, "Death Sentence Vacated Because Study Reveals Juror Misunderstanding," *Wall Street Journal*, September 28, 1992, B6.

32. *Moore v. U.S.*, 345 F.2d 97 (D.C. Cir. 1965).

33. Annin and Morganthau, "The Verdict: Death," 41.

34. For an excellent classic study of jury behavior, see Harry Kalven, Jr., and Hans Zeisel, *The American Jury* (Boston: Little, Brown, 1966).

35. "Overheard," *Newsweek*, October 16, 1989, 23.

36. Norman J. Finkel, *Commonsense Justice: Jurors' Notions of the Law* (Cambridge, Mass.: Harvard University Press, 1995), 146–150.

37. James Q. Wilson, *Moral Judgment* (New York: HarperCollins, 1997), 91.

38. In discussing the justification for sentences we have borrowed from David W. Neubauer, *America's Courts and the Criminal Justice System*, 5th ed. (Belmont, Calif.: Wadsworth, 1996), 269–274.

39. However, according to a 1994 law passed by Congress (18 USC Sec. 3593 and 3594), in capital cases only a jury can hand down a death sentence.

40. David Mulholland, "Judges Finding Creative Ways of Punishment," *Wall Street Journal*, May 24, 1994, B1.

41. "News from the Sentencing Commission," *The Third Branch* 19 (May 1987): 3–4.

42. Ibid., 5.

43. Jonathan M. Moses, "Many Judges Skirt Sentencing Guidelines," *Wall Street Journal*, May 7, 1993, B2.

44. Michael Tonry, "Twenty Years of Sentencing Reform: Steps Forward, Steps Backward," *Judicature* 78 (1995): 171.

45. Richard S. Frase, "State Sentencing Guidelines: Still Going Strong," *Judicature* 78 (1995): 177.

46. "Study: Prisoners Serving 45% of Terms," *Houston Chronicle*, December 31, 1987, 1:9.

47. A petition for habeas corpus is a civil petition by either a state or a federal prisoner, usually filed after he or she has been convicted and has had that conviction upheld by an appellate court. The petition does not focus on whether the evidence supported a conviction but rather challenges the constitutionality of various police, lawyer, or judicial practices that supposedly violated the rights of the defendant.

48. *McCleskey v. Zant*, 499 U.S. 467 (1991).

49. David A. Kaplan, "Life and Death Decisions," *Newsweek*, June 16, 1997, 28–30.

50. *Miranda v. Arizona*, 384 U.S. 436 (1966).

SUGGESTED READINGS

Cole, George F. *Criminal Justice: Law & Politics*, 6th. ed. Belmont, Calif.: Wadsworth, 1993. A reader containing articles by America's top experts on topics such as police behavior, defense attorneys, and corrections.

Eisenstein, James, and Herbert Jacob. *Felony Justice: An Organizational Analysis of Criminal Courts.* Boston: Little, Brown, 1977. Discusses how judges, prosecutors, defense attorneys, and others in the criminal court system interact as members of work groups that serve to reinforce each other's roles.

Hastie, Reid, Steven D. Penrod, and Nancy Pennington. *Inside the Jury.* Cambridge, Mass.: Harvard University Press, 1983. An excellent discussion of the history of and legal constraints on jury behavior; presents a sophisticated, data-containing behavioral model of how a jury functions.

Judicature 78, no. 4 (January–February 1995). The entire issue of this journal examines the current status of sentencing and efforts at reform.

Judicature 79, no. 5 (March–April 1996). The entire issue of this journal is dedicated to the work of juries and to thought on jury reform.

Levine, James P. *Juries and Politics.* Pacific Grove, Calif.: Brooks/Cole, 1992. A concise, comprehensive review of the legal and social science literature on juries.

Myren, Richard A. *Law and Justice: An Introduction.* Pacific Grove, Calif.: Brooks/Cole, 1988. A look at the criminal justice system from a more traditional, jurisprudence point of view that emphasizes the interrelationship between law and society.

Neubauer, David W. *America's Courts and the Criminal Justice System,* 5th ed. Belmont, Calif.: Wadsworth, 1996. A classic political science textbook on all the major stages present in the criminal justice process.

Walker, Samuel. *Sense and Nonsense about Crime and Drugs,* 3d ed. Belmont, Calif.: Wadsworth, 1994. Discusses the pros and cons of both liberal and conservative approaches to preventing and punishing criminal behavior.

CHAPTER 7

The Civil Court Process

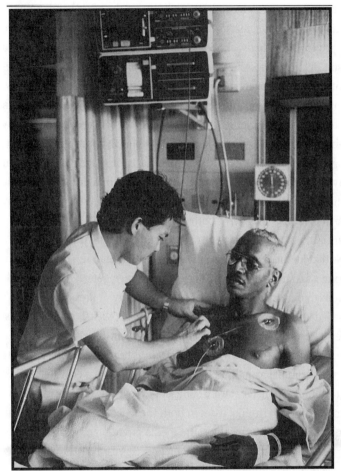

The numbers of medical malpractice suits are rising, as are the sizes of monetary awards to successful plaintiffs.

THIS CHAPTER CONTINUES OUR examination of courts from a judicial process perspective, focusing on the civil courts. After discussing how civil law differs from criminal law and describing the most important categories of civil law, we will proceed step by step through the civil trial process and then consider alternatives to trials.

The Nature and Substance of Civil Law

The American legal system observes several important distinctions between criminal and civil law. As we saw in the last chapter, criminal law is concerned with conduct that is offensive to society as a whole. Civil law, on the other hand, pertains primarily to the duties of private citizens to each other. In civil cases the disputes are usually between private individuals, although the government may sometimes be a party in a civil suit. Just the opposite is true with criminal cases, which always involve government prosecution of an individual for an alleged offense against society.

Civil actions are completely separate and distinct from criminal proceedings. In a civil case the court attempts to settle a particular dispute between the parties by determining their legal rights. The court then decides upon an appropriate remedy, such as awarding monetary damages to the injured party or issuing an order that directs one party to perform or refrain from a specific act. In a criminal case the court decides whether the defendant is innocent or guilty. A guilty defendant may be punished by a fine, imprisonment, or both.

In some instances the same act may give rise to both a criminal proceeding and a civil suit. Suppose that Joe and Pete, two political scientists attending a convention in Atlanta, are sharing a taxi from the airport to their downtown hotel. During the ride they become involved in a heated discussion over the quality of President Clinton's appointees to the federal courts. By the time the taxi stops at their hotel, the discussion has become so heated that Joe suggests they settle their differences right then and there. If Pete strikes Joe in the ribs with his briefcase as he gets out of the taxi, Pete may be charged with criminal assault. In addition, Joe might file a civil suit against Pete in an effort to obtain a monetary award sufficient to cover his medical expenses.

Civil cases far outnumber criminal cases in both the federal and state courts, although they generally do not attract the same media attention as criminal trials. Still, they often raise important policy questions and cover a broad range of disagreements in society. One leading judicial scholar summarizes the breadth of the civil law field as follows:

Every broken agreement, every sale that leaves a dissatisfied customer, every uncollected debt, every dispute with a government agency, every libel and slander, every accidental injury, every marital breakup, and every death may give rise to a civil proceeding.[1]

Thus, virtually any dispute between two or more persons may provide the basis for a civil suit. The number of suits is huge, but most of them fall into one of five basic categories.[2]

The Main Categories of Civil Law

Contract Law

Contract law is primarily concerned with voluntary agreements between two or more people. Some common examples familiar to us all include agreements to perform a certain type of work, to buy or sell goods, and to construct or repair homes or businesses. Basic to these agreements are a promise by one party and a counterpromise by the other party, usually a promise by one party to pay money for the other party's services or goods. For example, assume that Mr. Burns and Ms. Colder enter into an agreement whereby Colder agrees to pay Burns $125 if he will cut and deliver a cord of oak firewood to her home on December 10. If Burns does not deliver the wood on that date he has "breached" the contract and Colder may sue him for damages.

Although many contracts are relatively simple and straightforward, some rather complex fields also build on contract law or contract ideas. One such field is commercial law, which focuses primarily on sales involving credit or the installment plan. Commercial law also deals with checks, promissory notes, and other negotiable instruments.

Another closely related field—one that has become especially prominent in recent years—is bankruptcy and creditors' rights. Bankrupt individuals or businesses may go through a process that essentially wipes the slate clean and allows the person filing for bankruptcy to begin again. The bankruptcy process is also designed to ensure fairness to creditors. As we noted in Chapter 2, bankruptcy law has been a major concern of legislators for several years, and there are now a large number of special bankruptcy judges attached to the U.S. district courts.

The final area is the insurance contract, which is important because of its applicability to so many people. The insurance industry is regulated by government agencies and subject to its own distinct rules.

Tort Law

Tort law may generally be described as the law of civil wrongs. It concerns conduct that causes injury and fails to measure up to some standard set by society.

Actions for personal injury or bodily injury claims are at the heart of tort law, and automobile accidents have traditionally been responsible for a large number of these claims. One of the most rapidly growing subfields of tort law is product liability. This category has become an increasingly effective way to hold corporations accountable for injuries caused by defective foods, toys, appliances, automobiles, drugs, or a host of other products. This type of case is what many have in mind when they complain about a "litigation explosion" in the United States or describe America as a "litigious society" (see Chapter 1).

Perhaps one reason for the tremendous growth in product liability cases is a change in the standard of proof. Traditionally, negligence (generally defined as carelessness or the failure to use ordinary care, under the particular circumstances revealed by the evidence in the lawsuit) must be proven before one person is able to collect damages for injuries caused by someone else. However, it has been argued that for many years reliance on the negligence concept has been declining, especially in product liability cases. In its place, the courts often use a strict liability standard, which means that a victim can recover even if there was no negligence and even if the manufacturer was careful.

Another reason commonly suggested for the growth in the number of product liability cases finding their way into court is the size of jury awards when the decision favors the plaintiff. Jury awards for damages may be of two types: compensatory and punitive. Compensatory damages are intended to cover the plaintiff's actual loss. Examples include repair costs, doctor bills, and hospital expenses. Punitive (or exemplary) damages are designed to punish the defendant or serve as a warning against such behavior in the future.

Data from the National Center for State Courts allow us to put the problem in perspective.[3] In product liability cases involving a jury trial the plaintiff wins in 40 percent of the cases. That figure alone may not sound too impressive when compared to other types of cases. For example, in cases involving toxic substances, plaintiffs win 73 percent of the time; plaintiffs in automobile cases win 60 percent of the time. It is the size of jury awards in product liability cases that make people sit up and take notice. The $260,000 median jury award in these cases tops the National Center for State Court's list. In contrast, toxic substance and automobile cases receive median jury awards of $101,000 and $29,000, respectively. Another source reported that the size of jury verdicts in product liability lawsuits jumped 44 percent in 1996, although the number of actual awards declined.[4] Finally, the National Center for State Court's data show that fully 15 percent of product liability case awards come in at over $1 million. Medical malpractice cases top the list in this category, with 25 percent of the awards going over the $1 million mark. By contrast, only 4 percent of jury awards in automobile cases are over $1 million.

Some have argued that the potential for large awards in tort cases encourages plaintiffs to file suits that are not very strong or lack merit altogether. Others lay much of the blame on plaintiff's attorneys who are willing to pursue cases on a contingency fee basis (see Chapter 5).

As a result of concern over large jury awards and the increasing number of so-called frivolous cases, government officials, corporate executives, interest groups, and members of the legal community have called for legislation aimed at tort reform.[5] In fact, over the past ten or so years, a number of states have enacted a variety of tort reform measures. The American Tort Reform Association, which serves as an advocate of tort reform, reports that in the last ten years 9 states have limited awards of noneconomic damages, 31 states have modified their laws governing punitive damages, and 29 states have enacted statutes penalizing plaintiffs who file frivolous lawsuits.[6] At the national level, however, despite calls for action, Congress has yet to enact comprehensive tort reform legislation.

In short, American courts have increasingly been called upon to protect consumers against defective products. Although it has long been argued that consumers should have freedom of choice in the marketplace, there is now less freedom to make an unsafe choice.[7]

Still another rapidly growing subfield of tort law is the medical malpractice category. Ironically, the number of medical malpractice claims has increased even as great advances have been made in medicine. Yet two ongoing problems in contemporary medicine are the increased risk imposed by new treatments and the impersonal character of specialists and hospitals.[8] Patients today have high expectations, and when a doctor fails them their anger may lead to a malpractice suit.[9]

Courts generally use the traditional negligence standard rather than the strict liability doctrine in resolving medical malpractice suits. This means that the law does not attempt to make doctors guarantee successful treatment, but instead tries to make the doctor liable if the patient can prove that the physician failed to perform in a manner consistent with accepted methods of medical practice. The injured patient must demonstrate that the doctor's conduct was unreasonably negligent and that this negligence was the cause of the specific injury that occurred. The notion of acceptable practice is a rather slippery one that varies from state to state, and such questions must be resolved by the courts on a case-by-case basis. It should be noted, however, that there is customarily a presumption that the conduct of professionals, including doctors, is reasonable in nature. This means that to prevail against the doctor in court, the injured patient needs at least the testimony of one or more expert witnesses stating that the doctor's conduct was not reasonable.[10]

Property Law

There has traditionally been a distinction between real property and personal property. The former normally refers to real estate, that is, land, houses, and buildings; traditionally it has also included growing crops. Basically everything else is considered personal property. Included, then, would be such things as money, jewelry, automobiles, furniture, and bank deposits.

All of us have some involvement with both real estate and personal property during our lives. Most of us are renters or homeowners, or we live with someone who is. However, for most Americans personal property—our possessions—means more to us. Yet, "as far as the law is concerned the word *property* means primarily real property; personal property is of minor importance."[11] In fact, there is no single special field of law devoted to personal property. Instead, personal property is generally considered under the rubric of contract law, commercial law, and bankruptcy law.

Property rights have always been important in this country. It has been argued, for instance, that the protection of property rights was the major motivation of the framers of the U.S. Constitution.[12] Another pertinent example is that in the early days of this country only male *landowners* were eligible to vote.

Today, property rights have reached the point of being far more complex than mere ownership of something. The notion of property now includes, among several other things, the right to use that property.[13]

One important branch of property law today deals with land use controls. Zoning is the most familiar type of land use restriction. Zoning ordinances are generally considered to have had their beginning about the time of World War I, and are now found in cities, towns, and villages throughout the country. The zoning ordinances divide a municipality into districts designated for different uses. For instance, one neighborhood may be designated as residential, another as commercial, and yet another as industrial.

Early zoning laws were challenged on the ground that restrictions on land use amounted to a "taking" of the land by the city in violation of the Fifth and Fourteenth Amendments. A provision of the Fifth Amendment, made applicable to the states by the Fourteenth Amendment, says: "Nor shall private property be taken for public use without just compensation." In a sense, zoning laws do "take" from the owners of land the right to use their property in any way they see fit. Nonetheless, courts have generally ruled that zoning laws are not regarded as a "taking" in violation of the Constitution.[14]

Although the courts have given zoning authorities rather broad powers, they do not have unlimited powers. According to the Supreme Court, the regulations must "bear a substantial relation to the public health, safety, morals, or general welfare."[15]

Today, zoning is a fact of life in cities and towns of all sizes throughout the United States. City planners and other city officials recognize zoning ordinances as necessary to the planned and orderly growth of urban areas. In fact, it is a constant source of amazement to many that Houston, one of the nation's largest cities, does not have a comprehensive zoning ordinance.

The Law of Succession

The law of succession considers how property is passed along from one generation to another. The American legal system recognizes a person's right to dispose of his or her property as he or she wishes. One common way to do this is to execute a will. If a person leaves behind a valid will, the courts will enforce it. However, if someone leaves no will (or has improperly drawn it up), then the person has died "intestate," and the state must dispose of the property.

The state's disposition of the property is carried out according to the fixed scheme set forth in the state statutes. By law, intestate property passes to the deceased person's heirs, that is, to his or her nearest relatives. Occasionally a person who dies intestate has no living relatives. In that situation the property *escheats,* or passes, to the state in which the deceased resided. State statutes often prohibit the more remote relatives, such as second cousins and great uncles and aunts, from inheriting.[16]

Increasingly, Americans are preparing wills to ensure that their property is disposed of according to their wishes, not according to a scheme determined by the state. A will is a formal document. It must be very carefully drafted, and in most states it must be witnessed by at least two persons. In some jurisdictions it is possible to execute a will without witnesses. Such a document is known as a holographic will, and it must be written by hand by the *testator,* the person whose will it is.

Generally speaking, if you have a valid will you may disinherit any relatives you choose, with the general exception of a husband or wife. Laws in most states allow the spouse to contest the will in court and receive up to one-half of the deceased's property.[17]

Family Law

Family law concerns such things as marriage, divorce, child custody, and children's rights. It is, clearly, a field that touches the lives of a great number of Americans each year.

The conditions necessary for entering into a marriage are spelled out by state law. These laws traditionally cover the minimum age of the parties, required blood tests or physical examinations, mental conditions of the parties, license and fee requirements, and waiting periods.

The termination of a marriage was once very rare. In the early nineteenth century, some states granted divorces only through special acts of the legislature; one state, South Carolina, simply did not allow divorce. Even in the other states, divorces were granted only when one party proved some grounds for divorce. In other words, divorces were available only to "innocent" parties whose spouses were guilty of such things as adultery, desertion, or cruelty.

The twentieth century has seen an enormous change in divorce laws. The movement has been away from restrictive laws and toward a concept known as no-fault divorce. This trend is the result of two factors. First, for many years there has been an increasing demand for divorces. Second, the stigma once attached to divorced persons has all but disappeared.

The no-fault divorce system means that the traditional grounds for divorce have been eliminated. Basically, the parties simply explain that "irreconcilable differences" exist between them and that the marriage is no longer viable. In some states the defendant is not even required to appear in court. In short, the no-fault divorce system has put an end to the adversarial nature of divorce proceedings.

Not so easily solved are some of the other problems that may result from an ended marriage. Child custody battles, disputes over child support payments, and disagreements over visitation rights still find their way into court on a regular basis. In fact, custody disputes are probably more common and more contentious today than before the no-fault divorce. The child's needs come first, and courts no longer automatically assume that this means granting custody to the mother. Fathers are increasingly being granted custody, and it is also now common for courts to grant joint custody to the divorced parents.

The Courts and Other Institutions Concerned with Civil Law

Disagreements are common in the daily lives of Americans. Usually these disagreements can be settled outside the legal system. Sometimes they are so serious, however, that one of the parties sees no alternative but to file a lawsuit. The decision whether to file a suit and the institutions involved in resolving such disputes are examined in this section.

Deciding Whether to Go to Court

Every year thousands of potential civil cases are resolved without a trial because the would-be litigants settle their problems in another way or because the prospective plaintiff decides not to file suit. When faced with a decision to call upon the courts, to try to settle differences, or to simply forget the problem, many people resort to a simple cost-benefit analysis. That is, they weigh the costs associated with a trial against the benefits they are likely to gain if they win. Should a quick calculation indicate that the tangible and intangible costs in terms of such things as time, money, publicity, stress, and anxiety outweigh the benefits, then most people will opt for an alternative to a trial. On the other hand, if the prospective plaintiff perceives the costs to be low enough, then he or she might well file suit against the defendant.

One study of civil litigation patterns relied upon a telephone survey of approximately 1,000 households selected at random in each of the following five federal judicial districts: South Carolina, Eastern Pennsylvania, Eastern Wisconsin, New Mexico, and Central California.[18] The authors of the study tell us that about 40 percent of the households reported a grievance totaling $1,000 or more during the previous three years, and approximately 20 percent reported two or more such grievances.

Figure 7-1 presents a dispute pyramid that indicates what happens to 1,000 typical grievances. Although many grievances are never pursued any further, some result in the plaintiff's initiating a claim. A claim may be accepted, partially accepted, or rejected. Claims that are met with a partial or total rejection move on to become disputes. The odds that a claim will become a dispute are quite high. In the survey under discussion, approximately 63 percent of the claims became disputes (met with partial or total rejection).

The authors of the study next focused on the extent to which disputants hired attorneys and took their cases to court. Overall, they found that attorneys were hired in less than one-fourth of the disputes and that only about 11 percent of the disputants reported taking their dispute to court. This finding should not be seen as minimizing the importance of lawyers and judges, however. Each party's understanding of everyone's legal position is based on the lawyer's advice, which is in turn based on an understanding of previous court decisions.

Disputes that become court cases may go into a variety of courts, depending upon the nature of the dispute and the type of damages being sought. Furthermore,

FIGURE 7-1   Typical Dispute Pyramid for 1,000 Grievances

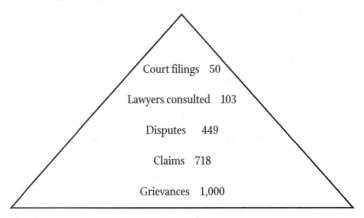

SOURCE: Richard E. Miller and Austin Sarat, "Grievances, Claims, and Disputes: Assessing the Adversary Culture," *Law and Society Review* 15 (1980–1981): 544. Reprinted by permission of the Law and Society Association.

most disputes do not go all the way through the trial process. Instead, they are dropped by the litigants or settled prior to trial.

Specialized Courts

The state court systems are frequently characterized by a number of specialized courts that are set up to handle specific types of civil cases. Domestic relations courts are often established to deal with such matters as divorce, child custody, and child support. In many jurisdictions one also finds probate courts to handle the settlement of estates and the contesting of wills.

Perhaps the best known of the specialized courts are the small-claims courts. These courts have jurisdiction to handle cases when the money being sued for is not above a certain amount. The amount varies by jurisdiction, but the maximum is usually $500 or $1,000. The first small-claims court, established in Cleveland, Ohio, in 1913 had a simplified process, a nominal filing fee, and no requirement that the parties be represented by a lawyer. By 1920 other major cities, including Chicago, Minneapolis, New York, and Philadelphia, as well as the state of Massachusetts, had set up small-claims courts based on the Cleveland model.[19]

Today, small-claims courts allow less complex cases to be resolved more informally than in most other trial courts. Filing fees are still low and the summons to the other party to appear in court can often be served by certified mail. Pleadings are often not required and the use of attorneys is often discouraged.

These courts are not without their problems, however. One complaint prevalent in a number of large cities is that collection agencies use these courts as a relatively cheap and efficient way to collect small debts. New York has enacted legislation to prohibit this use of small-claims courts.[20] And because lawyers are often not used in small-claims court, those who are not familiar with their legal rights and do not know much about preparing their cases may be at a disadvantage, especially when the other party is experienced in such courts.

Administrative Bodies

A number of government agencies have also established administrative bodies with quasi-judicial authority to handle certain types of cases. At the federal level, for example, agencies such as the Federal Trade Commission and the Federal Communications Commission carry out an adjudication of sorts within their respective spheres of authority. As noted in Chapter 2, an appeal of the ruling of one of these agencies may be taken to a federal court of appeals.

At the state level, a common example of an administrative body that aids in the resolution of civil claims is a workers' compensation board. This board determines whether an employee's injury is job related and thus whether the person is entitled to workers' compensation. Many state motor vehicle departments have hearing boards to make determinations about revoking driver's licenses. Another type of administrative board commonly found in the states rules on civil rights matters and cases of alleged discrimination.

The Civil Trial Process

In this section we will describe the steps in resolving a typical civil case. As with criminal cases, most civil cases are resolved by the parties without their actually going to trial; some are resolved after the trial has begun but before it is concluded. We will have more to say about the resolution of civil cases without trial in a later section.

Generally speaking, the adversarial process used in criminal trials is also used in civil trials, with just a few important differences. First, a litigant must have *standing*. This concept, which was discussed in detail in Chapter 4, means simply that the person initiating the suit must have a personal stake in the outcome of the controversy. Otherwise, there is no real controversy between the parties and thus no actual case for the court to decide.

A second major difference is that the standard of proof used in civil cases is a *preponderance of the evidence*, rather than the more stringent beyond-a-reasonable-doubt standard used in criminal cases. "A preponderance of the evidence" is generally taken to mean that there is sufficient evidence to overcome doubt or speculation. It clearly means that less proof is required in civil cases than in criminal cases.

A third major difference is that many of the extensive due process guarantees that a defendant has in a criminal trial do not apply in a civil proceeding. For example, neither party is constitutionally entitled to counsel. The Seventh Amendment does guarantee the right to a jury trial in lawsuits "where the value in controversy shall exceed twenty dollars." Although this amendment has not been made applicable to the states, most states have similar constitutional guarantees.[21]

Filing a Civil Suit

The person initiating the civil suit is known as the *plaintiff*, and the person being sued is the *defendant* or the *respondent*. A civil action is known by the names of the plaintiff and the defendant, such as *Jones v. Miller*. The plaintiff's name appears first. In a typical situation, the plaintiff's attorney pays a fee and files a *complaint* or *petition* with the clerk of the proper court. The complaint states the facts on which the action is based, the damages alleged, and the judgment or relief being sought.

It is useful to understand how a decision is made about which court should actually hear the case. Such a decision involves the concepts of jurisdiction and venue: *jurisdiction* deals with a court's authority to exercise judicial power, and *venue* means the *place* where that power should be exercised.

Jurisdictional requirements are satisfied when the court has legal authority over both the subject matter and the person of the defendant. This means that it is possible for several courts to have jurisdiction over the same case. Suppose, for example, that you are a resident of Dayton, Ohio, and are seriously injured in an automobile accident in Tennessee when the car you are driving is struck from the rear by a car driven by a resident of Kingsport, Tennessee. Total damages to you and your car run about $80,000. A state trial court in Ohio has subject matter jurisdiction, and Ohio can in all likelihood obtain jurisdiction over the defendant. In addition, the state courts of Tennessee probably have jurisdiction. Federal district courts in both Ohio and Tennessee also have jurisdiction because diversity of citizenship exists and the amount in controversy is over $75,000. Assuming that jurisdiction is your only concern, you, as plaintiff, can sue in any of these courts.

Other questions are raised by this hypothetical example: Which of these courts is the proper one to handle the case? Which is the best place for this case to be tried? These questions bring up the problem of venue.

Venue is often a matter of convenience since improper venue can be waived. In other words, if a court has proper jurisdiction, and the parties do not object to venue, then the court can render a valid judgment.

The determination of proper venue may be prescribed by statute, based on avoiding possible prejudice, or it may simply be a matter of convenience. The federal law states that proper venue is the district in which either the plaintiff or defendant resides, or the district where the injury occurred. State venue statutes vary somewhat, but usually provide that where land is involved, proper venue is the county where the land is located. In most other instances venue is the county where the defendant resides.

Venue questions may also be related to the perceived or feared prejudice of either the judge or the prospective jury. Attorneys sometimes object to trials being held in a particular area for this reason and may move for a change of venue. Although this type of objection is perhaps more commonly associated with highly publicized criminal trials, it is also found in civil trials.

Still another ground for change of venue is the doctrine of *forum non conveniens*, which simply means that the place selected for trial is not convenient. In deciding whether to grant the change, the judge considers the relative cost and inconvenience to the parties and to the witnesses.

Once the appropriate court has been determined and the complaint has been filed, the court clerk will attach a copy of the complaint to a summons, which is then issued to the defendant. The summons may be served by personnel from the sheriff's office, a U.S. marshal, or a private process-service agency.

The summons directs the defendant to file a response, known as a pleading, within a certain period of time (usually thirty days). If the defendant does not do so, then he or she may be subject to a default judgment.

These simple actions by the plaintiff, clerk of the court, and a process server set in motion the civil case. What happens next is a flurry of activities that precedes an actual trial and may last for several months. Approximately 75 percent of cases are resolved *without a trial* during this time.[22]

Pretrial Activities

Motions. Once the summons has been served on the defendant, there are a number of motions that can be made by the defense attorney. A *motion to quash* requests that the court void the summons on the ground that it was not properly served. For example, a defendant might contend that the summons was never delivered to her personally as required by the law in her state.

Next we find two types of motions that are meant to clarify or to object to the plaintiff's petition. A *motion to strike* requests that the court excise, or strike, certain parts of the petition because they are prejudicial, improper, or irrelevant. Sometimes the defense attorney will file a *motion to make more definite*. This simply asks the court to require the plaintiff to be more specific about the complaints. For instance, the defendant's attorney may ask that the alleged injuries be described in greater detail.

A fourth type of motion often filed in a civil case is a *motion to dismiss.* This type of motion may argue, for example, that the court lacks jurisdiction. Or it may insist that the plaintiff has not presented a legally sound basis for action against the defendant even if the allegations are true. This action is called a *demurrer* in many state courts.

The Answer. If the complaint survives the judge's rulings on the motions listed above, then the defendant submits an answer to the complaint. The response may contain admissions, denials, defenses, and counterclaims. When an *admission* is contained in an answer, there is no need to prove that fact during the trial. A *denial,* on the other hand, brings up a factual issue to be proven during the trial. A *defense* says that certain facts set forth in the answer may bar the plaintiff from recovery.

The defendant may also create a separate action by seeking relief against the plaintiff. This is known as a *counterclaim.* In other words, if the defendant thinks that a cause of action against the plaintiff arises from the same set of events, then he or she must present the claim to the court in response to the plaintiff's claim. Of course, the plaintiff may want to file a reply to the defendant's answer. In that reply, the plaintiff may admit, deny, or defend against the allegations of fact contained in the answer.

Discovery. Although surprise was once a legitimate trial tactic, our present legal system provides "discovery" procedures that "take the sporting aspect out of litigation and make certain that legal results are based on the true facts of the case—not on the skill of the attorneys."[23] In other words, to prevent surprise at the trial and to encourage settlement, each party is entitled to information in the possession of the other. The term *discovery* "encompasses the methods by which a party or potential party to a lawsuit obtains and preserves information regarding the action."[24]

There are several tools of discovery. A *deposition* is testimony of a witness taken under oath outside the court. The same question-and-answer format as in the courtroom is used. All parties to the case must be notified that the deposition is to be taken so that their attorneys may be present to cross-examine the witness.

A second tool of discovery is known as *interrogatories*, written questions that must be answered under oath. Interrogatories can be submitted only to the parties in the case, not to witnesses. They are very useful in obtaining descriptions of evidence held by the opposing parties in the suit.

The *production of documents* is a third tool used in the discovery process. Often, one of the parties may request an inspection of documents, writings, drawings, graphs, charts, maps, photographs, or other items held by the other party.

Finally, when the physical or mental condition of one of the parties is at issue, the court may order that person to submit to an examination by a physician.

What happens if a party refuses to comply with discovery requests? The judge may compel compliance, deem the facts of the case established, dismiss the cause of action, or enter judgment by default.

The Pretrial Conference. As a result of the discovery phase, surprise is no longer a major factor in civil cases; therefore, a large number of cases are settled without going to trial.[25] In the event the parties do not reach a settlement of their own accord, the judge may try to facilitate such an agreement during a pretrial conference.

Judges call such conferences to discuss the issues in the case informally with the opposing attorneys. The general practice is to allow only the judge and the lawyers to attend the conference, which is normally held in the judge's chambers. As federal district judge J. Skelly Wright put it, "If you bring the lawyer's litigants in there, the clients, well the lawyers will begin to act like thespians, in front of their clients."[26]

The judge and the attorneys use the conference to try to come to some agreement on uncontested factual issues, which are known as *stipulations.* The purpose of stipulations is to make the actual trial more efficient. The attorneys also share with each other a list of witnesses and documents that are a part of each case. In the words of Judge Wright, "We make each side disgorge completely and absolutely everything about its case. There can't possibly be surprise, if the lawyers know what they are doing."[27]

Lawyers and judges may also use the pretrial conference to try to settle the case. In fact, some judges actively work to bring about a settlement so the case does not have to go to trial. That Wright was such a judge is indicated by his own account of the pretrial conference:

After we set the case for trial, we talk about settlement. I say, "Well have you exhausted the possibility of settlement?" Then I say to the plaintiff's lawyer: "You brought this suit, how much is it worth?" And then they begin to talk; and then I actually find out that they have discussed settlement, and they have reached a stand-off with reference to the offer of settle-ment: One having made an offer in X amount, and the other having countered in Y amount. So, if it's a personal injury case, I look at the doctor's reports—just the last paragraph, where they show the extent of injury—I tell them. "This case is worth $20,000 for the settlement," and I tell them why; and I tell them further to go tell their clients that I said so. And the fun-ny thing is, the lawyers in our district want the judge to do that. They want to be able to go back to their clients and have some of the load taken off their shoulders. They say, "This is what I think, but the judge says this." And, by and large, these cases are settled.[28]

The Civil Trial

Selection of Jury. As we noted above, the right to a jury trial in a civil suit in a fed-eral court is guaranteed by the Seventh Amendment. State constitutions likewise provide for such a right. A jury trial may of course be waived, in which case the judge decides the matter. Although the jury traditionally consists of twelve persons, today the number varies. Most of the federal district courts now use juries of fewer than twelve persons in civil cases. A majority of states also authorize smaller juries in some or all civil trials.

As we saw in Chapter 6, jurors must be selected in a random manner from a fair cross-section of the community. A large panel of jurors is called to the courthouse, and when a case is assigned to a court for trial, a smaller group of prospective jurors is sent to a particular courtroom.

Following the voir dire examination, which may include challenges to certain jurors by the attorneys, a jury to hear the particular case will be seated. Recall that lawyers may challenge a prospective juror for cause, in which case the judge must determine whether the person challenged is impartial. Each side may also exercise a certain number of peremptory challenges, that is, excusing a juror without stat-ing any reason. However, the U.S. Supreme Court has recently ruled that the equal protection guarantee of the Fourteenth Amendment prohibits the use of such challenges to disqualify jurors from civil trials because of their race or sex.[29] Peremptory challenges are fixed by statute or court rule and normally range from two to six.

Opening Statements. After the jury has been chosen, the attorneys present their opening statements. The plaintiff's attorney begins. He or she explains to the jury what the case is about and what the plaintiff's side expects to prove. The defen-dant's lawyer can usually choose either to make an opening statement immediately after the plaintiff's attorney finishes or to wait until the plaintiff's case has been completely presented. If the defendant's attorney waits, he or she will present the entire case for the defendant continuously, from opening statement onward. Opening statements are valuable because they outline the case and make it easier for the jury to follow the evidence as it is presented.

Presentation of the Plaintiff's Case. In the normal civil case, the plaintiff's side is first to present and attempt to prove its case to the jury and last to make closing arguments. In presenting the case, the plaintiff's lawyer will normally call witnesses to testify and produce documents or other exhibits.

When a witness is called, he or she will undergo direct examination by the plaintiff's attorney. Then the defendant's attorney will have the opportunity to ask questions or cross-examine the witness. The Arizona Supreme Court recently took steps to help jurors do a better job of making decisions in civil cases. Among other things, the state's highest court voted to allow jurors to pose written questions to witnesses through the judge.[30] Other states are considering implementing Arizona's new practice. Following the cross-examination, the plaintiff's lawyer may conduct a redirect examination, which may then be followed by a second cross-examination by the defendant's lawyer.

Generally speaking, witnesses may testify only about matters they have actually observed; they may not express their opinions. However, there is a very important exception to this general rule: expert witnesses are specifically called upon to give their opinions in matters within their areas of expertise.

In order to qualify as an expert witness, a person must possess substantial knowledge about a particular field. Furthermore, this knowledge must normally be established in open court. Both sides often present experts whose opinions are contradictory. When this happens, the jury must ultimately decide which opinion is the correct one.

Rule 706 of the Federal Rules of Evidence permits federal district judges to appoint experts to assist in deciding cases. A recent study relied on a survey mailed to federal district judges to determine how often they had invoked the rule and appointed an expert. The authors found that only 20 percent of the 431 judges who responded to the survey had made such appointments, and, of that number, less than half had appointed an expert more than once. Slightly over half of the judges (52 percent) mentioned patent cases as suitable for the appointment of experts, followed by product liability (41 percent) and antitrust (33 percent) cases. In telephone interviews with sixty-eight of the judges who responded to the survey, the authors found that the expertise most frequently sought came from the fields of medicine, engineering, and accounting.[31]

When the plaintiff's side has presented all its evidence, the attorney rests the case. It is now the defendant's turn.

Motion for Directed Verdict. After the plaintiff's case has been rested, the defendant will often make a motion for a directed verdict. With the filing of this motion, the defendant is saying that the plaintiff has not proved his or her case and thus should lose. The judge must then decide whether the plaintiff could win at this point if court proceedings were to cease. Should the judge determine that the plaintiff has not presented convincing enough evidence, he or she will sustain the motion and direct the verdict for the defendant. Thus the plaintiff will lose the case.

The motion for a directed verdict is similar to the pretrial motion to dismiss, or demurrer. Essentially, each says "So what?" to the plaintiff—the former in court and the latter before trial.

Presentation of the Defendant's Case. Assuming that the motion for a directed verdict is overruled, the defendant then presents evidence. The defendant's case is presented in the same way as the plaintiff's case. That is, there is direct examination of witnesses and presentation of documents and other exhibits. The plaintiff has the right to cross-examine witnesses. Re-direct and re-cross questions may follow.

Plaintiff's Rebuttal. After the presentation of the defendant's case, the plaintiff may bring forth rebuttal evidence, which is aimed at refuting the defendant's evidence.

Answer to Plaintiff's Rebuttal. During this stage of the process the defendant's lawyer presents evidence to counter the rebuttal evidence. This rebuttal/answer pattern may continue until the evidence has been exhausted.

Closing Arguments. After all the evidence has been presented, the lawyers make closing arguments, or summations, to the jury. The plaintiff's attorney speaks both first and last. That is, he or she both opens the argument and closes it, and the defendant's lawyer argues in between. In this stage of the process each attorney attacks the opponent's evidence for its unreliability and may also attempt to discredit the opponent's witnesses. In doing so, the lawyers often wax eloquent or deliver an emotional appeal to the jury. However, the arguments must be based upon facts supported by the evidence and introduced at the trial. In other words, they must stay within the record.

Instructions to the Jury. Assuming that a jury trial has not been waived, the instructions to the jury follow the conclusion of the closing arguments. The judge informs the jury that it must base its verdict on the evidence presented at the trial. The judge's instructions also inform the jurors about the rules, principles, and standards of the particular legal concept involved. Recall that in civil cases a finding for the plaintiff is based on a preponderance of the evidence. This means that the jurors must weigh the evidence presented during the trial and determine in their minds that the greater weight of the evidence, in merit and in worth, favors the plaintiff.

The Verdict. The jury retires to the seclusion of the jury room to conduct its deliberations. The members must reach a verdict without outside contact. In some instances the deliberations are so long and detailed that the jurors must be provided meals and sleeping accommodations until they can reach a verdict. The verdict, then, represents the jurors' agreement after detailed discussions and analyses of the evidence. It sometimes happens that the jury deliberates in all good faith but cannot reach a verdict. When this occurs, the judge may declare a mistrial. This means that a new trial may have to be conducted.

After the verdict is reached, the jury is conducted back into open court, where it delivers its verdict to the judge. The parties are informed of the verdict. It is then customary for the jury to be polled—the jurors are individually asked by the judge whether they agree with the verdict.

Posttrial Motions. Once the verdict has been reached, a party not satisfied may pursue a variety of tactics. The losing party may file a motion for judgment notwithstanding the verdict. This type of motion is granted when the judge decides that reasonable persons could not have rendered the verdict the jury reached. Put another way, this decision says that the verdict is unreasonable in light of the facts presented at the trial and the legal standards to be applied to the case.

The losing party may also file a motion for a new trial. The usual basis for this motion is that the verdict goes against the weight of the evidence. The judge will grant the motion on this ground if he or she agrees that the evidence presented simply does not support the verdict reached by the jury. A new trial may also be granted for a number of other reasons: excessive damages, grossly inadequate damages, the discovery of new evidence, and errors in the production of evidence, to name a few.

In some cases the losing party also files a motion for relief from judgment. This type of motion may be granted if the judge finds a clerical error in the judgment, discovers some new evidence, or determines that the judgment was induced by fraud.

Judgment and Execution. A verdict in favor of the defendant ends the trial. However, a verdict for the plaintiff requires yet another stage in the process. There is no sentence in a civil case, but there must be a determination of the remedy or damages to be assessed. This determination is called the *judgment*.

In situations where the judgment is for money damages and the defendant does not voluntarily pay the set amount, the plaintiff can ask to have the court clerk issue an order to execute the judgment. The execution is issued to the sheriff and orders the sheriff to seize the defendant's property and sell it at auction to satisfy the judgment. An alternative is to order a lien, which is the legal right to hold property that may be used for the payment of the judgment.

Appeal. If one party feels that an error of law was made during the trial, and if the judge refuses to grant a posttrial motion for a new trial, then the dissatisfied party may appeal to a higher court. Probably the most common grounds for appeal are that the judge allegedly admitted evidence that should have been excluded, refused to admit evidence that should have been introduced, or failed to give proper jury instructions.

An attorney lays the groundwork for an appeal by objecting to the alleged error during the trial. This objection goes into the trial record and becomes a part of the trial transcript, which may be reviewed by an appellate court. The appellate court decision may call for the lower court to enforce its earlier verdict or to hold a new trial.

Alternative Dispute Resolution

As we have noted above, in practice very few persons make use of the entire judicial process. Instead, most cases are settled without resort to a full-fledged trial. In civil cases, a trial may be both slow and expensive. As the statistics on judicial work load presented in Chapters 2 and 3 indicate, most of our courts are hard pressed to keep up with their dockets. In many areas the backlogs are so enormous that it takes three to five years for a case to come to trial.

Many civil suits today are also exceedingly complex. Although the following example is certainly not typical, we think it provides a vivid illustration of a complex case that taxed the resources of thousands of people:

The [Judicial] Conference approved a recommendation that the trial of *In re Washington Public Power Supply Sys. Securities* Litig., No. MDL 551, be videotaped. The case, trial of which is expected to start in Tucson this year, involves more than 125,000 plaintiffs, multi-billion-dollar claims, more than 200 defendants, and the expected presence in the courtroom of more than 100 attorneys. Since the trial will necessarily be protracted and some jurors or counsel may therefore miss a portion of it due to health reasons or emergencies, they will be given access to the videotapes for the times they were absent, but the videotapes will not be made public.[32]

Often, the expense of a trial is enough to discourage potential plaintiffs. There is always the possibility of losing; even if a plaintiff wins, there is always the possibility of a long wait before the judgment is satisfied—if indeed it is ever completely satisfied. In other words, a trial may simply create a new set of problems for the parties concerned. For all these reasons, we have recently begun to hear more and more about alternative methods of resolving disputes.

The alternative dispute resolution (ADR) movement is now well established in the United States. From major corporations to attorneys to individuals, support for alternative ways to resolve disputes has been growing. Corporate America is interested in avoiding prolonged and costly court battles as the only way to settle complex business disputes. In addition, attorneys are more frequently considering alternatives such as mediation and arbitration where there is a need for faster resolution of cases or confidential treatment of certain matters. And individual citizens are increasingly turning to local mediation services for help in resolving family disputes, neighborhood quarrels, and consumer complaints.

Alternative dispute resolution processes are carried out under a variety of models. These models are commonly classified as "private, court-referred, and court-annexed, but the latter two together often are called court-connected."[33] In other words, there are some private ADR processes that function completely independently of the courts. A court-referred ADR process is one that operates outside the court itself, but still has some relationship to the court. In some instances the relationship is rather formal. For example, the court may contract for ADR services with the stipulation that they be provided according to rules and procedures specified by the court. In another jurisdiction the relationship may be less formal. The court might simply refer parties to an ADR provider without monitoring the progress of the case. The court actually administers the ADR process in a court-annexed program. In this scenario, the authority flows from statute or court rules. Case progress is supervised by the court and the individuals providing the ADR service are directly responsible to the court. Depending on the model and the issue, "ADR processes may be voluntary or mandatory; they may be binding or allow appeals from decisions rendered; and they may be consensual, adjudicatory, or some hybrid of the two."[34]

Proponents point to several generally recognized goals that may be accomplished by alternative dispute resolution procedures. Among these are

to provide readily accessible, fair, and appropriate means to resolve disputes; to increase the parties' participation in the dispute resolution process; to reduce litigant costs; to relieve congestion and demands on court resources; and to avoid delay in resolving disputes.[35]

We will now turn our attention to a more detailed examination of some commonly used ADR processes. We begin with mediation.

Mediation. Mediation is a private, confidential process in which an impartial person helps the disputing parties identify and clarify issues of concern and reach their own agreement. The mediator does not act as a judge. Instead, the parties themselves maintain control of the final settlement.

Although almost any type of dispute may be resolved through mediation, it is especially appropriate for situations where there is an ongoing relationship between the disputants. Examples include disputes between family members, neighbors, employers and employees, and landlords and tenants. Mediation is also useful in divorce cases because it changes the procedure from one of confrontation to one of cooperation. Child custody and visitation rights are frequently resolved through mediation as well. And in many areas, personal injury and property claims involving insurance companies are settled through mediation. In short, a wide variety of disputes that once found their way into courts are now being settled through mediation.

Arbitration. The arbitration process is similar to going to court. After listening to both parties in a dispute, an impartial person called an arbitrator decides how the controversy should be resolved. There is no judge or jury. Instead, the arbitrator, selected by both parties, makes the final decision. Arbitrators are drawn from all different types of professional backgrounds and frequently volunteer their time to help people resolve their problems.

Disputants choose arbitration because it saves time and money and is more informal than a court hearing. Most arbitrations are completed in four months or less; this is compared to six months to several years for court decisions.

Arbitration is used privately to resolve a variety of consumer complaints. Examples include disputes over poor automobile repairs, problems with the return of faulty merchandise, and overcharging for services. Arbitration is also being used in court-referred and court-annexed processes to resolve several types of disputes. Business, commercial, and employment disputes are examples of issues courts are now trying to resolve by arbitration.

Neutral Fact-Finding. This is an informal process whereby an agreed-upon neutral party is asked to investigate a dispute. Usually, the dispute involves complex or technical issues. The neutral third party analyzes the disputed facts and issues his or her findings in a nonbinding report or recommendation.

This process can be particularly useful in handling allegations of racial or gender discrimination within a company since such cases often provoke strong emotions and internal dissension. If both parties are employees of the same company, there may be conflicts of interest that would interfere with a supervisor or manager's ability to conduct an impartial investigation of alleged discrimination. In order to avoid the appearance of unfairness, a company may turn to a neutral third party in hopes of reaching a settlement all the employees can respect.

An interesting variation of neutral fact-finding is Early Neutral Evaluation (ENE). Parties using ENE have their attorney present the basic core of the dispute to a neutral evaluator in the presence of the parties. This takes place after the case is filed in court but before discovery of facts is conducted. The neutral evaluator provides a candid assessment of the strengths and weaknesses of the case. Then, if the parties cannot reach a settlement, the neutral evaluator helps narrow the dispute and suggests guidelines for managing the discovery process.

Mini-Trial. In a mini-trial each party presents its position in a trial-like fashion before a panel that consists of selected representatives for both parties and neutral third parties. Every panel has one neutral advisor. Mini-trials are designed to help define the issues and develop a basis for realistic settlement negotiations. The representatives from the two sides present an overview of their positions and arguments to the panel. As a result, each party becomes more knowledgeable about the other party's position. Having heard each side's presentation, the panel, including the advisor, meets to develop a compromise solution. The neutral advisor may also issue an advisory opinion regarding the merits of the case. This advisory opinion is nonbinding unless the parties have agreed beforehand to be bound by it in a written settlement agreement.

The primary benefit of a mini-trial is that both parties have an opportunity to develop solutions. This is enhanced by the fact that each has representation and access to detailed information.

Summary Jury Trial. A summary jury trial involves a court-managed process that takes place after a case has been filed, but before it reaches trial. In a summary jury trial each party presents its arguments to a jury (normally six persons). An overview of each side's argument as well as abbreviated opening and closing arguments are presented. Attorneys are typically given a rather short amount of time (an hour or less) for their presentations. They are limited to the presentation of information that would be admissible at trial. There is no testimony from sworn witnesses and proceedings are generally not recorded. Since the proceedings are nonbinding, rules of procedure and evidence are more flexible than in a normal trial.

The jury hands down an advisory, nonbinding decision based on the arguments presented. In this setting, the verdict is designed to give the attorneys and their clients insight into their cases. It may also suggest a basis for settlement of the dispute. If the dispute is not resolved during or immediately following the summary jury trial proceeding, a pretrial conference is held before the court to discuss settlement.

One of the major advantages of a summary jury trial is the time involved. A summary jury trial is typically concluded in less than a day compared to several days or weeks for full-fledged trials.

Private Judging. This version of alternative dispute resolution makes use of retired judges who offer their services in a variety of ADR processes. In California, for example, a number of retired superior court judges offer their services for a fee. Advocates claim that there are several advantages to using a private judge rather than a sitting court judge. First, the parties are able to select a person with the right qualifications and experience to handle the matter. Second, the parties can be assured that the matter will be handled when first scheduled and not be continued because the court's calendar is too crowded. Finally, the cost can be less than that incurred in full litigation.

Private judging is not without its problems, however. Some critics point to the high fees charged by the retired judges as an area of concern. In a recent California appellate court decision criticizing "rent-a-judge" rulings, it was noted that some of the retired judges may charge $500 or more per hour.[36] In fact, the appellate court pointed out that some sitting judges were leaving the bench for greener pastures.

Summary

In this chapter we focused on the handling of civil cases. We began by looking at some of the important categories of civil law: contracts, torts, property, the law of succession, and family law.

Next we examined the procedure followed in resolving civil cases. Once a complaint has been filed in a civil case, a number of pretrial motions may narrow the scope of the dispute or lead to a settlement of the case. As in criminal cases, most civil cases never actually go to trial. The discovery process is also useful in narrowing the scope of the case and preventing surprises should the case proceed to trial.

The cases that are not settled prior to trial become part of a fairly standard process, which was discussed step by step. Where appropriate, we pointed out the differences between a civil trial and a criminal trial.

Finally, we discussed in some detail the alternative dispute resolution movement, which has been around for quite some time but has only recently captured significant attention from the courts. We described several ADR techniques that are now being used by federal and state courts to solve the problems of increasing caseloads and troublesome backlogs.

NOTES

1. Herbert Jacob, *Justice in America*, 4th ed. (Boston: Little, Brown, 1984), 210.

2. We are indebted to Lawrence M. Friedman, from whom we borrowed the classifications and on whose work our discussion is based. See Friedman, *American Law* (New York: W. W. Norton, 1984), 141–153.

3. All figures were obtained from the Caseload Statistics Project, National Center for State Courts Home Page, July 16, 1997. The National Center for State Court's Internet address is *http://www.ncsc.dni. us/research/csp/tortperc.htm.*

4. See "Product-Liability Awards Increased 44% Last Year," *Wall Street Journal*, June 27, 1997, B17.

5. For example, Republican members of the U.S. House of Representatives made legal reform a part of their famous "Contract With America." See Ed Gillespie and Bob Schellhas, *Contract With America* (New York: Time Books, 1994), 143–155.

6. These figures were obtained from the American Tort Reform Association's home page on July 16, 1997. The Internet address is *http://www.atra.org/atra/atra.htm.*

7. William T. Schantz, *The American Legal Environment* (St. Paul, Minn.: West, 1976), 565.

8. See L. Lander, *Defective Medicine* (New York: Farrar, Straus & Giroux, 1978), chap. 1.

9. Mitchell S. G. Klein, *Law, Courts, and Policy* (Englewood Cliffs, N.J.: Prentice-Hall, 1984), 196.

10. See S. Law and S. Polan, *Pain and Profit: The Politics of Malpractice* (New York: Harper & Row, 1978), 7, 8.

11. Friedman, *American Law*, 146.

12. See Charles A. Beard, *An Economic Interpretation of the Constitution of the United States* (New York: Macmillan, 1913).

13. Klein, *Law, Courts, and Policy*, 183.

14. See *Village of Euclid v. Ambler Realty Co.*, 272 U.S. 365 (1926).

15. See *Nectow v. City of Cambridge*, 277 U.S. 188 (1928).

16. See Schantz, *The American Legal Environment*, 291.

17. Ibid., 292.

18. Richard E. Miller and Austin Sarat, "Grievances, Claims, and Disputes: Assessing the Adversary Culture," *Law and Society Review* 15 (1980–1981): 525–566.

19. See Howard Abadinsky, *Law and Justice*, 2d ed. (Chicago: Nelson-Hall, 1991), 273; and Christine B. Harrington, *Shadow Justice: The Ideology and Institutionalization of Alternatives to Court* (Westport, Conn.: Greenwood, 1985).

20. See Abadinsky, *Law and Justice*, 273.

21. See Jack H. Friedenthal, Mary Kay Kane, and Arthur R. Miller, *Civil Procedure* (St. Paul, Minn.: West, 1985).

22. See Abadinsky, *Law and Justice*, 268.

23. Schantz, *The American Legal Environment*, 169.

24. Friedenthal, Kane, and Miller, *Civil Procedure*, 380.

25. See Kenneth M. Holland, "The Federal Rules of Civil Procedure," *Law and Policy Quarterly* 3 (1981): 212.

26. J. Skelly Wright, "The Pretrial Conference," in *American Court Systems: Readings in Judicial Process and Behavior,* ed. Sheldon Goldman and Austin Sarat (San Francisco: Freeman, 1978), 120.

27. Ibid.

28. Ibid.

29. See *Edmondson v. Leesville Concrete Co.,* 500 U.S. 614 (1991) and *J.E.B. v. Alabama Ex Rel. T.B.,* 511 U.S. 127 (1994), respectively. Interestingly, the Supreme Court declined to hear a case from Minnesota that raised the question of whether the same principle should be extended to religion. See *New York Times,* July 3, 1994, 4E.

30. See Margaret A. Jacobs, "Arizona High Court Alters Jury Practices," *Wall Street Journal,* November 2, 1995, B4.

31. See Joe S. Cecil and Thomas E. Willging, "The Use of Court-Appointed Experts in Federal Courts," *Judicature* 78 (1994): 41–42.

32. See *The Third Branch* 20 (April 1988): 2.

33. Susan L. Keilitz, "Alternative Dispute Resolution in the Courts," in *Handbook of Court Administration and Management,* ed. Steven W. Hays and Cole Blease Graham, Jr. (New York: Marcel Dekker, 1993), 384.

34. Ibid.

35. Ibid.

36. "Judge Slams Rent-a-Judge Rulings," *The National Law Journal,* November 11, 1996, A8. The case is *McMillan v. Superior Court,* B105356 (1996).

SUGGESTED READINGS

Alfini, James J. "Alternative Dispute Resolution and the Courts: An Introduction." *Judicature* (1986): 252. Provides a good introduction to arbitration and mediation.

Friedenthal, Jack H., Mary Kay Kane, and Arthur R. Miller. *Civil Procedure.* St. Paul, Minn.: West, 1985. The authors discuss the rules relating to civil procedures in the courts.

Friedman, Lawrence. *American Law.* New York: W. W. Norton, 1984. Offers a good introduction to the nature and substance of civil law in the United States.

Harrington, Christine B. *Shadow Justice: The Ideology and Institutionalization of Alternatives to Court.* Westport, Conn.: Greenwood, 1985. The book focuses on the various alternatives available to people in resolving disputes.

Jacob, Herbert. *Silent Revolution: The Transformation of Divorce Law in the United States.* Chicago: University of Chicago Press, 1988. A detailed account of reforms in divorce law in the United States.

Kritzer, Herbert M. *The Justice Broker: Lawyers and Ordinary Litigation.* New York: Oxford University Press, 1990. A book that focuses on civil proceedings in the United States.

Miller, Richard E., and Austin Sarat. "Grievances, Claims, and Disputes: Assessing the Adversary Culture." *Law and Society Review* 15 (1980–1981): 525–566. A study of the evolution of civil cases from grievances to court cases.

Ostrom, Brian J., and Neal B. Kauder. *Examining the Work of State Courts, 1993: A National Perspective from the Court Statistics Project.* Williamsburg, Va.: National Center for State Courts, 1995. In addition to a general analysis of state court caseloads, the book's specific focus is on tort litigation and domestic violence cases.

CHAPTER 8

Federal Judges

President Clinton's appointments of women and minorities to the federal bench far surpass his three predecessors. Judge Vanessa Gilmore of Houston smiles during a round of applause after her swearing in.

IN PREVIOUS CHAPTERS WE EXPLORED the history, organization, and workload of the federal judiciary and identified those staff and support agencies that make the wheels of American justice spin with at least a modicum of efficiency. It is now time to focus upon the main actors in the federal system—the men and women who serve as judges and justices.

As we take an analytical look at the black-robed decision makers to whom most Americans still look with such reverence, we will keep several questions in mind: What characteristics do these people have that distinguish them from the rest of the citizenry? What are the qualifications—both formal and informal—for appointment to the bench? How are the judges selected and who are the participants in the process? Is there a policy link between the citizenry, the appointment process, and the subsequent decisions of the jurists? How are they socialized into their judicial roles—that is, how do judges learn to be judges? Finally, we shall say a few words about how and when judges stop being judges—the retirement, discipline, and removal of jurists.

Background Characteristics of Federal Judges

In the United States we still cling eagerly to the log cabin-to-White House myth of attaining high public office—that is, to the notion that someone born in the humblest of circumstances (like Abraham Lincoln) may one day grow up to be the president of the United States, or at least a U.S. judge. As with most myths, there is a kernel of truth to it. In principle virtually anyone can become a prominent public official, and there are in fact a few well-known examples of people who came from poor backgrounds yet climbed to the pinnacle of power. One example is former justice Thurgood Marshall, the great-grandson of a slave and the son of a Pullman car steward. Another is former chief justice Warren Burger, whose father earned his daily bread as a traveling salesman and as a railroad car inspector. More typical, however, is the most recent Supreme Court appointee, Stephen Breyer. A multimillionaire whose wife is from a family of British nobility, the main criticism levelled against him prior to his appointment was that he was overinvested in the wealthy insurance firm of Lloyds of London. For a long time uncontested data have clearly shown that America's federal judges, like other public officials and the captains of commerce and industry, come from a very narrow stratum of American society. As we shall momentarily see, although potential judges are not necessarily the sons and daughters of millionaires, it is at least helpful if they come from a special segment of the nation's middle and upper-middle classes.

District Judges

Before we can offer some generalizations about who U.S. trial judges are and where they come from, we need some facts and figures. Background data for all federal district judges for the past 200 years have never been collected, but about judges who have served in recent decades we know a good deal. Table 8-1 profiles some key characteristics of trial jurists appointed by Presidents Carter, Reagan, Bush, and Clinton.

In terms of their primary occupation before assuming the federal bench, a plurality had been judges at the state or local level. About 37 percent of Reagan's judges had had extensive judicial experience, and almost 45 percent of Carter's judicial team had previously worn the black robe. The next largest blocs were employed either in the political or governmental realms or in moderate- to large-sized law

TABLE 8-1 Background Characteristics of Presidents' District Court Appointees, 1977–1997

Characteristic	Clinton	Bush	Reagan	Carter
Occupation				
Politics/government	10.7%	10.8%	13.4%	5.0%
Judiciary	44.4	41.9	36.9	44.6
Large law firm				
100+ members	8.3	10.8	6.2	2.0
50–99	5.3	7.4	4.8	6.0
25–49	3.6	7.4	6.9	6.0
Moderate size firm				
10–24 members	8.3	8.8	10.0	9.4
5–9	8.3	6.1	9.0	10.4
Small firm				
2–4	5.3	3.4	7.2	10.9
solo	2.4	1.4	2.8	2.5
Professor of law	2.4	0.7	2.1	3.0
Other	1.2	1.4	0.7	0.5
Experience				
Judicial	49.7	46.6	46.2	54.0
Prosecutorial	37.9	39.2	44.1	38.1
Neither	31.4	31.8	28.6	30.7
Undergraduate education				
Public	44.4	44.6	36.6	56.4
Private	40.8	41.2	49.7	33.7
Ivy League	14.8	14.2	13.8	9.9
Law school education				
Public	42.6	52.7	42.4	50.5
Private	37.3	33.1	45.9	32.7
Ivy League	20.1	14.2	11.7	16.8
Gender				
Male	69.8	80.4	91.7	85.6
Female	30.2	19.6	8.3	14.4
Ethnicity/race				
White	72.2	89.2	92.4	78.7
African American	19.5	6.8	2.1	13.9
Hispanic	6.5	4.0	4.8	6.9
Asian	1.2	—	0.7	0.5
Native American	0.6	—	—	—
Percentage white male	47.3	73.0	84.8	68.3
ABA rating				
Exceptionally well qualified/well qualified	63.9	57.4	53.5	51.0
Qualified	34.3	42.6	46.6	47.5
Not qualified	1.8	—	—	1.5

Table continues on next page

TABLE 8-1   Background Characteristics of Presidents' District Court Appointees, 1977–1997 *(continued)*

Characteristic	Clinton	Bush	Reagan	Carter
Political identification				
Democrat	90.5	5.4	4.8	90.6
Republican	2.4	88.5	91.7	4.5
Other	0.6	—	—	—
None	6.5	6.1	3.4	5.0
Past party activism	53.9	60.8	59.0	60.9
Net worth				
Less than $200,000	17.2	10.1	17.6	35.8[a]
$200–499,999	22.5	31.1	37.6	41.2
$500–999,999	28.4	26.4	21.7	18.9
$1+ million	32.0	32.4	23.1	4.0
Average age at nomination	48.7	48.1	48.7	49.6
Total number of appointees	169	148	290	202

SOURCE: Sheldon Goldman and Elliot Slotnick, "Clinton's First Term Judiciary: Many Bridges to Cross," *Judicature* 80 (1997): 261.

[a]These figures are for appointees confirmed by the 96th Congress for all but six Carter district court appointees (for whom no data were available).

firms. Those working in small law firms or as professors of law made up the smallest bloc.

Their educational background reveals something of their elite nature. All obviously graduated from college; about half attended either the costly Ivy League schools or other private universities to receive their undergraduate and law degrees. Most adult Americans have never gone to college, and of those who have, only a tiny portion could meet the admission requirements—not to mention the expense—of most private or Ivy League schools.

Almost half of the district judges had had some experience on the bench, and well over a third had served at one time as a public prosecutor. This recent phenomenon has caused some court observers to conclude that "we may be evolving toward the European system of a career judiciary."[1]

Judges differ in yet another way from the population as a whole. Among trial judges—and all U.S. judges for that matter—there is a strong tendency toward "occupational heredity"—that is, for judges to come from families with a tradition of judicial and public service.[2] One of former president Reagan's trial court appointees, Howell Cobb of Beaumont, Texas, is typical of this phenomenon. The nominee's hometown paper said of him:

The appointee is the fourth generation of a family of lawyers and judges. His great-grandfather, a Confederate officer, served as secretary of the Treasury under President James Buchanan and was governor of Georgia and speaker of the U.S. House of Representatives. Cobb's grandfather was a justice on the Georgia Supreme Court, and his father was a circuit judge in Georgia. Cobb's son, a lawyer in El Paso, also follows tradition. "Most trial lawyers aspire to a seat on the bench," Cobb said.[3]

Traditionally being a woman and/or a racial minority has not been an asset if one coveted a judicial robe. Although the United States is about 51 percent female, judging has been almost exclusively a man's business. Until the Carter presidency less than 2 percent of the lower judiciary was female, and even with conscious effort to change this phenomenon, only 14.4 percent of Carter's district judges were women. The same holds for racial minorities, whose numbers on the trial bench have always been small, not only in absolute numbers but also in comparison with figures for the overall population. Until the present time only Jimmy Carter, who made affirmative action a cornerstone of his presidency, had appointed a significant number of non-Anglos to the federal bench—over 21 percent. Under the Clinton administration, however, a complete about-face has taken place. At the end of his first term the official count reveals that *a majority*—some 53 percent—of his judicial appointees have been either women or minorities. This figure (which represents both district and appeals court judges) is compared with percentages of only 28, 14, and 34 for Presidents Bush, Reagan, and Carter, respectively. The impact of Clinton's revolutionary appointment strategy on the policy output of the federal courts is currently under study by judicial scholars.

The American Bar Association (ABA) ratings reveal that few make it to the federal bench who are not rated as "qualified" by this self-appointed evaluator of judicial fitness. The difference in quality between the Republican and Democratic appointees is trivial; Clinton's appointees have received comparatively strong ratings.

More than nine out of ten district judges have been of the same political party as the appointing president, and until the Clinton administration about 60 percent had had a record of active partisanship. The Clinton cohort so far has contained fewer active partisans—about 54 percent.

That district judge nominees constitute an elite group is clearly revealed in the statistics for their net worth at the time of their appointment to the bench. Although these figures do not prove that all potential jurists were wealthy, they do suggest that few candidates for the bench had to ponder the source of their next meal. The Carter cohort seems to have been the least wealthy when they assumed the bench, whereas a third of Bush and Clinton's judicial nominees were millionaires at the time they took the judicial oath.

As for age, the typical judge has been forty-nine at the time of appointment. Age variations from one presidency to another have been small, and the only trend worth noting is that over time there has been a slight tendency to appoint judges of a somewhat younger age. This is potentially significant in that the younger the president's judicial cohort, the longer they would presumably remain on the bench, thereby extending the impact of the appointing president's judicial legacy.

Appeals Court Judges

Because the statistics and percentages of the appellate court appointees of the four presidents from Carter through Clinton are quite similar to those for the trial judges, we shall offer some commentary only on those figures that suggest a difference between the two sets of judges (see Table 8-2).

Appeals judges are much more likely to have previous judicial experience than their counterparts on the trial court bench. Also, Presidents Carter, Reagan, and Clinton were more apt to look to the ranks of law school professors for their appeals court appointments than was President Bush.

If the trend toward seeking out private school and Ivy League graduates was strong for trial judge appointments, it is even more pronounced for those selected for seats on the appeals courts. The only exception is for the Clinton appellate cohort. Only 48 percent of the Clinton jurists gained admittance to such schools, while 70 percent of Bush judges attended elite undergraduate institutions. Still, compared with the population at large or even U.S. district judges, appellate court jurists appear to be solid members of America's social and economic elite.

In terms of opposite-party selections, there is little difference between trial and appellate court appointments. However, there is a slight tendency for appeals judges to be more active in their respective parties than their colleagues on the trial bench. The Clinton cohort is an exception. His appellate judges are even less politically active than his trial jurists.

The Clinton initiative to make the bench more accurately reflect U.S. gender and racial demographics is evident in the ranks of the trial judges as well. Almost a third of his jurists are women. This is compared to just 19, 5, and 20 percent of the Bush, Reagan, and Carter judges, respectively. And the Clinton team is composed of more African Americans, Hispanics, and Asians than the cohorts of any other president. When the gender and race variables are combined, the contrast between

TABLE 8-2   Background Characteristics of Presidents' Appeals Court Appointees, 1977–1997

Characteristic	Clinton	Bush	Reagan	Carter
Occupation				
Politics/government	3.4%	10.8%	6.4%	5.4%
Judiciary	58.6	59.5	55.1	46.4
Large law firm				
100+ members	13.8	8.1	5.1	1.8
50–99	—	8.1	2.6	5.4
25–49	3.4	—	6.4	3.6
Moderate size firm				
10–24 members	3.4	8.1	3.9	14.3
5–9	6.9	2.7	5.1	1.8
Small firm				
2–4	—	—	1.3	3.6
solo	—	—	—	1.8
Professor of law	10.3	2.7	12.8	14.3
Other	—	—	1.3	1.8
Experience				
Judicial	69.0	62.2	60.3	53.6
Prosecutorial	37.9	29.7	28.2	32.1
Neither	20.7	32.4	34.6	39.3
Undergraduate education				
Public	51.7	29.7	24.4	30.4
Private	27.6	59.5	51.3	51.8
Ivy League	20.7	10.8	24.4	17.9
Law school education				
Public	41.4	29.7	41.0	39.3
Private	31.0	40.5	35.9	19.6
Ivy League	27.6	29.7	23.1	41.1
Gender				
Male	69.0	81.1	94.9	80.4
Female	31.0	18.9	5.1	19.6
Ethnicity/race				
White	72.4	89.2	97.4	78.6
African American	13.8	5.4	1.3	16.1
Hispanic	10.3	5.4	1.3	3.6
Asian	3.4	—	—	1.8
Percentage white male	44.8	70.3	92.3	60.7
ABA rating				
Exceptionally well qualified/				
well qualified	82.8	64.9	59.0	75.0
Qualified	17.2	35.1	41.0	25.0

Table continues on next page

TABLE 8-2 Background Characteristics of Presidents' Appeals Court Appointees, 1977–1997 *(continued)*

Characteristic	Clinton	Bush	Reagan	Carter
Political identification				
Democrat	86.2	5.4	—	82.1
Republican	3.4	89.2	96.2	7.1
Other	—	—	1.3	—
None	10.3	5.4	2.6	10.7
Past party activism	48.3	70.3	65.4	73.2
Net worth				
Less than $200,000	6.9	5.4	15.6[a]	33.3[b]
$200–499,999	10.3	29.7	32.5	38.5
$500–999,999	44.8	21.6	33.8	17.9
$1+ million	37.9	43.2	18.2	10.3
Average age at nomination	51.3	48.7	50.0	51.8
Total number of appointees	29	37	78	56

SOURCE: Sheldon Goldman and Elliot Slotnick, "Clinton's First Term Judiciary: Many Bridges to Cross," *Judicature* 80 (1997): 269.

[a]Net worth was unavailable for one appointee.

[b]Net worth only for Carter appointees confirmed by the 96th Congress with the exception of five appointees for whom net worth was unavailable.

the Clinton team and other presidential cohorts is even more vivid. Only 49 percent of Clinton's appellate judges are white males. This was true of 70, 92, and 61 percent of the judges appointed by Bush, Reagan, and Carter, respectively.

Finally, candidates for the appeals courts seem to be as blessed with financial resources as their brothers and sisters selected to preside over the trial courts. For example, about 43 percent of Bush's nominees to the appellate court bench and 38 percent of Clinton's nominees had a net worth of over $1 million at the time of their appointment.

Supreme Court Justices

Since 1789, 106 men and 2 women have sat on the bench of America's highest judicial tribunal. If we have suggested that judges of the trial and appeals courts have been culled primarily from America's cultural elite, then members of the U.S. Supreme Court are truly the crème de la crème. Let's take a look at the Court's collective portrait.

Although perhaps 10 percent of the justices were of essentially humble origin, the remainder "were not only from families in comfortable economic circumstances, but were chosen overwhelmingly from the socially prestigious and politically influential gentry class in the late 18th and early 19th century, or the professionalized upper class thereafter."[4] A majority of the justices came from politically active families, and about a third were related to jurists and closely connected with families with a tradition of judicial service. Thus the justices were reared in far from commonplace American families.

Until the 1960s the High Court had been all white and all male, but in 1967 President Johnson appointed Thurgood Marshall as the first black member of the Court; when Marshall retired in 1991, President Bush replaced him with Clarence Thomas (a man who shared Marshall's ethnic heritage, though not his liberal views). In 1981 the gender barrier was broken when President Reagan named Sandra Day O'Connor to the Court, and thirteen years later she was joined by Ruth Ginsburg. In terms of religious background, the membership of the Court has been overwhelmingly Protestant, and most of these have been affiliated with the more prestigious denominations (such as the Episcopal, Presbyterian, and Unitarian churches). Thus in terms of ethnicity, gender, and religious preference, the Court is by no means a cross-section of American society.

As for the nonpolitical occupations of the justices, all 108 had legal training and all had practiced law at some stage in their careers. An inordinate number had served as corporation attorneys before their appointments. Only 22 percent had state or federal judicial experience *immediately* prior to their appointments, although more than half had served on the bench at some time before their nomination to the Supreme Court. As with their colleagues in the lower federal judiciary, the justices were much more likely to have been politically active than the average American, and virtually all shared many of the ideological and political orientations of their appointing president.

An Appraisal of the Statistics

Several conclusions are readily apparent from the summary data we have just presented. First, it is clear that federal judges in the United States are an elite within an elite. They come from upper- or upper-middle-class families that are politically active and that have a tradition of public and, often, judicial service. Is the narrow judicial selection process the result of pure chance? Has there been a sinister conspiracy for the past two centuries to keep women, blacks, Roman Catholics, the poor, and so on out of the U.S. judiciary, or are the causes more subtle and complex? We think the evidence points to the latter explanation. Let us look at a few variables indicative of the selection route to the federal bench—race, family background, and gender.

Legislation has never been passed that forbade non-Anglos to wear the black robe. But there have been laws, traditions, and unwritten codes that have kept them from entering the better law schools, from working in the more prestigious law firms and corporations, and from making the kind of social and political connections that may lead to nomination to judicial office. Likewise, no statutes have excluded the children of the poor from consideration for a seat on the bench. But few youngsters from impoverished homes can afford expensive, high-quality colleges and law schools that would give them the training and the contacts they would need. Traditionally, too, many more young men than young women were encouraged to apply to law school. For instance, Supreme Court Justice Ruth Ginsburg remembers that while she was at Harvard Law School during the 1950s, the dean held a reception for the nine women in her class of more than 500. "After dinner," she recalled, "the dean asked each of us to explain what we were doing at the law school occupying a seat that could have been filled by a man. When my turn came, I wished I could have pushed a button and vanished through a trapdoor."[5] The process of exclusion, then, has not been part of a conscious, organized conspiracy; rather, it has been the inevitable consequence of more subtle social and economic forces in our society.

Another observation about the background profile of our federal judges is worthy of mention. Because they tend to come from the same kinds of families, to go to the same universities and law schools, and to belong to churches, clubs, and societies that uphold similar values, federal judges generally are much more alike than they are different. There may be Democrats and Republicans, former defense attorneys and former prosecutors on the bench, but to a significant degree virtually all play the game by the same rules. What one scholar has said about the recruitment process for the appeals courts is true for federal judgeships in general:

Broadly speaking [the recruitment process] tends to reward supporters of the presidential party; weed out incompetents, mavericks, and ideological extremists; and ensure substantial professional and political experience among those who wield federal appellate power. Forged thereby are continuous links between judges and their political and professional surroundings. Restricted thereby are the types of persons inducted into Courts of Appeals. The multiple filters through which recruits must pass put a premium on moderate, middle-class, and political lawyers, successful people advantaged in life.[6]

The fact that the recruitment process produces a corps of jurists who agree on how the judicial game is to be played is the primary reason why the loosely organized judicial hierarchy, outlined in Chapter 2, does not come flying apart. It is a key explanation for the predictability of most judicial decisions, a subject that we shall explore in later chapters. The judicial machinery runs as smoothly and consistently as it does not because of outside watchdogs or elaborate enforcement mechanisms but because the principal participants largely share the same values and orientations and are working to further similar goals.

Formal and Informal Qualifications of Federal Judges

Formal Qualifications

Students often torture one another with horror stories of the hurdles to be overcome in order to achieve success in a particular profession. Would-be medical students are awed by the high grade-point averages and aptitude scores required for admission to medical schools; potential university professors shrink at the thought of the many years of work necessary to obtain a Ph.D., only to face the publish-or-perish requirements for a tenured position. It would be logical, then, to assume that the formal requirements for becoming a federal judge—and surely a Supreme Court justice—must be formidable indeed. Not so. There are in fact no constitutional or statutory qualifications for serving on the Supreme Court or the lower federal courts. The Constitution merely indicates that "the judicial Power of the United States, shall be vested in one supreme Court" as well as in any lower federal courts that Congress may establish (Article III, Section 1) and that the president "by and with the Advice and Consent of the Senate, shall appoint . . . Judges of the supreme Court" (Article II, Section 2). Congress has applied the same selection procedure to the appeals and the trial courts. There are no exams to pass, no minimum age requirement, no stipulation that judges be native-born citizens or legal residents, nor is there even a requirement that judges have a law degree. Despite the absence of formal qualifications for a federal judgeship, there are nevertheless some rather well-defined informal requirements.

Informal Requirements

It is possible to identify at least four vital although informal factors that determine who sits on the federal bench in America: professional competence, political qualifications, self-selection, and the element of pure luck.

Professional Competence. Although candidates for U.S. judicial posts do not have to be attorneys—let alone prominent ones—it has been the custom to appoint lawyers who have distinguished themselves professionally—or at least not to appoint those obviously without merit. *Merit* may mean no more than an association with a prestigious law firm, publication of a few law review articles, or respect among fellow attorneys; a potential judge need not necessarily be an outstanding legal scholar. Nevertheless, one of the unwritten codes is that a judicial appointment is different from run-of-the-mill patronage. Thus although the political rules may allow a president to reward an old ally with a seat on the bench, even here tradition has created an expectation that the would-be judge have some reputation for professional competence, the more so as the judgeship in question goes from the trial court to the appeals court to the Supreme Court level.

A modern-day example of the unwritten rule that potential judges be more than just warm bodies with a law degree is found in President Nixon's nomination of G. Harrold Carswell to the Supreme Court in 1970. After investigations by the press and the Senate Judiciary Committee revealed that Carswell's record was unimpressive at best, his nomination began to stall on the floor of the Senate. To his aid came the well-meaning senator Roman Hruska of Nebraska, who stated in part: "Even if Carswell were mediocre, there are a lot of mediocre judges and people and lawyers. They are entitled to a little representation, aren't they, and a little chance? We can't have all Brandeises, and Frankfurters, and Cardozos and stuff like that there."[7] With such support Carswell must have wondered why he needed any detractors. In any case the acknowledgment by a friendly senator that the Supreme Court nominee was "mediocre" probably did more than anything else to prompt the Senate to reject Carswell. Although tradition may allow judgeships to be political payoffs and may not require eminence in the nominee, candidates for federal judicial posts are expected to meet a reasonable level of professional competence.

Political Qualifications. When at least 90 percent of all federal judicial nominees are of the same political party as the appointing president, it must strike even the most casual observer that there are certain political requirements for a seat on the bench. The fact that well over half of all federal judges were "politically active" before their appointments—in comparison with a 10 percent figure for the total population—is further evidence of this phenomenon. What are the political criteria? In some cases a judgeship may be a reward for major service to the party in power or to the president or a senator. For example, when federal judge Peirson Hall (of the Central District of California) was asked how important politics was to his appointment, he gave this candid reply:

I worked hard for Franklin Roosevelt in the days when California had no Democratic Party to speak of. In 1939 I began running for the Senate, and the party convinced me it would be best if there wasn't a contest for the Democratic nomination. So I withdrew and campaigned for Martin Downey. They gave me this judgeship as sort of a consolation prize—and one, I might add, that I have enjoyed.[8]

Although examples like this are not uncommon, it would be a mistake to think of federal judgeships merely as political plums handed out to the party faithful. As often as not, a seat on the bench goes to a reasonably active or visible member of the party in power but not necessarily to someone who has made party service the central focus of a lifetime.

Political activity that might lead to a judgeship includes service as chair of a state or local party organization, an unsuccessful race for public office, or financial backing for partisan causes.

The reason most nominees for judicial office must have some record of political activity is twofold. First, to some degree judgeships are still considered part of the political patronage system; those who have served the party are more likely to be rewarded with a federal post than those who have not paid their dues. Second, even if a judgeship is not given as a direct political payoff, some political activity on the part of a would-be judge is often necessary, because otherwise the candidate would simply not be visible to the president or senator(s) or local party leaders who send forth the names of candidates. If the judicial power brokers have never heard of a particular lawyer because that attorney has no political profile, his or her name will not come to mind when a vacancy occurs on the bench.

Self-Selection. For those seeking the presidency or running for Congress, shyness doesn't pay. One needs to declare one's candidacy, meet a formal filing deadline, and spend considerable time and money to advertise one's qualifications. Although Americans profess to admire modesty and humility in their leaders, *successful* candidates for elected office do well not to overindulge these virtues. With the judiciary, however, the informal rules of the game are a bit different. Many would consider it undignified and "lacking in judicial temperament" for someone to announce publicly a desire for a federal judgeship—much less to campaign openly for such an appointment.

We know, however, that some would-be jurists orchestrate discreet campaigns on their own behalf or at least pass the word that they are available for judicial service. Few will admit to seeking an appointment actively, but credible anecdotes suggest that attorneys often position themselves in such a way that their names will come up when the powers-that-be have a vacant seat to fill. In 1993, for instance, the *Wall Street Journal* carried a story about a vacancy on the U.S. Court of Appeals for the Federal Circuit, a court that deals with an inordinate number of patent appeals and one that is followed closely by business interests. The article noted that "a lively battle" had broken out among business groups over who should occupy the vacant seat and that

even major corporations have taken the highly unusual step of weighing in for their favored candidates, while some other candidates have taken to fairly aggressive self-promotion. . . . Among those pushing for such a judge [one committed to science and technology] is John B. Pegram. His preferred choice: himself. In the past few months, Mr. Pegram . . . has written to the White House, offering himself up as a candidate, and made contact with a number of members of Congress, trumpeting his credentials.[9]

At judicial swearing-in ceremonies it is often said that "the judgeship sought the man (or woman) rather than vice versa," and surely this does happen. But sometimes the judgeship does its seeking with a little nudge from the would-be jurist.

The Element of Luck. If all that were involved in the picking of a Supreme Court justice or a lower-court judge were professional and political criteria, the appointment process would be much easier to explain and predict. If, for instance, one wanted to know who was going to be appointed to a vacancy on the Sixth Circuit bench, one would need only to identify the person in the Sixth Circuit to whom the party was most indebted and who had a reputation for legal competence. The problem is that there would be hundreds of capable attorneys in the Sixth Circuit to whom the prevailing party owed much. Why should one of them be selected and several hundred not? Until judicial scholarship becomes more of a science and less of an art, we cannot make accurate predictions about who will wear the black robe; there are just too many variables and too many participants in the selection process. Let us look at the example of President Truman's appointment of Carroll O. Switzer to fill a vacant judgeship in 1949.

The story begins in 1948 when Truman was seeking a full term as president. The campaign had not gone well from the start. Even the party faithful could barely muster a faint cheer when Truman proclaimed to sparse crowds, "We're gonna win this election and we're gonna make those Republicans like it. Just you wait 'n' see." Almost everyone predicted Truman would lose, and lose badly. Then one morning his campaign train stopped in the little town of Dexter, Iowa. An unexpectedly large number of farmers had put aside their milking chores and the fall corn harvest to see the feisty little man from Missouri "give those Republicans hell." Truman picked up a real sense of enthusiasm among the cheering crowd, and for the first time in the campaign he smelled victory.

On the campaign platform with Truman that morning was Carroll Switzer, a bright young Des Moines attorney who was the (unsuccessful) Democratic candidate for Iowa governor that year. No evidence exists that Truman met Switzer before or after that one propitious day. But when a vacancy occurred on the U.S. bench a year later, Truman's mind jumped like a spring to the name of his lucky horseshoe, Carroll Switzer. A longtime administrative assistant to an Iowa senator related the story as follows:

I am sure that this day at Dexter was the first time President Truman and his staff were sure he could win—later proved right. I am sure that he recalled that day favorably when an appointment . . . came up in the Iowa judgeship. . . . Every time the Iowa judgeship came up, Truman would hear of no one but Switzer. Truman would say "That guy Switzer backed me when everyone else was running away, and, by God, I'm going to see that he gets a judgeship."[10]

That morning in Dexter was Switzer's lucky day. Although he had the professional and political credentials for a judicial post, no one could have foreseen that he would happen to appear with Truman the day the national winds of political fortune began to blow in the president's favor. Had it been any other day, Switzer might never have been more than just a bright attorney from Des Moines.

This account illustrates the point that there is a good measure of happenstance in virtually all judicial appointments. Being a member of the right party at the right time or being visible to the power brokers at a lucky moment often has as much to do with becoming a judge as the length and sparkle of one's professional résumé.

The Federal Selection Process and Its Participants

The skeletal framework of judicial selection is the same for all federal judges, although the roles of the participants vary depending on what level of the U.S. judiciary we are considering. All nominations are made by the president after due consultation with the White House staff, the attorney general's office, certain senators, and other politicos; it has been customary for the FBI to perform a routine security check. After the nomination is announced to the public, various interest groups that believe they have a stake in the appointment may lobby for or against the candidate. Also, the candidate's qualifications will be evaluated by a committee of the American Bar Association. The candidate's name is then sent to the Senate Judiciary Committee, which conducts an investigation of the nominee's fitness for the post. If the committee's vote is favorable, the nomination is sent to the floor of the Senate, where it is either approved or rejected by a simple majority vote. In the next sections we will take a close look at the role of the various participants in the selection process.

The President

Technically, the chief executive nominates all judicial candidates, but history has shown that the president manifests greater personal involvement in appointments to the Supreme Court than to the lower courts. This is so for two major reasons. First, Supreme Court appointments are seen by the president—and by the public at large—as generally more important and politically significant than openings on the lesser tribunals. Presidents often use their few opportunities for High Court appointments to make a political statement or to set the tone of their administration. For example, during the period of national stress prior to U.S. entry into World War II, Democratic president Franklin D. Roosevelt elevated Republican Harlan Stone to chief justice as a gesture of national unity; in 1969 President Nixon used his appointment of the conservative Warren Burger to make good on his campaign pledge to restore "law and order"; and President Reagan hoped to dispel his reputation for being unsympathetic toward the women's movement by being the first to name a woman to the High Court. Likewise, President Clinton's appointment to the Court of two political moderates, Ruth Ginsburg and Stephen Breyer, has been viewed by many as an attempt to demonstrate to the public that he is truly a "new Democrat" and not a left-wing radical. Because appointments to the lower judiciary are less newsworthy, they are less likely to command the personal involvement of the president, who will probably rely much more heavily on the judgment of the White House staff or the Justice Department in selecting and screening candidates for appeals and trial court benches.

A second reason why presidents are less likely to devote much attention to lower-court appointments is that tradition has allowed for individual senators and local party bosses to influence and often dominate such activity. In fact, the practice known as *senatorial courtesy* is a major restriction on the president's capacity to make district judge appointments. The conditions of this unwritten rule of the game are these: Senators of the president's political party who object to a candidate that the president wishes to appoint to a district judgeship in their home state have a virtual veto over the nomination. They exercise this veto through use of the "blue slip"—the printed form that a senator from the nominee's state is supposed to return to the Senate Judiciary Committee to express his or her views about the particular candidate.[11] So significant a restriction is this on the chief executive's appointing prerogatives that it caused one former assistant attorney general to quip: "The

Constitution is backwards. Article II, Section 2 should read: 'The senators shall nominate, and by and with the consent of the President, shall appoint.'"[12] Many senators in fact regard their prerogatives in this realm to be ordained by the Founders. For example, under the Reagan administration when Texas senator Phil Gramm was asked to defend his key role in the appointment of district judges in his state, he said, "I'm given the power to make the appointment. . . . The people elected me to do that."[13] Senatorial courtesy does not apply to appellate court appointments, although it is customary for presidents to defer to senators of their party from states that make up the appellate court circuit. Thus in lower-court appointments presidents have less incentive to devote effort to a game in which they are not the star player.

The president also has authority "to fill up all Vacancies that may happen during the recess of the Senate, by granting Commissions which shall expire at the End of their next Session" (Article II, Section 2). One reason a chief executive may wish to make a *recess appointment* is to fill a judicial vacancy on a court that has a large backlog of business. The other reason is more political. A president may find it easier to secure confirmation for a "sitting" judge than for a candidate named while the Senate is in session—that is, the Senate might be less likely to reject a *fait accompli*. For example, when President Kennedy selected Judge Irving Ben Cooper to fill an opening on the federal bench in New York State, the nomination stirred up great opposition in the Senate Judiciary Committee. Although Cooper enjoyed a good public image, he was not well liked by lawyers and other judges.[14] Most observers felt that the fact that Cooper was then serving an interim appointment was extremely useful, if not essential, to his subsequent confirmation. If the Senate had rejected Cooper, a new jurist would have had to be nominated, causing further delay in an urgent appointment.

The Department of Justice

Assisting the president and the White House staff in the judicial selection process are the two key presidential appointees in the Justice Department—the attorney general of the United States and the deputy attorney general. Their primary job is to seek out candidates for federal judicial posts who conform to general criteria set by the president. For example, if a vacancy were to occur on the Seventh Circuit appellate bench, the attorney general (or a staff member) might phone the U.S. attorneys in the states of Illinois, Wisconsin, and Indiana and ask, "Are there some attorneys in your district who would make good judges and who are members of our political party or who at least share the president's basic philosophy?" Once several names are obtained, the staff of the Justice Department will subject each candidate to further scrutiny. They may order an FBI investigation of the candidate's character and background; they will usually read copies of all articles or speeches the candidate has written or evaluate a sitting judge's written opinions; they might check with local party leaders to determine that the candidate is a party faithful and is in tune with the president's major public policy positions.

In the case of district judge appointments, where names are often submitted by home-state senators, the Justice Department's function is more that of screener than of initiator. But regardless of who comes up with a basic list of names, the Justice Department's primary duty is to evaluate the candidates' personal, professional, and political qualifications. In performing this role the department may work closely with the White House staff, with the senators involved in the nomination, and with party leaders who may wish to have some input in choice of the potential nominee.

Under the Clinton administration jurists are selected jointly by the White House Counsel's Office and the Justice Department's Office of Policy Development. At the Justice Department each potential judge is assigned to a particular attorney who examines the candidate's professional credentials, including any relevant judicial decision making. At the Office of White House Counsel candidates are screened for their political credentials; for example, the Office makes sure that the Republican chair of the Senate Judiciary Committee would have no objection to the nominee.[15]

State and Local Party Leaders

Regional party politicos have little to say in the appointment of Supreme Court justices, where presidential prerogative is dominant, and their role in the choice of appeals court judges is minimal. However, in the selection of U.S. trial judges their impact is formidable, especially when appointments occur in states in which neither senator is of the president's political party. In such cases the president need not fear that senatorial courtesy will be invoked against a district court nominee and thus will be more likely to consult with state party leaders rather than with the state's senators. For example, during the Kennedy and Johnson presidencies the Democratic mayor of Chicago, Richard J. Daley, personally approved every federal judge appointed in the Northern District of Illinois.

Interest Groups

A number of pressure groups in the United States, representing the whole political spectrum from left to right, often lobby either for or against judicial nominations. Leaders of these groups—civil liberties, business, organized labor, civil rights—have little hesitation about urging the president to withdraw the nomination of someone whose political and social values are different from their own, or from lobbying the Senate to support the nomination of someone who is favorably perceived. When President Bush nominated Clarence Thomas for a Supreme Court position in 1991, a variety of interest groups clamored to make their views known. For example, Dr. William F. Gibson, speaking for the liberal National Association for the Advancement of Colored People, said that "Thomas' judicial philosophy is simply inconsistent with the historical positions taken by the NAACP." Coordinating his action with the NAACP announcement, the voice of organized labor, President Lane Kirkland of the AFL-CIO, declared that the "president's apparent resolve to make the court the preserve of the far right wing leaves us no other choice [but to oppose the nomination]."[16] However, conservative interest groups rallied to Thomas's support. John Motley, the top lobbyist for the nation's largest association of small businesses (the National Federation of Independent Business), said of Thomas:

Some of the individual-freedom views he holds would call into question some labor-management decisions past courts have reached and affect the minimum-wage issue. If that's true, it provides one of the strongest arguments I've seen in a long time for the small business community to get involved in a high court nomination.[17]

There is evidence that interest groups lobby for and against nominees at all levels of the federal judiciary. As one scholar has noted, pressure-group activity to influence the selection process "has long been characteristic of American politics."[18]

The American Bar Association

For more than four decades, the Committee on the Federal Judiciary of the ABA has played a key role in evaluating the credentials of potential nominees for positions on the federal bench. The committee, whose fifteen members represent all the U.S. circuits, evaluates candidates on the basis of numerous criteria, including judicial temperament, age, trial experience, character, and intelligence. A candidate approved by the committee is rated either "qualified" or "well qualified," whereas an unacceptable candidate is stamped with a "not qualified" label. (Traditionally the committee rated the very best candidates as "exceptionally well qualified," but this category was dropped in 1991.)

The traditional composition of the committee has made it the subject of some controversy. Because it has been made up largely of older, well-to-do, Republican, business-oriented corporation attorneys, some observers have argued that their evaluation of potential judicial candidates has been biased in favor of their peers. There is a strong suspicion that the committee has seen being wealthy and conservative as positive traits and being liberal and outspoken as uncharacteristic of "a sound judicial temperament." It should come as no surprise, then, that the ABA's committee has generally worked more closely with Republican presidents than with Democratic administrations.

Bucking the recommendations of the committee is a risky business, and presidents are likely to think long and hard before nominating a candidate tagged with the "not qualified" label.[19] President Kennedy in 1962 successfully pushed for the appointment of Sarah T. Hughes (of the Northern District of Texas) despite opposition from the ABA, which argued that she was too old. Nevertheless it required lobbying from none other than the vice president (Lyndon Johnson) and the Speaker of the House (Sam Rayburn) to ease the nomination through.[20]

Some presidents have gone back and forth in terms of their willingness to be bound by the pronouncements of the ABA committee. For example, when he first took office, President Nixon indicated that he would appoint no one who did not have the blessing of the ABA. However, after Senate defeat of two of Nixon's Supreme Court nominees, Clement Haynsworth and G. Harrold Carswell, the ABA began to cast a more critical eye on Nixon's choices. (The ABA had approved the Haynsworth and Carswell nominations and felt somewhat humiliated when investigations by the press and the Senate turned up a variety of negative factors overlooked by the committee.) Late in 1971, when he was trying to fill two vacancies on the Supreme Court, Nixon brought up the possibility of nominating Senator Robert Byrd of West Virginia. Attorney General John Mitchell told Nixon that there would be a real problem securing ABA approval because Byrd had attended a "night law school" and had little experience as a practicing attorney. Nixon's reported reply to Mitchell indicates that the president's total confidence in the judgment of the ABA had waned. "Fuck the ABA," said Nixon. And indeed, from that time on, the president refused to submit names to the ABA committee until *after* he had already selected and publicized them.

Since President Nixon and Watergate, two changes seem to have occurred in the ABA. First, it appears to have severed some of its close ties to the conservative establishment and taken stands on public policy issues that offend traditional dogma. For instance, it has come out for federal support of legal aid for the poor. Second, its impact on the judicial selection process may be a bit less now than in past decades. President Carter's setting up of the U.S. Circuit Judge Nominating Commission was seen in part as a successful end run around the bar association, and when President Reagan appointed Sandra Day O'Connor to the Supreme Court, the ABA was not even consulted.

The relationship between the Bush administration and the ABA was generally a comfortable one, despite some minor initial conflict over whether or not the Bar Association should consider the nominees' political philosophy and ideology. (Bush's advisors called for less emphasis on such matters.) Under President Clinton a similar climate of quiet harmony has prevailed. For example, during his first term in office 64 percent of his district court nominees and 83 percent of his appellate court nominees received the ABA's "well-qualified" label—percentages higher than Carter, Reagan, or Bush's first-term nominees received.

The Senate Judiciary Committee

The rules of the Senate require its Judiciary Committee to pass on all nominations to the federal bench and to make recommendations to the Senate as a whole. Its role is thus to screen individuals who have already been nominated, not to suggest names of possible candidates. The committee by custom holds hearings on all nominations, at which time witnesses are heard and deliberations take place behind closed doors. The hearings for district court appointments are largely perfunctory because the norm of senatorial courtesy has, for all intents and purposes, already determined whether the candidate will pass senatorial muster. However, for appeals court nominees—and surely for an appointment to the Supreme Court—the committee hearing is a serious proceeding.

Acting as a sort of watchdog of the Senate, the committee can affect the selection process in several ways. "First, it can delay Senate action on confirmation in the hope of embarrassing the president or to test his determination to make a particular appointment." As a general rule, the longer the delay, the poorer the nominee's chances are of securing approval. The failure of Reagan's two Supreme Court nominees, Robert Bork and Douglas Ginsburg, to receive Senate approval was the result, in part, of the elongated committee hearings, which permitted the opposition forces to gather negative data and flex their lobbying muscles. Second, the committee can simply recommend against Senate confirmation. Finally, committee opponents of the nomination might engage in an extensive Senate floor debate, which "affords still another opportunity for senators to seek to embarrass the administration by questioning the wisdom of a particular appointment."[21]

Historically the Judiciary Committee has had a distinctly Southern and conservative flavor. As a result, it often did not look kindly upon appointees to the appeals courts and the Supreme Court who were thought to be too liberal—particularly on civil rights matters. Senator James Eastland of Mississippi, the powerful committee chair for many years, often exacted a terrible toll from presidents who sought to put integrationists on the upper federal courts. For example, when President Kennedy tried to secure the appointment of the black and liberal Thurgood Marshall for a seat on the appellate court bench, Senator Eastland refused to support the nomination unless he could get his old college chum, William Harold Cox, a seat on the federal district court in Mississippi. Cox, who on the bench referred to blacks as "niggers" and "chimpanzees," is regarded as the worst of several racist judges Kennedy was "forced" to appoint in the South. As one black civil rights leader put it: "The brothers had to pay a lot of dues" to get Thurgood Marshall appointed to the bench.[22]

Perhaps the most vivid reminder of the power of the Senate Judiciary Committee came in the fall of 1991, in its much-publicized (and perhaps overly thorough) hearings on the nomination of Clarence Thomas to the Supreme Court. Even before public hearings began, the committee had requested some 30,000 pages of documentation from Thomas! During weeks of intense questioning, the committee investigated almost every conceivable aspect of the nominee's background, philosophy, and credentials. The committee concluded its work with a dramatic weekend-long, televised hearing concerning sexual harassment charges brought by a former employee of Thomas, Anita Hill. Although the conduct of the committee during these proceedings is still being debated, few Americans came away from the spectacle unacquainted with the Judiciary Committee of the United States Senate.

After the Republican takeover of Congress in the 1994 elections, control of the Judiciary Committee passed into the hands of conservative GOP senator Orrin Hatch of Utah. Between 1994 and 1996 the relationship between the Clinton administration and Hatch was relatively good, although Clinton's success rate in getting his nominees approved by the Republican Senate did decline markedly.[23] The unwritten rule said that if Clinton did not send up for consideration the names of any potential jurists who were too overtly liberal, then Hatch would grease the skids for easy committee approval. This arrangement seemed to work well for Clinton, whose main objective was to put more women and minorities on the bench rather than to fill the judiciary with left-of-center judges.

All this changed abruptly during the 1996 presidential election campaign when Republican candidate Robert Dole began charging that Clinton was filling the judiciary with highly activist, liberal judges. Although as a senator Dole had voted to confirm both of Clinton's Supreme Court appointees (Ginsburg and Breyer) and virtually all of Clinton's lower-court appointees, and although the empirical evidence suggested that the Clinton judges were not all that liberal,[24] Dole as a candidate continued to charge that Clinton's judicial appointments were an "all-star team of liberal leniency" that had set off a "crisis" in the courts.[25]

The acrimony between Clinton and the GOP over judicial appointments continued after the 1996 election. In fact, by the summer of 1997 the Judiciary Committee had entered a state of virtual paralysis on the matter of confirming Clinton's judicial nominations. Currently, some 100 judicial vacancies remain unfilled, and there is a record wait of 183 days from nomination to confirmation.[26] Wrangling between Republicans and Democrats has increased, while in the House of Representatives right-wing legislators (such as House Majority Whip Tom DeLay) have mounted a drive to impeach activist-liberal judges.[27] Judiciary Chairman Hatch has acknowledged that the refusal of his committee to expedite the confirmation process has caused delays in the courts. "Playing politics with judges is unfair, and I am sick of it," he said in March 1997. But insiders note that the right wing has been upping the pressure, and indeed his rhetoric has become increasingly combative. In mid-May Hatch told a group of judges that he would refuse "to stand by to see judicial activists named to the federal bench."[28] Whether the president will continue to have problems with the Judiciary Committee now seems to be more a function of the power struggle between moderate and conservative Republican senators than of which kinds of individuals Clinton taps for judicial service.

The Senate

The final step in the judicial appointment process for federal judges is a majority vote by the Senate. As we have indicated, the Constitution states that the Senate must give its "advice and consent" to judicial nominations made by the president. Historically there have been two general views of the Senate's prescribed role. Presidents, from the time of George Washington, and a few scholars have taken the position that the Senate ought quietly to go along with the presidential choices unless there are overwhelmingly strong reasons to the contrary. Other scholars and, not unexpectedly, most senators have held to the views of Senator Birch Bayh of Indiana and Senator Robert Griffin of Michigan that the Senate "has the right and the obligation to decide in its own wisdom whether it wishes to confirm or not to confirm a Supreme Court nominee."[29] In practice the role of the Senate in the judicial confirmation process has varied, depending on the level of the federal judgeship that is being considered.

For district judges the norm of senatorial courtesy prevails. That is, if the president's nominee is acceptable to the senator(s) of the president's party in the state in which the judge is to sit, the Senate is usually happy to give its advice and consent with a quiet nod. For appointments to the appeals courts, as noted earlier, senatorial courtesy does not apply, since the vacancy to be filled covers more than just the state of one or possibly two senators. But it is customary for senators from each state in the circuit in which the vacancy has occurred to submit names of possible candidates to the president. An unwritten rule is that each state in the circuit should have at least one judge on that circuit's appellate bench, a practice often followed when the vacancy is that of a state's only representative on the circuit bench. As long as the norms are adhered to and the president's nominee has reasonably good qualifications, the Senate as a whole usually goes along with the recommendations of the chief executive.

It has been mainly with Supreme Court nominations that the Senate has been inclined traditionally to go toe-to-toe with the president if there is disagreement over the candidate's fitness for the High Court. Since 1789, presidents have sent the names of 144 persons to the Senate for its advice and consent. Of this number some 30 were either rejected or "indefinitely postponed" by the Senate, or the names were withdrawn by the president. Thus presidents have been successful about 79 percent of the time, and in fact their batting average seems to be improving, since as many as *one-third* of the nominations were rejected by the Senate in the last century. The record shows that presidents have met with the most success in getting their High Court nominations approved when (1) the nominee comes from a non-controversial background and has middle-of-the-road political leanings, and (2) the president's party also controls the Senate, or at least there is a majority that shares the president's basic attitudes and values. As one study of 2,054 Senate roll call votes on Supreme Court nominations from Earl Warren to Anthony Kennedy concluded: "When a strong president nominates a highly qualified, ideologically moderate candidate, the nominee passes the Senate in a lopsided, consensual vote. Presidents have often nominated this type of candidate and consequently consensual votes have been fairly common. When presidents nominate a less well qualified, ideologically extreme candidate, especially when the president is in a weak position, then a conflictual vote is likely." [30]

Policy Links Between the Citizenry, the President, and the Federal Judiciary

Because this book is about policy making, it is appropriate to examine the links between the policy values of the elected chief executive and the decisional propensities of federal judges. If in electing one presidential candidate over another, the citizenry expresses its policy choices, is there evidence that such choices spill over into the kind of judges presidents appoint and the way those judges decide policy-relevant cases? For instance, if the people decide in an election that they want a president who will reduce the size and powers of the federal bureaucracy, does that president subsequently appoint judges who share that philosophy? And, equally important, when those judges hear cases that give them the opportunity either to expand or to reduce the extent of a bureaucrat's power, do they opt for the reduction of authority? Although we are a long way from having complete answers to these questions, recent evidence suggests the existence of some policy links.

We shall look at this phenomenon by exploring two questions. First, what critical factors must exist for presidents to be able to obtain a judiciary that reflects their own political philosophy? Second, what empirical evidence is there to suggest that judges' decisions to some degree carry the imprint of the presidents who selected them?

The President and the Composition of the Judiciary

We suggest that there are four general factors that determine whether chief executives can obtain a federal judiciary that is sympathetic to their political values and attitudes.

Presidential Support for Ideologically Based Appointments. One key aspect of the success of chief executives in appointing a federal judiciary that mirrors their own political beliefs is the depth of their commitment to do so. Some presidents may be content merely to fill the federal bench with party loyalists and pay little attention to their nominees' specific ideologies. Some may consider ideological factors when appointing Supreme Court justices but may not regard them as important for trial and appellate judges. Other presidents may discount ideologically grounded appointments because they themselves tend to be nonideological; still others may place factors such as past political loyalty ahead of ideology in selecting judges.

Bill Clinton is a chief executive in the first category—that is, he is a president without a clearly defined set of ideological positions. More than once he has acknowledged that he will probably go down in history as the most conservative Democrat who has occupied the White House during this century. Frequently referring to himself as a "new Democrat," Clinton has tried to distance himself from the more liberal image that characterized the Democratic party during most of the twentieth century. Throughout his first term Clinton sought to establish a judicial cohort that "looks like America," that is, a team reflective of the nation's diverse ethnicity and gender rather than a cohort characterized by any singular ideological perspective.

As a president, Harry Truman had strong political views, but when selecting judges he placed loyalty to himself ahead of the candidate's overall political orientation. We noted earlier in this chapter how eager Truman was to appoint Carroll O. Switzer to fill the judicial vacancy in Iowa. Truman's premium on personal loyalty rather than ideology is generally reflected in the group of men he put on the bench. For example, there was scant linkage between Truman's personal liberal stance on civil rights and equal opportunity and his judicial selections: he appointed no blacks and no women at all, and at least three of his key Southern district court appointees have been identified as having been very unfriendly to the cause of civil rights.[31]

If Clinton and Truman exemplify presidents who eschewed ideological criteria, Ronald Reagan provides a good example of a chief executive who selected his judicial nominees with a clear eye toward their compatibility with his own conservative philosophy. During his two terms, Reagan appointed 368 judges to the district and appeals courts. Of these, 94 percent were Republicans, 93 percent were white, and 92 percent were males; the majority were well-off (46 percent had net worths of over $500,000 and more than one in five were millionaires); virtually all had established records as political conservatives and as apostles of judicial self-restraint. Indeed, as the Reagan administration's conservative programs began to bog down in the more liberal-minded Congress, the Reagan team looked more and more toward implementing their values through their judicial appointment strategy. As former White House communications director Patrick J. Buchanan put it, "[Our conservative appointment strategy] . . . could do more to advance the social agenda—school prayer, anti-pornography, anti-busing, right-to-life and quotas in employment—than anything Congress can accomplish in 20 years."[32] President Reagan was not the only modern president to pack the bench with those who shared his political and legal philosophies: Presidents Johnson and Carter both successfully appointed activist liberal judges.

The Number of Vacancies to Be Filled. A second element affecting the capacity of chief executives to establish a policy link between themselves and the judiciary is the number of appointments available to them. Obviously, the more judges a president can select, the greater the potential of the White House to put its stamp on the judicial branch. For example, George Washington's influence on the Supreme Court was significant because he was able to nominate ten individuals to the High Court. Jimmy Carter's was nil, on the other hand, because no vacancies occurred during his term as president.

The number of appointment opportunities depends, of course, on several factors: how many judicial vacancies are inherited from the previous administration

(Clinton, for example, was left with a whopping 100 district and trial court vacancies—14 percent of the total—by former President Bush), how many judges and justices die or resign during the president's term, how long the president serves, and whether Congress passes legislation that significantly increases the number of judgeships. Historically, the last factor seems to have been the most important in influencing the number of judgeships available, and, as one might expect, politics in its most basic form permeates this process. A study of proposals for new-judges bills in thirteen congresses tested the following two hypotheses: (1) "proposals to add new federal judges are more likely to pass if the party controls the Presidency and Congress than if different parties are in power," and (2) "proposals to add new federal judges are more likely to pass during the first two years of the President's term than during the second two years." The author concluded that his "data support both hypotheses—proposals to add new judges are about 5 times more likely to pass if the same party controls the Presidency and Congress than if different parties control, and about 4 times more likely to pass during the first two years of the President's term than during the second two years." He then noted that these findings serve "to remind us that not only is judicial selection a political process, but so is the creation of judicial posts."[33] Thus the number of vacancies that a president can fill—a function of politics, fate, and the size of the judicial workloads—is another variable that helps determine the impact a chief executive has on the composition of the federal judiciary.

The President's Political Clout. Another factor is the scope and proficiency of presidential skill in overcoming any political obstacles. One such stumbling block is the U.S. Senate, as we have noted previously. If the Senate is controlled by the president's political party, the White House will find it much easier to secure confirmation than if opposition forces control the Senate. Sometimes when the opposition is in power in the Senate, presidents are forced into a sort of political horse trading to get their nominees approved. For example, when the Democrats controlled the Senate during the Nixon and Ford administrations, those two presidents had to make a political deal for the district judgeships in California: the state's two Democratic senators were permitted to appoint one of their own for every three Republicans that were put on the bench. As for President Clinton, we have already noted that during the second half of his first term Clinton was obliged to abide by the unwritten but firm rule that he could appoint whomever he wished to the federal bench as long as the nominees' ideological orientations did not clash with those of the powerful, conservative Republican leaders.

The Senate Judiciary Committee is another roadblock preventing a president who has the requisite will from placing his chosen men and women on the federal bench. Some presidents have been more adept than others at easing their candidates through the jagged rocks of the Judiciary Committee rapids. Both Presidents Kennedy and Johnson, for example, had to deal with the formidable committee chairman James Eastland of Mississippi, but only Johnson seems to have had the political adroitness to get most of his liberal nominees approved. Kennedy lacked this skill, and we have mentioned the kinds of judges he was often obliged to appoint. It remains to be seen whether Clinton is able to parlay his considerable political acumen into the clout necessary to get his judicial nominees past an increasingly hostile Judiciary Committee.

The president's personal popularity is another element in the political power formula. Chief executives who are well liked by the public and command the respect of opinion makers in the news media, the rank-and-file of their political party, and the leaders of the nation's major interest groups are much more likely to prevail over any forces that seek to thwart their judicial nominees. Personal popularity is not a stable factor and is sometimes hard to gauge, but there is little doubt that presidents' standing with the electorate helps determine the success of their efforts to influence the composition of the American judiciary. For example, in 1930, President Hoover's choice for a seat on the Supreme Court, John J. Parker, was defeated in the Senate by a two-vote margin. It is likely that had the nomination been made a year or so earlier, before the onset of the depression took Hoover's popularity by the throat, Parker might have gotten on the Supreme Court. Likewise, in 1968 President Johnson's low esteem among voters and the powers-that-be may have been partially responsible for Senate rejection of Johnson's candidate for chief justice, Abe Fortas, and also for the Senate's refusal to replace Fortas with Johnson's old pal Homer Thornberry. As one observer commented, "Johnson failed largely because most members of the Senate 'had had it' with the lame-duck President's nominations." [34] Conversely, President Eisenhower's success in getting approval for an inordinately large number of nominees dubbed "not qualified" by the ABA (13.2 percent) may be attributed, in part at least, to Ike's great popularity and prestige.

The Judicial Climate the New Judges Enter. A final matter affects the capacity of chief executives to secure a federal judiciary that reflects their own political values: the current philosophical orientations of the sitting district and appellate court judges with whom the new appointees would interact. Since federal judges serve lifetime appointments during good behavior, presidents must accept the composition and value structure of the judiciary as it exists when they first take office. If the existing judiciary already reflects the president's political and legal orientation, the impact of new judicial appointees will be immediate and substantial. On the other hand, if new chief executives face a trial and appellate judiciary whose values are radically different from their own, the impact of their subsequent judicial appointments will be weaker and slower to materialize. New judges must respect the controlling legal precedents and the constitutional interpretations that prevail in the judiciary at the time they enter it, or they risk being overturned by a higher court. Such a reality may limit the capacity of a new set of judges to get in there and do their own thing—at least in the short run.

When Franklin Roosevelt became president in 1933, he was confronted with a Supreme Court and a lower federal judiciary that had been solidly packed with conservative Republican jurists by his three GOP predecessors in the White House. A majority of the High Court and most lower-court judges viewed most of Roosevelt's New Deal legislation as unconstitutional, and indeed it was not until 1937 that the Supreme Court began to stop overturning virtually all of FDR's major legislative programs.

To make matters worse, his first opportunity to fill a Supreme Court vacancy did not come until the fall of 1937. Thus, despite the ideological screening that went into the selection of FDR's judges, it seems fair to assume that, at least between 1933 and 1938, Roosevelt's trial and appellate judges had to restrain their liberal propensities in the myriad of cases that came before them. This may explain in part why the voting record of the Roosevelt court appointees is not much more liberal than that of the conservative judges selected by Roosevelt's three Republican predecessors; the Roosevelt team just didn't have much room to move in a judiciary dominated by staunch conservatives.

The decisional patterns of the Eisenhower judges further serve to illustrate this phenomenon. Although the Eisenhower appointees were more conservative than those selected by Presidents Truman and Roosevelt, the differences in their rulings are pretty small. One major reason was that the Eisenhower jurists entered a realm that was dominated from top to bottom by Roosevelt and Truman appointees, who were for the most part liberals. Ike's generally conservative judges didn't have much more room to maneuver than did Roosevelt's liberal jurists in the face of a conservative-dominated judiciary.

President Reagan's impact on the judicial branch continues to be substantial. By the end of his second term, he had appointed an unprecedented 368 federal judges,

50 percent of those on the bench. When he entered the White House, the Supreme Court was already teetering to the right because of Nixon's and Ford's conservative appointments. Although Carter's liberal appointees still had places on the trial and appellate court benches, Reagan found a good many conservative Nixon and Ford judges on the bench when he took office. Thus he has had a major role in shaping the entire federal judiciary in his own conservative image for some time to come. The Bush judges had a much easier time making their impact felt, since they entered a judicial realm wherein well over half the judges already professed conservative, Republican values. On the other hand, President Clinton's impact on the judiciary has been slower to manifest itself because his judicial nominees entered an arena in which over 75 percent of the trial and appellate court seats were held by judges appointed by prior GOP presidents with very conservative orientations. Still, bit by bit the more ideologically moderate thrust of the Clinton cohort is making itself felt. Between 1993 and 1997 President Clinton made more first-term nominations—202—than any other president except Carter, and by the end of his second term at least half of the federal judiciary will bear the Clinton stamp. What will happen to the ideological orientation of the courts after Clinton? If a Republican is elected in 2000, this will serve quickly to mute the Clinton effect. On the other hand, if a moderate-to-liberal Democrat enters the White House, this will accentuate whatever moderate ideological flames the Clinton cohort may have kindled.

Presidents' Values and Their Appointees' Decisions

We now know the conditions that must be met if presidents are to secure a judiciary in tune with their own policy values and goals. What evidence is there that presidents have in fact been able to do so? Or, to return to our original question, when the people elect a particular president, is there reason to believe that their choice will be expressed in the kinds of judges that are appointed and the kinds of decisions that those judges render?

To answer these questions we shall look at an investigation of the liberal-conservative voting patterns of the teams of district court judges appointed by fifteen presidents during this century. This comprehensive study is the only one that covers enough presidents, judges, and cases to allow us to make some meaningful generalizations. In essence we shall see whether liberal presidents appointed trial judges who decided cases in a more liberal manner and whether conservative chief executives were able to obtain district court jurists who followed their policy views.

To begin, we will offer some examples to define the sometimes slippery terms *liberal* and *conservative*. In the realm of civil rights and civil liberties, liberal judges

# Waiting for
# Cataloging
ov=.b _____

OCLC 38353782
OP ✓
EXP _____
UPD _____
LBL _____

PROCESSING WORKFORM:

OCLC # _____ Complete By: _____

ORDER .o _____ RECORD .b _____

Add Book Flaps/Cover? _____ Item Record Created? _____

Copy: 1 or _____ Barcode: YES _____ or NO _____

Call Number: (090 or 092 or 099)

KF
8700
.C37
1998

LOCATION	ITYPE	STATUS	OPACMSG
mustk	12	p	-
muqua	40	p	-
muref	53	-	o
muspe	2	-	o
muvid	132	p	-
mucdm	111	p	-
mudvd	112	p	-
mucdr	109	p	-
muqus	40	p	-
mucmc	12	p	-
mujuf	12	p	-
mujuv	12	p	-
muamp	2	-	o
muarc	2	-	o

Ref Book Pocket _____
Check Order Record _____

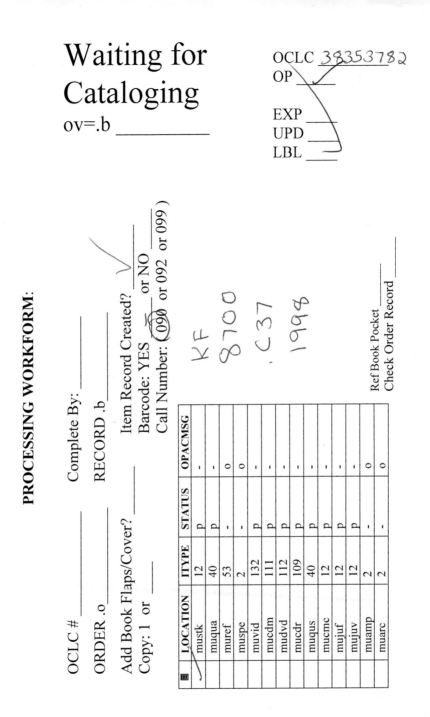

Ready to finish processing

would generally take a broadening position—that is, they would seek in their rulings to extend these freedoms; conservative jurists, by contrast, would prefer to limit such rights. For example, in a case in which a government agency wanted to prevent a controversial person from speaking in a public park or at a state university, a liberal judge would be more inclined than a conservative to uphold the right of the would-be speech giver. Or in a case concerning school integration, a liberal judge would be more likely to take the side of the minority petitioners. In the area of government regulation of the economy, liberal judges would probably uphold legislation that benefited working people or the economic underdog. Thus, if the secretary of labor sought an injunction against an employer for paying less than the minimum wage, a liberal judge would be more disposed to endorse the labor secretary's arguments whereas a conservative judge would tend to side with business, especially big business. Another broad category of cases often studied by judicial scholars is criminal justice. Liberal judges are, in general, more sympathetic to the motions made by criminal defendants. For instance, in a case in which the accused claimed to have been coerced by the government to make an illegal confession, liberal judges would be more likely than their conservative counterparts to agree that the government had acted improperly.

Figure 8-1 indicates the percentage of liberal decisions rendered by the district court appointees of Presidents Wilson through Clinton. Forty-nine percent of the decisions of the Wilson judges are liberal, which puts these jurists almost on a

FIGURE 8-1   Percentage of Liberal Decisions Rendered by District Court Appointees of Presidents Wilson through Clinton

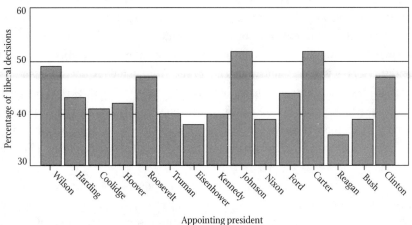

SOURCE: Unpublished data collected by Robert A. Carp and Ronald Stidham.

par with those of Lyndon Johnson and Jimmy Carter for having the most liberal voting record. The liberal pattern of the Wilson judges is not surprising: Wilson was one of the staunchest liberal presidents of this century—particularly on economic issues. Moreover, he chose his judges on a highly partisan, ideological basis: 98.6 percent of his appointments to the lower courts were Democrats—still the record for any president in this century.

Succeeding Wilson in the White House were the three Republican chief executives of the 1920s: Harding and his "return to normalcy" in 1921, followed by the equally conservative Coolidge and Hoover. The right-of-center policy values of these three presidents (and the undisputed Republican domination of the Senate during their incumbencies) are mirrored in the decisional patterns of the trial judges they selected. The liberalism score drops by 6 points from Wilson to Harding, 49 to 43 percent, and stays around that same level for the Coolidge and Hoover judicial teams.

With Franklin D. Roosevelt's judges there is a shift back to left-of-center. At 47 percent liberal, the Roosevelt jurists are five points more liberal than those of his immediate predecessor, Herbert Hoover. We have good evidence that FDR used ideological criteria to pick his judges and that he put the full weight of his political skills behind that endeavor. He once instructed his dispenser of political patronage, James Farley, in effect to use the judicial appointment power as a weapon against senators and representatives who were balking at New Deal legislation: "First off, we must hold up judicial appointments in States where the [congressional] delegation is not going along [with our liberal economic proposals]. We must make appointments promptly where the delegation is with us. Second, this must apply to other appointments. I'll keep in close contact with the leaders."[35]

At first the comparatively conservative voting record of the Truman judges seems a bit strange in view of Truman's personal commitment to liberal economic and social policy goals. Only 40 percent of the Truman judges' decisions were liberal, a full seven points less than Roosevelt's jurists—and even two points below the Hoover nominees. As we noted earlier, however, Truman counted personal loyalty much more heavily than ideological standards when selecting his judges, and as a result many conservatives found their way into the ranks of the Truman judges.

Because of Truman's lack of interest in making policy-based appointments, coupled with strong opposition in the Senate and lack of popular support throughout much of his administration, his personal liberalism was generally not reflected in the policy values of his judges. Eisenhower's judges were more conservative than

Truman's, as expected, but the difference is not very great. This is due in part to the fact that Eisenhower paid little attention to purely ideological appointment criteria and also because his judges had to work in the company of an overwhelming Democratic majority throughout the federal judiciary. These factors must have many of the conservative inclinations of the Eisenhower jurists.

The 40 percent liberalism score of the Kennedy judges represents a swing to the left. This is to be expected, and at first blush it may appear strange that John Kennedy's team on the bench was not even more left of center. However, we must keep in mind Kennedy's problems in dealing with the conservative, Southern-dominated Senate Judiciary Committee; his lack of political clout in the Senate, which often made him a pawn of senatorial courtesy; and his inability to overcome the stranglehold of local Democratic bosses, who often prized partisan loyalty over ideological purity—or even competence—when it came to appointing judges.

Lyndon Johnson's judges moved impressively toward the left, and, as we noted, his judges were more liberal than Wilson's and much more so than Kennedy's. We can account for this on the basis of the four criteria discussed earlier in this chapter that predict a correspondence between the values of chief executives and the orientation of their judges. Johnson knew well how to bargain with individual senators and was second to none in his ability to manipulate and cajole those who were initially indifferent or hostile to issues (or candidates) he supported; his impressive victories in Congress—for example, the antipoverty legislation and the civil rights acts—are monuments to his skill. Undoubtedly, too, he used his political prowess to secure a judicial team that reflected his liberal policy values. In addition, Johnson was able to fill a large number of vacancies on the bench, and his liberal appointees must have felt right at home ideologically in a judiciary headed by the liberal Warren Court.

If the leftward swing of the Johnson team is dramatic, it is no less so than the shift to the right made by the Nixon judges. Only 39 percent of the decisions of Nixon's jurists were liberal. Nixon, of course, placed enormous emphasis on getting conservatives nominated to judgeships at all levels. He possessed the political clout to secure Senate confirmation for most lower-court appointees—at least until Watergate, when the Nixon wine turned to vinegar—and the rightist policy values of the Nixon judges must have been prodded by a Supreme Court that was growing more and more conservative.

The 44 percent liberalism score of the Ford judges puts them right between the Johnson and Nixon jurists in terms of ideology. That Ford's jurists were less conservative than Nixon's is not hard to explain. First, Ford himself was much less of a political ideologue than his predecessor, as reflected in the way in which he screened his nominees and in the type of individuals he chose. (Ford's appointment of the moderate John Paul Stevens to the Supreme Court versus Nixon's selection of the highly conservative William H. Rehnquist illustrates the point.) Also, because Ford's circuitous route to the presidency did not enhance his political effectiveness with the Senate, he would not have had the clout to force highly conservative Republican nominees through a liberal, Democratic Senate, even if he had wished to.

With a score of 52 percent, Jimmy Carter shares with Lyndon Johnson the record for having appointed judges with the most liberal voting records of the fifteen presidents under consideration. Despite Carter's call for an "independent" federal judiciary based on "merit selection," it is clear that his judges were selected with a keen eye toward their potential liberal voting tendencies.[36] That there is a correspondence between the values of President Carter and the liberal decisional patterns of his judges should come as no surprise. Carter was clearly identified with liberal social and political values, and although his economic policies were perhaps more conservative than those of other recent Democratic presidents, there is little doubt about Carter's commitment to liberal values in the areas of civil rights and liberties and of criminal justice. Carter, too, had ample opportunity to pack the bench: The Omnibus Judgeship Act of 1978 passed by a friendly Democratic Congress created a record 152 new federal judicial openings for Carter to fill. Carter also possessed a fair degree of political clout with a Judiciary Committee and Senate controlled by Democrats. Finally, the Carter judicial team found many friendly liberals (appointed by Presidents Johnson and Kennedy) already sitting on the bench.

Reagan's judicial team has the distinction of having the most conservative voting record of all the judicial cohorts in our study. Only 36 percent of their decisions bear the liberal stamp. President Reagan's conservative values and his commitment to reshaping the federal judiciary in his own image were well known. Early in his first presidential campaign Reagan had inveighed against left-leaning activist judges, and he promised a dramatic change. As did his predecessor, Reagan had the opportunity, through attrition and newly created judgeships, to fill the judiciary with persons of his own inclinations. (At the end of his second term about half the federal judiciary bore the Reagan label.) This phenomenon was aided by Reagan's great personal popularity throughout most of his administration and a Senate that his party controlled during six of his eight years in office. Finally, the Reagan cohort entered the judicial realm with conservative greetings from the sitting right-of-center Nixon and Ford judges.

The judicial cohort appointed by President Bush continues in the conservative vein established by the Reagan administration, although at 39 percent the Bush cohort reflects the more moderate center of the Republican party that characterized the appointees of Presidents Eisenhower and Nixon. The fact that the Bush team is a tad more liberal than the Reagan cohort may be explained in two ways. First, on the policy issues of the day Bush was generally more moderate than Reagan; his critics in the Republican party were those on the far right who claimed he was too liberal, that he had often abandoned the "conservative revolution" that Reagan had set in motion. Second, as the Bush judges have increasingly interacted with the more moderate and diverse Clinton jurists, their voting behavior has been nudged a bit to the left.

President Clinton and the Federal Judiciary

What kind of men and women has President Clinton selected for service on the federal bench and what has been the ideological direction of their decision making? Figure 8-1 shows us that the behavior of Clinton's judges has resulted in 47 percent liberal decision making. While this is certainly more progressive than the 36 and 39 percent figures for Presidents Reagan and Bush, respectively, it is decidedly more conservative than the 52 percent liberal landmarks of Presidents Johnson and Carter. In a word, the Clinton judges are moderate. This comes as no surprise, given the explanatory model that we have set forth.

First, we have already noted that Clinton has not manifested any desire to make ideologically based judicial appointments; rather, his goal has been to put more women and minorities on the federal bench. As for ideology, one key member of the president's judicial selection team who worked in both the Justice Department and the White House put it this way: "Neither side is running an ideology shop. Neither of us consider ourselves to be the guardians of some kind of flame. . . . [T]his is not a do or die fight for American Culture. This is an attempt to get . . . highly competent lawyers on the federal bench so they can resolve disputes."[37]

While Clinton did inherit a large number of unfilled judicial slots from the Bush administration, the current Republican Congress has been loath to enact any type of omnibus judgeship bill that would enhance his capacity to pack the judiciary. Clinton has also evinced little desire to expend political muscle in pushing through "controversial" candidates over Judiciary Committee and Senate objections. The woman primarily in charge of Clinton's judicial selections, Eleanor Dean Acheson, confirmed the administration's unwillingness to do major battle over judicial appointments: "There are a couple of cases in which we decided that even if we thought we had a shot at winning a fight . . . that it was not worth the time and re-sources . . . because these fights go for months and months, and during that period it is very difficult to concentrate." [38]

Finally, the climate into which the Clinton judges entered was not very con-ducive to liberal decision making. When the Clinton cohort took their seats on the federal bench, about three-quarters of sitting judges—including the supervisory appellate panels—were conservative Republicans appointed primarily by Presi-dents Reagan and Bush. Thus even if the Clinton judges had been "closet liberals," they would have little opportunity to vent these values in a judiciary so dominated by those of a more conservative persuasion.

Given the quite moderate nature of the Clinton judges' decision making, it seems a bit strange that his jurists are coming under such great criticism from Re-publican senators and representatives, some of whom are even calling for the im-peachment of Clinton's so-called "liberal-activist judges." To explore this topic in greater depth, Table 8-3 breaks down the totality of decision making for the six most recent presidencies into three categories of cases: criminal justice (such as motions made by criminal defendants), civil rights and liberties (such as freedom of speech, abortion, and racial discrimination), and labor and economic regulation (such as disputes between labor and management and governmental efforts to reg-ulate the economy). If the Clinton judges are really inordinately liberal, we should see some evidence of it as we turn our analytic microscope up this additional notch.

In the realm of criminal justice 34 percent of the Clinton judges' decisions are liberal. This is certainly greater than the 29 percent figure for the Bush judges, but it is decidedly less than the 38 percent for Carter's judicial team. In the area of civil

TABLE 8-3   Percentage of Liberal District Court Decisions for Three Categories of Cases, Presidents Nixon through Clinton

Appointing president	Criminal justice	Civil rights and liberties	Labor and economic regulation
Nixon	30	37	48
Ford	32	39	55
Carter	38	52	62
Reagan	23	33	49
Bush	29	33	51
Clinton	34	39	62

SOURCE: Unpublished data collected by Robert A. Carp and Ronald Stidham.

rights and liberties 39 percent of Clinton's judges voted on the liberal side—the same figure as for Gerald Ford's cohort. Again, this number is indeed more liberal than the 33 percent figure for the Bush and Reagan jurists, but it is markedly more conservative than the 52 percent number for Jimmy Carter's judges. Finally, in the realm of labor and economic regulation decisions, Clinton's team, at 62 percent, does manifest a liberal tendency, equalling the trend of Carter's judges. This is somewhat ironic because it is the criminal justice and civil liberties decisions of the Clinton judges that the Republicans are currently attacking—not the fact that his jurists are more inclined to support employees in their disputes with management and the government in its efforts to regulate the environment. In sum, the data suggest that the Clinton judges are on the whole not particularly liberal in their decision making. Clinton judges are ideologically moderate.

The Judicial Socialization Process

The central focus of this chapter is on the judges and justices themselves. We continue our look at the judges by examining a critical period in their professional life—the judicial socialization process, the time during which new appointees learn to be judges.

When scholars use the term *socialization,* they are referring to the process whereby individuals acquire the values, attitudes, and behavior patterns of the existing social system. Factors that aid the process include family, friends, education, coworkers, religious training, political party affiliation, and the communications media. Social scientists also apply the term *socialization* to the process by which a person is formally trained to perform the specific tasks of a particular profession. It is the second meaning of the term, then, that will concern us.

Prior to looking at judges' on-the-job training, we must acknowledge that much significant socialization occurs before the judges first mount the bench. From their parents, teachers, exposure to the news media, and so on, future judges learn the rules of the American political game. That is, by the time they are teenagers they have absorbed key values and attitudes that will circumscribe subsequent judicial behavior: "the majority should rule on general matters of public policy, but minorities have their rights, too"; "judges ought to be fair and impartial"; or "the Constitution is an important document and all political leaders should be bound by it." In college and law school future judges acquire important analytic and communications skills, in addition to the basic substance of the law. After a couple of decades of legal practice, the preparation for a judgeship is in its final stage; the future judge has learned a good bit about how the courts and the law actually work and has specialized in several areas of the law. Despite all this preparation, sometimes called "anticipatory socialization," [39] most new judges in America still have a lot to learn even after donning the black robe.

In many other countries, preparing to be a judge is like preparing to be a physician, an engineer, or a pharmacist—that is, one goes to a particular professional school in which one receives many years of in-depth training and perhaps an on-the-job internship. Since 1959 in France, for example, all would-be judges are intensively trained for a minimum of twenty-eight months in the prestigious Ecole Nationale de la Magistrature; they enter judicial service only after passing rigorous, competitive examinations. Not only does the United States lack formalized training procedures for the judicial profession, but there is the naive assumption that being a lawyer for a decade or so is all the experience one needs to be a judge. After all, don't most lawyers, like judges, work in the courtroom? Isn't it enough for the lawyer-turned-judge just to mount the bench and put on a new hat? To the contrary, becoming a judge in America requires a good deal of *freshman socialization* (short-term learning and adjustment to the new role) and *occupational socialization* (on-the-job training over a period of years).

Let us examine what it is like to become a new judge and why socialization must continue well into the novice jurist's career. Typical new trial court appointees may be first-rate lawyers and experts in a few areas of the law in which they have specialized. As judges, however, they are suddenly expected to be experts on *all* legal subjects, are required to engage in judicial duties usually quite unrelated to any tasks they performed as lawyers (for example, sentencing), and are given a host of administrative assignments for which they have had no prior experience (for example, learning how to docket efficiently several hundred diverse cases.)[40] The following statements by U.S. trial judges reveal what it was like for them as the new kid on the judicial block. (Virtually all the judges who were interviewed for this book were promised anonymity, and thus no references will appear.)

Before I became a federal judge I had been a trial lawyer dealing mainly with personal injury cases and later on with some divorce cases. Needless to say, I knew almost nothing about criminal law. With labor law I had had only one case in my life on this subject, and that was a case going back to the early days of World War II. In other words when I became a federal judge I really had an awful lot to learn about many important areas of the law.

My legal background and experience really didn't prepare me very well for the kind of major judicial problems I face. For instance, most lawyers don't deal with constitutional issues related to the Bill of Rights and the Fourteenth Amendment; rather they deal with much more routine questions, such as wills and contracts. Civil liberties questions were really new to me as a judge, and I think this is true for most new judges.

A report about a Bush appointee to the trial bench confirms the persistence of this phenomenon. Before becoming a U.S. district judge, Melinda F. Harmon

was a Houston attorney for Exxon for 12 years. She had no experience in criminal litigation or in constitutional law, fields that will make up a significant portion of her case load as a federal judge. Harmon acknowledged at her confirmation hearing that she would have to rely on "on-the-job training" to become prepared for the federal bench. She said she used part of her trip to Washington to stop by the federal judicial training center and check out seven videotapes to help her prepare.[41]

At the appeals court level there is also a period of freshman socialization—despite the circuit judge's possible prior judicial experience—and former trial judges appear to make the transition with fewer scars. As a couple of appeals judges said of their first days on the circuit bench: "I was no blushing violet in fields I knew something about. How effective I was is another question." Even an experienced former trial judge recalled his surprise that "it takes a while to learn the job—and I'm not addressing myself to personal relationships. . . . That's a very different job." Another appeals judge, regarded by his peers as a leader from the beginning, said, "I don't know how I got through my first year." [42] During the transition time—the period of learning the appellate court ropes—circuit judges tend to speak less for the court than their more experienced colleagues; they often take longer to write opinions, defer more often to senior colleagues, or just wallow about in indecision.

The learning process for new Supreme Court justices is even harder—if the personal testimonies of justices as diverse as Benjamin Cardozo, Frank Murphy, Harlan F. Stone, Earl Warren, William Brennan, and Arthur Goldberg are to be believed. As one scholar has noted, "Once on the Court, the freshman Justice, even if he has been a state or lower federal court judge, moves into a strange and shadowy world." [43] Perhaps this is the metaphor that Chief Justice William Howard Taft had in mind when he confided that in joining the Court he felt that he had come "to live in a monastery." As with new appeals court judges, novice Supreme Court justices tend to defer to senior associates, to write fewer majority and dissenting opinions, and to manifest a good deal of uncertainty. New High Court appointees may have more judicial experience than their lower-court colleagues, but the fact that the Supreme Court is involved in broad judicial policy making—as opposed to the error correction of the appeals courts and the norm enforcement of the trial courts—

may account for their initial indecisiveness. Still, not all new justices experience what scholars have come to call "the freshman effect," and of those who do, not all manifest it in the same way.[44]

Supreme Court appointee David Souter's first year on the Court provides a good example of "the freshman effect phenomenon." Near the end of his first term on the Court, one observer noted that "Souter has gotten off to a notably slow start and written only one opinion of the 64 released this term, a unanimous ruling on a procedural point about jury selection" (hardly a bombshell case).[45] It was pointed out in *Newsweek* that

He may be a New Englander, but Justice David Souter hasn't shown much Yankee independence in his first term. . . . So far Souter has voted with the majority in all 40 of the decisions in which he has participated. Each of the other eight justices has written at least one dissenting opinion and joined the dissenting side several other times. Souter also lags behind in writing majority decisions—producing only one while the other justices have averaged six each. In the next few weeks, Souter may catch up; but some blame his anemic output for the court's end-of-term gridlock. "There's just one reason and that's the total breakdown in one chamber," says a former court clerk.[46]

Given the need on the part of all new federal jurists for both freshman and occupational socialization, where do they go for instruction? Although there are many agents of socialization for novice judges, the evidence is pretty strong that the older, more experienced judges have the primary responsibility for this task: the system trains and nurtures its own. As one trial judge told us, "My prime sources of help were the two judges here in [this city]. They sent me various things even before I was appointed, and I was glad to get them." Another recalled, "I had the help I needed right down here in the corner of this building on this floor," pointing in the direction of another judge's chambers. One district judge gave a more graphic description of his "schooling":

They [the other trial judges] let me sit next to them in actual courtroom situations, and they explained to me what they were doing at every minute. We both wore our robes and we sat next to each other on the bench. I would frequently ask them questions and they would explain things to me as the trial went along. Other times I would have a few free minutes and I would drop into another judge's courtroom and just sit and watch. I learned a lot that way.

For both the rotating appeals court judges and their trial court peers, then, the lion's share of training comes from their more senior, experienced colleagues on the bench—particularly the chief judge of the circuit or district.[47] One scholar has noted that "the impact of chief judges was most noticeable on freshmen. . . . ('If all the judges are new, he'll pack a wallop out of proportion to one vote.')"[48] Likewise on the Supreme Court there is evidence that older associates, often the chief justice, play a primary part in passing on to novice justices the essential rules and values on which their very serious game is based.[49]

The training seminars provided by the Federal Judicial Center for newly appointed judges should also be mentioned again in this regard because over the years the center has played an ever increasing role in the training and socialization of new jurists. Although some of these seminars are conducted by "outsider" specialists—subject matter experts in the law schools—the key instructors still tend to be seasoned judges whose real-life experience on the bench commands the respect of the new members of the federal judiciary.

The fact that judges in America still require socialization even after their appointments is interesting in and of itself, but we might well ask: What is the significance of all this for the operation of our judicial-legal system? First, the agents of socialization that are readily available to the novice jurists allow the system to operate more smoothly, with a minimum of down time. If new judges were isolated from their more experienced associates, geographically or otherwise, it would take them much longer to learn the fine points of their trade and presumably there would be a greater number of errors foisted upon hapless litigants.

There is a second consequence of the socialization process. As noted in Chapter 2, the judicial system is a rather loose hierarchy that is constantly subjected to centrifugal and centripetal forces from within and without. The fact that the system is able to provide its own socialization—that the older, experienced jurists train the novices—serves as a sort of glue that helps bond the fragmented system together. It allows the judicial values, practices, and orientations of one generation of judges to be passed on to another. It gives continuity and a sense of permanence to a system that operates in a world where chaos and random behavior appear to be the order of the day.

The Retirement and Removal of Judges

We have reached the final stage in our look at the judges themselves—the time when they cease performing their judicial duties, by choice, or because of ill health or death, or the disciplinary actions of others.

Disciplinary Action Against Federal Judges

All federal judges appointed under the provisions of Article III of the Constitution hold office "during good Behavior," which means in effect for life or until they choose to step down. The only way they can be removed from the bench is by impeachment (indictment by the House of Representatives) and conviction by the Senate. In accordance with constitutional requirements (for Supreme Court justices) and legislative standards (for appeals and trial court judges), impeachment may occur for "Treason, Bribery, or other high Crimes and Misdemeanors." An impeached jurist would face trial in the Senate, which could convict by a vote of two-thirds of the members present.[50]

The impeachment of a federal judge is a fairly rare event, although recently it has become a more familiar topic. In October 1989, the Senate voted to convict Judge Alcee L. Hastings on eight of the seventeen charges brought in impeachment proceedings against him. The case against the judge was filed less than two years after this black Carter appointee assumed the bench. The matter began when a convicted felon with long-standing associations with organized crime walked into the U.S. Attorney's Office in Miami and asked for a plea bargain. If drug charges would be reduced or dropped against him, he would be willing to provide information about a bribery scheme in Judge Hastings's court. An investigation followed, and criminal charges were brought against the judge, who was accused of soliciting and accepting a bribe and of "corruptly influencing and impeding the administration of justice." Ironically the judge was found not guilty of the charges, but during the course of the trial he had inadvertently revealed information that suggested that he ran his courtroom in an unethical, though not criminal, manner. Less than one month after the trial an investigation was commenced into Hastings's behavior by the chief judge of the Eleventh Circuit, John Godbold. A circuit judicial council called more than 110 witnesses and examined more than 2,800 exhibits. The committee found against Hastings and then officially informed the House of Representatives that Hastings had engaged in conduct that "might constitute one or more grounds for impeachment." The House of Representatives conducted an inquiry through the use of a subcommittee and on its recommendation voted 413 to 3 to impeach the judge. A trial was then held in the Senate. While some of the charges were thrown out, Judge Hastings was convicted on several counts and was promptly stripped of his judgeship.[51] Two weeks later the same fate befell Judge Walter L. Nixon, who was convicted on two of three impeachment charges. However, since 1789 the House has initiated such proceedings against only thirteen jurists—although about an equal number of judges resigned just before formal action was taken against them. Of these thirteen cases, only seven resulted in a conviction, which removed them from office. Considering all the men and women who have sat on the federal bench during the past two centuries, that's not a bad record. (In the past decade, four members of Congress were convicted of felonies in a single session!)

Although outright acts of criminality by those on the bench are few, a gray area of misconduct may put offending judges somewhere in the twilight zone between acceptable and impeachable behavior. What to do with the federal jurist who hears a case despite an obvious conflict of interest, who consistently demonstrates biased behavior in the courtroom, who too often totters into court after a triple-martini lunch? A case in point is Judge Willis Ritter, who used to sit on the federal bench in Salt Lake City. One observer described Ritter as

ecumenically mean, which is to say he seems to dislike most persons who come into his court, be they defendant, government lawyer, private trial attorney, or ordinary citizen. Ritter is also selective about his fellow judges. He was once so estranged from another Utah federal judge that they wouldn't ride on the elevator together, much less speak; for a while the court clerk divided cases so that they didn't have to appear in the courthouse on the same day. . . . Ritter is one of the few federal judges in the nation who becomes so emotionally involved in his hearings that appeals courts often order him not to retry cases when they are reversed.[52]

One lawyer who had managed to fall from Judge Ritter's graces recalled an incident. As the lawyer was starting to present his case in open court, from out of the blue the judge began to hiss at him and continued to do so throughout the attorney's presentation. "Like a snake, he was going 'ssssss' all the time I was speaking," the astounded lawyer recounted later. "I never ever have been before a judge of this kind."[53]

Had Ritter committed impeachable offenses? Surely he had not been guilty of "Treason, Bribery, or other high Crimes and Misdemeanors," although one could well question whether he was indeed serving "during good Behavior." Historically, little has been done in such cases other than issuance of a mild reprimand by colleagues (a useless gesture for a Judge Ritter) or impeachment (a recourse considered too drastic in most cases). In recent decades, however, actions have been taken to fill in the discipline gap. In 1966, for example, the Supreme Court upheld an action taken by the Tenth Circuit Judicial Council against U.S. District Judge Stephen S. Chandler of Oklahoma. The council had stripped him of his duties and authority (while permitting him to retain his salary and title) for a series of antics both on and off the bench that made Judge Ritter seem venerable by comparison.

In addition, on October 1, 1980, a new statute took effect, on which Congress had labored for several years. Titled the Judicial Councils Reform and Judicial Conduct and Disability Act, the law has two distinct parts.[54] The first authorizes the Judicial Council in each circuit, composed of both appeals and trial court judges and presided over by the chief judge of the circuit, to "make all necessary and appropriate orders for the effective and expeditious administration of justice within its circuit." The second part of the act establishes a statutory complaint procedure against judges. Basically, it permits an aggrieved party to file a written complaint with the clerk of the appellate court. The chief judge then reviews the charge and may dismiss it if it appears frivolous, or for a variety of other reasons. If the complaint seems valid, the chief judge must appoint an investigating committee consisting of himself or herself and an equal number of trial and circuit court judges. After an inquiry the committee reports to the council, which has several options: (1) the judge may be exonerated; (2) if the offender is a bankruptcy judge or magistrate, he or she may be removed; and (3) an Article III judge may be subject to private or public reprimand or censure, certification of disability, request for voluntary resignation, or prohibition against further case assignments. However, removal of an Article III judge is not permitted; impeachment is still the only recourse. If the council determines that the conduct "might constitute" grounds for impeachment, it will notify the Judicial Conference, which in turn may transmit the case to the U.S. House of Representatives for consideration.

Since the act went into effect there has been no shortage of complaints: between 1983 and 1990 some 1,586 were filed, an average of more than 200 each year. Of these, the chief judges dismissed the lion's share (1,224), and the circuit councils dismissed another 290. While some cases are still pending, we do know that some type of action was taken against 54 judges. (For example, the councils publicly censured one judge, privately censured another, issued a private warning to two more, and recommended that two be impeached by the House of Representatives.) Because of the confidential nature of this process, it is difficult to keep a hard count of all the disciplinary actions. Still, we do know that at least eleven judges chose to retire after judicial conduct complaints were filed and quite a number of others took senior status or reduced workloads because of deteriorating physical or mental health.[55] Thus, there is reason to believe that the Judicial Conduct Act is having some meaningful impact, although its effects cannot be measured with total precision.

Disability of Federal Judges

Perhaps the biggest problem has not been the removal of criminals and crackpots from the federal bench; rather, it has been the question of what to do with jurists who have become too old and infirm to carry out their judicial responsibilities effectively. As the former chief judge of the Fifth Circuit Court of Appeals, John Brown, tersely put it, "Get rid of the aged judges, and you get rid of most of the problems of the federal judiciary: drunkenness, incompetence, senility, cantankerous behavior on the bench." [56] For example, Justice William O. Douglas suffered a stroke while on the Supreme Court but refused afterward to resign, even when it was clear to all that he should do so. In 1974 Chief Justice Burger "believed Douglas was developing the paranoid qualities of many stroke victims. Douglas complained that there were plots to kill him and to remove him from the bench. Once he was wheeled into the Chief's chambers and maintained it was his. Rumors circulated among the staff that Douglas thought he was the Chief Justice." But he stayed on. A year later he was still interpreting the Constitution for over 200 million Americans although he "was in constant pain and barely had the energy to make his voice audible. He was wheeled in and out of conference, never staying the entire session, leaving his votes with Brennan to cast. Powell counted the number of times Douglas fell asleep. Brennan woke him gently when it came time to vote." Eventually Douglas resigned, but surely he remained on the bench longer than he should have. On the Court at the same time as Douglas were Justices John Harlan and Hugo Black. The latter, at eighty-five, was in such poor health that Douglas was counseling *him* to resign. "But Black would not accept the advice." [57]

In contrast to Black, Harlan continued to run his chambers from his hospital bed. Nearly blind, he could not even see the ash from his own cigarette, but he doggedly prepared for the coming term. One day a clerk brought in an emergency petition. Harlan remained in bed as he discussed the case with the clerk. They agreed that the petition should be denied. Harlan bent down, his eyes virtually to the paper, wrote his name, and handed the paper to his clerk. The clerk saw no signature. He looked over at Harlan. "Justice Harlan, you just denied your sheet," the clerk said, gently pointing to the scrawl on the linen. Harlan smiled and tried again, signing the paper this time.[58]

Although the federal judiciary as a whole is not proportionally in the same state of ill health and advanced age as was the Supreme Court during the early 1970s, the problem of what to do with the aged or mentally disabled judge has not disappeared. Congress has tried with some success to tempt the more senior judges into retirement by making it financially more palatable to do so. Since 1984 federal judges have been permitted to retire with full pay and benefits under what is called "the rule of eighty"—that is, when the sum of a judge's age and number of years on the bench is eighty. Congress has also permitted judges to go on "senior" status instead of accepting full retirement: In exchange for a reduced caseload they are permitted to retain their office and staff and—equally important—the prestige and self-respect of being an active judge. Despite the congressional inducements to retire, "more vacancies occur as a result of death in harness, particularly at the higher levels, than in any other way." [59]

We conclude this discussion of federal judicial tenure on a more political note. There is some credible evidence that judges often time their resignations to occur when their party controls the presidency so that they will be replaced by a jurist of similar political and judicial orientation. As one researcher concluded, "Among the Appeals and District judges there is a substantial contingent who bring to the bench political loyalties that encourage them, more often than not, to maneuver their departure in such a way that will maximize the chance for the appointment of a replacement by a president of their party." [60] This observation has been given even greater weight by a 1990 study that correlated federal trial judges' retirement patterns with a wide variety of variables. The study found, among other things, that especially since 1954, "judicial retirement/resignation rates have been strongly influenced by political/ideological considerations, and infused with partisanship." [61] Predicting electoral outcomes can sometimes be problematic, however, as indicated by this account of an Iowa district judge's decision about retirement:

By 1948 Iowa Southern District Federal Judge Charles A. Dewey had decided that the time had come for him to retire. The seventy-one-year-old jurist had served on the federal bench for two full decades, and he felt that he had earned the right to his government pension. As a good Republican, however, he felt that it would be best to withhold his resignation until after the November election when "President Thomas E. Dewey" would be in a position to fill the vacancy with another "right-minded" individual like himself. Much to Judge Dewey's chagrin, his namesake did not receive the popular mandate in the presidential election, and Judge Dewey did not believe that he could carry on for another four years until the American people finally "came to their senses" and put a Republican in the White House. Therefore, shortly after the November election, Judge Dewey tendered his resignation.[62]

A similar note is sounded by former chief justice William Howard Taft, who clung to his High Court position lest he be replaced with someone whose policy values were more progressive than his own: "As long as things continue as they are, and I am able to answer in their place, I must stay in the Court in order to prevent the Bolsheviki [that is, American Communists] from gaining control." [63] And more recently the liberal black Supreme Court justice Thurgood Marshall vowed not to "retire from the Court as long as Reagan remains in the White House." [64] (He kept his pledge throughout the Reagan years, but finally, in June 1991, a rather bitter and decrepit Thurgood Marshall yielded to Father Time and announced his resignation, saying, "I'm old and I'm coming apart.")

These illustrations provide further evidence that many jurists view themselves as part of a policy link between the people, the judicial appointment process, and the subsequent decisions of the judges and justices.

Summary

This chapter began with a collective portrait of the men and women who have served in the federal judiciary. We noted that despite the occasional maverick, the jurists have come from quite a narrow stratum within America's social and economic elite. The result is a core of judges who share similar values and who therefore strive, with minimal coercion, to keep the judicial system functioning in a relatively harmonious manner. Though formal qualifications for a seat on the bench are few, tradition has established several informal criteria, including a reasonable degree of professional competence, the right political affiliation and contacts, at least some desire for the job itself, and a bit of luck thrown in for good measure.

At the national level the judicial selection process includes a variety of participants, despite the constitutional mandate that the president shall do the appointing with the advice and consent of the Senate. If presidents are to dominate this process and name individuals having similar policy values to the bench, several conditions must be met: Chief executives must desire to make ideologically based appointments, they must have an ample number of vacancies to fill, they must be adroit leaders with political clout, and the existing judiciary must be attuned to their policy goals. If most of these conditions are met, presidents tend to get the kind of judges they want. In other words, there is an identifiable policy link between the popular election of the president, the appointment of judges, and the substantive content of the judges' decisions.

Although much judicial socialization occurs before the judges don their black robes, a good deal of learning takes place after they assume the bench. Because both freshman socialization and occupational socialization are furthered by senior colleagues, the values and practices of one generation of judges are smoothly passed on to the next. Thus continuity in the system is maintained.

The disciplining and removal of corrupt or mentally unfit judges is still a problem, although at the national level it may be eased as the Judicial Conduct Act of 1980 seems to be having some effect. The fact that so many judges time their resignations to allow a president (or a governor) of similar party identification and values to appoint a replacement is further evidence that the jurists themselves see a substantive link between the appointment process and the content of many of their decisions.

NOTES

1. Richard A. Posner, *The Federal Courts: Challenge and Reform* (Cambridge, Mass.: Harvard University Press, 1996), 20.

2. For a more extensive study of this subject, particularly as it pertains to the U.S. appeals courts and the Supreme Court, see John R. Schmidhauser, *Judges and Justices: The Federal Appellate Judiciary* (Boston: Little, Brown, 1979), 55–58.

3. Debra Sharpe and Peggy Roberson, "Tower Backs Cobb for Federal Judge," *Beaumont Enterprise,* May 4, 1984, A1.

4. Schmidhauser, *Judges and Justices,* 49.

5. Jill Abramson, "Ruth Bader Ginsburg Has Spent Her Career Overcoming the Odds," *Wall Street Journal,* June 15, 1993, A6.

6. J. Woodford Howard, Jr., *Courts of Appeals in the Federal Judicial System* (Princeton, N.J.: Princeton University Press, 1981), 121.

7. Howard Ball, *Courts and Politics: The Federal Judicial System* (Englewood Cliffs, N.J.: Prentice-Hall, 1980), 201–202.

8. As quoted in Joseph C. Goulden, *The Benchwarmers: The Private World of the Powerful Federal Judges* (New York: Weybright & Talley, 1974), 33.

9. Richard F. Schmitt, "Battle Erupts Over Federal Circuit Seat," *Wall Street Journal,* October 21, 1993, B8.

10. As quoted in Robert A. Carp and C. K. Rowland, *Policymaking and Politics in the Federal District Courts* (Knoxville: University of Tennessee Press, 1983), 55.

11. As a standard procedure, the Senate Judiciary Committee sends to the senator(s) of the state in which a district court vacancy exists a request, printed on a blue form, to approve or disapprove the nomination being considered by the committee. If approval is not forthcoming, the senator simply retains the slip; but if there is no objection, the blue form is returned to the committee.

12. As quoted in Ball, *Courts and Politics,* 176.

13. Cragg Hines, "Dispensing Legal Plums," *Houston Chronicle,* April 21, 1985, A1.

14. Goulden, *The Benchwarmers,* 65. The reason Kennedy was under pressure to appoint Cooper in the first place was that Cooper was the choice of Rep. Emanuel Celler, titular leader of New York State's congressional delegation and chairman of the House Judiciary Committee.

15. Sheldon Goldman and Elliot Slotnick, "Clinton's First Term Judiciary: Many Bridges to Cross," *Judicature* 80 (1997): 254–255.

16. Judy Wiessler, "NAACP, AFL-CIO Join Anti-Thomas Fray," *Houston Chronicle,* August 1, 1991, A1.

17. Jeanne Saddler, "Support for High-Court Nominee," *Wall Street Journal,* July 17, 1991, B2.

18. John R. Schmidhauser, *The Supreme Court: Its Politics, Personalities, and Procedures* (New York: Holt, Rinehart and Winston, 1960), 21.

19. The classic study of the role of the ABA is Joel B. Grossman, *Lawyers and Judges: The ABA and the Politics of Judicial Selection* (New York: Wiley, 1965).

20. For the humorous and interesting details of this controversy, see Goulden, *The Benchwarmers,* 61–62.

21. Harold W. Chase, *Federal Judges: The Appointing Process* (Minneapolis: University of Minnesota Press, 1972), 21, 23.

22. As quoted in Donald Dale Jackson, *Judges* (New York: Atheneum, 1974), 122.

23. Goldman and Slotnick, "Clinton's First Term Judiciary," 254–273.

24. Ronald Stidham, Robert A. Carp, and Donald R. Songer, "The Voting Behavior of President Clinton's Judicial Appointees," *Judicature* 80 (1996): 16–21.

25. Richard L. Berke, "A Missing Issue in the Big Race," *New York Times*, October 13, 1996, Sec. 4, 1.

26. Viveca Novak, "Empty-Bench Syndrome," *Time*, May 26, 1997, 37.

27. Greg McDonald, "Conservative Lawmakers Propose Impeachment of Activist Judges," *Houston Chronicle*, March 13, 1997, A6.

28. Novak, "Empty-Bench Syndrome," 38.

29. As quoted in Ball, *Courts and Politics*, 167.

30. Charles M. Cameron, Albert D. Cover, and Jeffrey A. Segal, "Senate Voting on Supreme Court Nominees: A Neoinstitutional Model," *American Political Science Review* 84 (1990): 532. For a more recent and equally sophisticated study of this phenomenon, see Jeffrey A. Segal, Charles M. Cameron, and Albert D. Cover, "A Spatial Model of Roll Call Voting: Senators, Constituents, Presidents, and Interest Groups in Supreme Court Confirmations," *American Journal of Political Science* 36 (1992): 96–121.

31. "Judicial Performance in the Fifth Circuit," *Yale Law Review* 73 (1963): 90–133.

32. Jack Nelson, "Courts Main Hope for Reagan Social Stand," *Houston Chronicle*, March 18, 1986, A6.

33. Jon R. Bond, "The Politics of Court Structure: The Addition of New Federal Judges," *Law and Policy Quarterly* 2 (1980): 182, 183, 187.

34. Henry J. Abraham, *The Judicial Process*, 3d ed. (New York: Oxford University Press, 1975), 77.

35. James A. Farley, "Why I Broke with Roosevelt," *Collier's*, June 21, 1947, 13.

36. See Jon Gottschall, "Carter's Judicial Appointments: The Influence of Affirmative Action and Merit Selection on Voting on the U.S. Courts of Appeals," *Judicature* 67 (1983): 165–173.

37. Goldman and Slotnick, "Clinton's First Term Judiciary," 256.

38. Ibid., 257.

39. This phenomenon also appears to occur among U.S. appeals court judges. See, for example, Stephen L. Wasby, "'Into the Soup?': The Acclimation of Ninth Circuit Appellate Judges," *Judicature* 73 (1989): 13. (This article is a good discussion of the socialization process of appeals court judges in general.)

40. New federal district judges with prior state court experience have a somewhat easier time of it, particularly in terms of the psychological adjustment to the judgeship and dealing with some of the administrative problems. However, prior state court experience seems to be of little help in the jurist's efforts to become expert in *federal* law. See Robert A. Carp and Russell R. Wheeler, "Sink or Swim: The Socialization of a Federal District Judge," *Journal of Public Law* 21 (1972): 367–374.

41. "Easy OK Seen for Houston Judge," *Houston Chronicle*, April 6, 1989, A6.

42. All quoted in Howard, *Courts of Appeals in the Federal Judicial System*, 224.

43. Walter F. Murphy, *Elements of Judicial Strategy* (Chicago: University of Chicago Press, 1964), 50.

44. For a recent and sophisticated study of this subject, see Timothy M. Hagle, "'Freshman Effects' for Supreme Court Justices," *American Journal of Political Science* 37 (1993): 1142–1157. Also, see Terry Bowen, "Consensual Norms and the Freshman Effect on the United States Supreme Court," *Social Science Quarterly* 76 (1995): 222–231.

45. Ruth Marcus, "Souter Draws Clear Bench Marks," *Houston Chronicle*, May 28, 1991, A4. Note, however, that not all Supreme Court appointees appear to manifest "the freshman effect." See, for example, Albert P. Melone, "Revisiting the Freshman Effect Hypothesis: The First Two Terms of Justice Anthony Kennedy," *Judicature* 74 (1990): 6–13.

46. "Souter: Slow Off the Mark," *Newsweek*, May 27, 1991, 4.

47. For the best discussion of this training, see Howard, *Courts of Appeals in the Federal Judicial System*, chap. 8.

48. Ibid., 229.

49. For examples of this, see Murphy, *Elements of Judicial Strategy*, 49–51.

50. For a good discussion of the impeachment process, including information on what the Founding Fathers had in mind regarding the terms "High Crimes and Misdemeanors," see "Impeaching Federal Judges: Where Are We and Where Are We Going?" *Judicature* 72 (1989): 359–365. (The article is an edited version of a panel discussion.) Also see Mary L. Volcansek, *Judicial Impeachment* (Urbana: University of Illinois Press, 1993).

51. Information about the Hastings impeachment was taken from Volcansek, *Judicial Impeachment*, chaps. 4 and 5.

52. Goulden, *The Benchwarmers*, 298.

53. Philip Hager, "Legal Leaders Seek Way to Unseat Unfit Federal Judges," *Houston Chronicle*, October 2, 1977, A6.

54. For a good discussion of this subject, see Collins T. Fitzpatrick, "Misconduct and Disability of Federal Judges: The Unreported Informal Responses," *Judicature* 71 (1988): 282–283.

55. All data in this paragraph derive from Volcansek, *Judicial Impeachment*, 13–14.

56. As quoted in Goulden, *The Benchwarmers*, 292.

57. Bob Woodward and Scott Armstrong, *The Brethren* (New York: Simon & Schuster, 1979), 361, 392, 156.

58. Ibid., 157.

59. Henry J. Abraham, *The Judicial Process*, 4th ed. (New York: Oxford University Press, 1980), 41.

60. R. Lee Rainey, "The Decision to Remain a Judge: Deductive Models of Judicial Retirement" (Paper delivered at the annual meeting of the Southern Political Science Association, Atlanta, 1976), 16.

61. Deborah J. Barrow and Gary Zuk, "An Institutional Analysis of Turnover in the Lower Federal Courts, 1900–1987," *Journal of Politics* 52 (1990): 457.

62. Robert A. Carp, "The Function, Impact, and Political Relevance of the Federal District Courts: A Case Study," Ph.D. dissertation, University of Iowa, 1969, 76.

63. As quoted in C. Herman Pritchett, *The Roosevelt Court: A Study of Judicial Votes and Values, 1937–1947* (New York: Macmillan, 1948), 18.

64. "Grading the Presidents," *Newsweek*, September 21, 1987, 33.

SUGGESTED READINGS

Abraham, Henry J. *Justices & Presidents: A Political History of Appointments to the Supreme Court*, 3d ed. New York: Oxford University Press, 1992. Offers an indepth political history of appointments to the U.S. Supreme Court.

Goldman, Sheldon, and Elliot Slotnick. "Clinton's First Term Judiciary: Many Bridges to Cross." *Judicature* 80 (1997): 254–278. Provides a background profile of the socioeconomic characteristics of the district and appeals court judges appointed by Presidents Carter through Clinton.

Goulden, Joseph C. *The Benchwarmers: The Private World of the Powerful Federal Judges*. New York: Weybright & Talley, 1974. A readable, journalistic account of the behind-the-scenes world of federal jurists.

Judicature 77 (1994). The entire issue is dedicated to discussion of electing, selecting, and retaining judges.

Posner, Richard A. *The Federal Courts: Challenge and Reform.* Cambridge, Mass.: Harvard University Press, 1996. A perceptive account of how the federal courts function and the problems they face, written by a judge who is also a judicial scholar.

Ryan, John Paul, et al. *American Trial Judges: Their Work Styles and Performance.* New York: Free Press, 1980. A classic analysis of the role of American trial judges and the ways that their performance might be evaluated.

Stidham, Ronald, et al. "The Voting Behavior of President Clinton's Judicial Appointees," *Judicature* 80 (1996): 16–20. Discusses the impact of the appointing president on the judicial voting behavior of his federal trial and appellate judges.

Twentieth Century Fund Task Force on Judicial Selection. *Judicial Roulette.* New York: Priority Press Publications, 1988. A concise, sophisticated review of the politics of federal judicial selection in recent decades.

Volcansek, Mary L. *Judicial Impeachment: None Called It Justice.* Urbana: University of Illinois Press, 1993. A comprehensive discussion of the removal of federal judges from office for misconduct.

CHAPTER 9

State Judges

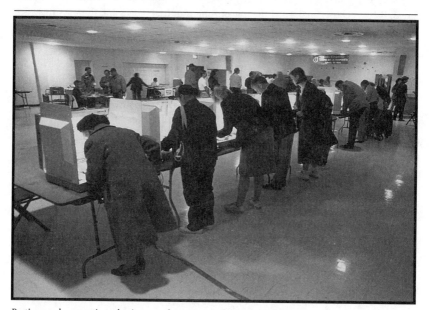

Partisan and nonpartisan elections are the most popular methods of choosing state judges. Some states allow voters to determine whether sitting judges should be retained.

IN THE PREVIOUS CHAPTER WE LOOKED at the women and men who serve as judges and justices in the federal courts. In this chapter our focus will be on those who wear the black robe in the numerous trial and appellate courts throughout the states.

Qualifications and Backgrounds of State Judges

Although the selection process for state judges varies from that of the federal model, the men and women who are tapped for judicial service reflect a familiar profile. State jurists, like their counterparts on the federal bench, are overwhelmingly older, white, male, and Protestant. They tend to be home-grown fellows who are moderately conservative and staunchly committed to the status quo. They believe in the basic values and tradition of the legal and political communities from which they come. State judges, then, share with their federal colleagues the distinction of being local boys who made good.

Most state laws and constitutions provide few rigid conditions for being a state judge. The vast majority of the states do not require their justices of the peace or magistrates to have law degrees, but such degrees are virtually required (either formally or in practice) for trial and appellate judges. Some states require their judges to be U.S. citizens.

The informal qualifications for being a state jurist are reflected in the socioeconomic profile that seems to hold throughout the United States. Although women constitute a scant majority of the American population, this fact is of little use to them if they seek judicial service—still very much a man's game. Despite the upsurge in recent decades in the number of women in the legal profession, women are still significantly underrepresented on the bench.

A recent study noted that only fifty-nine women served as state supreme court justices between 1922 and 1992.[1] Given the complex network of state courts, especially at the trial level, an exact figure on the number of female judges who have served as intermediate appellate court or trial court judges is more difficult to obtain. As one judicial scholar noted after Ruth Bader Ginsburg became the second woman appointed to the U.S. Supreme Court (thus doubling the number of female justices),

... the number of women judges on courts other than the U.S. Supreme Court has also doubled. In fact, the number of women judges has probably tripled, but accurate figures are hard to come by.[2]

Despite these improvements it is still noteworthy that women are disproportionately more likely to serve at the lower levels of the state judiciary than on the supreme courts, although even this phenomenon varies greatly from one state to the next. For example, some states have no women at all serving on their supreme courts while in Minnesota a majority of the justices are women. In the same vein, being non-Anglo is clearly not an asset if one yearns to wear a black robe: Less than 6 percent of all state judges are members of racial minorities.

State judges, like their federal counterparts, have never wandered far from the region in which they grew up and were educated. About three-fourths of all state jurists were born in the state in which they serve, and less than a third went out of state for their undergraduate degrees or even for their law degrees. This penchant for localism is also reflected in the patterns of work experience that state judges bring to the bench. For example, of those serving on the state supreme court bench, only 13 percent have any form of prior federal experience, whereas 93 percent have some type of prior state experience.

Judges tend to be middle-aged when they assume the bench. State trial judges come to the bench at about age forty-six, which corresponds roughly to the figure of forty-nine for federal trial judges. State appellate court judges tend to be a tad older than their trial court colleagues when they become jurists—about fifty-three, which is approximately the same as their federal equivalents.

In terms of political party affiliation, state judges, whether they be elected or appointed, tend to mirror the party that dominates in the judge's state. Since in the past more states have been controlled by Democrats than by Republicans, this fact is reflected in the partisan affiliation of the judges. Perhaps the key point here is that the vast majority of state judges had been politically active before assuming the bench. Whether they were elected to the bench or whether a governor placed them there, state judges in America tend to know which way the political wind is blowing at any given moment.

Over half the state trial judges come to the bench from the private practice of law, and about a quarter were elevated from a lower-court judgeship, such as a magistrate's position. Of those who practiced law, most reported a general practice without specialization. About one in five were recruited from the ranks of district attorneys, and only 3 percent come from private criminal law practice. Of those serving on state supreme courts, almost two-thirds came from the ranks of the intermediate appellate courts or from the state trial courts.[3]

What one keen observer has said about state trial judges is true about state judiciaries as a whole:

General trial judges, then, like their appellate brethren, represent a comparatively narrow group of legal professionals. White, middle-aged male lawyers in private practice (or sitting on lower courts or working in district attorney's offices) constitute the bulk of the pool. If you are young, female, a member of a racial minority, are of the wrong political party, or presumably have few contacts within the organized legal community in your state, the chances of making it to the trial bench are slight.[4]

The Selection Process for State Judges

At the state level a variety of methods are used to select jurists, and each of these has many permutations. Basically there are five routes to a judgeship in any one of the fifty states: partisan election, nonpartisan election, merit selection, gubernatorial appointment, and appointment by the legislature. Tables 9-1 and 9-2 indicate how many states fall into each category, for general trial courts and for the appellate courts. Note that there is a rough regional pattern to the distribution. The South still has a penchant for selecting judges with a party label, the upper Midwest

TABLE 9-1   Selection Processes for General Trial Courts

Method	State(s)
Partisan election	Alabama, Arkansas, Illinois, Indiana, Mississippi, New York, North Carolina, Pennsylvania, Tennessee, Texas, West Virginia
Nonpartisan election	Arizona, Florida, Georgia, Idaho, Kentucky, Louisiana, Michigan, Minnesota, Montana, Nevada, North Dakota, Ohio, Oklahoma, Oregon, South Dakota, Washington, Wisconsin
Merit selection	Alaska, Colorado, Connecticut, Delaware, Hawaii, Iowa, Kansas, Maryland, Massachusetts, Missouri, Nebraska, New Mexico, Utah, Vermont, Wyoming
Gubernatorial appointment	California, Maine, New Hampshire, New Jersey, Rhode Island
Legislative appointment	South Carolina, Virginia

SOURCE: Council of State Governments, *The Book of the States 1996–97* (Lexington, Ky.: Council of State Governments, 1996), 133–135. Reprinted with permission from *The Book of the States.*

TABLE 9-2   Selection Processes for Appellate Courts

Method	State(s)
Partisan election	Alabama, Arkansas, Illinois, Mississippi, North Carolina, Pennsylvania, Tennessee (Supreme Court), Texas, West Virginia
Nonpartisan election	Georgia, Idaho, Kentucky, Louisiana, Michigan, Minnesota, Montana, Nevada, North Dakota, Ohio, Oregon, Washington, Wisconsin
Merit selection	Alaska, Arizona, Colorado, Connecticut, Delaware, Florida, Hawaii, Indiana, Iowa, Kansas, Maryland, Massachusetts, Missouri, Nebraska, New Mexico, Oklahoma, South Dakota, Tennessee (Intermediate Appellate Court), Utah, Vermont, Wyoming
Gubernatorial appointment	California, Maine, New Hampshire, New Jersey, New York
Legislative appointment	Rhode Island, South Carolina, Virginia

SOURCE: Council of State Governments, *The Book of the States 1996–97* (Lexington, Ky.: Council of State Governments, 1996), 133–135. Reprinted with permission from *The Book of the States.*

and the West seem to like nonpartisan selection schemes, states west of the Mississippi often opt for the merit selection plans, and the East is partial to appointments made by either the governor or the state legislature.

But as is often the case in the political world, things are not always what they seem. For instance, in states that officially choose their judges by partisan elections, the vast majority of judges may actually receive their initial position through gubernatorial appointment. This occurs because a sitting judge may die or resign or a new judicial vacancy may occur, and the position is filled by the governor in accordance with state law. The newly appointed judge may eventually have to run for another term in a general election, but most incumbent judges are easily reelected. Thus a state listed in the partisan election column may in reality be a "gubernatorial appointment state." Likewise in states that are officially in the nonpartisan election category—for example, Minnesota—it is often no secret which judicial candidate is the Democrat and which is the Republican, and the voters respond accordingly.

Election of Judges

The election of judges, on either a partisan or a nonpartisan ballot, is the norm in the states. Although it was almost unheard of in colonial days, this method became popular during the time of President Andrew Jackson—an era when Americans sought to democratize the political process, probably thinking that "If only the average person in his simple innate wisdom could choose the judges, this would put an end to corruption and control of the government by the special (moneyed) interests." In practice things have not always worked this way, however. There is evidence that party bosses often regard judicial elections as indirect patronage to reward the party faithful. Also, judges who must run for election are often forced to solicit campaign contributions from the lawyers and law firms that will eventually appear before them in court—an obvious potential source of conflict of interest. Finally, the data overwhelmingly indicate that voter turnout in judicial elections is extremely low. Voters may know whom they prefer for president or member of Congress or state senator, but when presented with a long list of persons running for state judgeships, they often resort to the method used for so long by the grandmother of one of the authors: "I voted for the men who had honest-sounding names."[5]

As part of the Progressive movement at the turn of the century, reformers sought to take some of the raw partisanship out of judicial elections by having judges run on a nonpartisan basis. In principle they would run on their ideas and qualifications, not on the basis of which party they belonged to. But as with many a good idea, some little demon got hold of this one and ruined it in practice. One judicial scholar has noted that in about half of the "states that use nonpartisan judicial ballots, parties [still] play some role in the selection of judges."[6] That is, in these technically nonpartisan states, the political parties still endorse individual judicial candidates and contribute to their campaigns so that by the time of the election, only a dullard would fail to distinguish the "nonpartisan" Republican from the "nonpartisan" Democrat.

Merit Selection

Undaunted, reformers have come up with a method other than nonpartisan elections to accomplish the goal of obtaining good-quality state judges free from the taint of political bias. Merit selection, by whatever name, has been around since the early 1900s as a preferred method of selecting judges. The first state fully to adopt such a method was Missouri in 1940, and ever since such schemes have come to be known as generic variants of "the Missouri Plan."

The states with Missouri-type plans use a combination of elections and appointments; in effect this type of plan provides for much greater influence from lawyers than any other selection method. In essence the governor appoints a judge from among several candidates recommended by a nominating panel of five or more people, usually including attorneys (often chosen by the local bar association), non-lawyers appointed by the governor, and sometimes a senior local judge. Either by law or by implicit agreement, the governor will appoint someone from the recommended list. After serving for a short period of time, often a year, the newly appointed judge must stand for a special election, at which time he or she in effect runs on his or her record. (The voters are asked, "Shall Judge X be retained in office?") If the judge's tenure is supported by the voters, as is virtually always the case, the judge will serve for a regular and fairly long term. Does a Missouri plan take politics out of the judicial selection process? Well, yes and no. After an exhaustive study of how the plan had operated in Missouri over a quarter century, two observers concluded:

It is naive to suggest . . . that the Plan takes the "politics" out of judicial selection. Instead, the Plan is designed to bring to bear on the process of selecting judges a variety of interests that are thought to have a legitimate concern in the matter and at the same time to discourage other interests. It may be assumed that these interests will engage in the "politics" of judicial selection, that is, they will maneuver to influence who will be chosen as judges (1) because such judgeships constitute prestigious positions for aspiring lawyers, and (2) because, in the course of making decisions, judges inevitably affect the fortunes of persons and groups involved in the litigation process.[7]

A recent judicial contest in Tennessee shows what can happen when a judge is asked merely to run on her own record. Supreme Court Justice Penny White, who had been appointed to Tennessee's High Court in 1994 after previously serving as a trial and court of criminal appeals judge, faced a retention election in August 1996. The retention election became a referendum on the death penalty.[8] Justice White's most vocal opponents included the Tennessee Conservative Union, the Republican party, and Republican governor Don Sundquist. The Republican party mailed a brochure to voters that carried the slogan "Vote for Capital Punishment by Voting NO on August 1 for Supreme Court Justice Penny White." The brochure described three cases as evidence that Justice White placed the rights of criminals before the rights of victims. One case was described as follows:

Richard Odom was convicted of repeatedly raping and stabbing to death a 78 year old Memphis woman. However, Penny White felt the crime wasn't heinous enough for the death penalty—so she struck it down.[9]

Supporters of Justice White mounted a counterattack based on three arguments. First, they noted that Odom's case was reversed because all five members of the Tennessee Supreme Court agreed that there had been at least one legal error requiring a new sentencing hearing. Second, they pointed out that the court affirmed Odom's conviction and remanded the case only for a new sentencing hearing. In fact, they argued, the remand made it clear that the court did not find the death penalty inappropriate for Odom. Finally, White's supporters tried to make voters aware of the fact that she did not write the majority opinion, a concurring opinion, or a dissenting opinion in the case. The arguments in Justice White's behalf were to no avail, however, and she was removed from the bench.

Despite the unhappy anomalies that occasionally accompany this form of judicial selection and retention (à la Justice White), there is still a weak consensus among judicial scholars that the pluses of this method do outweigh the negatives. Nevertheless, these same scholars have been unable to document empirically any significant differences in the behavior of elected judges versus those selected under merit systems.[10] Thus, support for merit selection is more an act of faith than an argument based on well-documented findings. What Winston Churchill said about democracy (that it is the worst form of government—except for all the other forms) is possibly true of plans for the merit selection of judges.

Gubernatorial Appointment and Legislative Appointment

In the early days of the Republic, judges were chosen either by the governor or by the state legislature, but today such methods are used in only a handful of states. When judges are appointed by the governor, politics almost invariably comes into play. In the dozens of appointment opportunities that come their way, governors tend to select individuals who have been active in state politics and whose activity has benefited either the governor personally or the governor's political party or allies. Also, in making judicial appointments the governor often bargains with local political bosses or with state legislators whose support he or she needs. A governor may also use a judgeship to reward a legislator or local politico who has given faithful political support in the past.

Only a few states still allow their legislators to appoint state judges. Although a variety of criteria may be used in choosing members of the state supreme courts, when it comes to filling the state trial benches, state legislators tend to turn to former members of the legislature.[11] This does not mean that in these legislative-appointment states judges are merely political hacks in need of a job, but it is evidence that friends and colleagues do take care of their own when given the opportunity to do so.

Judicial Selection Methods and the Recruitment of Women and Minorities

We have already noted that in terms of gender and ethnicity, state (and federal) judiciaries are highly unrepresentative of the country as a whole. As of the mid–1990s, only about 14 percent of all state judges were women and 6 percent were either black, Hispanic, or Asian. Most advocates of increased ethnic and gender diversity on the bench have argued that at the very least it is essential out of basic fairness to these groups. Others point to the *symbolic importance* of having our judiciary better reflect the gender and ethnic makeup of society as a whole. Whether the decision making of women and ethnic minorities is—or should be—different from that of white males is still the subject of much debate. A few preliminary studies have suggested that with minor exceptions, women judges and judges belonging to racial minorities decide cases about the same way as their Anglo, male colleagues.[12] However, in more recent years there has been an increasing body of scholarship indicating that on some narrow but key issues women on the bench do indeed decide cases differently from their male colleagues. For example, a study of voting behavior of judges on the U.S. Courts of Appeals found no differences between male and female judges on obscenity and on search and seizure cases, but in employment discrimination cases female jurists were significantly more liberal than their male counterparts.[13] Why this should be so is still the subject of some debate.

But if, for the sake of fairness and political symbolism, we ought to have a more diverse judiciary, which selection method is most likely to achieve this aim? Scholars are hardly of one mind on this subject, and indeed the author of one study of the subject concluded, "Judicial selection methods alone do not explain differential representation of women, blacks, and Hispanics on state judiciaries." He further noted that selection methods that work for one group do not necessarily work for another, and that indeed minorities "may rationally choose to pursue different policy alternatives in their attempts to increase their representation on state judiciaries." But at the very least, women and minorities might try to increase the size of their ranks among attorneys in the states. The scholar concluded, "the significant, positive effects found . . . between both groups' shares of states' lawyers and their shares of state judgeships make this a rational coalitional goal."[14]

A 1991 U.S. Supreme Court decision might well be a boon for increased minority (and possibly women's) representation on the state bench.[15] The Court ruled that the Voting Rights Act of 1965 applies fully to the election of state court judges. This decision opened the doors to a panoply of suits against state governments pertaining to the way they choose their judges.[16] However, since some of the challenges under the Voting Rights Act are still working their way through the courts, it is still too early to fully assess the impact of the Supreme Court decision.

Some efforts to diversify the bench have been successful. A recent Louisiana Supreme Court decision illustrates. In 1992, the Louisiana legislature added an eighth seat to the state's seven-member highest court in order to settle a federal civil rights claim filed in 1986. The group filing the suit claimed that African Americans were not properly represented on the supreme court because of the way the state elects its justices. The parties agreed that adding a third justice from the New Orleans area would ensure African-American representation. The law was challenged on the ground that the Louisiana constitution stipulates a seven-member court. U.S. district judge Charles Schwartz, Jr., who handled the federal suit, asked the state Supreme Court to review the settlement. On July 1, 1997, the court found that the constitution does indeed limit the Louisiana Supreme Court to seven members. However, the court ruled that the change will not occur until the term for that seat expires in the year 2000. The seat in question has been held since 1994 by Bernette J. Johnson, the first African American to serve on the Louisiana Supreme Court.[17]

The Retirement and Removal of Judges

We have reached the final stage in our look at the judges themselves—the time when they cease performing their judicial duties, by choice, or because of ill health or death, or the disciplinary actions of others.

Being burdened with judges too old and unfit to serve seems to be less of a problem at the state level than at the federal level. This is so perhaps because a goodly number of states (thirty-five in all) have mandatory retirement plans; in 1991 the Supreme Court gave a major boost to such plans by ruling that they do not violate federal law or the equal protection clause of the Fourteenth Amendment.[18] Minimum ages for retirement range from sixty-five to seventy-five, with seventy being the most common. Some states even go so far as to have declining retirement benefit plans for judges who serve beyond the desired tenure—that is, the longer you stay on the bench, the lower your retirement benefits. Observers say that such plans are often quite effective in getting old, workaholic jurists to start examining travel brochures.

Retirement plans, no matter how effective in getting the older judge to resign, are still of little use against the younger jurist who is incompetent, corrupt, or unethical. Throughout American history the states have used procedures such as impeachment, recall elections, and concurrent resolutions of the legislature to rid themselves of the judge gone bad. For example, in 1992 the Florida Supreme Court demoted Judge John Santora as chief judge in his northeast Florida district for allegedly racist remarks made in a newspaper interview in which he blamed school violence on integration, opposed interracial marriage, and complained that most welfare recipients are black.[19] Nevertheless, the evidence suggests that these methods were only minimally effective, either because they proved to be politically difficult to put into operation or because of their time-consuming, cumbersome nature. (Sometimes, however, recall elections can be keenly effective—particularly when there is an ideological motive behind them. For example, in California in 1986, three justices on the state supreme court, including its chief justice, Rose Bird, were turned out of office by a conservative wave of voters who objected to the justices' liberal voting record.)

More recently, the states have begun to set up special commissions, often made up of the judges themselves, to police their own members. Reformers have given such commissions only fair-to-poor marks, however. The reason is that the persons most familiar with the problem—the judges themselves—are often loath to expose a colleague to public censure and discipline. One state judge anonymously told one of us about a fellow jurist who was an alcoholic:

We all know he's on the bottle and the [chief court] administrator no longer assigns him any real cases. He just signs grand jury indictments and stuff like that. The tragedy is that he was a great man and a very good judge before he turned to drink. He recently has had a lot of sorrow in his life, you see, and no one wants to be the one known as the mean bastard who went public with what we know. We [all the judges] just cover for him and hope he will either lay off the booze or resign.

Policing the state judiciaries remains a challenge that beckons champions of good government.

Summary

This chapter began with a collective portrait of the men and women who have served in the state judiciaries. We noted that state jurists generally have had strong ties to the locales in which they've served, and like their federal counterparts have come from a distinct stratum of American society. The result is a core of judges who share similar values and who therefore strive, with minimal coercion, to keep the judicial system functioning in a relatively harmonious manner. Though formal qualifications for a seat on the bench are few, tradition has established several informal criteria, including a reasonable degree of professional competence, the right political affiliation and contacts, at least some desire for the job itself, and a bit of luck thrown in for good measure.

Politics and the judiciary go hand in glove. If the governor appoints the judges, then similarity between the values of the governor and of the judicial nominees is the norm. If judges are elected—even on "nonpartisan" ballots—the political and judicial processes are still inexorably intertwined. Judicial decisions by state judges reflect both the process by which the judges are chosen and the values of those who choose them.

Retention elections, such as the one involving Justice Penny White in Tennessee, frequently reflect struggles between politically diverse groups in the state. In California, another effort is under way to remove a judge: Orange County Superior Court Judge Nancy Wieben Stock, the judge who awarded O.J. Simpson custody of his two youngest children, was served with recall papers by the Women's Progress Alliance on April 7, 1997. Judge Stock responded to the recall petition by stating that she "had no discretion to ignore the law of parental preference."[20]

The disciplining and removal of corrupt or mentally unfit judges is still a problem. However, implementation of mandatory retirement plans and the establishment of peer policing commissions illustrate the states' commitment to addressing this problem.

NOTES

1. David W. Allen and Diane E. Wall, "Role Orientations and State Supreme Court Justices," *Judicature* 77 (1993): 156.

2. Elaine Martin, "Women on the Bench: A Different Voice?" *Judicature* 77 (1993): 126.

3. The statistics for the background characteristics of the state judges are taken from these sources: Beverly Blair Cook, "Women Judges: The End of Tokenism," in *Women in the Courts*, ed. Winifred L. Hepperle and Laura Crites (Williamsburg, Va.: National Center for State Courts, 1978), 84–105; Bradley C. Canon, "Characteristics and Career Patterns of State Supreme Court Justices," *State Government* 45 (Winter 1972): 34–41; Susan Carbon, "Women in the Judiciary," *Judicature* 65 (1982): 285; Henry Glick and

Craig Emmert, "Stability and Change: Characteristics of Contemporary State Supreme Court Judges," *Judicature* 70 (1986): 107–112; John Paul Ryan, Allan Ashman, and Sandra Shane Du Bow, *American Trial Judges: Their Work Styles and Performance* (New York: Free Press, 1980); and Harry P. Stumpf and John H. Culver, *The Politics of State Courts* (White Plains, N.Y.: Longman, 1992).

4. Harry P. Stumpf, *American Judicial Politics* (San Diego: Harcourt Brace Jovanovich, 1988), 184.

5. Still, there is encouraging evidence to suggest that those voters who do trouble themselves to vote in the low-turnout elections for judicial candidates are much better informed about the candidates and the issues than voters in general. See, for example, Nicholas P. Lovrich, John C. Pierce, and Charles H. Sheldon, "Citizen Knowledge and Voting in Judicial Elections," *Judicature* 73 (1989): 28–33.

6. Herbert Jacob, *Justice in America*, 4th ed. (Boston: Little, Brown, 1984), 124.

7. Richard A. Watson and Rondal G. Downing, *The Politics of the Bench and the Bar* (New York: Wiley, 1969), 331–332.

8. Our account of Justice White's retention election is drawn from Stephen B. Bright, "Political Attacks on the Judiciary," *Judicature* 80 (1997): 165–173.

9. Ibid., 168–169.

10. For example, a good study of this subject concluded in part that "as far as responsiveness to public opinion is concerned, merit judges are indistinguishable from their 'non-merit' colleagues." Jerome O'Callaghan, "Another Test for the Merit Plan," *Justice System Journal* 14, no. 3 and 15, no. 1 (1991): 477.

11. Herbert Jacob, "The Effect of Institutional Differences in the Recruitment Process: The Case of State Judges," *Journal of Public Law* 13 (1964): 104–119; Bradley C. Canon, "The Impact of Formal Selection Process on the Characteristics of Judges—Reconsidered," *Law and Society Review* 6 (1972): 575–593; and Henry R. Glick and Craig F. Emmert, "Selection Systems and Judicial Characteristics," *Judicature* 70 (1987): 228–235.

12. See Cassia Spohn, "The Sentencing Decisions of Black and White Judges: Expected and Unexpected Similarities," *Law and Society Review* 24 (1990): 1197–1216; and David W. Allen and Diane E. Wall, "The Behavior of Women State Supreme Court Justices: Are They Tokens or Outsiders?" *Justice System Journal* 12 (1987): 232–245.

13. See Sue Davis, Susan Haire, and Donald R. Songer, "Voting Behavior and Gender on the U.S. Courts of Appeals," *Judicature* 77 (1993): 129–133. For additional research on outcome differences see Malcolm D. Holmes, Harmon M. Hosch, Howard C. Daudistel, and Joseph B. Graves, "Judges' Ethnicity and Minority Sentencing: Evidence Concerning Hispanics," *Social Science Quarterly* 74 (September 1993): 496–506; Martin, "Women on the Bench: A Different Voice?"; and Donald R. Songer, Sue Davis, and Susan Haire, "A Reappraisal of Diversification in the Federal Courts: Gender Effects in the Courts of Appeals," *Journal of Politics* 56 (1994): 425–439.

14. Nicholas O. Alozie, "Distribution of Women and Minority Judges: The Effects of Judicial Selection Methods," *Social Science Quarterly* 71 (1990): 321, 324. In a recent study focusing on the representation of women on state courts of last resort, Alozie again confirms that formal selection systems may not provide the answer to increasing the role of women on such courts. See Alozie, "Selection Methods and the Recruitment of Women to State Courts of Last Resort," *Social Science Quarterly* 77 (1996): 110–126.

15. *Chisom v. Roemer; Houston Lawyers' Association v. Texas Attorney General*, 499 U.S. 935 (1991).

16. See Anna M. Scruggs, Jean-Claude Mazzola, and Mary E. Zaug, "Recent Voting Rights Act Challenges to Judicial Elections," *Judicature* 79 (1995): 34–41.

17. Our discussion of this case is based on Mark Ballard, "Louisiana High Court Loses a Seat," *The National Law Journal*, July 14, 1997, A7. The case is *Perschall v. State*, 96-CC-0322.

18. *Gregory v. Ashcroft*, 498 U.S. 979 (1991).

19. "Remarks Get Judge Demoted," *Houston Chronicle*, January 18, 1992, A8.

20. B.J. Palermo, "O.J. Custody Judge Targeted," *The National Law Journal*, April 28, 1997, A8.

SUGGESTED READINGS

Baum, Lawrence. "Electing Judges." In *Contemplating Courts*, ed. Lee Epstein, 18–43. Washington, D.C.: CQ Press, 1995. Addresses the question of how voters choose between candidates for Ohio Supreme Court judgeships.

Judicature 77 (1994). The entire issue is dedicated to discussion of electing, selecting, and retaining judges.

Ryan, John Paul, Allan Ashman, and Sandra Shane Du Bow. *American Trial Judges: Their Work Styles and Performance.* New York: Free Press, 1980. A classic analysis of the role of American trial judges and the ways that their performance might be evaluated.

Sheldon, Charles H., and Nicholas P. Lovrich, Jr. "State Judicial Recruitment." In *The American Courts: A Critical Assessment*, ed. John B. Gates and Charles A. Johnson, 161–188. Washington, D.C.: CQ Press, 1991. A good general review of the major selection methods for judges in the states and their advantages and disadvantages.

Watson, Richard A., and Rondal G. Downing. *The Politics of the Bench and the Bar.* New York: Wiley, 1969. A study of the impact of merit selection in Missouri.

CHAPTER 10

Decision Making by Trial Court Judges

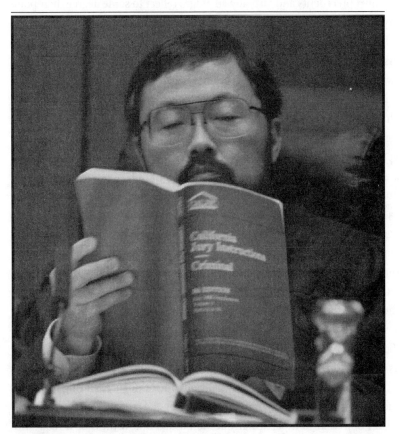

Judges must take special care with the instructions they provide to the jury because decisions are reversed for improper instructions more than for any other reason. Here, Judge Lance Ito reviews California jury instructions during the O.J. Simpson murder trial.

ON WHAT BASIS AND FOR WHAT reasons do judges in the United States rule the way they do on the motions, petitions, and judicial policy questions with which they must deal? We shall respond to this query by summarizing the theories and research findings of a large number of judicial scholars who have tried to find out what makes judges tick. (Chapter 11 will examine the special case of decision making on the *collegial* appellate courts at the state and federal levels.) In this chapter we will examine federal and state jurists as a group because, to a large extent, the variables that influence judicial decision making are the same for judges at both levels of the judiciary. For instance, both types of judges tend to be strongly governed by court precedents and virtually all judges reflect to some degree their political party affiliation. Where differences between federal and state judges can be anticipated, we will take note of it. For example, one would expect public opinion to have less effect on federal judges who are appointed for life than on those state judges who must regularly stand for reelection.

It is useful to begin with a brief discussion of the decision-making environment in which trial judges and their appellate colleagues operate. Because of the differing purposes and organizational frameworks of trial and appellate courts, judges of each type face particular kinds of pressures and expectations. As the chapter emphasizes, however, all jurists are subject to two major kinds of influences: the legal subculture and the democratic subculture. It is often difficult to determine, in any given case, the relative weight that any specific influence has on a judge. Studies have suggested, though, that when judges, especially trial judges, find no significant precedent to guide them—that is, when the legal subculture cupboard is bare— they tend to turn to the democratic subculture, an amalgam of determinants that include their own political inclinations.

At the base of the federal and state judicial hierarchies are the trial court judges who preside over the judicial process and who corporately make hundreds of millions of decisions each year. Some pertain to legal points and procedures raised by litigants even before a trial begins, such as a motion by a criminal defendant's lawyer to exclude from trial a piece of illegally obtained evidence. During the actual trial a judge must rule on scores of motions made by the attorneys in the case—for example, an objection to a particular question asked of a witness or a request to strike from the record a contested bit of testimony. Even after a verdict has been rendered, a trial judge may be beset with demands for decisions—for instance, the request by a litigant to reduce a monetary award made by a civil jury.

Trial judges can and occasionally do take ample time to reflect on their more important decisions and may consult with their staff or other judges about how to handle a particular legal problem. Nevertheless, a significant portion of their decision making must be done on the spur of the moment, without the luxury of lengthy reflection or discussion with staff or colleagues. As one trial judge told us: "We're where the action is. We often have to 'shoot from the hip' and hope you're doing the right thing. You can't ruminate forever every time you have to make a ruling. We'd be spending months on each case if we ever did that." (Again, virtually all of the judges interviewed for this study were promised anonymity.)

Decision making by the appeals courts and the supreme courts is different in several important respects. By the time a case reaches the appellate levels, the record and facts have already been established. The jurists' job is to review dispassionately the transcript of a trial that has already occurred, to search for legal errors that may have been committed by others. Few snap judgments are required. And although the appeals courts and a supreme court may occasionally hear oral arguments by attorneys, they do not examine witnesses and they are removed from the drama and confrontations of the trial courtroom. Another difference in the decision-making process between the trial and appellate levels is that the former is largely individualistic, whereas the latter is to some degree the product of group deliberation (discussed in Chapter 11).

Despite the acknowledged differences between trial and appellate judge decision making, there are many factors common to all American jurists, and we shall examine several studies that have sought to explain why judges in general think and act as they do. As we shall see, the thrust of these scholarly attempts at explanation has differed. Some view judges as judicial computers who take in a volume of facts, law, and legal doctrines and spew out "correct" rulings—determinations that are virtually independent of the judges' values and characteristics as human beings. Other researchers tend to explain judicial decision making in terms of the personal orientations of the judges themselves. A decision is seen not so much as the product of some unbiased, exacting thought process that judges learn in law school but rather as being affected by the judge's life experiences, prejudices, and overall social values. As with most explanatory theories of human behavior, each of these approaches has its fair share of the truth, but none accounts for the whole story of the activity in question.

One simple but comprehensive model for explaining judicial decision making was developed by Richard Richardson and Kenneth Vines almost three decades ago.[1] These two judicial scholars argued that judges are influenced in their decision making by two separate but overlapping sets of stimuli: the legal subculture and the democratic subculture. We shall use their basic analytic framework, with updated research findings, to offer an account of how and why judges make decisions the way they do.

The Legal Subculture

In examining the legal subculture as a source of trial judge decision making, it is useful to focus on a number of specific questions. What are the basic rules, practices, and norms of this subculture? Where do judges learn these principles, and what groups or institutions keep judges from departing from them? How often and under what circumstances do judges respond to stimuli other than those from the traditional legal realm?

The Nature of Legal Reasoning

In a popular television series of the 1970s, "The Paper Chase," the formidable Professor Kingsfield promises his budding law students that if they work hard and turn their mush-filled brains over to him, he will instill in them the ability "to think like a lawyer." How *do* lawyers and judges think when they deliberate in their professional capacities? In one classic answer to this question, we are told that "the basic pattern of legal reasoning is reasoning by example. It is a three-step process described by the doctrine of precedent as follows: (1) similarity is seen between cases; (2) the rule of law inherent in the first case is announced; and (3) the rule of law is made applicable to the second case."[2]

Let us look at an example. The cases of *Lane v. Wilson* and *Gomillion v. Lightfoot* had similar arguments and factual situations.[3] In the former case a black citizen of Oklahoma brought suit in federal court alleging that he had been deprived of the right to vote. In 1916 the legislature of that state had passed a law, ostensibly designed to give formerly disenfranchised black citizens the right to vote, that required them to register—but the registration period was only *twelve days!* (White voters were for all practical purposes exempted from this scheme through the use of a "grandfather clause.") If blacks did not sign up within that short interval, never again would they have the right to vote. The Oklahoma legislature clearly realized that a twelve-day period was wholly inadequate for blacks to mount a voter registration drive and that the vast majority would not acquire the franchise. The plaintiff in this case did not get on the registration rolls in 1916. When he was thereafter forbidden ever to vote, he brought suit claiming the Oklahoma registration scheme to be unconstitutional. The Supreme Court agreed with the plaintiff; in striking down the statute, it set forth this principle, or rule of law: "The Fifteenth Amendment nullifies sophisticated as well as simple-minded modes of discrimination."[4]

Two decades later another black citizen, Charles Gomillion, brought suit in the federal courts alleging a denial of his right to vote as secured by the Fifteenth Amendment. Here an Alabama statute altered the Tuskegee city boundaries from a square to a twenty-eight-sided figure, allegedly removing "all save only four or five of its 400 Negro voters while not removing a single white voter or resident." Although not denying the right of a legislature to alter city boundaries "under normal circumstances," the Court saw through this thinly disguised attempt by the Alabama legislature to deny the suffrage to the black citizens of Tuskegee. Reasoning that the situation in *Gomillion* was analogous to that in the Oklahoma case, the Court used the precedent of *Lane v. Wilson* to strike down the Alabama law: "It is difficult to appreciate what stands in the way of adjudging a statute having this inevitable effect invalid in light of the principles of which this Court must judge, and uniformly has judged, statutes that, howsoever speciously defined, obviously discriminate against colored citizens. 'The Fifteenth Amendment nullifies sophisticated as well as simple-minded modes of discrimination.' *Lane v. Wilson.*" Here is one example of the judicial reasoning process—of thinking like Professor Kingsfield's lawyer. Two cases are compared because the facts or principles are similar; a rule of law gleaned from the first case is applied to the second. This step-by-step process is the essence of proper and traditional legal reasoning.

Adherence to Precedent

A related value held by trial and appellate judges is a commitment to follow *precedents*—that is, decisions rendered on similar subjects by judges in the past. The sacred doctrine of *stare decisis* ("stand by what has been decided") is a cardinal principle of our common law tradition. In a series of interviews, William Kitchin asked federal district judges to rate the importance of "clear and directly relevant" precedents in their decision-making process. Precedent attained a score of 90.44 on a 100-point scale, whereas the judge's "personal, abstract view of justice in the case" was ranked only 60.69.[5] As for appellate court judges, a 1981 study of appeals courts in the Second, Fifth, and District of Columbia Circuits concluded that "adherence to precedent remains the everyday, working rule of American law, enabling appellate judges to control the premises of decision of subordinates who apply general rules to particular cases."[6] The U.S. Supreme Court, although technically free to depart from its own precedents, does so very seldom, for when "the Court reverses itself or makes new law out of whole cloth—reveals its policy-making role for all to see—the holy rite of judges consulting a higher law loses some of its mysterious power."[7]

Ideally, adherence to past rulings gives predictability and continuity to the law and reduces the dangerous possibility that judges will decide cases on a momentary whim or with a totally individualistic sense of right and wrong. Not all legal systems have placed such emphasis on *stare decisis*, however. In early Greek times, for example, the judge-kings decided each case on the basis of what appeared fair and just to them at the moment. When a judge-king resolved a dispute, the judgment was assumed to be the result of direct divine inspiration.[8] The early Greek model is thus the antithesis of the common law tradition. As we shall momentarily see, however, strict adherence to past precedent may be something of a legal fiction. We have long known that judges can and do distinguish among various precedents in creating new law. This helps to keep the law flexible and reflective of changing societal values and practices. Indeed, many scholars have argued that the readiness of common law judges occasionally to discard or ignore precedents that no longer serve the public has contributed to the very survival of the common law tradition.

Constraints on Trial Judge Decision Making

Another significant element of the legal subculture—found under the heading of what one prominent scholar has called the "great maxims of judicial self-restraint"[9]—we have already examined, in Chapter 4. These maxims derive from a variety of sources—the common law, statutory law, legal tradition—but each one serves to limit and channel the decision making of state and federal judges. Because we have discussed these various principles in detail, we shall merely reiterate here a few of the major themes of judicial self-restraint.

Before a judge will agree even to hear a case, there must exist a definite "case" or "controversy" at law or in equity between bona fide adversaries under the Constitution. The case must concern the protection or enforcement of valuable legal rights or the punishment, prevention, or redress of wrongs directly related to the litigants in the case. Allied with this maxim is the principle that U.S. judges may not render "advisory opinions"—that is, rulings on abstract, hypothetical questions. (As noted in Chapter 4, this rule is not followed as strictly in many state systems.) Also, all parties to a lawsuit must have "standing," or a substantial personal interest infringed by the statute or action in question.

The rules of the game also forbid jurists to hear a case unless all other legal remedies have been exhausted. In addition, the legal culture discourages the judiciary from deciding "political questions," or matters that ought to be resolved by one of the other branches of government, by another level of government, or by the voters. Judges are also obliged to give the benefit of the doubt to statutes and to official actions whose constitutionality is being questioned. A law or an executive action is presumed to be constitutional until proven otherwise. (Some judges adhere to this principle on economic issues but not on matters of civil rights and civil liberties, believing that in these matters the burden of proof is on the government.) In this same realm, judges feel bound by the norm that if they must invalidate a law, they will do so on as narrow a ground as possible or will void only that portion of the statute that is unconstitutional.

Finally, America's jurists may not throw out a law or an official action simply because they personally believe it to be unfair, stupid, or undemocratic. In order for a statute or an official deed to be invalidated, it must be clearly unconstitutional. Of course, judges do not always agree about what is a "clearly unconstitutional" act, but most acknowledge that broad matters of public policy should be determined by the people through their elected representatives—not by the judiciary.

The Impact of the Legal Subculture: An Example

Because the principles that make up the legal subculture—reasoning, precedent, and restraint—tend to be abstract, it is useful to illustrate them with a real-life example. The 1964 case of *Evers v. Jackson Municipal Separate School District* is a case in point.[10] It was an uncomplicated school integration case in which a group of black children and their parents sought to enjoin the "district and its officials from operating a compulsory biracial school system." The facts and controlling precedents were clear enough: (1) Jackson, Mississippi, was overtly maintaining a segregated public school system; (2) the U.S. Supreme Court had ruled a decade previously in *Brown v. Board of Education* that such segregation was unconstitutional; and (3) the U.S. Court of Appeals for the Fifth Circuit, which has jurisdiction over Mississippi, had handed down a string of rulings ordering the integration process to go ahead.

The federal trial judge in this case, Sidney Mize, did not like the commands he heard from the legal subculture. Appointed to the federal bench in 1937, Mize was an unabashed segregationist, as his written opinion in this case clearly shows. After discussing a score of alleged physical and mental differences between blacks and whites, Mize argued further that

in the case of Caucasians and Negroes, such differences may be directly confirmed by comparative anatomical and encephalographic measurements of the correlative physical structure of the brain and of the neural and endocrine systems of the body. The evidence was conclusive to the effect that the cranial capacity and brain size of the average Negro is approximately ten per cent less than that of the average white person of similar age and size, and that brain size is correlated with intelligence.[11]

On an ostensibly more positive and benign note, Judge Mize also argued, "From the evidence I find that separate classes allow greater adaptation to the differing educational traits of Negro and white pupils, and actually result in greater scholastic accomplishments for both."[12]

It seems clear where this decision is headed. But wait: Enter the legal subculture. After fourteen single-spaced printed pages of argument against the integration of the Jackson schools, Mize yielded to the requirements of legal reasoning, respect for precedent, and judicial self-restraint. Almost sheepishly he concluded his decision with these unexpected words:

Nevertheless, this Court feels that it is bound by what appears to be the obvious holding of the United States Court of Appeals for the Fifth Circuit that if disparities and differences such as that reflected in this record are to constitute a proper basis for the maintenance of separate schools for the white and Negro races it is the function of the United States Supreme Court to make such a decision and no inferior federal court can do so.[13]

Mize then quietly enjoined the school district and its officials from operating a compulsory biracial school system: The legal subculture tiptoed to victory.

Wellsprings of the Legal Subculture

We have examined some of the major threads of the tapestry of America's legal subculture; we will now point briefly to the institutions that instill and maintain the legal values in this country—"the law schools, the bar associations, the judicial councils, and other groups that spring from the institutionalization of the 'bench and the bar.'"[14]

"The purpose of law school," we are told, "is to change people; to turn them into novice lawyers; and to instill in them a nascent self-concept as a professional, a commitment to the value of the calling, and a claim to that elusive and esoteric style of reasoning called 'thinking like a lawyer.'"[15] The world just does not look the same to someone on whom law school has worked its indoctrinating magic. Facts and relationships in the human arena that formerly went unnoticed suddenly become "compelling" and "controlling" to the fledgling advocate. Likewise other facets of reality that previously had been important in one's world view are now dismissed as "irrelevant and immaterial."

Besides the indoctrination that occurs in law school, the values of the legal subculture are maintained by the state and national bar associations[16] and by a variety of professional-social groups whose members are from both bench and bar—for example, the honorary Order of the Coif. We have already documented in Chapters 8 and 9 how the values and practices of jurists are handed down from one generation to another. Thus the traditions and tenets of the American legal subculture are well tended by powerful support groups. They are rightly accorded ample deference if one is to understand judicial decision making in America.

The Limits of the Legal Subculture

Despite the taut nature of judicial reasoning and the importance of *stare decisis* and of judicial self-restraint, the legal subculture does not totally explain the behavior of American jurists. If "objective facts" and "obvious controlling precedents" were the only stimuli to which jurists responded, then the judicial decision-making process would be largely mechanical and all judicial outcomes would be quite predictable. Yet even the legal subculture's most loyal apologists would concede that judges often distinguish among precedents and that some judges are more inclined toward self-restraint than others.

To understand the thinking of judicial decision makers and the evolution of the law, we must consider more than law school curricula and the canons of the bar associations. One of the first great minds to realize this was Justice Oliver Wendell Holmes, Jr., who over a century ago wrote that

the life of the law has not been logic; it has been experience. The felt necessities of the time, the prevalent moral and political theories, intuitions of public policy, avowed or unconscious, even the prejudices which judges share with their fellow-men have had a good deal more to do than syllogism in determining the rules by which men should be governed. The law embodies the story of a nation's development through many centuries, and it cannot be dealt with as if it contained only the axioms and corollaries of a book of mathematics. In order to know what it is, we must know what it has been, and what it tends to become. . . . The very considerations which judges most rarely mention, and always with an apology, are the secret root from which the law draws all the juices of life. I mean, of course, considerations of what is expedient for the community concerned.[17]

By about the 1920s a whole school of thought had developed that argued that judicial decision making was as much the product of human, extralegal stimuli as it was of some sort of mechanical legal thought process. Adherents of this view, who were known as "judicial realists," insisted that judges, like other human beings, are influenced by the values and attitudes learned in childhood. As one of these "realists" put it, a judge's background "may have created plus or minus reactions to women, or blonde women, or men with beards, or Southerners, or Italians, or Englishmen, or plumbers, or ministers, or college graduates, or Democrats. A certain facial twitch or cough or gesture may start up memories, painful or pleasant."[18]

Since the late 1940s, the study of the personal, extralegal influences on decision making has become more rigorous. Often calling themselves "judicial behavioralists," modern-day advocates of the realist approach have improved on it in two ways. First, they have tried to test empirically many of the theories and propositions advanced by the realist school; second, they have attempted to relate their findings to more scientifically grounded theories of human behavior. Thus, whereas a realist might have asserted that a Democratic judge would probably be more supportive of labor unions than a Republican jurist, a judicial behavioralist might go a step further by taking a generous random sample of labor union-versus-management decisions and statistically determining whether Democratic judges are significantly more likely to back the union position than their GOP counterparts. Thus it is one thing to intuitively ascribe a cause for human behavior; it is another to subject an assertion to careful empirical analysis.

In the next section we shall discuss the many extralegal stimuli that the realists and behavioralists have shown to impinge upon trial judge decision making. In the last section of the chapter, we shall explore questions such as: Which is the more compelling explanation for judicial decision making—the one provided by the legal subculture model or the one offered by the realist-behavioralist school? Does the efficacy of the model depend on the type of case(s) we are attempting to analyze? Does the way that judges view their judicial role help to determine which mode of explanation is the more compelling?

The Democratic Subculture

We know that the legal subculture has an impact on American jurists. There is evidence, too, that popular, democratic values—manifested in a variety of ways through many different mediums—have an influence as well. Indeed, some scholars have argued that the only reason courts have maintained their significant role in the American political system is that they have learned to bend when the democratic winds have blown—that is, that judges have tempered rigid legalisms with common-sense popular values and have maintained "extensive linkages with the democratic subculture":

Very often, legal elites such as bar associations and judicial councils are more noticeable spokesmen for the federal judiciary than are the spokesmen of the democratic subculture. However, representatives of the democratic subculture, such as members of political parties, members of social and economic groups, and local state political elites, can also be observed commenting on controversial questions. In matters like staffing the courts, determining their structure and organization, and fixing federal jurisdiction, democratic representatives have access through Congress and through other institutions that are influential in establishing judicial policy. Although Congress provides a main channel to the federal courts, access for democratic values is also obtained through the President, the attorney general, and through nonlegal officials who deal with the judiciary. In addition, the location of federal courts throughout the states and regions renders them unusually susceptible to local and re-gional democratic forces.[19]

In our discussion of the democratic subculture, we shall focus on the influences most often observed by students of the American court system—political party identification, localism, public opinion, and the legislative and executive branches of government.

The Influence of Political Party Affiliation

Do judges' political party affiliations affect the way they decide certain cases? The question is straightforward enough, but those who reply to it are by no means unanimous in their response. To most attorneys, judges, and court watchers among the general public, the question rings with outright impertinence, and their answer is usually something like this: After taking the sacred judicial oath and donning the black robe, a judge is no longer a Republican or a Democrat. Former affiliations are (or at least certainly should be) put aside as the judge enters a realm in which deci-sions are the product of evidence, sound judicial reasoning, and precedent rather than such a base factor as political identification. Or, as Donald Dale Jackson quipped in his perceptive book *Judges,* "Most judges would sooner admit to grand larceny than confess a political interest or motivation."[20]

Despite the cries of indignation from those who contend that the legal subcul-ture explains virtually all judicial decision making, a mounting body of evidence strongly suggests that judges' political identification does indeed affect their behav-ior on the bench. Studies have shown that other personal factors—such as religion, sex, race, pre-judicial career, and the level of prestige of their law school educa-tion—may also play a role. However, only political party affiliation seems to have any significant and consistent capacity to explain and predict the outcome of judi-cial decisions.[21] One prominent student of American politics explains why there may be a cause-and-effect relationship between judges' party allegiance and their decisional patterns:

If judges are party identifiers before reaching the bench, there would be a basis for believing that they—like legislators—are affected in their issue orientations by party. . . . Further-more, judges are generally well educated and the vote studies show that the more educated tend to be stronger party identifiers, to cast policy preferences in ideological terms, to have clearer perceptions of issues and of party positions on those issues, to have issue attitudes consistent with the positions of the party with which they identify, and to be more interest-ed and involved in politics. For judges, even more than for the general population, party may therefore be a significant reference group on issues.[22]

Federal District Court Judges. In examining what we have learned about the relationship between party affiliation and court decision making, we can begin with an observation that should come as no surprise: As a whole, Democratic trial judges on the U.S. district courts are more liberal than their Republican colleagues. In a study of more than 57,000 published district court decisions reached between 1932 and 1995, it was determined that Democratic judges took the liberal position 48 percent of the time whereas Republican jurists did so in only 39 percent of the cases.[23] Thus, for almost a half-century, the Democrats' ratio of liberal-to-conservative opinions has been 1.46 times greater (more liberal) than the Republican ratio.[24] Although the overall differences cannot be called overwhelming, neither can we dismiss them as inconsequential.

As the data in Table 10-1 suggest, differences between Republicans and Democrats depend considerably on what type of cases we are talking about. In analyzing partisan voting patterns in twenty-four separate case categories, we can see that differences between judges from the two parties were greatest for cases concerning the right to privacy (e.g., abortion, gay and lesbian rights), disputes about state and local government efforts to regulate the economic lives of their citizens, and discrimination against racial minorities. On the other hand, partisan differences were quite modest when cases involved rent control and excess profits, matters concerning state habeas corpus pleas, and in disputes between union members and their union hierarchy.

All these facts and figures would become more meaningful if we could enter into the minds of typical Republican and Democratic judges and view the world from their perspectives. The closest we can come is to report the partial contents of interviews with a lifelong member of each of the two parties. The two jurists, sitting in the same city and on the same day, discussed a subject that in recent decades has divided Republican from Democratic judges—their philosophy of criminal justice and, more specifically, their views about sentencing convicted felons. The rank-and-file Democrat (appointed by Lyndon Johnson) said in part:

You know, most of the people who appear before me for sentencing come from the poorer classes and have had few of the advantages of life. They've had an uphill fight all the way and life has constantly stepped on them. . . . . I come from a pretty humble background myself, and I know what it's like. I think I take all this into consideration when I have to sentence someone, and it inclines me towards handing down lighter sentences, I think.

One hour later a lifelong Republican (appointed by Richard Nixon) addressed the same issue but with quite a different twist at the end:

When I was first appointed, I was one of those big law-and-order types. You know—just put all those crooks and hippies in jail and all will be right with the world. But I've changed a lot.

TABLE 10-1   Liberal Decisions of Federal District Judges in Order of Magnitude of Partisan Differences for Twenty-Four Types of Cases, 1932–1995

Type of case	Overall	Demo-crat	Repub-lican	Partisan difference	Odds ratio[a]
Right to privacy	52%	69%	39%	30%	3.47
Local economic regulation	67	78	57	21	2.65
Race discrimination	47	56	34	22	2.50
Rights of the handicapped	51	62	44	18	2.07
Women's rights	51	59	43	16	1.93
Freedom of religion	51	57	42	15	1.85
Fourteenth Amendment	37	44	31	13	1.78
Criminal convictions	37	43	30	13	1.73
Freedom of expression	56	63	49	14	1.72
Age discrimination	37	44	32	12	1.68
U.S. habeas corpus pleas	27	30	22	8	1.52
Environmental protection	63	67	58	9	1.45
Employee v. employer	38	42	34	8	1.40
U.S. commercial regulation	69	72	65	7	1.39
Criminal court motions	30	33	27	6	1.38
Voting rights cases	51	54	47	7	1.36
NLRB v. employer	65	69	62	7	1.34
Indian rights and law	49	53	46	7	1.32
Union v. company	50	53	47	6	1.30
Secretary of labor or NLRB v. union	64	63	57	6	1.30
Alien petitions	41	43	37	6	1.29
Union members v. union	44	46	41	5	1.22
State habeas corpus pleas	25	26	23	3	1.21
Rent control, excess profits	60	61	58	3	1.17

SOURCE: Unpublished data collected by Robert A. Carp and Ronald Stidham.

[a]The odds ratio, also called the cross-product ratio, is a measure of the relationship between two dichotomous variables. Specifically, it is a measure of the relative odds of respondents from each independent variable category being placed in a single dependent variable category.

I never realized what poor, pathetic people there are who come before us for sentencing. My God, the terrible childhoods and horrendous backgrounds that some of them come from! Mistreated when they were kids and kicked around by everybody in the world for most of their lives. Society has clearly failed them. As a judge there's only one thing you can do: *send them to prison for as long as the law allows because when they're in that bad a state there's nothing anyone can do with them. All you can do is protect society from these poor souls for as long as you can.* [Emphasis added.]

Although we would not contend that all Republican and all Democratic trial judges think precisely in these terms, we believe that something of the spirit of partisan differences is captured in these two quotations.

Federal Appeals Court Judges. As for partisan variations in the voting patterns of U.S. appeals court judges, here, too, there is evidence that the judges' (prior) party affiliation tempers their decision making to some degree.[25] Studies conducted during the 1960s by Sheldon Goldman and others concluded that "on balance, the findings underscore the absence of a sharp ideological party cleavage in the United States but also give support to the contention that the center of gravity of the Democratic party is more 'liberal' than that of the Republican party."[26] These early studies showed that partisan differences tended to be greatest on economic issues— that is, GOP jurists were more likely than their Democratic counterparts to oppose government efforts to regulate the economy and to support business in its judicial tussles with labor. More recently, however, the field of battle has switched from the economic realm to that of the rights of criminal defendants and civil rights and liberties. Studies show that Democratic judges on the whole tend to be more supportive of the rights of criminal defendants and of those seeking to expand First and Fourteenth Amendment freedoms.[27]

For example, a 1990 study of voting patterns among appellate court judges was conducted for decisions made *en banc,* that is, by all or a specified number of the judges in a circuit court of appeals instead of by the usual three-judge panels. This study focused primarily on partisan differences in cases dealing with criminal justice and civil liberties issues. The researchers found that support for criminal appellants by the Democrats (in effect, the Carter appointees) was 58.9 percent, whereas for Republican appointees the figures were significantly lower—19.9 percent for Nixon's judicial team and 22.3 percent for Reagan's. Likewise, the Carter Democrats supported the civil liberties petitioners 67.1 percent of the time, whereas Nixon's cohort did so 38.5 percent of the time and Reagan's team took the stance in only 29.8 percent of the cases.[28]

U.S. Supreme Court Justices. Does political party affiliation affect the way members of the U.S. Supreme Court decide some of their cases? Although scholars have found this to be a hard subject to investigate, the evidence suggests a mild but positive yes. The research hurdle stems, in part, from the fact that at any given time there are only nine justices on the Court, and it is virtually impossible to generalize about the behavior of groups this small. Moreover, numerous political parties have been represented on the Court in its nearly two-century history, and the definitions of *Federalist, Democrat, Whig, Republican, liberal,* and *conservative* have varied so over time that generalizations become very difficult. For example, prior to the 1920s most mainstream Democrats opposed civil rights for blacks; since that era most champions of the civil rights movement have been Democrats. In the jargon of the trade: The variables are so numerous and the *n*'s (number of justices) are so small that statistically significant observations are extremely difficult to make.

Despite the methodological problems involved, some judicial scholars have gone where even angels fear to tread and have sought to explore this subject. In a comprehensive study of the relationship between party affiliation and the liberal-conservative voting patterns of the justices in this century, one scholar found that between 1903 and 1939, party identification was "clearly a good cue for selecting judicial decision-makers with the proper values"—that is, on matters of support for the economic underdog, Democratic justices were more liberal than their Republican colleagues. Since 1940 the greater liberalism of Democratic Court members has extended as well to matters of civil rights and liberties, thereby reaffirming "the concept that judges are not random samples of their group." But even this scholar concedes, as did those who studied partisan voting by the appeals court and trial court judges, that the relationships are weak:

The inability to predict at high rates of probability is not surprising when one considers the assumptions that must be made and the variety of other influences on the Court such as political and environmental pressures, social change, precedent, reasoned argument [the "legal subculture" for these last two], intracourt social influences and idiosyncrasy.[29]

A recent major study of partisan voting patterns on the Supreme Court focused on criminal justice cases. Among other things, the researchers found that "Democratic control of the Court and the White House, coupled with a high proportion of the Court's docket devoted to criminal issues, results in significantly higher support levels for criminal defendants than under the condition of the Republicans occupying the presidency and a majority of the Supreme Court seats with a relatively low priority placed on criminal justice appeals."[30] Still, some scholars urge caution before making a flat-out pronouncement about the relationship between the justices' backgrounds and their subsequent voting patterns. For example, one prominent researcher has argued that previous studies may be time-bound, that is, during some time periods decisional differences among the justices might well be explained by background characteristics, whereas during others background is only a modest predictor of behavior.[31] When we are faced with such conflicting and tentative studies, it is clear that the final chapter of a book on this subject is yet to be written.

Partisanship in State Courts. The federal courts are not the only arena in which Republican and Democratic jurists sometimes square off against one another. There is evidence that partisan voting patterns often occur as well among the men and women who sit on the trial and appellate court benches. Still, the evidence at the state level is weaker, for three general reasons. First, the state courts have not been studied as extensively and systematically as have the federal courts. This may be either because some political scientists have held the (mistaken) view that state judiciaries are less important than their federal counterparts or because many state court decisions are unpublished and therefore much more difficult to acquire and study. Second, we know for a fact that partisanship among state jurists is not strongly uniform across the country. In some states, for instance, judicial selection is truly bipartisan (or nonpartisan) and both political parties may support the same candidates. Also, many state judges do not have extensive relationships with a political party; though they may have partisan identifications, they might not see judicial questions as being reflective of their party's ideology. Finally, there are still quite a number of one-party states in America in which virtually all judges bear the same party label. Thus it would make little sense to study partisan differences among judges in states like Mississippi or West Virginia, where almost all the jurists are Democrats. Still, keen levels of partisanship have been documented in some jurisdictions—particularly in the states with big cities.

Michigan is a state in which partisan voting patterns among the judges, especially on the state supreme court, have been noteworthy. Studies have shown that on labor-management issues, for example, Democrats on the bench were significantly more likely to support the side of the worker in unemployment compensation cases and in issues dealing with workers' compensation (on-the-job injuries). Democratic judges are also more likely to support criminal defendants seeking a new trial, to favor government efforts to regulate business, and to side with persons who sue business enterprises—all consistent with the voting behavior of Democrats on the federal bench.[32]

In a study of partisan conflict on a California intermediate court of appeals, significant differences were found between Democrats and Republicans in both criminal and civil cases.[33] Studying issues such as votes in criminal justice cases, labor-management disputes, debtor/creditor disagreements, and consumerism, the author concluded that "as previous research . . . would have predicted, the results are in the expected direction, with Republican panels significantly more likely to reach conservative outcomes than Democratic panels."[34]

Illinois, Pennsylvania, Iowa, Maryland, and New York are examples of other states for which researchers have reported meaningful partisan differences between Republican and Democratic judges.[35]

An Appraisal. Let us stop for a moment to look back on what we have said. Our basic point is that the political party affiliation of the judges and justices can well make a difference in the way they decide cases. Of all the background variables studied, it seems to be the most compelling and consistent. But a word of caution is in order, too. Although evidence of partisan influence on judicial behavior is convincing, it by no means suggests that Democrats always take the liberal position on all issues whereas Republicans always opt for the conservative side. Rather, we are talking about tendencies—that is, where the decision is a close call, a Democrat on the bench tends to be more liberal than a GOP judge. When controlling precedents are absent or ambiguous or when the evidence in the case is about evenly divided, Democrats more than Republicans are inclined to be supportive of civil rights and liberties, to support government regulation that favors the worker or the economic underdog, and to turn a sympathetic ear toward the pleas of criminal defendants.

The Impact of Localism

A wide range of influences are included in the term *localism*, and we shall regard it as a broad second category of factors that affect federal and state judicial decision making. First, let's examine localism at the federal level. An accumulating body of literature suggests that judges are influenced by the traditions and mores of the region in which their courts are located or, in the case of Supreme Court justices, by the geographic area in which they were reared. Indeed, for trial and appeals court judges, geographical differences define both the legal and the democratic subcultures as well as the nature of the questions they must decide. Historically, such judges have had strong ties with the state and the circuit in which their courts are situated, and on many issues judicial decision making reflects the parochial values and attitudes of the region. As two leading students of the subject have noted:

A persistent factor in the molding of lower court organization has been the preservation of state and regional boundaries. The feeling that the judiciary should reflect the local features of the federal system has often been expressed by state officials most explicitly. Mississippi Congressman John Sharp Williams declared that he was "frankly opposed to a perambulatory judiciary, to carpetbagging Nebraska with a Louisianian, certainly to carpetbagging Mississippi or Louisiana with somebody north of Mason and Dixon's line."[36]

Why should judges in one district or circuit decide cases differently from their colleagues in other localities? Why should a Supreme Court justice make decisions differently from colleagues who hail from other parts of the United States?[37] Richardson and Vines have put the matter succinctly:

Since both district and appeals judges frequently receive legal training in the state or circuit they serve, the significance of legal education is important. If a federal judge is trained at a state university, he is exposed to and may assimilate state and sectional political viewpoints, especially since state law schools are training grounds for local political elites. . . . Other than education, different local environments provide different reactions to policy issues, such as civil rights or labor relations. Indeed, throughout the history of the lower court judiciary there is evidence that various persons involved in judicial organization and selection have perceived that local, state, or regional factors make a difference and have behaved accordingly.[38]

Moreover, as we noted in Chapters 8 and 9, trial and appellate judges tend to come from the district or state in which their courts are located, and the vast majority were educated in law schools of the state or circuit they work in. (For example, two-thirds of all district judges in one study were born in the state where their court is located, and 86 percent of all circuit judges attended a law school in their respective circuits.[39]) Also, the strong local ties of many judges tend to develop and mature even after their appointment to the bench.[40]

In their identification with their regional base, judges in fact are similar to other political decision makers. We have long known that public attitudes and voting patterns on a wide range of issues vary from one section of America to another.[41] As for national political officials, there is evidence that regionalism affects the voting patterns of members of Congress on many important issues—for example, civil rights, conservation, price controls for farmers, and labor legislation.[42] Furthermore, sectional considerations have their impact within each political party—for instance, Northern Democrats are more liberal than their Southern counterparts on many significant issues.

Regionalism at the Three Judicial Levels. We noted in Chapter 2 that when President Washington appointed the first Supreme Court, half of its members were Northerners and the other half were Southerners. Surely Washington's choice was more than just a symbolic gesture to give a superficial balance to the Court. Washington, who had successfully led a group of squabbling former colonies during the Revolutionary War, understood that the attitudes and mores of his fellow citizens differed widely from one locale to another and that justices would not be immune to these parochial influences. Indeed, studies of the early history of the High Court reveal that sectionalism did creep into its decision-making patterns—particularly along North-South lines. For example, from a study of Supreme Court voting patterns in the sectional crisis that preceded the Civil War, we note that the four justices who were most supportive of Southern regional interests were all from the South, whereas those jurists from the Northern states usually favored the litigants from that region.[43]

In this century, too, there is evidence for the belief that where the justices come from tempers their decision making to some degree.[44] A fairly dramatic manifestation of this principle is found in President Nixon's famous "southern strategy." After the appointment of Warren Burger as chief justice in 1969,

pressure had been building on Nixon to name a southerner to the Court. Though he had never publicly promised a southern nominee, Nixon's intentions were never seriously doubted. Aware that a judge in the South enjoyed a prestige unrivaled in any other section of the country, Nixon advisors believed that he could do southerners no higher favor than to appoint one of their own to the highest court in the land. Even before Nixon assumed office, he had successfully identified with the southern cause. "The one battle most white southerners feel they are fighting is with the Court and Nixon has effectively identified himself with that cause," wrote election analyst Samuel Lubell. "Only Nixon can change the makeup of the Court to satisfy southern aspirations."[45]

Nixon then nominated Clement Haynsworth, Jr., of South Carolina, who was turned down by the Senate. Next he sent forth the name of G. Harrold Carswell of Florida, but this nomination met the same fate as Haynsworth's. An angry Nixon then stated, "As long as the Senate is constituted the way it is today, I will not nominate another southerner."[46]

Although political leaders and much of the general public believe that there is a relationship between the justices' regional backgrounds and their judicial decisions, scholars have had difficulty in documenting this phenomenon. First, links between the justices' regional heritage and their subsequent voting behavior are very difficult to pinpoint, and they exist at most for probably a few regionally sensitive issues. Also, there is reason to believe that after Supreme Court justices are appointed and move to Washington, over time they may take on a more national perspective, loosening to a significant degree the attitudes and narrow purview of the region in which they were reared and educated. For example, in his early days in Alabama, Hugo Black had been a member of the Ku Klux Klan, but after his judicial appointment in 1937, Justice Black became one of the most articulate advocates of civil rights ever to sit on the Supreme Court.

Some evidence exists that regionalism pervades the federal judicial system at the appeals court level as well. A 1981 study noted regional differences on such important questions as rights of the consumer, pleas by criminal defendants, petitions by workers and by blacks, public rights in patent cases, and immigration litigation. The author of this study concluded that "regionalism is an inescapable adjunct of adjudicating appeals in one of the oldest regional operations of federal power in existence." He observed that although the appeals courts may adhere to national standards, such norms are nevertheless "regionally enforced. In the crosswinds of office and constituencies, Courts of Appeals may mediate cultural values—national and local, professional and political—in federal appeals."[47] In a recent study of regional variations in the voting of court of appeals judges, Susan Haire noted, for example, that "in search and seizure cases, Western judges were more liberal than their counterparts in the East (including the South) whereas in race-based employment discrimination cases Western judges adopted positions that were more conservative than their colleagues in the East."[48]

Federal district judges appear to reflect their sectional heritage in decisional patterns even more distinctly than their colleagues on the appellate bench. In an analysis of trial judge decision making between 1933 and 1987, one research team compared the ratio of liberal to conservative opinions for Northern and Southern judges (see Table 10-2). They learned that the Northerners were 1.2 times more liberal than their colleagues in the South. However, it was also learned that North-South differences have declined in recent years. Between 1969 and 1977 the ratio was 1.41, but in the interval between 1978 and 1987 it declined to a mere 1.07—the smallest ratio of all the time periods studied. East-West differences among the district judges have been almost negligible for all the time periods studied since 1933. On questions of criminal justice, judges in the North have historically been somewhat more liberal, although this trend has reversed itself since 1977. In cases that pertain to civil rights and liberties, Northern jurists have been on the liberal side more often since 1969, although this was not the case in earlier time spans. Finally, on issues concerning government regulation of the economy and labor, judges in the North were more liberal prior to 1978, but since that time the North-South split has been negligible. A 1990 study showed that in the more conservative South, federal district judges were almost 70 percent more likely to take an antiabortion stance in their decisions than their colleagues in the North. This was found to be consistent with the values of the region as measured by public opinion polls and other data.[49]

Regional differences within the parties have also been observed over the years—mainly between judges in the North and South. In the past half century, Northern Democrats have been the most liberal group of judges. This group is followed by Southern Democrats, Northern Republicans, and then Southern Republicans. The difference between Southern Republicans and Northern Democrats is 14 percentage points—that is, Northern Democrats are 40 percent more liberal than Southern Republicans.[50]

Variances in Judicial Behavior Among the Circuits. Not only does judicial decision making vary from one region of the land to another, but studies reveal that, for numerous reasons, each of the circuits has its own particular way in which its appellate and trial court judges administer the law and make decisions. One reason, of

TABLE 10-2   Liberal Decisions of Federal District Judges, Controlled for Region, 1933–1987

	1933–1953	1954–1968	1969–1977	1978–1987	All years
All cases					
North (%)	46	42	47	46	45
South (%)	43	37	38	44	41
α	1.14	1.22	1.41	1.07	1.20
East (%)	46	42	43	43	43
West (%)	44	39	44	47	44
α	1.08	1.08	0.90	0.83	0.93
Criminal justice					
North (%)	26	23	31	31	28
South (%)	27	21	24	35	26
α	0.93	1.12	1.40	0.85	1.12
East (%)	23	23	27	28	25
West (%)	29	23	30	35	29
α	0.66	0.94	0.89	0.72	0.81
Civil rights and liberties					
North (%)	39	39	53	48	47
South (%)	45	42	45	41	43
α	0.79	0.88	1.39	1.30	1.20
East (%)	39	39	51	44	44
West (%)	42	41	49	46	46
α	0.80	0.86	1.00	0.90	0.92
Labor and economic regulation					
North (%)	58	64	61	55	58
South (%)	49	55	55	54	53
α	1.48	1.40	1.30	1.01	1.22
East (%)	62	65	61	53	59
West (%)	51	58	58	55	55
α	1.59	1.32	1.08	0.93	1.18

SOURCE: Unpublished data collected by Robert A. Carp, Ronald Stidham, and C. K. Rowland.

NOTE: All figures except the odds ratio are given in percentages.

course, is that circuits tend to follow sectional lines that mark off historical, social, and political differences. Another reason is that the circuit courts of appeals tend to be idiosyncratic, and thus the standards and guidelines they provide the trial judges will reflect their own approach.[51] In a recent study of variations in the behavior of appellate judges from one circuit to another, the "findings . . . strongly suggest judges' decisional tendencies are shaped by the circuit." In her analysis Haire found "meaningful policy differences" in such fields as search and seizure cases, obscenity rulings, and cases dealing with employment discrimination.[52] Similarly, the behavior of U.S. trial judges has been observed to vary on a circuit-by-circuit basis. In the First Circuit, for example, which covers several New England states, 50 percent of the judges' decisions have been liberal. In the Fourth Circuit, on the other hand (Maryland, North and South Carolina, Virginia, and West Virginia), only 37 percent of the judges' decisions have been liberal.[53]

Variances in Trial Judge Behavior Among the States. At first blush it may appear strange to argue that U.S. judicial decisions vary significantly by state, since the state is not an official level of the federal judicial hierarchy, which advances from district to circuit to nationwide system. Still, direct and indirect evidence suggests that each state is unique in the way its federal judges administer justice. There are several reasons why this is so. First, a state, like a circuit or a region, is often synonymous with a particular set of policy-relevant values, attitudes, and orientations. One would automatically expect, for instance, that on some issues U.S. trial and appellate judges in Texas would act differently from Massachusetts jurists, not so much because they are from different states but because they are from different political, economic, legal, and cultural milieus. Second, many judges regard their states as meaningful boundaries and behave accordingly. For example, a U.S. trial judge in Louisiana told us: "One thing I frequently discuss with the other judges here is sentencing matters. Judge X has been a big help with this. I wouldn't want to hand down a sentence which is way out of line with what the other judges are doing here in this state for the same crime."[54] Comments from a jurist indicate that the same phenomenon occurs in the U.S. Eighth Circuit. For instance, in Iowa the federal trial judges

were anxious that their sentencing practices be reasonably similar, particularly where the facts of a case were almost identical. They . . . believed that if a person committed a federal crime in Iowa, the criminal should expect nearly equal treatment regardless of whether he was tried in the Northern or Southern federal districts of the state. This mutual belief is nicely illustrated in these remarks made by Judge Graven to Judge Riley in 1954:

"I have coming before me at Sioux City for sentencing on December 14 one . . . who apparently was splitting $20 [bills] and passing them. I am informed that there is a similar charge against him in the Southern District which is being transferred to this District under Rule 20 and that it is expected that that charge will also be disposed of at Sioux City on December 14th.

"I note that you have two defendants who were associates of Mr. ___ coming up before you for sentencing. Since all the defendants committed the same crimes and presumably have much the same background, I would not want my sentence of Mr. ___ to be out of line with the sentence you impose. If you impose your sentences before December 14th at 10:00 a.m., I wish you would let me know what your sentences are."[55]

Third, we would note the impact upon federal judicial behavior of diversity of citizenship cases—suits that constitute a quarter of the district courts' civil business and about a sixth of civil appeals to circuit courts (see Chapter 2). Because the Supreme Court requires the lower courts to apply *state* rather than federal law in such cases, it behooves U.S. trial judges to keep abreast of and be sensitive to the latest developments in state law. The effect may be the same for circuit judges as well. For example, when three-judge appellate panels are appointed for diversity of citizenship cases, there is a tendency to name circuit judges from states whose law governs. As one scholar observed: "A 'slight local tinge' thus colored diversity opinions as part of a general tendency of members to defer to colleagues most knowledgeable about the subject."[56]

We would also note that quantitative studies of federal trial judges' voting behavior substantiate the proposition that there are meaningful differences on a state-by-state basis. In fact, such differences have been increasing since the late 1960s. Also, it has been observed that in both circuits that cross North-South boundaries, the Sixth and the Eighth, the district courts in the border and Southern states are markedly more conservative than those in the other states.[57] This suggests that local and regional values—as personified by the state—have a greater influence on trial judge decision making than do those of the circuit as a whole.

Localism and the Behavior of State Judges. If regional factors leaven the bread of federal judicial decisions, there is every reason to believe that this phenomenon is even more pervasive for state jurists. As we noted in Chapter 9, state judges, even more than their federal counterparts, tend to be local folks—born, bred, educated, and socialized in the locale in which they preside. Whether they be elected directly by the people or appointed as a result of their political connections with the governor or the local political machine, state judges are likely to mirror the values and attitudes of their environment. Let us look at an example from a study by Martin A. Levin, who compared and contrasted judges and justices in Minneapolis and Pittsburgh.[58]

In Minneapolis the state trial judges are elected on a nonpartisan ballot, and in practice the political parties have almost no role in the selection of judges. "The socialization and recruitment of [the] . . . judges reflect this pattern of selection. Most of these judges [as the majority of the local population] have Northern European-Protestant and middle-class backgrounds, and their pre-judicial careers have been predominantly in private legal practice. . . . Such career experiences seem to have stimulated these judges to be interested more in 'society' than in the defendant." Minneapolis's conservative, middle-class environment, from which its judges come, is reflected in the law-and-order, no nonsense grist of the judicial mill.

This pre-judicial experience, reinforced by their lack of party or policy-oriented experiences and their middle-class backgrounds, seems to have contributed to the legalistic and universalistic character of their decision-making and their eschewal of policy and personal considerations. In their milieu, rules were generally emphasized, especially legal ones, and these rules had been used to maintain and protect societal institutions. Learning to "get around" involved skill in operating in a context of rules. The judges' success seems to have depended more on their objective achievements and skills than on personal relationships.[59]

The environment of the Pittsburgh jurists is in stark contrast. The highly partisan (Democratic) judges reflect the working-class, ethnic-group-based values of the political machine that put them on the bench. These jurists were likely to have held public office before becoming judges, and they were thus much more people oriented than their counterparts in Minneapolis. They often felt that their own "minority ethnic and lower-income backgrounds and these government and party experiences had developed their general attachment to the problems of the 'underdog' and the 'oppressed.'" Levin concludes this about the judicial behavior that is reflected by the local environment and recruitment process:

Their political experiences and lack of much legalistic experience apparently contributed to the highly particularistic and nonlegalistic character of their decision-making, their emphasis on policy considerations, and their use of pragmatic criteria. . . . Personal relationships, especially with constituents, were emphasized, and focused on particular and tangible entities. Success depended largely on the ability to operate within personal relationships. It depended on *whom* one knew, rather than on *what* one knew. Abstractions such as "the good of society as a whole" seem to have been of little concern.[60]

Although social science still needs to develop more systematic empirical evidence for the relationship between the local environment and the "output" of state courts, these two brief case studies are indicative of the kind of phenomena we are describing.

The Impact of Public Opinion

If one were to approach a typical judge or justice and ask whether public opinion affected the decisions made from the bench, the jurist might well respond with a fair measure of indignation. We might hear an answer something like this: "Look, as a judge with a lifetime appointment, I'm expected to be free from the pressures of public opinion. That's part of what we mean when we say that we're a 'government of laws—not of men.' When I decide a case, I look at the law and the facts. I don't go out into the streets and take some sort of public opinion poll to tell me what to do."

Yet there is reason to believe that to some degree and on certain issues, American judges do temper their decision making with public opinion. Before we look at the specific evidence for this, let us outline our intuitive reasons for asserting some role for public opinion. First, judges as human beings, as parents, as consumers, as residents of the community are themselves part of public opinion. Putting on a black robe may stimulate a greater concern for responsible, objective decision making, but it does not void a judge's membership in the human race. As one judicial scholar has noted, "Since judges, both appointed and elected, usually have been born and reared locally and recruited from a local political system, it seems likely that public opinion would have an effect, especially in issues that are locally visible and controversial. In addition . . . many judges seem to consider themselves independent judicial officials who represent local populations in the courts. Consequently, judges may feel that they ought to take local values into account."[61] Even a conservative, strict-constructionist such as Supreme Court Chief Justice William Rehnquist has acknowledged this in a very revealing statement:

Judges, so long as they are relatively normal human beings, can no more escape being influenced by public opinion in the long run than can people working at other jobs. And, if a judge on coming to the bench were to decide to hermetically seal himself off from all manifestations of public opinion, he would accomplish very little; he would not be influenced by current public opinion, but instead would be influenced by the state of public opinion at the time he came to the bench.[62]

The following is an example of a judge's keen sensitivity to local public opinion. When the media reported that U.S. district judge William Overton was involved in rendering a decision that overturned Arkansas's creation-science law, the judge received over 500 letters, most of them highly critical. (The Arkansas law required that the teaching of evolution in schools be accompanied by the teaching of creation science, a theory that life is of recent, supernatural, sudden origin, as related in the book of Genesis; Overton's position was that the law violated the principle of separation of church and state.) The judge was so overwhelmed by the outpouring of negative public opinion that he took the unusual step of making the letters available to reporters and to the University of Arkansas at Little Rock. "How many monkeys are in your family tree?" asked one angry letter writer from Richmond, Virginia. "Repent!" And from Benton, Arkansas, came a clipping that included a picture of three persons who filed suit, and the sender wrote: "I hope the souls of you and these 3 goons rot in Hell for eternity."[63]

A second reason for suggesting the influence of public opinion on judicial behavior is that in many instances it is actually supposed to be an official factor in the decision-making process. For example, when it came to implementing the famous *Brown v. Board of Education* school desegregation ruling, the Supreme Court refused to set strict national guidelines for how their ruling was to be carried out. Rather, it was left up to individual federal district judges to implement the High Court decision based on the judges' determination of local moods, conditions, and traditions.[64] Likewise, when the Supreme Court ruled that it was permissible for federal courts to hear cases concerning malapportionment of state legislatures, it refused to indicate how its decision was to be carried out. Instead it was, in effect, left to the lower federal courts to implement the ruling in accordance with the way they viewed local needs, conditions, and the state political climate.[65] A further example may be found in the obscenity rulings of the Burger Court, in which the justices determined that the courts should use community values and attitudes in determining what materials are obscene.[66]

Thus, not only is it humanly impossible for judges to rid themselves of the influence of public opinion, but indeed in many important types of cases judges are obliged to consider the attitudes and values of the public. This does not mean they go out and take opinion polls whenever they face a tough decision, but it does mean that public opinion is often one ingredient in the decision-making calculus.

Third, both federal and state judges are surely aware that ultimately their decisions cannot be carried out unless there is a reasonable degree of public support for them. As Lawrence Baum has noted, "Justices care about public regard for the Court, because high regard can help the Court in conflicts with the other branches of government and increase people's willingness to carry out its decisions."[67] It has been an open secret for a long time that when the Court is about to hand down a bombshell decision likely to be unpopular among many groups of Americans, the author of the majority opinion takes great pains to word the decision in such a way as to generate popular support for it—or at least to salve the wounds of those potentially offended by it. Examples of High Court decisions in which the author is thought to have written as much for the public at large as for the usual narrow audience of lawyers and lower-court judges include the following: *Marbury v. Madison,* in which the Court claimed for itself the right to declare acts of Congress unconstitutional; *Brown v. Board of Education,* which called for an end to racial segregation in the public schools; *Roe v. Wade,* in which the Court upheld a woman's right to an abortion; and *United States v. Nixon*—the Watergate case—in which the justices ordered the president of the United States to yield to the authority of the courts.[68]

The *empirical* evidence for the impact of public opinion is suggestive but hardly conclusive, in part because there are relatively few comprehensive studies of the phenomenon and because the proposition is very difficult to prove. While many of the earliest studies of this subject came up with conflicting conclusions,[69] more recent and exhaustive investigations have begun to map a very real, albeit imperfect, relationship between public opinion and jurists' decisional patterns. In 1993 two Supreme Court researchers concluded that popular sentiment "exercises important influence on the decisions of the Court even in the absence of changes in the composition of the Court or in the partisan and ideological make up of Congress and the presidency."[70] However, they qualified their findings by noting that there was a fairly lengthy lag time—three to seven years—between a change in the public mood and a corresponding alteration in justices' voting behavior.[71] Likewise these voting changes tended to be concentrated among only a handful of justices.[72]

The most recent team of researchers to address this phenomenon came up with a set of conclusions that were more emphatic and contained fewer qualifications about the link between public mood changes and Supreme Court decisional patterns. Roy B. Flemming and B. Dan Wood discovered that "public opinion *directly* affects decisions by individual members of the Court," and furthermore that "the result holds across various issue areas, is not restricted to only a few justices, and that the justices' responses are relatively quick with a lag of only one term."[73] Research is now also under way to determine whether shifts in public opinion affect the decision making of federal appeals court judges[74] as well as U.S. trial jurists.[75]

Researchers have also explored this phenomenon at the state level. For example, a study of California state courts noted that sentencing in marijuana cases often changed in severity soon after a popular referendum was held on reducing criminal penalties for personal use of the drug. For example, judges who had given light sentences prior to the referendum sometimes gave harsher sentences if the local vote was in favor of maintaining criminal penalties. Conversely, harsh-sentencing jurists sometimes became more lenient when the vote indicated that the public favored reducing the penalties.[76]

Given the fact that in a majority of the states judges must periodically run for election (see Tables 9-3 and 9-4), there is good reason to believe that they are more attuned to public opinion than federal judges, with their lifetime tenure. In fact a recent study of elected state supreme court justices found that "in order to appease their constituencies, justices who have views contrary to those of the voters and the court majority, and who face competitive electoral conditions will vote with the court majority instead of casting unpopular dissents on politically volatile issues."[77] Here is an example that we believe illustrates a state judge's greater grass-roots political awareness and also the greater degree to which elected jurists interact with the local environment.

On November 28, 1988, Jack Hampton, a state district court judge in Dallas, Texas, gave a thirty-year prison sentence to a defendant who had been convicted of murdering two gay men. The killer, Richard Bednarski, had testified in court that he and some friends went to a central Dallas park to "pester homosexuals" and ended up killing two of them in what authorities called an execution-style slaying. (Bednarski placed a gun in one victim's mouth and pulled the trigger; he then coldly shot the other man several times.) Because of the heinous and unprovoked nature of the crime and because Hampton is known as a "hanging judge" who usually gives life sentences for murder, the *Dallas Times Herald* decided to interview the judge about his lighter-than-usual sentence. During the interview Judge Hampton said that the murder victims more or less got what they asked for, since they were "queers" who "wouldn't have been killed if they hadn't been cruising the streets picking up teenage boys."[78]

Immediately after the interview was published, public protests were staged by human rights groups, local church leaders, and various gay rights organizations. Protest rallies were held, including one attended by 500 people at the City Hall Plaza, where letters of support were read from Sen. Edward Kennedy of Massachusetts and then Texas state treasurer Ann Richards. Also, formal complaints were filed with the Texas Commission on Judicial Conduct, calling for Hampton to be disciplined. Realizing that he had perhaps bitten off more than he could chew, this elected judicial official issued a four-paragraph letter to a group of eight Methodist ministers. Judge Hampton said he wished "to apologize" for his "poor choice of words that appeared in a recent newspaper story...." He promised that in his court "everyone is entitled to and will receive equal protection."

Was the judge's public apology in response, at least in part, to his perception of public opinion and the effect that it might have on his bid for reelection? This might well be surmised from a later statement made by the judge when he was asked about possible political fallout from the incident: "If it makes anybody mad, they'll forget it by 1990" (when Judge Hampton was up for reelection).[79]

We are not suggesting that this particular incident is typical of the behavior of state judges, but we do believe that it demonstrates the degree to which locally elected judicial officials respond to the tides of public opinion. Very rarely indeed do *lifetime judicial appointees,* such as federal judges, feel the need to justify their sentencing behavior in interviews with the local press or to issue public apologies when public opinion turns critical of their behavior. For better or worse, public opinion does affect judicial behavior, and this is particularly true when judges must be accountable directly to the electorate.

Thus, despite the traditional notion of the blindfolded justice weighing only the facts in a case and the relevant law, there is common-sense and statistical support for the assertion that jurists do keep their eyes (and ears) open to public opinion.

The Influence of the Legislative and Executive Branches

We shall now look at one final set of stimuli that the democratic subculture may bring to bear on the behavior of American judges—the executive and the legislative branches. We shall first explore this phenomenon at the national level and then indicate how it is equally prevalent at the state and local levels.

Congress and the President. Perhaps the most obvious link between the values of the democratic subculture and the output of the federal courts is the fact that the people elect the president and members of the Senate, and the president appoints judges and justices with the advice and consent of the Senate. We have already noted in Chapter 8 the substantial capacity of the chief executive and certain key senators to influence what kind of men and women will sit on the bench, but even after judges have been appointed, the president and the Congress may have an impact on the content and direction of judicial decision making.

First, as we discussed in Chapter 4, to a very large degree the jurisdiction of the federal trial and appellate courts is determined by the Congress of the United States. Congress has the authority to decide which types of issues may become appropriate matters for judges to resolve. For example, in 1994 Congress passed the Violence Against Women Act, which made crimes motivated by gender a violation of civil rights. (A woman could now claim, for instance, that her civil rights had been violated if her husband had raped her during the course of their marriage.) In doing so, Congress in effect expanded the jurisdiction of the federal courts to hear a large number of disputes that previously had been outside the purview of the federal judiciary. Conversely, Congress may restrict the jurisdiction of the federal courts. In response to popular dissatisfaction with many court rulings on busing, abortion, school prayer, and so on, Congress has considered passage of a number of bills designed to restrict the right of the courts to render decisions on these subjects.[80] Even if Congress does not actually pass such legislation, one may speculate that the threat to do so may cause the federal courts to pull in their horns when it comes to deciding cases in ways that are not in accord with the will of the president or Congress.

Second, there is evidence that judicial decision making is likely to be bolder and more effective if it has the active support of at least one other branch of the federal government, and ideally both of them.[81] School integration is a case in point. When the federal courts began to order desegregation of the public schools after

1954, we know that they met with considerable opposition—primarily from those parts of the country most affected by the Supreme Court ruling in the *Brown* case. It is doubtful whether the federal courts could have overcome this resistance without the support given them (sometimes reluctantly) by the president and Congress. For example, in 1957 Arkansas governor Orville Faubus sought to obstruct a district judge's order to integrate Little Rock's Central High School. President Eisenhower then mobilized the National Guard and in effect used federal bayonets to implement the judge's ruling. President Kennedy likewise used federal might to support a judge's decision to admit a black student to the University of Mississippi in the face of massive local resistance. Congress also lent its hand to federal desegregation rulings. For instance, it voted to withhold federal aid to school districts that refused to comply with district court desegregation decisions. Surely White House and congressional support emboldened the Supreme Court and the lower judiciary to carry on with their efforts to end segregation in the public schools.

Sometimes presidential and congressional actions may in fact *lead* rather than just implement judicial decision making. One study analyzed the impact on trial judge behavior of the 1937 Supreme Court decisions that permitted much greater government regulation of the economy.[82] As expected, federal district judge support for government regulation increased markedly after the Supreme Court gave its official blessing to the government's new powers. However, it was also learned that district court backing for labor and economic regulation had been building *before* the Supreme Court's decisions: pro regulation decisions by U.S. trial judges increased from 44 percent in 1936 to 67 percent in 1937—a change of 23 points. The authors attributed this at least in part to the fact that prior to 1937, the president and Congress, in response to public opinion, were strongly pushing legislation that favored an expanded federal role in labor and economic regulation.[83]

Thus the Supreme Court and the lower courts are not, and cannot be, immune to the will of Congress and of the chief executive as they go about their judicial business. Not only does the president, with the advice and consent of the Senate, select all members of the federal judiciary, but to a large degree the Congress prescribes the jurisdiction of the federal courts and often the qualifications of those who have standing to sue in these tribunals. Moreover, many court decisions cannot be meaningfully implemented without the support of the other two branches of government—a fact not lost on the judges and justices themselves. Sometimes, too, the courts appear to follow the lead of the president and Congress on various public policy matters. Whichever set of circumstances is the case, it is clear that the legislative and executive branches of government constitute an important source of nonjudicial influence on court behavior.

The State Legislature and the Governor. Just as the legislative and executive branches affect judicial decision making at the national level, so, too, do their counterparts at the state and local levels. In almost half of the jurisdictions the popularly elected governor (or the state legislature) makes the selection of the state judges (see Tables 9-3 and 9-4), and there is every reason to suggest a policy link between the value sets of the voters, the appointing officials, and the judges who render subsequent decisions. More specifically, the authors of one study tell us that there are three major ways that the political branches affect the role of the state courts.[84]

First, legislation sponsored by the governor or passed by the legislature regulates the sorts of claims that can be adjudicated in state courts and also brought to the state appellate courts. For example, let us look at the ease with which class action suits may be brought in state judicial tribunals. (Such suits facilitate access to the courts by allowing large numbers of potential litigants with individually small claims to band together, thereby reducing or eliminating entirely the financial costs of seeking redress.) Actions by the legislature determine who may bring such suits and under what circumstances. The evidence suggests that there is great variation from one state to another in this area: some states make it very easy to initiate such suits whereas in others access to the courts in this fashion is very difficult.[85]

Second, actions by the legislature (which may or may not be part of the governor's political agenda) determine the authority of the state supreme court to regulate its workload and focus on important cases. For example, it is generally accepted that for most cases litigants should have the right to appeal trial court decisions. In states that have an ample number of intermediate appellate courts this right to appeal is readily available. However, in states without sufficient numbers of intermediate appeals courts or in states where the supreme court is forced by law to deal with a succession of relatively minor disputes, the chances of litigants having their cases heard by the supreme court are slim indeed. This fact is significant in itself in terms of the distribution of justice, but it is important for another reason. In states where the supreme court is forced by the legislature into overwork on judicial trivia, the court does not have time to devote much attention to cases that raise important policy questions. For instance, after the legislature in North Carolina created intermediate courts of appeals, a study concluded that such action enabled the state high court to assume "a position of true leadership in the legal development of the state."[86] Thus actions by the legislature (supported or opposed by the governor) may well determine whether the supreme court plays a major or minor role in policy questions important to the state.

Finally, because a prime function of courts is to enforce existing legal norms, the sorts of issues that state courts address depend to a large degree on the substantive law of the state. For instance, seventeen state constitutions contain "little ERA's" (equal rights amendments); ten states specifically protect the right to privacy; and in some states there is a provision guaranteeing a right to quality of the environment.[87] Thus, a judge in a state in which good air quality is guaranteed will have a much greater opportunity and right to issue an injunction against a polluter than one in a state where such a right is not legally provided for. An example of a legislature's taking a subject matter out of the hands of its state judges occurred in Hawaii after its Supreme Court ruled in 1993 that same-sex couples could marry. Shortly after the Court's decision the legislature began a process to modify its state's constitution to deny marriage licenses to same-sex couples, thereby overruling the state supreme court and taking the subject matter out of its jurisdiction.[88] The point here is that judges render decisions within the existing constitutional and legal environment of their respective states. Such an environment is largely the product of political decisions made by the governor and the legislature as representatives of the electorate.

In sum, the output of the state courts, like that of federal tribunals, is to a significant degree the result of the political values and policy goals of the chief executive and the legislative branch of government.

The Subcultures as Predictors

Earlier in the chapter we indicated that there is scholarly divergence over the question of whether judicial decision making is essentially the product of facts, laws, and precedent (the legal subculture model), or whether the various extralegal factors we have examined carry more weight (the realist-behavioralist view). In other words, are court decisions better explained by understanding the facts and law that impinge upon a given case, or by knowing which newspaper the judge reads in the morning or how the judge voted in the last election?

The clue to answering the question lies in knowing what kind of case the judge is being asked to decide. In our discussion of the nature and scope of the federal judicial workload in Chapter 2, we indicated that the vast majority of the trial judge's cases and much appellate judicial business involve routine norm enforcement decisions. In cases in which the law and the controlling precedents are clear, the victor will be the side that is able to marshal better evidence to show that its factual case is stronger. In other words, in the lion's share of cases, the legal subculture model best explains and predicts judicial decision making. When traditional legal cues are ambiguous or absent, however, judges are obliged to look to the democratic subculture for guidance in their decision making. We will examine the types of situations in which the legal subculture model might give way to the democratic subculture as an explicator of judicial behavior.

When the Legal Evidence Is Contradictory

It is probably fair to say that in a majority of cases the facts, evidence, and controlling precedents distinctly favor one side. In such instances the judge is clearly obliged to decide for the party with the stronger case. Not to do so would violate the judge's legal training and mores; it would subject a trial or appeals court judge to reversal by a higher court, an event most jurists find embarrassing; and it would render the Supreme Court vulnerable to the charge that it was making up the law as it went along—an impression not flattering to the High Court justices. On the other hand, judges often find themselves in situations in which the facts and evidence are about equally compelling on both sides, or in which there are about an equal number of precedents to sustain a finding for either party. As one U.S. trial judge in Houston told us:

There are days when you want to say to the litigants, "I wish you guys would've settled this out of court because I don't know what to do with you." If I grant the petition's request, I can often modify the relief requested [in an attempt to even out the decision], but still one side has got to win and one side has got to lose. I could cite good precedents on either side, and it's no good worrying about the appeals court because there's no telling what they would do with it should the judge's decision be appealed.

The following is an example in which a U.S. trial judge was forced to decide a case by his own lights (that is, using his democratic subculture values) when the cues from the legal subculture were clearly contradictory or nonexistent. Judge Robert E. Coyle, who holds court in the Eastern District of California (Fresno), was presented with a case that stemmed from an employment discrimination complaint filed with the Equal Employment Opportunity Commission (EEOC) by Alicia Castrejon. She had been employed by the Tortilleria La Mejor of Farmersville, California, and claimed in her suit that she had been dismissed from her job because of previous complaints filed with the EEOC against her employer.

The legal issue was whether Alicia Castrejon had the right to file a suit in the first place since she was an undocumented immigrant. When Congress passed the Immigration Reform and Control Act of 1986, which prohibits employment of undocumented workers, it did not specify in the act whether immigrants who have applied for amnesty are protected in the period when their applications are being processed. Castrejon had in fact filed for amnesty, but her application had not been acted on at the time she filed her employment discrimination complaint.

The judge looked to the Department of Labor and to the EEOC for some legal guidance on the matter of the interim rights of undocumented residents. Both of these federal agencies maintained that workers *are* covered by federal labor and antidiscrimination laws even if they are here illegally. But the judge learned that many employers had been interpreting the Immigration Reform and Control Act of 1986 to mean that illegal immigrants are not protected, and they were able to point to a 1987 ruling by a federal district judge in Alabama. That decision dismissed an undocumented immigrant's claim for minimum wages and overtime because, the judge said, that would conflict with the congressional act of 1986. It was evident that the legal subculture was giving Judge Coyle few cues as to the "right" answer, and the existing cues were contradictory. It was also clear that in deciding this case, the judge had to tap attitudes and values derived from his democratic subculture and to put much of his legal subculture orientation "on hold."

After sitting on the case for more than two years, the judge finally issued a ruling in February 1991 that had significant immediate impact for hundreds of thousands of immigrants. For reasons known fully only to Judge Coyle, he ruled that undocumented workers do have the right to pursue discrimination suits against an employer—regardless of legal residency status. In his decision the judge acknowledged the seeming incongruity of discouraging illegal immigration while at the same time allowing undocumented workers to seek legal recourse against discrimination on the job: "We doubt, however, that many illegal aliens come to this country to gain the protection of our labor laws. Rather it is the hope of getting a job—at any wage—that prompts most illegal aliens to cross our borders."[89]

In situations such as the one just described, judges have little choice but to turn to their personal value sets to determine how to resolve the cases. We can assume that decision making is affected by local attitudes and traditions or by the judge's perception of the public mood or the will of the current Congress or state legislature or administration.

As we shall see in Chapter 11, since the advent of the Burger Court in 1969, and continuing throughout the Rehnquist Court, an inordinate number of the Supreme Court's decisions have been regarded as "ideologically imprecise and inconsistent," often sustained by weak, five-to-four majorities. This state of affairs has surely increased the likelihood that trial and appellate judges will respond to stimuli from the democratic rather than the legal subculture. That is, the confusion created by the Court in setting forth ambiguous or contradictory guidelines has meant that the lower federal and state courts—and perhaps even members of the Supreme Court—have been forced to rely on (or have felt free to give vent to) their own personal ideas about how the law should read. As one study concluded, "With the decline of the fact-law congruence after 1968 the . . . [lower courts] became more free to take their decision-making cues from personal-partisan values rather than from guidelines set forth by the Higher Court."[90]

When a Case Concerns New Areas of the Law

There is a second situation that causes researchers to set aside the legal subculture model and turn to the democratic subculture approach—when jurists are asked to resolve new types of policy questions for which statutory law and appellate court guidelines are virtually absent. Since about 1937, most new and uncharted areas of the law (at least at the federal level) have been in the realms of civil liberties and criminal justice rather than in the area of labor and economic regulation. As we noted in Chapter 2, since 1937 the federal courts have leaned toward self-restraint and deference to the elected branches when it comes to ordering the economic lives of the American people.[91] Moreover, in recent decades Congress has legislated, often with precision, in the areas of economic regulation and labor relations, and this has further restricted the discretion of judges in these fields. As a result, the noose of the legal subculture has been drawn tightly around trial judges' necks in this area, and there is little room for creative decision making or for responding to the tug of the heart rather than to the clear command of the law. Thus, since New Deal days the legal rather than the democratic subculture has been the better predictor of trial and appellate judge decision making in labor and economic regulation cases.

Since the 1930s the opposite trend has been observable for issues of criminal justice and civil rights and liberties:

The "great" and controversial decisions of the Stone, Vinson, Warren, and Burger Courts [and, one might add, the Rehnquist Court] focused primarily on issues of civil liberties and of the rights of criminal defendants, and it is precisely those sorts of issues which evoked the greatest partisan schisms among the justices. Research has shown that . . . [the lower courts] were by no means immune to the debates and divisions which racked the nation's High Court; they, too, seem to have split along "political" lines more often on criminal justice and on civil rights matters than they did with other sorts of cases.[92]

The ambiguity (or perhaps the constant state of flux) of the law on matters such as the rights of criminal defendants, First Amendment freedoms, and equal protection of the law has given the federal jurists greater opportunity to respond than in the labor and economic realms, where their freedom of action has been more circumscribed. Put another way, since the 1930s the democratic rather than the legal subculture model has become increasingly important as a predictor of judicial behavior on Bill of Rights matters.[93]

A series of interviews with a wide range of district and appellate court judges lends further credence to this notion. In William Kitchin's study, the trial judges were asked about their willingness to "innovate"—that is, their inclination to make new law in areas where appellate court or congressional guidelines were ambiguous or nonexistent. After asking why judges create new law through judicial innovation, Kitchin noted:

One answer is that the courts innovate because other branches of government ignore certain significant problems which, to individual judges, cry out for attention. Accordingly, the individual district judge innovates in an attempt to fill a legal vacuum, as one judge commented, "The theory is that judges should not be legal innovators, but there are some areas in which they have to innovate because legislatures won't do the job. Race relations is one of these areas. . . ." Other areas mentioned as needing judicial innovation because of legislative inaction were housing, equal accommodations, and criminal law (especially habeas corpus).[94]

Picking up the thread of these interviews, another study of decisional patterns and variations in U.S. district judge decision making showed that "the subjects that . . . [the Kitchin study] found to represent the greatest areas of freedom in judicial decision making are the very same subjects that we find to maximize partisan voting differences among the district judges. In situations where judges are more free to take their decision-making cues from sources other than appellate court decisions and statutes, they are more likely to rely on their personal-partisan orientations."[95]

Let us look at a relatively new area of the law in which appellate court and congressional guidelines are few and thus lower-court judges must fend for themselves—the definition of obscenity. Prior to 1957 there were no Supreme Court decisions of note on the matter of obscenity. In that year the nation's high court ruled that obscenity was not protected by the First Amendment and said that it could be defined as material that dealt with sex "in a manner appealing to prurient interest."[96] Seven years later, the Supreme Court said that in determining what appealed to the prurient interest of the average person, hypothetical "national standards" were to be used,[97] but nine years after that the Court changed its mind and ruled that "state community standards" could be employed."[98] But what is obscenity? No one seems to know with any greater certainty today than Justice Potter Stewart did in 1964 when he confessed that he could not intelligibly define obscenity but that "I do know it when I see it."[99] As U.S. District Judge José Gonzalez in 1990 wrote in determining that an album by the controversial Miami-based rap group 2 Live Crew was obscene, "It is an appeal to 'dirty' thoughts and the loins, not to the intellect and mind." (The 2 Live Crew's attorney defended the album as "art" and said that "Put in its historical context, it is a novel and creative use of sound and lyrics.")[100] Given the reluctance or the inability of Congress and the Supreme Court to define obscenity, America's trial and appellate judges have little choice but to look to their own personal values and perceptions of the local public need in order to determine what kinds of books, films, art, and plays the First Amendment protects in their respective jurisdictions.

Another lively new area of the law that is currently bedeviling federal judges is the subject of sexual harassment. Ever since Congress added sexual harassment to the list of items prohibited in the workplace by Title VII of the Civil Rights Act of 1964, federal jurists have had a difficult time defining what sexual harassment means. Obvious examples are clear enough (a boss explicitly telling a female employee that sexual favors were required for a pay raise), but the new "gray" areas are taxing judges' minds. For example, a U.S. trial judge in Los Angeles was recently asked to rule that there was sexual harassment in an office because women's breasts were being compared among female workers and sexual toys were being given as presents. The judge ruled that according to his lights, while the office in question had indeed been turned into a "bawdy sorority," still federal law did not provide a "cause of action for *embarrassment*." [Emphasis added.][101]

But confusion in this new realm by no means ends with trying to define traditional forms of sexual harassment. The federal courts are now trying to determine whether *same-sex* harassment can be understood to mean a violation of one's civil rights. For instance, in May of 1997 a U.S. appeals court in Atlanta considered a case involving a waiter at a hotel restaurant whose maitre d' had made sexual advances to him. This court said that such activity did come within the strictures of the 1964 Civil Rights Act, although other courts have clearly ruled to the contrary.[102] Even here the confusion and uncertainty does not end. What about sexually oriented "horse-play" among straight men? There is currently a suit being pressed in a federal courtroom in Denver against the United Parcel Service of America by Michael Garcia, a heterosexual maintenance mechanic. Garcia is claiming that his boss "tried to unnerve him by prodding him from behind with a radio antenna and touching him in front of co-workers." The company has claimed in similar cases that this amounted to no more than "locker-room" antics—not harassment—to which Garcia responded that "I've played many sports in my time and I've never seen that kind of action in any locker rooms I've been in."[103] What is the judge going to do in this case? With the legal subculture virtually silent in this realm, the jurist is going to have to look to the democratic subculture to find an answer.

Judicial innovation in new legal realms or in the absence of appellate court or legislative guidelines is by no means confined to federal jurists; the phenomenon is just as significant at the state court level. For example, in 1992 the supreme court of Tennessee had to decide the novel question of whether a state can force a man to become a father. The case revolved around a couple whose marriage had ended in a divorce. Prior to the divorce, however, the couple had placed in frozen storage seven of the woman's eggs that had been fertilized with the man's sperm—"children in vitro" as the courts came to call them. The woman wished to secure the right either to have the eggs implanted in her womb or to donate them to an anonymous childless couple. Her former husband objected, and the novel question became grist for the Tennessee judicial mill. Are embryos human beings with independent rights? Could the man be forced to become a father without his consent? With no clear legislative or judicial precedents to guide them the state's high court eventually ruled in favor of the former husband: "The state's interest in the potential life of these pre-embryos is not sufficient to justify any infringement upon the freedom of these individuals to [decide] whether to allow a process to continue that may result in such a dramatic change in their lives as becoming parents."[104] This case is a vivid reminder that judicial policy making in new legal realms is by no means the exclusive activity of the federal courts.

The Judge's Role Conception

In our discussion of which better explains judicial decision making—the rules of the legal subculture or stimuli from the democratic subculture—there is one additional factor to consider: how judges conceive of their judicial role. Judicial scholars often talk about three basic decision-making categories regarding whether judges should make law when they decide cases. "Lawmakers" are those who take a broad view of the judicial role. These jurists, often referred to as "activists" or "innovators," contend that they can and must make law in their decisions, because the statutory law and appellate or Supreme Court guidelines are often ambiguous or do not cover all situations and because legislative intent is frequently impossible to determine. In Kitchin's study of federal district judges, 14 percent were classified in this category, whereas in an investigation of appeals court judges, 15 percent were associated with this role.[105]

At the other end of the continuum are the "law interpreters," who take a very narrow, traditional view of the judicial function. Sometimes called "strict constructionists," they don't believe that judges should substitute judicial wisdom for the rightful power of the elected branches of government to make policy. They tend to eschew making innovative decisions that may depart from the literal meaning of controlling precedents. In the Kitchin study, 52 percent of the U.S. trial judges were found to be "law interpreters," whereas only 26 percent of the appeals court judges were so designated.[106] This finding is consistent with our discussion in Chapter 2 that federal district judges are more concerned with routine norm enforcement, whereas the appellate judges' involvement—and their perception of it—is with broader questions of judicial policy.

Midway between the law interpreters and the lawmakers are judges known as "pragmatists" or "realists," who believe that on occasion they are indeed obliged to make law, but that for most cases a decision can be made by consulting the controlling law or appellate court precedents. Studies have indicated that a third of federal district judges assume this moderate role, whereas a full 59 percent of their appellate court colleagues do so.[107] Comparing federal jurists with state judges, one scholar has noted, "A slightly greater number of federal than state judges take the pragmatist or realist views, possibly because they have more opportunities to make innovative decisions."[108]

Thus, whether judicial decisions are better explained by the legal model or by the democratic model depends not only on the nature of the cases and the state of the controlling law and precedents; it also depends to some degree on how the individual judges evaluate these factors. In virtually every case that comes before them, judges have to determine how much discretion they have and how they wish to exercise it. This is obviously a subjective process, and, as one research team put it, "activist judges will find more discretion in a given fact situation than will their more restrained colleagues."[109]

Summary

Federal and state judges make hundreds of millions of decisions each year, and scholars have sought to explain the thinking behind these decisions. Two schools of thought provide two explanations. One theory is based on the rules and procedures of the legal subculture. Judges' decisions, according to this model, are the product of traditional legal reasoning and adherence to precedent and judicial self-restraint. Another school of thought, the realist-behavioralist approach, argues that judges are influenced in their decision making by such factors as party affiliation, local values and attitudes, public opinion, and pressures from the legislative and executive branches. We asserted that in the vast majority of cases, the legal subculture model is the more accurate predictor of judicial decision making. However, stimuli from the democratic subculture often become useful in accounting for judges' decisions (1) when the legal evidence is contradictory or equally compelling on both sides; (2) if the situation concerns new areas of the law and significant precedents are absent; and (3) when judges are inclined to view themselves more as activist lawmakers than as law interpreters.

NOTES

1. Richard J. Richardson and Kenneth N. Vines, *The Politics of Federal Courts* (Boston: Little, Brown, 1970). Although Richardson and Vines developed their model primarily for federal courts, we feel that their hypotheses and conclusions are equally true for state judges.

2. Edward H. Levi, *An Introduction to Legal Reasoning* (Chicago: University of Chicago Press, 1948), 1–2.

3. *Lane v. Wilson*, 307 U.S. 268 (1939); *Gomillion v. Lightfoot*, 364 U.S. 339 (1960).

4. *Lane v. Wilson*, 307 U.S. 275 (1939).

5. William Kitchin, *Federal District Judges* (Baltimore: Collage Press, 1978), 71.

6. J. Woodford Howard, Jr., *Courts of Appeals in the Federal Judicial System: A Study of the Second, Fifth, and District of Columbia Circuits* (Princeton, N.J.: Princeton University Press, 1981), 187.

7. Walter F. Murphy, *Elements of Judicial Strategy* (Chicago: University of Chicago Press, 1964), 204.

8. Henry Sumner Maine, *Ancient Law* (Boston: Beacon Press, 1963), 3–19.

9. Henry J. Abraham, *The Judicial Process*, 4th ed. (New York: Oxford University Press, 1980), chap. 9.

10. *Evers v. Jackson Municipal Separate School District*, 232 F. Supp. 241 (1964).

11. Ibid., 247.

12. Ibid., 249.

13. Ibid., 255.

14. Richardson and Vines, *The Politics of Federal Courts*, 8–9.

15. Steven Vago, *Law and Society*, 5th ed. (Englewood Cliffs, N.J.: Prentice-Hall, 1997), 354.

16. For a good, current bibliography on this subject, see ibid., chap. 9.

17. Oliver Wendell Holmes, Jr., *The Common Law* (Boston: Little, Brown, 1881), 1–2.

18. Jerome Frank, *Courts on Trial: Myth and Reality in American Justice* (Princeton, N.J.: Princeton University Press, 1950), 151.

19. Richardson and Vines, *The Politics of Federal Courts*, 10.

20. Donald Dale Jackson, *Judges* (New York: Atheneum, 1974), 18.

21. Some studies suggest that age, socioeconomic status, and religion may influence some judges in some of their cases, but the associations are weak. For example, see Sheldon Goldman, "Voting Behavior on the United States Courts of Appeals Revisited," *American Political Science Review* 69 (1975): 491–506; John R. Schmidhauser, "The Justices of the Supreme Court: A Collective Portrait," *Midwest Journal of Political Science* 3 (1959): 1–57; and Donald Leavitt, "Political Party and Class Influences on the Attitudes of Justices of the Supreme Court in the Twentieth Century" (Paper delivered at the annual meeting of the Midwest Political Science Association, Chicago, 1972). Other studies suggest that these background factors have virtually no explanatory power—e.g., Howard, *Courts of Appeals in the Federal Judicial System*, chap. 6. For a more detailed discussion of this subject and a literature review, see C. K. Rowland and Robert A. Carp, *Politics & Judgment in Federal District Courts* (Lawrence: University Press of Kansas, 1996), chap. 2.

22. David W. Adamany, "The Party Variable in Judges' Voting: Conceptual Notes and a Case Study," *American Political Science Review* 63 (1969): 59.

23. These figures are based on unpublished data collected by Robert A. Carp and Ronald Stidham.

24. For a more extensive discussion of the "odds ratio" and methodology used in this study, see Rowland and Carp, *Politics & Judgment in Federal District Courts*, 180–181.

25. For a good review of the early literature on this subject, see Goldman, "Voting Behavior on the United States Courts of Appeals Revisited," 491, note 2. Also, see Howard, *Courts of Appeals in the Federal Judicial System*, chap. 6.

26. Sheldon Goldman, "Voting Behavior on the United States Courts of Appeals, 1961–1964," *American Political Science Review* 60 (1966): 384.

27. For example, see Donald Songer, "Consensual and Nonconsensual Decisions in Unanimous Opinions of the United States Courts of Appeals," *American Journal of Political Science* 26 (1982): 225–239; Donald Songer and Sue Davis, "The Impact of Party and Region on Voting Decisions in the United States Courts of Appeals, 1955–1986," *Western Political Quarterly* 43 (1990): 317–334; and Ronald Stidham, Robert A. Carp, and Donald R. Songer, "The Voting Behavior of President Clinton's Judicial Appointees," *Judicature* 80 (1996): 16–21.

28. Christopher E. Smith, "Polarization and Change in the Federal Courts: *En Banc* Decisions in the U.S. Courts of Appeals," *Judicature* 74 (1990): 137.

29. Leavitt, "Political Party and Class Influences on the Attitudes of Justices of the Supreme Court in the Twentieth Century," 18–19.

30. Lee Epstein, Thomas G. Walker, and William J. Dixon, "The Supreme Court and Criminal Justice Disputes: A Neo-Institutional Perspective," *American Journal of Political Science* 33 (1989): 838.

31. S. Sidney Ulmer, "Are Background Models Time-Bound?" *American Political Science Review* 80 (1986): 957–967.

32. S. Sidney Ulmer, "The Political Party Variable in the Michigan Supreme Court," *Journal of Public Law* 11 (1962): 352–362; and Malcolm M. Feeley, "Another Look at the 'Party Variable' in Judicial Decision-Making: An Analysis of the Michigan Supreme Court," *Polity* 4 (1971): 91–104.

33. Philip L. Dubois, "The Illusion of Judicial Consensus Revisited: Partisan Conflict on an Intermediate State Court of Appeals," *American Journal of Political Science* 32 (1988): 946–967.

34. Ibid., 953–954.

35. For a good, current bibliography of the literature on partisan voting patterns among state judges, see ibid., 965–967.

36. Richardson and Vines, *The Politics of Federal Courts*, 71.

37. For a more elaborate discussion of this phenomenon, see Robert A. Carp and C. K. Rowland, *Policymaking and Politics in the Federal District Courts* (Knoxville: University of Tennessee Press, 1983), chap. 4.

38. Richardson and Vines, *The Politics of Federal Courts*, 73.

39. Ibid., 72.

40. For example, see Robert A. Carp and Russell Wheeler, "Sink or Swim: The Socialization of a Federal District Judge," *Journal of Public Law* 21 (1972): 359–393. Also, Robert A. Carp, "The Influence of Local Needs and Conditions on the Administration of Federal Justice" (Paper delivered at the annual meeting of the Southwestern Political Science Association, Dallas, 1971).

41. For example, see Angus Campbell, Philip E. Converse, Warren E. Miller, and Donald E. Stokes, *The American Voter* (New York: Wiley, 1960); Everett Carll Ladd, Jr., and Charles D. Hadley, *Transformations of the American Party System*, 2d ed. (New York: W. W. Norton, 1978); V. O. Key, Jr., *Public Opinion and American Democracy* (New York: Knopf, 1967); and Robert S. Erikson and Kent L. Tedin, *American Public Opinion: Its Origins, Content, and Impact*, 5th ed. (Boston: Allyn Bacon, 1995).

42. Barbara Hinckley, *Stability and Change in Congress* (New York: Harper & Row, 1978); Randall B. Ripley, *Congress: Process and Policy*, 2d ed. (New York: W. W. Norton, 1978); V. O. Key, Jr., *Politics, Parties, and Pressure Groups*, 5th ed. (New York: Crowell, 1964), especially chaps. 9 and 24; and J. H. Fenton, "Liberal-Conservative Divisions by Sections of the United States," *Annals* 344 (1962): 122–127.

43. John R. Schmidhauser, "Judicial Behavior and the Sectional Crisis of 1837–1860," *Journal of Politics* 23 (1961): 615–640. To be more precise, Schmidhauser found that justices' party affiliations and their geographic orientations were highly interrelated. Because the four justices who were most supportive of Southern regional interests were all Southern Democrats, and since the two justices with the strongest pro-Northern voting patterns were Northern Whigs, Schmidhauser concluded that the effects of party and region were virtually inseparable.

44. Leavitt, "Political Party and Class Influences on the Attitudes of Justices of the Supreme Court in the Twentieth Century."

45. James F. Simon, *In His Own Image* (New York: David McKay, 1973), 103–104.

46. Ibid., 123.

47. Howard, *Courts of Appeals in the Federal Judicial System,* 55, 79, 156.

48. Susan Brodie Haire, "Judges' Decisions in the United States Courts of Appeals: A Reassessment of Geographic Patterns in Judicial Behavior," Ph.D. dissertation, University of South Carolina, 1993, 160.

49. Steve Alumbaugh and C. K. Rowland, "The Links Between Platform-Based Appointment Criteria and Trial Judges' Abortion Judgments," *Judicature* 74 (1990): 161.

50. Based on unpublished data collected by Robert A. Carp, Ronald Stidham, and C. K. Rowland.

51. For example, see Goldman, "Voting Behavior on the United States Courts of Appeals, 1961–1964," 370–385.

52. Haire, "Judges' Decisions in the United States Courts of Appeals," 163 and chap. 5.

53. Based on unpublished data collected by Robert A. Carp, Ronald Stidham, and C. K. Rowland.

54. Carp and Wheeler, "Sink or Swim," 376.

55. Carp, "The Influence of Local Needs and Conditions on the Administration of Federal Justice," 17–18.

56. Howard, *Courts of Appeals in the Federal Judicial System,* 234.

57. For example, see Carp and Rowland, *Policymaking and Politics in the Federal District Courts,* 106–116.

58. This discussion is based on material taken from Martin A. Levin, *Urban Politics and the Criminal Courts* (Chicago: University of Chicago Press, 1977).

59. Ibid., 136–142.

60. Ibid., 142–147.

61. Henry R. Glick, *Courts, Politics, and Justice,* 3d ed. (New York: McGraw-Hill, 1993), 321.

62. As quoted in William Mishler and Reginald S. Sheehan, "The Supreme Court as a Countermajoritarian Institution? The Impact of Public Opinion on Supreme Court Decisions," *American Political Science Review* 87 (1993): 89.

63. "Arkansas Judge Who Struck Down Creation-Science Law Condemned in Hundreds of Letters," *Houston Chronicle,* August 6, 1982, 1:9.

64. *Brown v. Board of Education,* 349 U.S. 294 (1955).

65. *Baker v. Carr,* 369 U.S. 186 (1962).

66. *Miller v. California,* 413 U.S. 15 (1973).

67. Lawrence Baum, *The Supreme Court,* 5th ed. (Washington, D.C.: CQ Press, 1995), 151. For a good discussion of this subject, see David G. Barnum, "Supreme Court and Public Opinion: Judicial Decision Making in the Post–New Deal Period," *Journal of Politics* 47 (1985): 652–666.

68. The full citations are as follows: *Marbury v. Madison,* 1 Cranch 137 (1803); *Brown v. Board of Education,* 347 U.S. 483 (1954); *Roe v. Wade,* 410 U.S. 113 (1973); and *United States v. Nixon,* 418 U.S. 683 (1974).

69. For examples of these earlier studies, see Glen T. Broach et al., "State Political Culture and Sentence Severity in Federal District Courts," *Criminology* 16 (1978): 373–382; and Ronald Stidham and Robert

A. Carp, "Trial Courts' Responses to Supreme Court Policy Changes: Three Case Studies," *Law & Policy Quarterly* 4 (1982): 215–235.

70. Mishler and Sheehan, "The Supreme Court as a Countermajoritarian Institution?" 96.

71. Ibid., 87–101; and Mishler and Sheehan, "Popular Influence on Supreme Court Decisions: A Response to Helmut Norpoth and Jeffrey A. Segal," *American Political Science Review*, 88 (1994): 716–724.

72. Mishler and Sheehan, "The Supreme Court as a Countermajoritarian Institution?" 87–101.

73. Roy B. Flemming and B. Dan Wood, "The Public and the Supreme Court: Individual Justice Responsiveness to American Policy Moods," *American Journal of Political Science* 41 (1997): 468–498.

74. For example, see Haire, "Judges' Decisions in the United States Courts of Appeals."

75. For example, see Kenneth Luis Manning, "Public Opinion and Gender Equality in the Federal District Courts" (Paper delivered at the annual meeting of the Midwest Political Science Association, Chicago, 1997).

76. James H. Kuklinski and John E. Stanga, "Political Participation and Government Responsiveness: The Behavior of California Superior Courts," *American Political Science Review* 73 (1979): 1090–1099.

77. Melinda Gann Hall, "Electoral Politics and Strategic Voting in State Supreme Courts," *Journal of Politics* 54 (1992): 427.

78. "Dallas Judge Apologizes for 'Poor Choice of Words,'" *Montrose Voice*, December 23, 1988, 5.

79. "Overheard," *Newsweek*, January 2, 1989, 13.

80. However, many constitutional scholars argue that the right of the federal courts to hear such cases stems directly from Article III of the Constitution and that therefore Congress could not legally curtail court jurisdiction over these subjects except by initiating an amendment to the Constitution.

81. For example, see Stephen L. Wasby, *The Impact of the United States Supreme Court* (Homewood, Ill.: Dorsey Press, 1970), especially 255–256; and Harrell R. Rodgers, Jr., and Charles S. Bullock III, *Coercion to Compliance* (Lexington, Mass.: Heath, 1976).

82. *National Labor Relations Board v. Jones and Laughlin Steel Corp.*, 301 U.S. 1 (1937); and *West Coast Hotel Co. v. Parrish*, 300 U.S. 379 (1937).

83. Stidham and Carp, "Trial Courts' Responses to Supreme Court Policy Changes," 218–222.

84. G. Alan Tarr and Mary Cornelia Aldis Porter, *State Supreme Courts in State and Nation* (New Haven, Conn.: Yale University Press, 1988), chap. 2.

85. Ibid., 45.

86. Roger D. Groot, "The Effects of an Intermediate Appellate Court on the Supreme Court Product: The North Carolina Experience," *Wake Forest Law Review* 7 (1971): 548–572.

87. Tarr and Porter, *State Supreme Courts in State and Nation*, 51.

88. Meki Cox, "Hawaii Starts Benefits to Gay Couples," *Houston Chronicle*, July 9, 1997, A5

89. This example is based on Jim Carlton and Amy Dockser Marcus, "Undocumented Worker's Suit Is Upheld," *Wall Street Journal*, February 25, 1991, B5. The case citation is *E.E.O.C. v. Tortilleria La Mejor*, 758 F. Supp. 585 (E.D. Cal. 1991).

90. Carp and Rowland, *Policymaking and Politics in the Federal District Courts*, 37.

91. However, on matters of *local* economic regulation, voting differences among judges are still sharp (see Table 10-1). Only at the national level have federal judges tended to refrain from substituting their own views for those of elected officials.

92. Carp and Rowland, *Policymaking and Politics in the Federal District Courts*, 39.

93. Of course, at the state level, whether high court ambiguity is thought to be greater on civil rights and liberties issues or in the labor and economic realm varies from one jurisdiction to another. Note the several areas discussed in Chapter 4, under the heading "Jurisdiction and Policy Making of State Courts," in which state courts have taken the lead in bringing about policy-making innovations.

94. Kitchin, *Federal District Judges*, 104.

95. Carp and Rowland, *Policymaking and Politics in the Federal District Courts*, 40.

96. *Roth v. United States* and *Alberts v. California*, 354 U.S. 476 (1957).

97. *Jacobellis v. Ohio*, 378 U.S. 184 (1964).

98. *Miller v. California*, 413 U.S. 15 (1973).

99. *Jacobellis v. Ohio*, 378 U.S. 184 (1964) at 197.

100. Laura Parker, "Federal Judge in Florida Rules 2 Live Crew Album Is Obscene," *Houston Chronicle*, June 7, 1990, A11.

101. Ann Davis, "When Ribaldry Among Men Is Sex Harassment," *Wall Street Journal*, June 5, 1997, B1.

102. "Same-Sex Harassment: Is It Illegal and Under What Circumstances?" *Wall Street Journal*, June 3, 1997, A1.

103. Davis, "When Ribaldry Among Men Is Sex Harassment."

104. Helene Cooper, "Tennessee Court Refuses to Give Custody of 7 Embryos to Mother," *Wall Street Journal*, June 2, 1992, B8.

105. Kitchin, *Federal District Judges*, 107.

106. Ibid.

107. Ibid.

108. Glick, *Courts, Politics, and Justice*, 335.

109. Carp and Rowland, *Policymaking and Politics in the Federal District Courts*, 14.

SUGGESTED READINGS

Burton, Steven J. *An Introduction to Law and Legal Reasoning.* Boston: Little, Brown, 1985. Explains what it has traditionally meant to "think like a judge"; explores the judicial reasoning process.

Carter, Lief H. *Reason in Law,* 5th ed. New York: HarperCollins, 1998. A short, excellent discussion of how judges think and reason; offers a good explication of the legal subculture.

Gates, John B., and Charles Johnson. *The American Courts: A Critical Assessment,* Part III. Washington, D.C.: CQ Press, 1991. A collection of essays by prominent political scientists on the various influences on judicial decision making.

Goldman, Sheldon, and Austin Sarat, eds. *American Court Systems: Readings in Judicial Process and Behavior,* 2d ed. White Plains, N.Y.: Longman, 1989. A reader containing contemporary approaches to explaining why judges think and act the way they do.

Richardson, Richard J., and Kenneth N. Vines. *The Politics of Federal Courts: Lower Courts in the United States.* Boston: Little, Brown, 1970. A classic discussion of the influences of both the legal subculture and the democratic subculture on judicial decision making.

Rowland, C. K., and Robert A. Carp. *Politics & Judgment in Federal District Courts.* Lawrence: University Press of Kansas, 1996. A comprehensive study of decision making at the federal district court level, based on a large data sample.

Schubert, Glendon. *Judicial Behavior: A Reader in Theory and Research.* Chicago: Rand McNally, 1964. A classic reader in judicial decision making; excellent essays introduce each separate chapter.

Tanenhaus, Joseph, and Walter F. Murphy. *The Study of Public Law.* New York: Random House, 1972. Systematically discusses the history of public law and examines the various approaches to its study.

CHAPTER 11

Decision Making in Collegial Courts

Chief Justice William Rehnquist, himself a former law clerk for Justice Robert Jackson, meets with his clerks to discuss cases before the Court.

UNTIL NOW WE HAVE TREATED decision making by American judges at all levels as if it were essentially the product of the same two influences—the legal and the democratic subcultures. To a substantial degree this is a valid approach to take. After all, jurists on multijudge appellate courts adhere to the same legal reasoning process as do their colleagues on the trial court bench; lower-court judges may be influenced in close cases by their political party affiliation just as are members of the appeals courts. But before an analysis of judicial decision making can be complete, we need to recognize one vital difference between trial courts on the one hand and the state and federal appellate courts on the other. The former render decisions that are largely the product of a single individual, whereas the latter are *collegial* courts, in which decision making is the product of group interaction. As one former trial judge, now a member of an appellate court, described it:

The transition between a district judge and circuit judge is not an easy one, primarily because of, shall I say, the autocratic position occupied by the district court judge. He is the sole decider. He decides as he sees fit, and files the decision in a form as he sees fit. *A Court of Appeals decides by committee.* One of the first traumas I had was when opinions were sent back by the other judges asking me to add this sentence, change that, etc., to get concurrence. I admit at the beginning I resisted that. It was pride. I learned it was a joint project, but it was a very difficult thing. I see the same in others.[1] [Emphasis added.]

What are the extra ingredients that go into a decision made by the nine-member Supreme Court or by a three-judge state appellate panel? What is the essence of the dynamics of multijudge decision making that distinguishes it from a judgment made by a single jurist? We shall discuss several theoretical approaches that have attempted to get a handle on this interesting but slippery subject. Although we shall continue to address these phenomena as they affect *both* state and federal judges, we shall not treat the several judicial systems as separate entities. This is because there is no reason to believe that the variables and forces we are exploring here affect state jurists differently from federal judges. For example, when we contend that the corporate decision of a collegial court is often the product of personal interaction among its judges, there is no reason to believe that such interpersonal variables differ to any significant degree whether we are talking about the U.S. Supreme Court or the highest tribunal of a given state.[2]

Cue Theory

We have noted that as long as trial and appeals courts have jurisdiction over a case, the judges must render some type of decision on the merits; they have little discretion about the composition of their dockets. If the judges view a particular case as presenting a trivial question, they will not spend time agonizing over it, but they are still obliged to provide some kind of formal ruling on the substance of the matter. Not so with the Supreme Court. Recall from Chapter 2 that of the approximately 5,000 petitions presented to the Court each year, the justices agree to hear only a few hundred on the merits—and in recent years fewer than a hundred of these carry with them full-blown written opinions. Since the passage of Public Law 100–352 in 1988, the Supreme Court has had complete control over its own docket—that is, the justices themselves decide which issues they want to tackle in a given term and which ones are not ripe for adjudication or must be summarily dismissed for "want of a substantial federal question." The importance of this is that what the Supreme Court decides *not* to rule on is often as significant as the cases it does summon forth for its scrutiny. (At the state level, as noted in the previous chapter, there is great variance in the amount of control that the supreme courts have over their dockets.[3])

Judicial scholars have sought to identify the reasons some petitions are culled for special attention and the rest never receive those important four votes that are needed for the Supreme Court to grant certiorari and decide the case. A pioneering study of this question was conducted by a research team during the early 1960s.[4] Analysts began by examining the Court's official reasons for granting certiorari as set forth in Rule 17, which specifies that the Court might hear a case if (1) an appeals court has decided a point of local law in conflict with local decisions, (2) a court of appeals has departed from "the usual course of judicial proceedings," (3) a conflict is perceived between a lower-court decision and a Supreme Court precedent, (4) a conflict exists on a point of law among the various federal circuits, or (5) there exists a really important question on which the Court feels it must have the final word.

The research team tested these official reasons by comparing the cases for which certiorari was granted with those in which review was denied. To their surprise (or maybe not), the official reasons did not prove to be a very accurate or useful guide to the Court's decision making. For example, in over 50 percent of the cases that were selected for review, the Court's official reason for its actions was that the cases were "important"—a nebulous adjective at best. The researchers thought they could do better. They set out to identify certain key characteristics of those cases for which review was and was not granted. They hoped to develop some predictive statements that were more precise and reliable than Rule 17. The result was cue theory.

Cue theory is based on the assumption that the Supreme Court justices have neither the time nor the desire to wade through the myriad of pages in the thousands of petitions presented to them each year. Therefore, it is logical to assume that they must have developed some sort of shortcut to help them select the petitions that are interesting and important. The justices must, the researchers hypothesized, look for cues in each petition—readily identifiable characteristics that trigger a positive response in the justices as they skim through the cumbersome assemblage of legal documents. After all, we ourselves have our own particular cue theories as we go about our daily lives. We wouldn't read through a four-page circular on a local store's white sale, for instance, if we already had an ample supply of bedding material. Just as we look for cues in sorting through the daily mail, so, too, do justices on the Supreme Court as they sort through the daily arrival of petitions for certiorari. At least this is what the research team reasoned.

The results of the team's hypotheses and investigations were encouraging. Of the several possible cues they tested for, three were found to contain substantial explanatory power. In order of importance they were (1) whether the U.S. government was a party to a case and was asking for Court review, (2) whether a civil rights or civil liberties issue was debated, and (3) whether there was dissension among the judges in the court that had previously heard the case (or disagreement between two or more courts and government agencies). If a case contained all three cues, there was an 80 percent chance that certiorari would be granted; if none were present, the chance dropped to a mere 7 percent. Clearly the researchers had developed a useful model to explain this one aspect of Supreme Court behavior.

During the past two decades judicial scholars have further tested, elaborated on, and revised cue theory. Some studies have found a relationship between the way the justices voted on a grant of certiorari and their eventual vote on the merits of the case at conference.[5] Additional studies have suggested that a fourth cue has considerable explanatory power—the ideological direction of the lower-court decision.[6] In comparing selected periods of the Warren Court (1967 and 1968 terms) and the Burger Court (1976 and 1977 terms) on certiorari voting, the analysts reached several conclusions. First, during the liberal Warren Court era, the justices were more likely to review economic cases that had been decided in a *conservative* manner by the lower court[7]—especially when the U.S. government was seeking Court review. Second, and conversely, the more conservative Burger Court tended to review *liberal* lower-court economic decisions. Third, the Burger Court was readier to scrutinize a civil libertarian position taken by a lower court than a lower-court decision limiting civil liberties.

A study of the first three terms of the Rehnquist Court reveals the presence of a new hybrid strategy for granting certiorari. Unlike the Warren and Burger Courts, the Rehnquist Court has not engaged in much "error correction" activity, that is, overturning lower-court decisions with which it disagrees. Rather it has chosen to affirm a tremendous percentage of conservative lower-court decisions with which it is in ideological harmony, thereby underscoring the values inherent in these cases. It is also more likely to accept cases that concern issues on which lower-court judges had rendered conflicting decisions. The researchers conceded that they could only speculate as to why the Rehnquist team had switched gears in this decision-making area.[8]

Cue theory, then, is one predictor of High Court voting behavior. One contemporary judicial scholar has summarized the certiorari behavior of the Court during the past several decades:

When the civil rights movement was building in importance (1950s), the Supreme Court, under the leadership of Chief Justice Earl Warren, paid special attention to cases involving civil liberties violations, and during the 1960s various underdog appellants, such as aliens, minorities, criminal defendants, laborers, and other have-nots, were more successful than others in getting *certiorari*. However, as the Supreme Court has shifted toward the conservatives, upperdogs such as governments at all levels and businesses have received more attention by the Supreme Court.[9]

In the remainder of the chapter we will examine several models of appellate court behavior that seek to explain how these collegial bodies make decisions once a case has been docketed. The models are small-group analysis, attitude theory and bloc-formation analysis, and fact pattern analysis.

Small-Group Analysis

As applied to the judiciary, most small-group research is based on the thesis that judges want to influence the judgments of their colleagues and to be on the winning side as often as possible. This school of thought assumes that judges' positions are not written in stone from the start but are susceptible to moderation or even to a 180-degree turn on occasion. More specifically, scholars believe that a good deal of interaction takes place among justices from the time a case is first discussed in conference to the moment the final decision is rendered in open court some weeks or months later. One researcher, in fact, has referred to the appellate judges' openness to change as "fluidity."[10]

It has been no secret that the way judges relate to one another affects their behavior on the court. Examination of the personal papers of members of the Supreme Court, interviews with appellate court jurists, and reminiscences of former law clerks all reveal the impact of group dynamics on voting behavior and on the content of written opinions.[11] Two characteristics in particular seem to carry weight when justices seek to influence their colleagues—personality and intellect. Judges who are considered to be warm, good-hearted, fair-minded, and so on seem able to put together winning coalitions and to hammer out compromises a bit more effectively than colleagues who have a reputation for condescension, self-righteousness, hostility, or vindictiveness.[12] As one researcher put it after interviewing supreme court justices in Louisiana, Pennsylvania, New Jersey, and Massachusetts:

Generally, the judges believed it is important for court members to moderate their own personal idiosyncrasies in order to maintain as much harmony in the group as possible. Such things as arrogance, pride, sense of superiority, and loss of temper were condemned. . . . A pleasing personality . . . can be particularly important on collegial courts because the judges interact on a continuous basis: they operate as a small, permanent committee.[13]

This reflection on human nature should come as no surprise. A student who had served on his university's multimember student court gave us an illustration of this phenomenon, and though a student tribunal is certainly not a state or federal appellate court, we think the dynamics are similar:

> We had this guy on the court . . . who was one of these people that you just kind of naturally take to. I mean, he had a good sense of humor and was real decent and outgoing. I don't think he was that much of a "brain" or anything, but you always felt that he honestly wanted to do the right thing. Well, when we were split on some case—especially on matters of what punishment to hand down—and he suggested a way out, I think we all listened pretty carefully to what he thought was fair. He was just that sort of person.

The other personal attribute that is part of small-group dynamics is the knowledge and intellectual capacity of the individual judge.[14] A justice with a superior intellect or wide experience in a particular area of the law has a good deal more clout than a jurist who is seen as an intellectual lightweight. As one appeals court judge observed:

> Personality doesn't amount to so much as opinion-writing ability. Some judges are simply better than others. Some know more, think better. It would be strange if among nine men all had the same ability. Some simply have more respect than others. . . . That's bound to be so in any group. The first thing, is the judge particularly broad and experienced in the field? A couple of judges are acknowledged masters in admiralty. What they think carries more weight. I don't have much trouble being heard on criminal law or state government. I've been there. Ex-district judges on Courts of Appeals certainly carry more weight in discussion of trial procedures, instructions to juries, etc. Every judge is recognized for a particular proficiency obtained before or after his appointment. It saves enormous spadework and drudgery [to assign opinions accordingly]. No one could develop an expertise in all these fields.[15]

The techniques or strategies that justices use in their conscious (or even unconscious) efforts to maximize their impact on multijudge courts can be grouped into three general categories: persuasion on the merits, bargaining, and threat of sanctions. Although the tactics overlap and are inherently interrelated, we shall take a look at their central focuses, which are in fact different.

Persuasion on the Merits

This aspect of small-group dynamics takes us right back to the *legal subculture* discussed in Chapter 10. Quite simply, it means that because of their training and values, judges are open to persuasion based on sound legal reasoning bolstered by legal precedents. Unless judges have taken a hard-and-fast position from the start, most can be swayed by an articulate and well-reasoned argument from a colleague with a differing opinion.

One study of the Supreme Court concluded that the justices

can be persuaded to change their minds about specific cases as well as about broad public policies, and intellectual persuasion can play an important role in such shifts. . . . Time and time again positions first taken at conference are changed as other Justices bring up new ar guments. Perhaps most convincing in demonstrating the impact of intellectual factors are the numerous instances on record in which the Justice assigned the opinion of the Court has reported back to the conference that additional study had convinced him that he and the rest of the majority had been in error.[16]

For example, Justice Robert Jackson, hardly a wilting violet when it came to holding fast to a judicial point of view, once commented: "I myself have changed my opinion after reading the opinions of the other members of this Court. And I am as stubborn as most. But I sometimes wind up not voting the way I voted in conference because the reasons of the majority didn't satisfy me."[17]

Judges on state appellate courts appear to be just as willing to have their positions altered by arguments well seasoned by the spices of precedent and sound judicial reasoning. After interviews with supreme court justices in four states, one scholar observed:

When differences become evident, members of the court may attempt to persuade other judges to adopt their view by vigorously presenting their position or arguing the merits of their way of analyzing the case. Because of different amounts of influence exerted by the chief justice or by judges who have special personal status on the court, certain members of the court may be "persuaded" to abandon their own position and adopt the views of others.[18]

The persuasion-on-merits phenomenon can't be pushed too far, however. If the facts and legal arguments are straightforward enough, a justice may simply not be open to change. And judges who are deeply committed to a specific point of view or whose egos are sufficiently great will probably be impervious to legal arguments inconsistent with their own views. For instance, former justices Thurgood Marshall and (later in his career) Harry Blackmun were profoundly and morally opposed to the principle of capital punishment and often said so in their opinions. It is doubtful that any amount of legal reasoning or any calling up of "sacred precedents" could alter their belief that executions constitute "cruel and unusual punishment" by contemporary standards.

Bargaining

Bargaining may sound like a strange word to use in talking about the personal interactions of judges on collegial courts. When students first hear the term, they often think of the vote-trading technique called *logrolling* that legislators sometimes use. For example, one lawmaker might say to another, "If you vote for a new federal dam in my district, I'll vote to build a couple of new post offices in yours." Is this what happens with judges, too? Is there evidence that they sometimes say to one another, "If you vote for me in this case, I'll decide with you in one of your 'pet cases'"? In fact, there is virtually *no* evidence for this in the judiciary. Bargaining does indeed take place, but it is more subtle and does not involve vote swapping. Although some bargaining occurs in the give-and-take that goes on in conference, when the initial votes are taken, most attention is focused on the scope and contents of the majority (or even the dissenting) opinion.

To understand how the bargaining process works, it is important to realize that usually much more is at stake in the outcome of a decision than merely whether party A or party B wins. Judges also have to discuss such questions as these: How broad should the decision be—that is, should we suggest in our written opinion that this case is unique, or should we open the gates and encourage other suits of this nature? Should we overturn what appears to be the obviously controlling precedent, or should we "distinguish around" it and let the precedent stand? Should we base our decision on constitutional grounds, or should we allow the victor to win on more technical and restrictive grounds? In other words, most decisions at the appellate level are not zero-sum games in which the winner automatically takes all; there are almost always important supplementary issues to be talked about or to be bargained for.

Two landmark cases of the 1970s provide a good example. In 1973 the Supreme Court handed down a joint decision on the matter of abortion.[19] To most citizens the only issue the Court had to decide was whether abortion was legal. Although that may have been the bottom-line question, many other issues were in fact at stake, and the bargaining over them among the majority justices was intense.[20] What is human life and when does it begin? Should the decision rest on the Ninth Amendment or should it be based on the due process clause of the Fourteenth Amendment? Does a fetus have any constitutional rights? Is it a greater health risk to a woman to have an abortion or to deliver a child after carrying it to full term? Can a woman decide to have an abortion on her own or does a physician have to concur? If the latter, how many doctors need concur? And this by no means completes the list!

For the abortion cases the justices spent over a year trying to hammer out a decision that would be acceptable to a majority. Draft opinions were sent around, altered, and changed again as the official opinion writer, Justice Harry Blackmun, tried to accommodate all views—or at least not to offend someone in the majority so strongly that he would join the dissenters. Bob Woodward and Scott Armstrong noted in *The Brethren* that the law clerks "in most chambers were surprised to see the Justices, particularly Blackmun, so openly brokering their decision like a group of legislators."[21] But the law clerks themselves were not immune to the bargaining process. In the Supreme Court's cafeteria, law library, and gymnasium the clerks asked one another whether "your Justice" could go along with this or that compromise or related that "my Justice" would never support an opinion containing such and such an offensive clause.

Bargaining of this nature is just as common on state collegial courts as it is at the national level. This statement by one state supreme court justice is quoted by a scholar who regards it as typical:

> You might say to another judge that if you take this line out, I'll go along with your opinion. You engage in a degree of compromise and if it doesn't hurt the point you're trying to make in an opinion, you ought to agree to take it out. . . . The men will write an opinion and circulate it. And then the other judges will write a letter or say at conference, can you change this or that, adjust the language here, etc. . . . Your object is to get a unanimous court. That's always best.[22]

In a significant portion of appellate court cases, then, bargaining is the name of the game—it is one way in which a group of jurists, in a unanimous or majority opinion, is able to present a united front. The author of one classic study that focused on the Supreme Court has observed:

> For Justices, bargaining is a simple fact of life. Despite conflicting views on literary style, relevant precedents, procedural rules, and substantive policy, cases have to be settled and opinions written; and no opinion may carry the institutional label of the court unless five Justices agree to sign it. In the process of judicial decision-making, much bargaining may be tacit, but the pattern is still one of negotiation and accommodation to secure consensus. Thus how to bargain wisely—not necessarily sharply—is a prime consideration for a Justice who is anxious to see his policy adopted by the Court. A Justice must learn not only how to put pressure on his colleagues but how to gauge what amounts of pressure are sufficient to be "effective" and what amounts will overshoot the mark and alienate another judge. In many situations a Justice has to be willing to settle for less than he wants if he is to get anything at all. As Brandeis once remarked, the "great difficulty of all group action, of course, is when and what concession to make."[23]

Appellate judges do most of their face-to-face bargaining at the three-judge conferences and then iron out the details of the opinion later on, using the telephone and short memos. As with Supreme Court decision making, a threat to dissent can often result in changes in the way the majority opinion is drafted.

When a conservative minority sought to amend a middle-of-the-road compromise by which the 5th circuit achieved unanimity in the Mississippi school case, for example, a former legislator reportedly threatened to bolt to the left. "They came back into the fold in a hurry," a colleague remarked. "So you see, the judicial process is like legislation. All decisions are compromises."[24]

Threat of Sanctions

Besides persuasion on the merits and bargaining, there is one other tactic that jurists use in their efforts to maximize their impact on the multimember appellate tribunals—the threat of sanctions. Basically there are three sanctions that a judge or justice can invoke against colleagues: the vote, the willingness to write a strong dissenting opinion, and the threat to "go public."

The Judge's Vote. The threat to take away one's vote from the majority, and thus dissent, may cause the majority to alter its views. For example, back in 1889 Justice Horace Gray sent this subtle (or perhaps not so subtle) message to Justice Samuel Miller:

After a careful reading of your opinion in *Shotwell v. Moore,* I am very sorry to be compelled to say that the first part of it . . . is so contrary to my conviction, that I fear, unless it can be a good deal tempered, I shall have to deliver a separate opinion on the lines of the enclosed memorandum. I am particularly troubled about this, because, if my scruples are not removed, and Justices Field, Bradley and Lamar adhere to their dissent, your opinion will represent only four judges, half of those who took part in the case.[25]

His back against the wall because of his narrow majority, Justice Miller was obliged to yield to his colleague's costly "scruples."

For the most part the potential effect of a threat to dissent from the majority depends on how small that majority is. Thus if the initial vote among a three-judge appellate panel were three-to-zero, the threat of one member to dissent would not be all that serious; there would still be a two-to-one majority. Conversely, if at a preliminary Supreme Court conference there were a five-to-four vote, the threat by one of those five to defect would be taken seriously indeed by the remaining four. At the end of the 1993–94 term, Justice Anthony Kennedy had voted with the majority in thirteen of the Court's fourteen cases decided by a five-to-four vote, and it seems fair to assume that his support in close cases was much sought after.

The newly acquired judicial papers of Thurgood Marshall provide a colorful example of how pivotal one justice's vote can be. In January of 1989 the Court decided to take the case of *Webster v. Reproductive Health Services,* which dealt with the constitutionality of Missouri's law that severely restricted abortions.[26] Many Court observers believed that there was finally a viable conservative majority on the Court that could strike down the 1973 *Roe* and *Doe* decisions that established the constitutional right to an abortion. Indeed, Justice Marshall's informal tally sheet dated April 28 indicated five tentative initial votes to uphold the law: Justices Rehnquist, White, Scalia, Kennedy, and O'Connor. Rehnquist assigned the majority opinion to himself, and Justice Blackmun penned a bitter dissent in which he said in part that the right to abortion "no longer survives."

"Over the course of two months, in flurries of court memos, the justices traded views and language. Throughout, O'Connor remained the pivotal swing vote. But she couldn't bring herself to join Rehnquist. Within days of the end of the term O'Connor changed her mind. She signaled her switch when she wrote that *Roe* was 'problematic,' rather than 'outmoded,' as she had said in an earlier draft."[27]

Still, "on June 27, Rehnquist circulated his fourth draft. The document still said, 'Chief Justice Rehnquist delivered the opinion of the Court,' traditional wording indicating that he had not given up his hopes of getting O'Connor's support. Then something definitive happened to the Rehnquist majority. On June 28, O'Connor and Blackmun submitted drafts referring to the Rehnquist opinion as a 'plurality,' rather than a majority."[28] The next day Rehnquist circulated his final draft in which, for the first time, he called his opinion the "judgment" of the Court rather than the majority opinion, meaning in effect that the Missouri law would be upheld but there would be no reversal of *Roe v. Wade.* This illustration shows vividly how important a single justice's vote can be when the Court is split evenly between one ideological camp and another.

Sometimes, however, the impact of one's vote is not merely a function of how divided the court is. On occasion the perceived need for unanimity may be so strong that *any* justice's threat to vote against the prevailing view may have a disproportionate effect. We know now, for example, that prior to the 1954 *Brown* decision, a majority on the Supreme Court opposed segregation in the schools. Chief Justice Warren and the other liberals believed, though, that a simple majority was not enough to confront the backlash expected if segregation were struck down; only a *unanimous* Court, they felt, could have any chance of seeing its will prevail throughout the nation. Therefore, the liberal majority bided its time during the early 1950s until the moment came when all nine justices were willing to take on the malignant giant of racial segregation.

A more recent example occurred when President Clinton wished to postpone the sexual harassment suit brought against him by Paula Jones. He argued that the president should be immune from such troublesome and time-consuming litigation during his tenure in the White House. Otherwise, he and his attorneys argued, chief executives would be plagued by scores of such suits brought by publicity-seeking troublemakers who would detract from his ability to devote his full time and energies to the task of governance. A district court judge rejected the president's motion to dismiss the case entirely, but the jurist did agree to postpone the case until the end of Clinton's presidency. Both parties were unhappy with the trial court's rulings and both appealed. A panel of the Eighth Circuit Court of Appeals ruled against the president in a very split vote, and Clinton appealed to the U.S. Supreme Court.

The High Court's decision was unanimous, and it went against the president. Speaking for the majority, Justice Stevens said in part: "We think the District Court may have given undue weight to the concern that a trial might generate unrelated civil actions that could conceivably hamper the President in conducting the duties of his office. If and when that should occur, the court's discretion would permit it to manage those actions in such fashion (including deferral of trial) that interference with the President's duties would not occur. But no such impingement upon the President's conduct of his office was shown here."[29] Besides the importance of the decision itself, what is equally important is that the decision was *unanimous;* even the president's two Supreme Court appointees (Ginsburg and Breyer) voted against him. A unanimous vote coming from the deeply divided Rehnquist Court underscored the legal principle involved in the case, and it quashed any notion that partisan politics was a variable in the decision. The defection of just a single vote, while not changing the outcome one wit, would have detracted from the decisive impact of a totally unified court.

State judges, too, may well feel the need for unanimity in certain types of cases. For example, one New Jersey supreme court justice told a researcher: "We did have a case where we felt a unanimous opinion was necessary. No one felt strongly about a dissent, so no dissents were made. . . . A religious case, for example, needs a unanimous decision. Courts don't try to be divisive on this."[30]

Thus although the impact of the threat to abandon the majority is usually in direct proportion to the closeness of the vote, there are occasions when a majority will pay top dollar to keep any judge or justice from breaking ranks.

The Willingness to Write a Strong Dissent. There are dissents and there are dissents. Appellate court jurists who intend to vote against the majority must decide whether to write a lengthy, assertive dissenting opinion or merely to dissent without opinion. If jurists are not regarded by other justices—or by the public at large—as being prestigious or articulate, their threat to write a dissenting opinion may be taken with the proverbial grain of salt. If, however, potential dissenters are respected jurists with a reputation for a keen wit or for often being right in the long run, the situation is quite different. The other judges may be willing to alter their views to accommodate potential dissenters' positions or at least to dissuade them from attacking the majority position. As one Court observer has noted:

There are factors which push the majority Justices, especially the opinion writer, to accept accommodation. An eloquent, tightly-reasoned dissent can be an upsetting force. Stone's separate opinions during the thirties pointed up more sharply the folly of the conservative Justices than did any of the attacks on the Court by elected politicians. The majority may thus find it profitable to mute criticism from within the Court by giving in on some issues.[31]

Thus the second sanction—the threat to write a dissenting opinion—depends on the circumstances for its effectiveness. Sometimes it may be regarded as no more than a nuisance or the fruit of judicial egomania; on other occasions it may be viewed as likely to weaken the impact of the majority opinion.

In state courts the impact of a threat to author a strong dissent is smaller simply because dissents are more infrequent at that level. Consensus and unanimity are norms in most of the state appellate tribunals, whereas this is clearly not the case at the federal level. Since the 1943 term at least 50 percent of Supreme Court decisions have produced dissents. However, using data from the early to mid-1960s, researchers have found that fewer than ten state supreme courts produced dissents in 20 percent or more of their cases, and only the high courts in Michigan, New York, and Pennsylvania produced dissents at or above the 40 percent mark.[32]

The Threat to "Go Public." On rare occasions an appellate judge may use the ultimate weapon against colleagues—public exposure. Such strong medicine is usually administered only when a jurist believes a colleague (or a group of judges) has violated the basic rules of the game; the judge then threatens to hang out the dirty linen for all to see. For example, one appeals court judge told how, as a newcomer to the bench, he had threatened public exposure to force a senior colleague to withdraw an opinion filed without his consent, a possibility he had been warned against by another judge on the court: "It was my first sitting as a circuit judge," he recalled. "It was not a major case. But there was strong give and take!"[33]

In 1967, Judges John Danaher and Warren Burger (soon to be Chief Justice Burger) accused three of their appellate court colleagues of consciously attempting to foist on the Washington, D.C. Circuit a minority position on criminal procedures.[34] Ironically, some four years later it was Burger who was threatened with public exposure by a Supreme Court colleague who felt that Burger was trying to turn his minority status on a case into a majority position.

The incident occurred as follows. When the vote had been taken at conference on the abortion cases (*Roe v. Wade*, considered jointly with *Doe v. Bolton*), Chief Justice Burger was in the minority. According to Supreme Court practice, this would have meant that the senior member of the majority—in this case William O. Douglas—would have been assigned to speak for the Court. Ignoring Court protocol, Burger assigned the official opinion writing to his alter ego Harry Blackmun. This enraged Douglas. But the pot didn't really boil over until several months later when Burger lobbied from his minority status to have the case postponed until the next term. (Douglas wanted the decision to be handed down immediately.) These extracts from *The Brethren* capture something of the drama of the confrontation:

This time Douglas threatened to play his ace. If the conference insisted on putting the cases over for reargument, he would dissent from such an order, and he would publish the full text of his dissent. Douglas reiterated the protest he had made in December about the Chief's assigning the case to Blackmun, Burger's response and his subsequent intransigence. . . . Douglas . . . continued: "When, however, the minority seeks to control the assignment, there is a destructive force at work in the Court. When a Chief Justice tries to bend the Court to his will by manipulating assignments, the integrity of the institution is imperiled."

Douglas's pen then became more acid:

Borrowing a line from a speech he had given in September in Portland, Douglas then made it clear that, despite what he had said earlier, he did in fact view the Chief and Blackmun as Nixon's Minnesota Twins. "Russia once gave its Chief Justice two votes; but that was too strong even for the Russians."[35]

Douglas was ultimately prevailed upon to refrain from publishing this petulant opinion, but this is nevertheless a classic example of the third sanction that one jurist can use against another—the threat to go public.

The threat to go public is probably a less potent weapon at the state level than it is for federal judges—particularly Supreme Court justices—because state appellate courts are generally much less visible to the general public except in the most unusual and controversial cases. Thus if a judge on a typical state appellate court threatened to go public and reveal to the populace some irregularity to which he or she had been subjected, the jurist might be told, "So, who cares?"

Despite the availability of several sanctions, it should be noted that they are usually invoked with varying degrees of hesitation—lest a judge or justice acquire a reputation for intransigence. For example, with regard to a justice's willingness to write a dissenting opinion, one perceptive scholar has noted:

Although dissent is a cherished part of the common law tradition, a Justice who persistently refuses to accommodate his views to those of his colleagues may come to be regarded as an obstructionist. A Justice whose dissents become levers for legislative or administrative action reversing judicial policies may come to be regarded as disloyal to the bench.[36]

Or, putting it in more human terms, one appeals court judge observed that "you have to keep on living with each other. In the next case the situations may be reversed."[37]

The Special Role of the U.S. Chief Justice, the U.S. Chief Judges, and State Supreme Court Chief Justices

As indicated in the previous chapters, the heads of the multijudge federal and state appellate tribunals have a number of special duties and responsibilities. At this point we shall examine their respective roles insofar as they constitute one more ingredient in the recipe for small-group interaction.

The Chief Justice of the United States. The Constitution makes only passing reference to this official whose stature has come to loom so large in the eyes of the American people. Despite the constitutional slight, the chief justice can have considerable impact on the decision-making process. The key seems to be whether the chief justice possesses the capacity and the will to use the formal and informal powers that have accrued to the office during the past two centuries.

The chief justice's greatest potential for leadership is at the conference, where the cases are discussed and where the initial votes are taken among the justices. Because the chief has the primary responsibility for setting the agenda of the conference and traditionally is the first to offer an opinion about each case, the potential for influencing both the format and the tone of the deliberation is significant. As noted earlier, David J. Danelski has identified two types of roles for justices at conference: social leader and task leader. The social leader "attends to the emotional needs of his associates by affirming their values as individuals and as Court members, especially when their views are rejected by the majority. Ordinarily he is the best liked member of the Court. . . . In terms of personality, he is apt to be warm, receptive and responsive." The task leader, on the other hand, is the intellectual force behind the conference deliberations, focusing on the actual decision and trying to keep the Court consistent with itself. Danelski describes how the two roles complement each other:

As presiding officer of the conference, the Chief Justice is in a favorable position to assert task and social leadership. His presentation of cases is an important task function. His control of the conference's process makes it easy for him to invite suggestions and opinions, seek compromises, and cut off debate which appears to be getting out of hand, all important social functions.[38]

One observer, commenting on the transition from the Burger to the Rehnquist Court, has noted these differences in leadership styles:

Differences are already apparent during oral arguments. Rehnquist is sharper, more thoughtful, more commanding and wittier than his predecessor in the center chair. And from the far right of the bench, Scalia almost bubbles over with energy and questions for counsel. No less revealing is that in the week before the start of the 1986–87 term on the first Monday in October, Rehnquist managed to get the justices to dispose of over 1,000 cases (granting 22 and denying or otherwise disposing of the rest). He did so in only two days, whereas it usually took Burger more than twice as long to get through about the same number.[39]

Not only does Rehnquist seem to possess the task leadership skills that provide the intellectual stimulus of his chief justiceship, but there is now good evidence to demonstrate his social leadership skills as well. One study noted that

Mr. Rehnquist's consensus-building is aided by the more friendly and informal style he has imposed at the court, which is for many a stark and pleasing contrast with the stiff and formal manner of former Chief Justice Warren Burger. Observers say this comfortable style, along with a powerful intellect, has made Mr. Rehnquist far more influential at the high court than Mr. Burger ever was. "The fact that he is agreeable, affable, well-liked, low-keyed, has made him a more effective leader as the court begins to emerge with what looks to be a conservative working majority," says A. E. Dick Howard, a University of Virginia Law School professor.[40]

In the past the chief justice has also had a key role in setting up what is called the *discuss list*—that is, special petitions selected out of the many to which the Court will give full consideration. The chief's law clerks obviously helped with this task, but the chief guided their judgment. In the Burger and Rehnquist Courts the chief justice has played much less of a role in establishing the discuss list. At the present time a majority of the justices pool their law clerks and give a single clerk the authority to summarize a particular petition for all the justices who participate in the pool. However, not all members of the Court participate in this practice—for example, the moderately liberal Justice Stevens has his clerks screen all petitions and write memos only on those they deem important enough for him to consider. Whether the chief justice chooses to play a major or minor role in this process, the activity is important because it determines which cases the Court will consider as a group and which are to be summarily dismissed.[41]

The final power of the chief justice is the assignment of opinions—that is, designation of who will write the official decision of the Court.[42] As noted earlier, this task falls to chief justices only if they are in the majority when the vote on a case is taken at conference; otherwise the most senior justice in the majority selects the opinion writer. The chief justices have the greatest control over an opinion when they assign it to themselves, and traditionally they have retained many important cases for that reason.[43] It will be recalled that in such cases as *Marbury v. Madison, Brown v. Board of Education,* and *United States v. Nixon,* the chief justice used his option to speak as the official voice of the Court.

Chiefs who choose not to write the opinion may assign it to that member of the majority whose views are closest to the dissenters', with the hope that some of the minority may subsequently switch their votes to the majority view.[44] Or, as has most often been the case in recent decades, chief justices will assign the opinion to an ideological alter ego so that the grounds for the decision will be favorable to their own. A 1996 study of opinion assignments made by Chief Justice Rehnquist indicated that he has utilized this power for institutional rather than policy reasons. For example, he has had an eye for evenly distributing the workload and for assigning opinions to justices who have an expertise in the subject matter of the case; he has not been motivated as keenly as other chief justices to assigning opinions to those whose ideologies are closest to his own. The authors of this study concluded: "Our model suggests that each justice's efficiency, expertise, and the number of majority opinion assignments by other justices—and not ideological compatibility—are the factors that shape Rehnquist's decisions. The only instance where Rehnquist demonstrates a bias related to ideology is when the initial majority coalition cannot afford to lose a single vote."[45]

Despite the considerable influence that a chief justice may have on the Court's small group, the crucial factor, as previously indicated, seems to be whether the chief has both the *capacity* and the *desire* to exert such potential authority. For example, the first great chief justice, John Marshall, possessed both these traits, and they helped fill the intellectual vacuum of the Court during the early 1800s:

Marshall, like the majority of justices in the court's history, was an experienced politician. . . . He guided the Court in a series of sweeping decisions . . . through force of personality and a talent for negotiation. Justice William Johnson, a Jefferson appointee, grumbled to his patron about Marshall's dominance. Wondering why Marshall invariably wrote the Court's opinions, Johnson reported to Jefferson that he had "found out the real cause. [William] Cushing was incompetent. [Samuel] Chase could not be got to think or write. [William] Paterson was a slow man and willingly declined trouble, and the other two judges [Marshall and Bushrod Washington] you know are commonly estimated as one judge."[46]

Although John Marshall had the skill and the desire to influence the Court, not all of his successors possessed these traits. For instance, the nation's chief justice between 1941 and 1946, Harlan Fiske Stone, had neither the talent nor the will for either task leadership or social leadership. As his biographer sadly wrote of him, "He was totally unprepared to cope with the petty bickering and personal conflict in which his court became engulfed."[47]

The Chief Judges of the U.S. Appeals Courts. As with the chief justice, the leadership potential of the administrative circuit heads is determined, in part, by their intellectual and negotiating skills and by their desire to put them to use. In reality, however, their potential effect on their respective circuits is probably less than the potential impact of the chief justice on the Supreme Court. First, since most appellate court decisions are made by three-judge panels on a rotating basis, the chief judge is not likely even to be a part of most circuit decision making. Second, the circuits are more decentralized than the Supreme Court. Finally, the chief judge is not nearly so prominent a figure in the eyes of the public or of other government decision makers. As one former chief judge said about the job: "The only advantage is that the title sounds more imposing if you are speaking in public or writing an article. Otherwise it's a pain in the ass."[48]

Much of a chief judge's work is administrative (such as docketing cases, keeping financial records, adjusting the caseloads), but it is also true that administration and policy making are not mutually exclusive endeavors. The chief judge of the former U.S. Fifth Circuit once acknowledged: "So many times judicial problems slop over into administrative problems and vice versa" that the real questions are when and where this effect occurs. Commenting on the influence of the chief judges, one observer has said:

As with strong presidents [or "as with strong chief justices," he might have added] . . . the spillover depends on the personality of the chief and the countervailing force of experienced colleagues. The impact of chief judges was most noticeable on freshmen and the composition of three-judge district courts. ("If all the judges are new, he'll pack a wallop out of proportion to one vote.") Southern judges made no bones about packing three-judge district courts in race relations cases. ([The liberal] "Tuttle was not about to set up a three-judge court with [segregationists like] Cameron and Cox on it; this occurs no more.") Of all administrative powers, plainly the most potent instruments of policy leadership involve the assignment of work.[49]

The State Supreme Court Chief Justices. To some extent the powers and leadership potential of state chief justices mirror those of the U.S. chief justice, but there are also significant differences, not only between the federal and state levels but also from one state to another. Recall that at the national level the chief justice is appointed by the president with the advice and consent of the Senate. In some states—Michigan, for example—the chief justice is chosen by fellow associate justices; in Texas and Ohio the chief justices are elected directly by the people.

The states also differ in regard to whether the chief justice has the most power in the assignment of opinions. There are only four states, including Hawaii, that follow very closely the opinion assignment practice of the U.S. Supreme Court. In more than a quarter of the states the chief justice assigns opinions in all cases, whether he or she is in the majority or not.[50] Well over half of the states use an automatic method of opinion assignment whereby a justice either draws cases by lot or, more often, receives them by rotation. In fewer than half of the twenty states that use the rotating system, the assignments hold only if the justice to whom the case is assigned is in the majority.

On the effectiveness of the chief justice under the different opinion assignment methods, one scholar has concluded:

A chief justice who is an extraordinary leader can make the court perform more effectively and efficiently by using selective opinion assignment. A court without an extraordinary leader may be better served by a rotational method of assignment. . . . Nondiscretionary methods best maintain social cohesion, but the chief justice's discretion in assigning opinions can best accomplish the efficient disposition of the workload.[51]

As with the U.S. chief justice, however, nothing inherent in the office guarantees that a chief justice will be an active and effective leader. Intellect, personality, political skills, and a fair degree of happenstance still interact and blend in mysterious ways to create chief justices whom court watchers term either "great" or "ineffectual." On the positive side, there have been people such as Arthur Vanderbilt, who became chief justice of the New Jersey Supreme Court in 1948. As one scholar observed of him:

Once installed as chief justice . . . he had to contend with a set of judges who had served under the old constitution and did not fully share either his vision or his aims. Nevertheless, Vanderbilt provided impetus and direction to the movement for judicial reform in the state, and, as chief justice, he secured the gains of the reform movement, gave the court stature, and ensured it the independence it needed to play a major role in the governance of the state. Despite the obvious differences, the comparison that springs to mind is with John Marshall, who—like Vanderbilt—assumed the leadership of a relatively moribund court and transformed it.[52]

Likewise one can point to Howell Heflin, chief justice of the Alabama Supreme Court, whose dynamic leadership and political skills during the 1970s brought about much-needed judicial reforms in the state and effective leadership on the court.[53]

On the negative side, there are many examples of persons who came to the state high court bench with great potential but who lacked the ability or the political savvy (and perhaps the luck) to provide leadership when confronted by opposition or political lethargy. For instance, when Frank D. Celebrezze headed the Ohio Supreme Court during the early 1980s, he blatantly politicized the court until he was driven from office by the voters in the 1986 election. One observer summarized the unhappy period of his chief justiceship:

Squabbles on the Celebrezze court were important because, owing to the Celebrezze agenda, the court was important. The irony of Celebrezze's stewardship is that as his court attained prominence, his actions, so visible on so many fronts, brought the court as an institution into disrepute. During [his term as chief justice] Ohioans perceived their court as a "circus."[54]

Evidence of Small-Group Interaction

We have argued that small-group dynamics include persuasion on the merits between individual judges, bargaining among the appellate jurists, and the threat of sanctions, such as a judge's vote, a willingness to write a strong dissent, and (at least for federal judges) the threat to go public. We have also contended that supreme court chief justices and chief judges of the appeals courts can potentially affect the decision making of their respective small judicial groups. The evidence we have cited for this so far has largely been anecdotal or subjective, but there are some more rigorous empirical data to back up our arguments.

One study compared U.S. Supreme Court justices' initial votes at conference with the final votes as they appeared in the published reports for the years 1946 to 1956.[55] Any change in the two sets of votes was attributed to small-group interaction. The findings tell us several things. First, there were vote changes in about 60 percent of all cases. Most of these changes occurred when a justice who had not participated in the first vote or who had been a dissenter opted to join the majority position.

But when one considers all votes for all cases, the justices changed positions only 9 percent of the time. In such instances of vote change, the initial majority position lost out in only 14 percent of the cases. A study of conference and final votes surely underestimates the extent of small-group interaction, because there is plenty of such interaction prior to the initial conference vote.[56] The most recent study of fluidity on the Supreme Court not only confirmed that it is an ongoing phenomenon, but revealed that most of the vote changes stem from justices who move from the minority to the majority positions rather than vice versa. The authors of the study suggested that "the majority opinion author has little incentive to be responsive to the suggestions of a dissenter. Since the majority opinion becomes the law of the land, justices who wish to shape the law have an incentive to be part of the majority. Consistent with this theory is the fact that justices who initially voted with the majority switched only 4.6% of the time, and justices who initially dissented switched 18.1% of the time."[57]

Many other empirical studies that deal with the federal appeals courts and with state supreme courts likewise suggest the importance of small-group dynamics as a factor in judicial decision making.[58]

Although it is unclear how many final outcomes are actually determined by small-group dynamics, we know that they are a major factor in the drawing up of the majority opinion and in setting forth its perimeters and corollaries. Scholars still lack a precise measure of the impact of small-group interaction, but it seems fair to say that it is considerable.

Attitude Theory and Bloc-Formation Analysis

Many judicial scholars have been dissatisfied with small-group analysis, arguing that the fruits of such exploration are barely worth their efforts. Although not denying that personal interactions make a difference in some cases and perhaps play a key role in a handful of decisions, they contend that the richest ore for explaining judicial behavior can be found in other mines. A decision-making model that claims greater explanatory power deals with the discovery of the justices' basic, judicially relevant attitudes and with the coalitions, or *blocs*, formed by jurists who share similar attitudes.[59] This approach rests on the assumption that judges—particularly appellate jurists—view cases primarily in terms of the broad political and socioeconomic issues they raise and that they generally respond to these issues in accordance with their own personal values and attitudes. The "official reasons" the justices give for their decisions (found in their published opinions) are regarded as "mere rationalizations." For example, let us suppose that Judge X strongly believes that the government should never tamper with freedom of the press. If a case comes before the court in which censorship is the central issue, then Judge X will go with his convictions and vote on the side of the news media. His written opinion may be full of impressive legal citations, quotations from eminent law reviews, or lofty discussions of the importance for democracy of a maximum of freedom of expression. But all this, the attitude scholars contend, is only a rationalization after the fact. The *real* reason for Judge X's vote was that he strongly dislikes the concept of government censorship.

The attitude theorists do not claim that their decision-making models explain everything, nor do they deny that judges must often decide cases *against* the grain of their personal values. For instance, a justice may be a strong environmentalist, but if a pro-environment petitioner has absolutely no standing to sue, it is not likely that the justice will yield to the tug of the heart. Nevertheless, supporters of the judicial attitude approach contend that it can explain a significant portion of judicial behavior and that it is well worth the research time and effort that such studies require.

Let us now examine some specific questions about this approach: Where do judicial attitudes originate? How does one learn about a judge's attitudes? What are some of the techniques that have been used to study attitudinal behavior and bloc formation, and what have these techniques uncovered in terms of substance?

First, as noted in Chapters 8, 9, and 10, appellate jurists acquire their relevant attitudes from the same sources that people in general do: from parents and friends, from educational institutions, from the media, from political activities, and so on. Thus, there is clearly an overlap between the attitude theorists and those who study judicial background characteristics. The difference is that the latter want to know *from what source* the justices acquire their values, whereas the attitude theorists concentrate on measuring the effects of judges' values—regardless of their origin—on collegial decision making. The attitude scholars acknowledge that some beliefs change during a jurist's tenure on the bench, but still they postulate "that attitudes are 'relatively enduring.'"[60]

Second, how can one compile a judge's attitudes in order to test for their manifestations in collegial court decisions? Unfortunately, judges have shown no willingness to answer the sort of in-depth questionnaires that might reveal judicially significant attitudes—particularly on matters that relate to issues that may come before them in court. Likewise judges are reluctant to give speeches, grant interviews, or write articles that bare their judicial souls. Judges consider such behavior inappropriate and many resist making it easy for reporters and social scientists to suggest a link between their personal values and the way they decide cases.

Third, for the most part, scholars have turned to the contents of written opinions to categorize judges' primary values. Thus a justice who writes a strong opinion attacking government interference with the free operation of the marketplace is said to have a conservative economic attitude. This sort of approach has opened the researchers to the charge that they have created a tautology: A justice writes several conservative economic opinions, is classified as an economic conservative, and, lo and behold, aggregate analysis of his or her voting patterns reveals that the judge is a conservative on economic issues. Such theorists respond that this criticism is unfair because the patterns they have uncovered have proved to be consistent over time and susceptible to duplication by other researchers using similar methodologies. Furthermore, the best and most recent study based on attitude theory successfully formulated and applied three separate and independent ways in which to eliminate the circular reasoning problem: using facts derived from lower court records of cases decided by the U.S. Supreme Court, conducting content analysis of editorials appearing in publications prior to a justice's confirmation, and employing the justices' prior voting behavior as a predictor of votes in subsequent cases.[61] The next section will examine some of the research techniques that have been useful in measuring judicial attitudes and, in particular, the degree to which these attitudes cause like-minded judges to vote as blocs on similar cases.

Content Analysis

One important method used by attitude theorists is *content analysis*—they search through hundreds of appellate court opinions for certain key words or phrases that indicate a particular judicial attitude.[62] For example, a judge whose opinions contain numerous references to "personal freedom" is probably going to be more of a civil libertarian than one whose published decisions are strewn with continual references to "law and order." Such an approach has been greatly enhanced by the advent of the computer; it has been possible to lay bare the attitudinal dimensions of scores of judges who jointly have rendered thousands of opinions.

Bloc Analysis

The publication in 1948 of C. Herman Pritchett's *The Roosevelt Court: A Study of Judicial Votes and Values, 1937–1947* is regarded as the first attempt to study, in a rigorous, quantitative manner, voting blocs on the Supreme Court. Pritchett discovered two basic attitudinal coalitions on the Court: those who voted to sanction the liberal economic reforms of Roosevelt's New Deal and those who believed that such measures were unconstitutional. Since the 1950s, the analysis of voting blocs based on similar attitudes has become more sophisticated.[63] For example, researchers not only tested for the existence of a cohesive bloc on the Court, but they began to introduce such factors as an index of interagreement—that is, a mean agreement score of the justices in the bloc.

The dean of the attitude-bloc approach, Glendon Schubert, has provided a classic outline of this mode of analysis:

Sociometric analysis of interagreement in voting behavior, which focused upon a pool of all the votes of all of the justices, in cases decided on the merits during a stipulated period, showed . . . that the Court characteristically divided into a liberal bloc and conservative bloc. But bloc analysis also showed that there were usually some justices who did not seem to affiliate with either bloc, and there seemed to be a considerable amount of inconsistent voting, even among the bloc members—inconsistent, that is, in the sense that in some decisions one or more justices would vote with members of the "opposing" bloc rather than with members of their own bloc. The latter findings were perplexing, and it was not until the introduction of more powerful research tools that they were understood. At first through linear cumulative scaling and subsequently through factor analysis and multidimensional scaling, studies of the voting behavior of Supreme Court justices have shown that there are three major attitudinal components of judicial liberalism and conservatism.

The three types of attitude dimensions developed by Schubert were political, social, and economic. The political liberal supports civil rights and liberties, while the conservative is more supportive of the law-and-order position. The social liberal upholds the egalitarian position on matters of voting, citizenship, and ethnic status; a conservative counterpart is more inclined to oppose equal access to the polity and the economic structure. Finally, the economic liberal is less of a defender of private property and vested interests than is a conservative colleague.[64]

The courts of appeals have also been subjected to bloc analysis during the past two decades, and there, too, researchers have been able to identify groups of judges with similar voting patterns on the same issue dimension.[65] Likewise state supreme courts have been subjected to this type of analysis, with results similar to those for federal appellate tribunals. For instance, in an early classic study of the Michigan supreme court, Schubert demonstrated the existence of liberal and conservative blocs on a variety of issues in workers' compensation cases and matters of contributory negligence in civil cases.[66] And more recent studies of the high court in Ohio have demonstrated the presence of ideologically based voting blocs.[67]

Scaling

Almost simultaneously with the development of bloc analysis came the application of scaling techniques to the study of judicial behavior on collegial courts.[68] *Scaling* is founded on several basic assumptions. One is that there exists an underlying attitudinal continuum of beliefs about a given subject—for example, support for civil rights and liberties. In principle the stronger one's support for these freedoms, the higher one would fall on the scale. On a hypothetical 10-point scale, a justice who was only moderately supportive of civil rights and liberties might be assigned a score of 3, whereas a justice who always voted on the libertarian side would be given a score of 10.

Scaling also assumes that there is a cutoff point somewhere along the scale for each justice—that is, the point at which the numerical value of the case stimuli will be so low that the justice will vote against rather than for the particular attitude dimension being studied. Judicial behavioralists like to use scaling because it permits them to predict how a judge or justice might vote (or would have voted) in any given case. For example, let us assume that Justice X can be assigned a 6 on a 10-point civil rights scale (with 1 representing total opposition to the cause and 10 indicating unqualified support for civil rights). Then let us suppose that a case comes up in which the stimuli to vote for the civil rights position will be only a 4. We would predict that the justice would *not* vote for the position because the stimuli to do so had not reached his threshold of 6. Scales are said to be accurate if their predictions are correct about 90 percent of the time, and to the delight of scholars most scales do meet this level of reliability.

Since 1946 two types of scales have worked particularly well in the analysis of nonunanimous Supreme Court decisions: the C scale (Schubert's scale for civil rights and liberties) and the E scale (Schubert's scale for matters in which an economic underdog is in litigation against a well-to-do opponent). Improving on his earlier analysis and techniques, Schubert developed what he called a "psychometric model." [69] In such a model justices hypothetically respond (in their votes) to various stimuli found in the cases. The key elements are (1) the nature of the stimulus and where it falls on the value continuum, and (2) the particular judge's attitude and where it appears on the value scale.

The use of the techniques of content analysis, bloc analysis, and scaling has greatly enhanced the capacity of judicial scholars to explain and predict the behavior of judges on collegial courts. One researcher, Harold Spaeth, has gained for himself a fair amount of popular acclaim for his accurate radio and newspaper predictions of pending Supreme Court decisions and votes. Using the very research techniques we have discussed here, he has scored hits on more than 9 out of 10 predictions of judicial behavior.[70]

Fact Pattern Analysis

There is another model for explaining the behavior of judges on collegial courts—*fact pattern analysis.* At first blush this approach seems to resemble that of the traditional legal subculture understanding of judicial decision making discussed in Chapter 10, because its central thesis is that the facts of a case are the primary determinants of how the case will be resolved. Recall that the legal subculture model contends that a judge will resolve an issue in favor of the side that is able to marshal the stronger set of factual evidence and legal precedents. Although fact pattern scholars also believe that the facts of a case determine its outcome, they quickly part company with the traditional approach after that point.[71]

Several basic assumptions of the fact pattern approach set it apart from other models of judicial behavior. First, when fact pattern scholars refer to the "facts of a case," they have in mind quite a different set of items from that of the legal subculture adherents. "Facts" to these scholars include the gender of the litigants, whether an attorney in a criminal case is court appointed or privately retained, the social status of the parties, and whether the petitioner is a member of a racial minority. According to traditional scholars, such information is not supposed to affect the outcome of a case, but to the fact pattern theorists, cases are often won or lost because of just such extrajudicial variables. Let us look at an example.

One classic study using this approach focused on the voting behavior of Supreme Court justice Felix Frankfurter. The author found that Frankfurter was favorably disposed toward a petitioner in cases containing certain basic facts, or "signs," as the writer called them. The signs included the terms *confession-counsel,* meaning that the defendant's confession may not have been voluntary; *Negro,* indicating the minority status of the accused; and *state,* suggesting an insensitivity to correct criminal procedure. Referring to these signs, the study noted that there was

a positive association between the presence of each and a favorable vote for civil liberties by Frankfurter in both years. Frankfurter's favorable vote was cast with the appearance of the "Negro" sign in 13 of 15 cases; with the appearance of the "state" sign 28 of 47 times; and with the appearance of the "confession-counsel" factor in 8 cases out of 9. These figures alone suggest that Frankfurter's willingness to draw negative inferences against a governmental unit in civil liberty cases might have been affected by the presence of these factors, with the presence of one or more of them improving the chances of a favorable vote.[72]

A second theoretical underpinning of fact pattern researchers is that they do not begin their analysis with any assumption

regarding the existence or nonexistence of consistent patterns in the acceptance of facts or in decisions based on facts. Whether or not consistency does exist in a given area of adjudication is determined by the use of the methods. If consistent patterns cannot be identified, it must be concluded that judicial action in the given area of law cannot be understood in terms of the dependence of decisions on facts. If, on the other hand, consistent patterns are found, an important implication of the proposed methods is apparent. Should it be possible to predict only later cases from earlier cases, the underlying pattern of consistency could be explained in terms of stare decisis. But if earlier cases could be predicted from later ones, adherence to precedent would have to be explained in terms of an independent—although convergent—recognition and acceptance of similar standards of justice by different judges at different times. Thus not only the existence of consistent patterns but also the basis for their consistency can be evaluated.[73]

Finally, the fact pattern scholars believe that to explain judicial behavior, they must learn how to weight each of the key facts of a case and also to learn how the facts combine to have the greatest (and the least) effect on any given judge. This is obviously a time-consuming and complicated procedure because the researcher is usually dealing with scores of possible facts and an enormous variety of possible weightings—combinations that literally run into the billions. Using sophisticated mathematical equations and the computer, fact pattern scholars have advanced into the unknown and achieved considerable success. One of the key exponents of the approach explains how

Each case is represented by an equation, in which an index denoting the acceptance or rejection of a fact by an appellate court is set equal to the combination of appearances, nonappearances, and denials of the fact at the preceding stages. The weights of the fact at the various stages—in the sense of how persuasive its appearance at the respective stages is toward its acceptance by the appellate court—are the *unknowns* in the equations. As the equations are solved, the weights are determined. To be sure, the complex procedures which are required for the solutions of the equations again necessitate the use of a computer, especially because there is a separate system of equations for each fact. By using the weights in a case not previously encountered, one can predict for each fact an acceptance or rejection that would be consistent with the established pattern of past cases.[74]

Fact pattern analysis, like the other approaches to collegial court decision making, does not claim to explain the whole of judicial behavior. But like the other models discussed in this chapter, it has provided some key insights during the past several decades as to how and why appellate judges act as they do.

Summary

We began this chapter with the observation that decision making by judges on collegial appellate courts is in some key ways different from the decisional behavior of judges acting alone on trial benches. Because of these differences scholars have devised theories and research techniques to capture the special reality of decision making by jurists on federal and state multijudge appellate courts. We took a close look at the discretionary review process of the Supreme Court and noted that the issues it decides *not* to rule on are often as substantively important as those cases it selects for full review. In this context we discussed the importance of cue theory—the attempt by scholars to learn the characteristics of those few cases chosen from the many for Supreme Court consideration.

We then focused on three separate theoretical approaches to explain and predict the decision making of multijudge courts: small-group analysis, attitude theory and bloc-formation analysis, and fact pattern analysis. Each of these has its own working assumptions and research techniques that are used to glean the explanatory data. Although it is tempting to speculate on which of these several approaches provides the best insights into appellate court behavior, it is probably fairest to say that the jury of judicial scholars is still out. Indeed, in recent years there has been an increasing belief that models that represent a *combination* of these approaches provide much greater explanatory power than any of them taken alone.[75]

NOTES

1. From an interview with an appeals court judge as quoted in J. Woodford Howard, Jr., *Courts of Appeals in the Federal Judicial System* (Princeton, N.J.: Princeton University Press, 1981), 135.

2. However, for a discussion of the causes of dissent in state supreme courts and of how such causes may differ from those at the federal level, see Paul Brace and Melinda Gann Hall, "Neo-Institutionalism and Dissent in State Supreme Courts," *Journal of Politics* 52 (1990): 54–70.

3. Alabama, for example, imposes a burdensome original jurisdiction on its supreme court, and Arizona requires its high court to hear appeals in a wide variety of cases. On the other hand, Florida has given its supreme court broad discretion in case selection. See G. Alan Tarr and Mary Cornelia Aldis Porter, *State Supreme Courts in State and Nation* (New Haven, Conn.: Yale University Press, 1988), 49.

4. Joseph Tanenhaus, Marvin Schick, Matthew Muraskin, and Daniel Rosen, "The Supreme Court's Certiorari Jurisdiction: Cue Theory," in *Judicial Decision-Making*, ed. Glendon Schubert (New York: Free Press, 1963), 111–132.

5. For example, see S. Sidney Ulmer, "The Decision to Grant Certiorari as an Indicator to Decision 'On the Merits,'" *Polity* 4 (1972): 429–447. Nevertheless, in a later study Ulmer found that despite the inordinate willingness of the High Court to hear cases brought by the U.S. government, such willingness did not translate into subsequent support for the government's position—at least in civil liberties cases. See Ulmer, "Governmental Litigants, Underdogs, and Civil Liberties in the Supreme Court: 1903–1968 Terms," *Journal of Politics* 47 (1985): 899–909.

6. For example, see Donald R. Songer, "Concern for Policy Outputs as a Cue for Supreme Court Decisions on Certiorari," *Journal of Politics* 41 (1979): 1185–1194; and S. Sidney Ulmer, "Selecting Cases for Supreme Court Review: An Underdog Model," *American Political Science Review* 72 (1978): 902–910.

7. Virginia C. Armstrong and Charles A. Johnson, "Certiorari Decisions by the Warren and Burger Courts: Is Cue Theory Time Bound?" *Polity* 15 (1982): 141–150.

8. Jeffrey A. Segal and Harold J. Spaeth, "Rehnquist Court Disposition of Lower Court Decisions: Affirmation Not Reversal," *Judicature* 74 (1990): 84–88.

9. Henry R. Glick, *Courts, Politics, and Justice*, 3d ed. (New York: McGraw-Hill, 1993), 280.

10. J. Woodford Howard, Jr., "On the Fluidity of Judicial Choice," *American Political Science Review* 62 (1968): 43–57.

11. For example, see Walter F. Murphy, *Elements of Judicial Strategy* (Chicago: University of Chicago Press, 1964); Bob Woodward and Scott Armstrong, *The Brethren: Inside the Supreme Court* (New York: Simon & Schuster, 1979); Howard, *Courts of Appeals in the Federal Judicial System;* Alpheus T. Mason, *Harlan Fiske Stone: Pillar of the Law* (New York: Viking, 1956).

12. In the parlance of judicial scholars, this is referred to as the *social leadership* function. See David J. Danelski, "The Influence of the Chief Justice in the Decisional Process," in *Courts, Judges, and Politics*, 3d ed., ed. Walter F. Murphy and C. Herman Pritchett (New York: Random House, 1979), 695–703. We will have more to say about Danelski's characterizations a little later in the chapter. For an empirical analysis of the phenomena discussed by Danelski, see Stacia L. Haynie, "Leadership and Consensus on the U.S. Supreme Court," *Journal of Politics* 54 (1992): 1158–1169.

13. Henry Robert Glick, *Supreme Courts in State Politics* (New York: Basic Books, 1971), 59.

14. This is termed the *task leadership* function. See Danelski, "The Influence of the Chief Justice in the Decisional Process."

15. Howard, *Courts of Appeals in the Federal Judicial System*, 230–231.

16. Murphy, *Elements of Judicial Strategy*, 44.

17. As quoted in ibid.

18. Glick, *Supreme Courts in State Politics*, 89.

19. *Roe v. Wade*, 410 U.S. 113 (1973); and *Doe v. Bolton*, 410 U.S. 179 (1973).

20. Woodward and Armstrong, *The Brethren*, chaps. entitled "1971 Term" and "1972 Term."

21. Ibid., 233.

22. Glick, *Supreme Courts in State Politics*, 66.

23. Murphy, *Elements of Judicial Strategy*, 57.

24. Howard, *Courts of Appeals in the Federal Judicial System*, 209.

25. As quoted in Charles Fairman, *Mr. Justice Miller and the Supreme Court, 1862–1890* (Cambridge, Mass.: Harvard University Press, 1939), 320.

26. *Webster v. Reproductive Health Services*, 492 U.S. 490 (1989).

27. David A. Kaplan, "A Legacy of Strife: Marshall's Papers Shed Light on the Court—and the Library of Congress," *Newsweek*, June 7, 1993, 69.

28. Benjamin Weiser and Bob Woodward, "Roe Decision Nearly Overturned 4 Years Ago, Justice's Files Show," *Houston Chronicle*, May 24, 1993, A2.

29. *Clinton v. Jones* (No. 95-1853), decided May 27, 1997.

30. Henry Robert Glick and Kenneth N. Vines, *State Court Systems* (Englewood Cliffs, N.J.: Prentice-Hall, 1973), 79.

31. Murphy, *Elements of Judicial Strategy*, 63–64.

32. Henry R. Glick and George W. Pruet, Jr., "Dissent in State Supreme Courts: Patterns and Correlates of Conflict," in *Judicial Conflict and Consensus: Behavioral Studies of American Appellate Courts*, ed. Sheldon Goldman and Charles M. Lamb (Lexington: University Press of Kentucky, 1986), 200.

33. As quoted in Howard, *Courts of Appeals in the Federal Judicial System*, 209.

34. *Ross v. Sirica*, 380 F.2d 557 (D.C. Cir. 1967).

35. Woodward and Armstrong, *The Brethren*, 187, 188.

36. Murphy, *Elements of Judicial Strategy*, 61.

37. As quoted in Howard, *Courts of Appeals in the Federal Judicial System*, 209.

38. Danelski, "The Influence of the Chief Justice in the Decisional Process," 696.

39. David M. O'Brien, "The Supreme Court: From Warren to Burger to Rehnquist," *PS* 20 (1987): 12.

40. Stephen Wermiel, "Consensus Builder: Rehnquist Emerges as a Skillful Leader of the Court's Majority," *Wall Street Journal*, June 29, 1989, A1.

41. For an excellent discussion of research findings about the "discuss list" and the U.S. Supreme Court, see Gregory A. Caldeira and John R. Wright, "The Discuss List: Agenda Building in the Supreme Court," *Law and Society Review* 24 (1990): 809–836.

42. For an excellent discussion of this subject, see David W. Rohde and Harold J. Spaeth, *Supreme Court Decision Making* (San Francisco: Freeman, 1976), chap. 8.

43. Elliot E. Slotnick, "The Chief Justice and Self-Assignment of Majority Opinions: A Research Note," *Western Political Quarterly* 31 (1978): 219–225.

44. However, some research has challenged the "conventional wisdom . . . that assignment of the majority opinion to the marginal member of the minimum winning original coalition might ensure its survival." In a study of the Warren Court the researchers found that "although the marginal justice is substantially advantaged in opinion assignment, coalition maintenance is not thereby enhanced." Saul Brenner and Harold J. Spaeth, "Majority Opinion Assignments and the Maintenance of the Original Coalition on the Warren Court," *American Journal of Political Science* 32 (1988): 72–81. Also, see Saul Brenner, "Reassigning the Majority Opinion on the United States Supreme Court," *Justice System Journal* 11 (1986): 186–195.

45. Forrest Maltzman and Paul J. Wahlbeck, "May It Please the Chief? Opinion Assignments in the Rehnquist Court," *American Journal of Political Science* 40 (1996): 438.

46. Donald Dale Jackson, *Judges* (New York: Atheneum, 1974), 329.

47. As quoted in Danelski, "The Influence of the Chief Justice in the Decisional Process," 698. For a good discussion of the importance of Stone's leadership style as it affected future chief justiceships, see Thomas G. Walker, Lee Epstein, and William J. Dixon, "On the Mysterious Demise of Consensual Norms in the United States Supreme Court," *Journal of Politics* 50 (1988): 361–389.

48. As quoted in Howard, *Courts of Appeals in the Federal Judicial System*, 228.

49. Ibid., 229. In a few instances the chief judges have been accused of "stacking" the three-judge panels, which are supposed to operate on a more or less random, rotational basis. For example, see *Armstrong v. Bd. of Educ. of Birmingham*, 323 F.2d 333, 352–361 (5th Cir. 1963); 48 F.R.D. 141, 182 (1969). See also, Burton M. Atkins and William Zavoina, "Judicial Leadership on the Court of Appeals: A Probability Analysis of Panel Assignment in Race Relations Cases on the Fifth Circuit," *American Journal of Political Science* 18 (1974): 701–711.

50. Victor E. Flango, Craig R. Ducat, and R. Neal McKnight, "Measuring Leadership through Opinion Assignments in Two State Supreme Courts," in Goldman and Lamb, eds., *Judicial Conflict and Consensus*, 217.

51. Ibid., 218–219.

52. Tarr and Porter, *State Supreme Courts in State and Nation*, 186.

53. Ibid., chap. 3.

54. Ibid., 148. For all the details, chap. 4.

55. Saul Brenner, "Fluidity on the United States Supreme Court: A Reexamination," *American Journal of Political Science* 24 (1980): 526–535.

56. For a more recent article on this subject, and one that addresses some aspects not included in Brenner's earlier article, see Robert H. Dorff and Saul Brenner, "Conformity Voting on the United States Supreme Court," *Journal of Politics* 54 (1992): 762–775.

57. Forrest Maltzman and Paul J. Wahlbeck, "Strategic Policy Considerations and Voting Fluidity on the Burger Court," *American Political Science Review* 90 (1996): 590–591.

58. For example, see Goldman and Lamb, *Judicial Conflict and Consensus*, pts. 2 and 3; and Glick, *Supreme Courts in State Politics*.

59. For the best statement of attitude theory, along with an excellent summary of the relevant literature, see Jeffrey A. Segal and Harold J. Spaeth, *The Supreme Court and the Attitudinal Model* (New York: Cambridge University Press, 1993). For a sophisticated and up-to-date debate among judicial scholars about the utility of various forms of attitudinal models, see the first six articles in *American Journal of Political Science* 40 (1996): 971–1083.

60. Rohde and Spaeth, *Supreme Court Decision Making*, 75.

61. Segal and Spaeth, *The Supreme Court and the Attitudinal Model*.

62. For example, see Glendon Schubert, "Jackson's Judicial Philosophy: An Exploration in Value Analysis," *American Political Science Review* 59 (1965): 940–963; and Werner F. Grunbaum, "A Quantitative Analysis of the 'Presidential Ballot' Case," *Journal of Politics* 34 (1972): 223–243.

63. For example, see Glendon Schubert, *Quantitative Analysis of Judicial Behavior* (New York: Free Press, 1959); and S. Sidney Ulmer, "The Analysis of Behavior Patterns in the United States Supreme Court," *Journal of Politics* 22 (1960): 629–653.

64. Glendon Schubert, *Judicial Policy Making* (Glenview, Ill.: Scott, Foresman, 1974), 160–161. For a good later study of this phenomenon, see Craig R. Ducat and Robert L. Dudley, "Dimensions Underlying Economic Policymaking in the Early and Later Burger Courts," *Journal of Politics* 49 (1987): 521–539; and Timothy M. Hagle and Harold J. Spaeth, "The Emergence of a New Ideology: The Business Decisions of the Burger Court," *Journal of Politics* 54 (1992): 120–134.

65. For example, see Sheldon Goldman, "Conflict on the U.S. Courts of Appeals, 1965–1971: A Quantitative Analysis," *University of Cincinnati Law Review* 42 (1973): 635–658; and Charles M. Lamb, "Warren Burger and the Insanity Defense: Judicial Philosophy and Voting Behavior on a U.S. Court of Appeals," *American University Law Review* 24 (1974): 91–128.

66. Schubert, *Quantitative Analysis of Judicial Behavior,* 129–141. For a more up-to-date analysis of the Michigan court (as contrasted with the Pennsylvania supreme court), see Flango, Ducat, and McKnight, "Measuring Leadership through Opinion Assignment in Two State Supreme Courts," 215–239.

67. For a discussion of these studies, see Tarr and Porter, *State Supreme Courts in State and Nation,* chap. 4.

68. For a good discussion of scaling and its application to judicial studies, see Joseph Tanenhaus, "The Cumulative Scaling of Judicial Decisions," *Harvard Law Review* 79 (1966): 1583–1594.

69. Schubert, *The Judicial Mind Revisited.*

70. "Computer Helps Predict Court Rulings," *New York Times,* August 15, 1971, 1:75; and "Court Handicappers: Computer Predictions of Supreme Court Decisions," *Newsweek,* August 12, 1974, 53.

71. One study combined fact pattern analysis with a study of judges' background variables. The researcher found that such a "combination . . . is more successful at explaining judicial voting in equal protection cases than either set of variables alone. This difference is particularly notable with respect to background variables. These traits alone allowed 63 per cent for the votes to be classified correctly, compared with 73 per cent of case variables and 80 per cent for a combination of the two sets of variables." Jilda M. Aliotta, "Combining Judges' Attributes and Case Characteristics: An Alternative Approach to Explaining Supreme Court Decisionmaking," *Judicature* 71 (1988): 277–281. Also see Jeffrey A. Segal, "Supreme Court Justices as Human Decision Makers: An Individual-Level Analysis of the Search and Seizure Cases," *Journal of Politics* 48 (1986): 938–955.

72. S. Sidney Ulmer, "The Discriminant Function and a Theoretical Context for Its Use in Estimating the Votes of Judges," in *Frontiers of Judicial Research,* ed. Joel B. Grossman and Joseph Tanenhaus (New York: Wiley, 1969), 365.

73. Fred Kort, "Quantitative Analysis of Fact-Patterns in Cases and Their Impact on Judicial Decisions," in *American Court Systems,* ed. Sheldon Goldman and Austin Sarat (San Francisco: Freeman, 1978), 334.

74. Ibid., 332.

75. For examples of these combined or "integrated" approaches, see Donald R. Songer and Susan Haire, "Integrating Alternative Approaches to the Study of Judicial Voting: Obscenity Cases in the U.S. Courts of Appeals," *American Journal of Political Science* 36 (1992): 963–982; and Paul Brace and Melinda Gann Hall, "Integrated Models of Judicial Dissent," *Journal of Politics* 55 (1993): 914–935.

SUGGESTED READINGS

Cannon, Mark W., and David M. O'Brien, eds. *Views from the Bench: The Judiciary and Constitutional Politics.* Chatham, N.J.: Chatham House, 1985. A collection of essays, mainly by appellate judges, about how such jurists ought to carry out their functions and duties.

Goldman, Sheldon, and Charles M. Lamb, eds. *Judicial Conflict and Consensus: Behavioral Studies of American Appellate Courts.* Lexington: University Press of Kentucky, 1986. An excellent collection of empirical studies on how appellate courts operate and how they are influenced by both internal and external factors.

Howard, J. Woodford, Jr. *Courts of Appeals in the Federal Judicial System.* Princeton, N.J.: Princeton University Press, 1981. A well-written study of decision making at the level of the U.S. appellate courts; contains both quantitative and anecdotal information.

Lamb, Charles M., and Stephen C. Halpern, eds. *The Burger Court: Political and Judicial Profiles.* Urbana: University of Illinois Press, 1991. Contains a series of sophisticated, nonquantitative articles on decision making by members of the Burger Court.

Murphy, Walter F. *Elements of Judicial Strategy.* Chicago: University of Chicago Press, 1964. Emphasizes the importance of interpersonal interactions on the outcome of collegial court decision making.

O'Brien, David M. *Storm Center,* 4th ed. New York: Norton, 1996. Offers a historical look at and contemporary discussion of the dynamics of decision making by the U.S. Supreme Court.

Perry, H. W., Jr. *Deciding to Decide: Agenda Setting in the United States Supreme Court.* Cambridge, Mass.: Harvard University Press, 1991. Emphasizes the importance of the Supreme Court's decisions with respect to which types of cases it will and will not hear; the author argues that these decisions are as important as the ultimate dispositions of those cases the Court does consider.

Tarr, G. Alan, and Mary Cornelia Aldis Porter. *State Supreme Courts in State and Nation.* New Haven, Conn.: Yale University Press, 1988. Analyzes decision making at the state supreme court level; offers specific analyses of three selected state courts.

Woodward, Bob, and Scott Armstrong. *The Brethren: Inside the Supreme Court.* New York: Simon & Schuster, 1979. A journalistic account of behind-the-scenes interpersonal interactions on the Burger Court.

CHAPTER 12

Implementation and Impact of Judicial Policies

State and local police officers have played an important role in implementing the Supreme Court's ruling that criminal suspects must be advised of their constitutional rights.

IN THE TWO PREVIOUS CHAPTERS we have focused on decision making by judges. In this chapter we extend the discussion to examine what happens *after* a decision is reached. Decisions made by judges are not self-executing, and a wide variety of individuals—other judges, public officials, even private citizens—may be called upon to implement a court's decisions. As we study the implementation process we will look at the various actors involved, their reactions to judicial policies, and the methods by which they may respond to a court's decision.

Depending upon the nature of the court's decision, the judicial policy may have a very narrow or a very broad impact. A suit for damages incurred in an automobile accident would directly affect only the persons involved, and perhaps their immediate families. But the famous *Gideon v. Wainwright* decision has directly affected literally millions of people in one way or another.[1] In *Gideon* the Supreme Court held that states must provide an attorney for indigent defendants in felony trials. Scores of people—defendants, judges, lawyers, taxpayers—have felt the effects of that judicial policy. As we discuss the implementation process, then, we will also look at the impact judicial policy making has had on society.

Lower-court judges are involved so frequently in enforcing a higher court's decision that they deserve especially careful attention. Therefore, we begin our analysis of the implementation process with the lower-court judges.

The Impact of Higher-Court Decisions on Lower Courts

As we noted in Chapter 2, Americans often view the appellate courts, notably the U.S. Supreme Court, as most likely to be involved in policy making. The trial courts, on the other hand, are frequently seen as norm enforcers rather than policy makers. Given this traditional view, the picture that often emerges is one in which the Supreme Court makes a decision that is then implemented by a lower court. In short, some envision a judicial bureaucracy with a hierarchy of courts much like superiors and subordinates.[2] More recent studies, however, have cast doubt on the bureaucracy theory, arguing that "most of the work of the lower courts seems less dependent on the Supreme Court than . . . bureaucracy [theory] would indicate."[3] In other words, we now realize that lower-court judges have a great deal of independence from the appellate courts and may be viewed as "independent actors . . . who will not follow the lead of higher courts unless conditions are favorable for their doing so."[4] For example, it is well known that not all federal district judges immediately enforced the Supreme Court's public school desegregation decision.[5] Some judges allowed school districts to engage in a variety of tactics ranging from evasion to postponement of the Supreme Court mandate.[6]

Lower-Court Discretion

Why do the lower-court judges have so much discretion when it comes to implementing a higher court's policy? In part, the answer may be found in the structure of our judicial system. You will recall from our discussions in Chapters 2 and 3 that the judiciary has always been characterized by independence, decentralization, and individualism. Federal judges, for example, are protected by life tenure and traditionally have been able to run their courts as they see fit. Disciplinary measures are not at all common, and federal judges have historically had little fear of impeachment. To retain their positions, the state trial court judges do not have to worry about the appellate courts in their system, either. They simply have to keep the electorate satisfied. In short, lower-court judges have a good deal of freedom to make their own decisions and to respond to upper-court rulings in their own way.

The discretion exercised by a lower-court judge may also be a product of the higher court's decision itself. Let us look at a couple of examples. Following the famous school desegregation decision in 1954, the Supreme Court heard further arguments on the best way to implement its new policy. In 1955 it handed down its decision in *Brown v. Board of Education of Topeka II*.[7] In that case the Court was faced with two major questions: (1) How soon are the public schools to start desegregating? and (2) How much time should they be given to complete the process? Federal district judges given the task of enforcing the High Court's ruling were told that the public schools were to make a prompt and reasonable start and then proceed with all deliberate speed to bring about desegregation. What constitutes a prompt and reasonable start? How rapidly must a school district proceed in order to be moving with all deliberate speed? Since the Supreme Court justices did not provide specific answers to these questions, many lower-court judges were faced with school districts that continued to drag their feet while at the same time claiming they were acting within the High Court's guidelines.

A second example concerns the Supreme Court's decision in the 1962 reapportionment case, *Baker v. Carr*.[8] In that case the Court held that allegations of malapportioned state legislative districts in Tennessee presented a justiciable rather than a political question; that is, apportionment cases could properly be litigated in the courts. The case was remanded (sent back down) to the federal court for the middle district of Tennessee in Nashville for implementation. Justice Brennan's opinion for the Court concluded with the statement, "The cause is remanded for further proceedings consistent with this opinion." No guidelines were provided; the federal district judge was not told how rapidly to proceed or what methods to use. Justice Clark, in a concurring opinion, pointed out that the Court "fails to give the District any guidance whatever."[9]

It is obvious, then, that federal district judges implementing either of the policies described above could exercise a high degree of freedom and still legitimately say that they were in compliance with the Supreme Court's mandate. Although not all High Court decisions allow such discretion, a good number of them do. Opinions that are ambiguous or simply poorly written are almost certain to encounter problems during the implementation process.

A court's decision may be unclear for several reasons. Sometimes the issue or subject matter may be so complex that it is difficult to fashion a clear policy. In obscenity cases, for instance, the Supreme Court has had little difficulty in deciding that pornographic material is not entitled to constitutional protection. Defining obscenity has proven to be another matter. Phrases such as "prurient interest," "patently offensive," "contemporary community standards," and "without redeeming social value" have become commonplace in obscenity opinions. Obviously, these terms leave a good deal of room for subjective interpretation. It is little wonder that a Supreme Court justice admitted that he could not define obscenity but added that "I know it when I see it."[10]

Policies established by collegial courts are often ambiguous because the majority opinion is written to accommodate several judges. At times such opinions read more like committee reports than forceful, decisive statements. The majority opinion may also be accompanied by several concurring opinions. When this happens, lower-court judges are left without a clear-cut precedent to follow. The death penalty cases serve as an example. In 1972 the Supreme Court struck down the death penalty in several states, but for a variety of reasons. Some justices opposed the death penalty per se, on the ground that it constituted cruel and unusual punishment in violation of the Eighth Amendment to the Constitution. Others voted to strike down the state laws because they were applied in a discriminatory manner.[11] The uncertainty created by the 1972 decision affected not only lower-court judges but also state legislatures. The states passed a rash of widely divergent death penalty statutes and caused a considerable amount of new litigation.

A lower-court judge's discretion in the implementation process may also be affected by the manner in which a higher court's policy is communicated. Quite obviously, the first step in implementing a judicial policy is actually to learn of the new appellate court ruling. Although we probably assume that lower-court judges automatically are made aware of a higher court's decision, that is not always the case. Certainly the court from which a case has been appealed will be informed of the decision. In our example above, the federal district court for the middle district of Tennessee was told of the Supreme Court's decision in *Baker v. Carr* because its earlier decision was reversed, and the case was remanded to it for further action. However, systematic, formal efforts are not made to inform other courts of the decision or to see that lower-court judges have access to a copy of the opinion. The decisions that contain the new judicial policy are simply made available to the public in printed form, and judges are expected to read them if they have the time and inclination.

Opinions of the Supreme Court, lower federal courts, and state appellate courts are available in a large number of courthouse, law school, and university libraries. They are also increasingly available on the Internet. Today, it is possible to read some court opinions the day after they are handed down, and others within a matter of a few days. This widespread availability does not guarantee that they will be read and clearly understood, however. One complication is that many lower-level state judges, such as justices of the peace and juvenile court judges, are nonlawyers who have little interest or skill in reading complex judicial decisions.[12] Finally, even those judges who have an interest in higher-court decisions and the ability to understand them do not have adequate time to keep abreast of all the new opinions.

Given the problems described above, how do judges become aware of upper-court decisions? One way is to hear of them through lawyers presenting cases in the lower courts. It is generally assumed that the opposing attorneys will present relevant precedents in their arguments before the judge. As we noted earlier, those judges who are fortunate enough to have law clerks may also rely upon them to search out recent decisions from higher courts.

Thus some higher-court policies are not quickly and strictly enforced simply because lower-court judges are not aware of them. Even those of which they are aware may not be as clear as a lower-court judge might like. Either reason contributes to the discretion exercised by lower-court judges placed in the position of having to implement judicial policies.

Interpretation by Lower Courts

A 1984 study noted that "important policy announcements almost always require interpretation by someone other than the policy maker."[13] This is certainly true in the case of judicial policies established by appellate courts. The first exercise of a lower-court judge's discretion may be to interpret what the higher court's decision actually means.

Consider for a moment an example from a famous Supreme Court decision concerning what types of speech are protected by the Constitution. In that 1919 case the Court announced that "the question in every case is whether the words used are used in such circumstances and are of such a nature as to create a clear and present danger that they will bring about the substantive evils that Congress has a right to prevent."[14] With that statement the Court announced what is known as the "clear-and-present-danger" doctrine. Although it may seem simple in the abstract to say that a person's right to speak is protected unless the words create a "clear and present danger," lower-court judges do not decide cases in the abstract. They must fit higher-court policy decisions to the concrete facts of an actual case. Place yourself in the position of a lower-court judge deciding a case shortly after the announcement of the clear-and-present-danger policy. Assume that you were presiding over the trial of an individual who, in the course of a speech to a group of onlookers on a busy street corner in a large city, advocated violent overthrow of the U.S. government. You might well have had to answer one or more of the following questions in your own mind as you tried to interpret the clear-and-present-danger doctrine:

(1) How well defined must the danger be in order for it to be clear? (2) How imminent must the danger be in order for it to be present? (3) Is the danger in question one the government has a right to prevent? (4) Did the speech actually bring about any danger? (5) At what point is the government allowed to intervene or stop the speech? As you can see, interpreting what is meant by the clear-and-present-danger policy is no simple task. In fact, modern courts grapple with the free speech question just as did the courts in 1919.

The manner in which a lower-court judge interprets a policy established by a higher court depends upon many factors. We have already noted that many policies are simply not clearly stated. Thus reasonable people may disagree over the proper interpretation. Even policy pronouncements that do not suffer from ambiguity, however, are sometimes interpreted differently by different judges.

A judge's own personal policy preferences will also have an effect upon the interpretation he or she gives to a higher-court policy. We saw in previous chapters that judges come to the courts with their own unique background characteristics. Some are Republican, others are Democrat; one judge may be liberal, another conservative. They come from different regions of the country. Some have been prosecutors; others have been primarily defense lawyers or corporate lawyers. In short, their backgrounds may influence their own particular policy preferences. Thus the lower-court judges, given their wide latitude anyway, may read their own ideas into a higher-court policy. The result is that a policy may be enthusiastically embraced by some judges yet totally rejected by others.

Strategies Employed by Lower Courts

We have seen that appellate court policies are open to different interpretations; we now turn our attention to the actual strategies employed by the implementing judges. Those who favor and accept a higher court's policy will naturally try to enforce it and perhaps even expand upon it. Those who do not like a higher court's policy decision may well implement it sparingly or only under duress.

We first examine the strategies that may be employed by a judge who basically disagrees with a policy established by a higher court. One rarely used strategy is defiance, whereby a judge simply does not apply the higher court's policy in a case before a lower court. One study of judicial implementation offers this example:

Desegregation brought out considerable trial court defiance; in one extreme case, a Birmingham, Alabama, municipal judge not only refused to follow Supreme Court decisions desegregating municipal facilities but also declared the Fourteenth Amendment unconstitutional.[15]

Such outright defiance is highly unusual; there are other strategies that are not quite so extreme. A study of the libel decisions of the U.S. courts of appeals between 1964 and 1974 did not find a single case of noncompliance with Supreme Court mandates.[16] Another study, focusing on compliance with the Supreme Court's *Miranda* decision, found only one instance of possible noncompliance and twelve decisions that could be classified as narrow compliance among the 250 cases studied.[17]

Another strategy often employed by judges not favorably inclined toward a higher-court policy is simply to avoid having to apply the policy. Sometimes a case may be disposed of on technical or procedural grounds so that the judge does not have to rule on the actual merits of the case. It may be determined, for example, that the plaintiff does not have standing to sue or that the case has become moot because the issue was resolved before the trial commenced. Lower-court judges sometimes avoid accepting a policy by declaring a portion of the higher-court decision to be "dicta." *Dicta* refers to the part of the opinion that does not contribute to the central logic of the decision. It may be useful as guidance but is not seen as binding. Obviously, what constitutes dicta is open to varying interpretations.

Yet another strategy often employed by judges who are in basic disagreement with a judicial policy is to apply it as narrowly as possible. One method is for the lower-court judge to rule that a precedent is not controlling because there are factual differences between the higher-court case and the case before the lower courts. In other words, because the two cases may be distinguished, the precedent does not have to be followed. Two good examples are provided by lower-court applications of the Supreme Court's decisions in *Escobedo v. Illinois* and *Miranda v. Arizona*.

The *Escobedo* decision held that a suspect being interrogated had to be allowed access to his lawyer. *Miranda* went a step further and declared that suspects taken into custody must be advised of their constitutional rights and that any confession made by a suspect who had not been so advised is invalid. A leading judicial scholar explains how these two landmark decisions were treated by some lower-court judges:

Lower court judges who did not like the *Escobedo* ruling . . . refused to apply *Escobedo* to anyone who did not already have a lawyer. Similarly, judges who did not like the *Miranda* ruling did not require warnings to be given to those not in custody, and then defined "in custody" as narrowly as possible.[18]

State court judges faced with interpreting or implementing civil liberties policies often rely on what is termed "new judicial federalism."[19] This idea originated in the early 1970s, primarily as a result of Warren Burger's appointment as chief justice of the U.S. Supreme Court. Many civil libertarians, fearful that the new Burger Court would erode or overturn major Warren Court decisions, began to look to state bills of rights as alternative bases for their court claims. The Burger Court in fact encouraged a return to state constitutions by pointing out that the states could offer greater protection under their own bills of rights than was available under the federal Bill of Rights.

In the beginning, state civil liberties suits focused most frequently on the rights of defendants, and only the supreme courts of California and New Jersey showed much interest in new judicial federalism. Initially, courts used this approach to circumvent specific Burger Court decisions. By the late 1980s, however, a national campaign to revive state civil liberties law was under way. Since 1970 there have been more than 300 decisions in which the state courts "have either afforded greater protection to rights under their state constitutions than was granted by the Supreme Court or have based their decisions upholding rights claims solely on state constitutional grounds."[20]

Recent studies, however, have cautioned against too much optimism among those who advocate reliance on state constitutions as a way to avoid conservative precedents espoused by the Burger and Rehnquist Courts. In separate examinations of criminal justice decisions from all fifty state high courts, both Barry Latzer and Michael Esler concluded that state supreme courts continue to rely on federal law in the vast majority of their decisions.[21]

Not all lower-court judges are opposed to a policy announced by a higher court. Some judges, as we have noted earlier, have risked social ostracism and various kinds of harassment in order to implement policies they believed in but that were not popular in their communities.[22]

A judge who is in basic agreement with a higher-court policy is likely to give that policy as broad an application as possible. In fact, the precedent might be expanded to apply to other areas. Let's look at one instance of judges expanding a precedent.

In *Griswold v. Connecticut* the Supreme Court held that a Connecticut statute forbidding the use of birth control devices was unconstitutional because it infringed upon a married couple's constitutional right to privacy.[23] In other words, the Court said that a decision whether to use birth control devices was a personal one to be made without interference from the state. Five years later, a three-judge federal district court expanded the *Griswold* precedent to justify its finding that the Texas abortion statute was unconstitutional.[24] The court ruled that the law infringed upon the right of privacy of an unmarried woman to decide, at least during the first trimester of pregnancy, whether to obtain an abortion. Thus the lower court actually went further than the Supreme Court in striking down state involvement in such matters.

Influences on Lower-Court Judges

It should be quite evident by now that lower courts are not slaves of the higher courts when it comes to implementing judicial policies but have a high degree of independence and discretion. At times the lower courts must decide cases for which no precise standards have been provided by the higher courts. Whenever this occurs, lower-court judges must turn elsewhere for guidance in deciding a case before them.

One study notes that lower-court judges in such a position "may take their cues on how to decide a particular case from a wide variety of factors including their party affiliation, their ideology, or their regional norms."[25] Several analyses, for example, point out that differences between Democratic and Republican lower-court judges are especially pronounced when Supreme Court rulings are ambiguous, when there is a transition from one Supreme Court period to another, or when the issue area is so new and controversial that more definite standards have not yet been formulated.[26]

Regional norms have also been mentioned prominently in the literature as having an influence on lower-court judges when they interpret and apply higher-court decisions.[27] One study found, for example, that "federal judges tend to be more vigilant in enforcing national desegregation standards in remote areas than when similar issues arise within the judge's immediate work/residence locale." In other words, the prevailing local norms may mean that "when faced with desegregating his own community a judge may be more concerned with public reaction than when dealing with an outlying area."[28]

To this point we have examined only one actor in the implementation process—the lower-court judge. It is now time to turn our attention to others in the political system who influence the way judicial policies are implemented. We begin our discussion with Congress because it is the body that most often registers and mirrors public reactions to major federal judicial policies.[29]

Congressional Influences on the Implementation Process

Once a federal judicial decision is made, Congress can offer a variety of responses. It may aid the implementation of a decision or hinder it. In addition, it can alter a court's interpretation of the law. Finally, Congress can mount an attack on individual judges. Naturally, the actions of individual members of Congress will be influenced by their partisan and ideological leanings.

In the course of deciding cases, the courts are often called upon to interpret federal statutes. On occasion the judicial interpretation may differ from what a majority in Congress intended. When that situation occurs, the statute can simply be changed in new legislation that in effect overrules the court's initial interpretation. A good example of this occurred in March 1988, when Congress effectively overruled the Supreme Court's decision in *Grove City College v. Bell*.[30] At issue in the case was the scope of Title IX of the 1972 Education Act Amendments, which forbids sex discrimination in education programs. In the *Grove City* case, which involved a small Pennsylvania college, the Court ruled that only the specific "program or activity" receiving federal aid was covered by Title IX. According to that interpretation only Grove City College's financial aid office was affected by the law. Many in Congress interpreted Title IX to mean that the entire college was subject to the act's prohibitions.

In order to overturn the Court's decision and restore the interpretation favored by many legislators, a bill known as the Civil Rights Restoration Act was passed by Congress. The bill was vetoed by President Reagan. However, on March 22, 1988, the House and Senate mustered the necessary two-thirds vote to override the president's veto. In this way Congress established its view that if one part of an entity receives federal funds, the entire entity is covered by Title IX of the Education Act.[31] Still, the vast majority of the federal judiciary's statutory decisions are not touched by Congress. A study focusing on the Supreme Court's labor and antitrust decisions in the period 1950–1972 found that only 27 of the 222 decisions were the objects of reversal attempts in Congress, and that only 9 of those attempts were successful.[32]

Besides ruling on statutes, the federal courts interpret the Constitution. There are two methods Congress can use to reverse or alter the effects of a constitutional interpretation it does not like. First, Congress can respond with another statute. On June 21, 1989, in *Texas v. Johnson,* the Supreme Court overturned a Texas flag desecration statute that made it illegal to "cast contempt" on the flag by "publicly mutilating, defacing, burning, or trampling" it. Gregory Lee Johnson had been found guilty of violating the law when he burned an American flag at the 1984 Republican National Convention in Dallas.[33] Although President Bush and some legislators argued in favor of a constitutional amendment to overturn the Court's decision, others preferred not to tinker with the Constitution. Instead, Congress enacted a statute that was designed to avoid the constitutional problems of the Texas law by eliminating any reference to the motives of the person who damages an American flag. The Flag Protection Act of 1989 was passed by Congress on October 12, 1989, and became effective on October 28 after President Bush allowed it to become law without his signature.[34] The new law was immediately challenged in several flag-burning exhibitions that were held in various parts of the country on October

28–30. In one of these exhibitions, held on the steps of the Capitol on October 30, 1989, Gregory Lee Johnson joined several others in igniting an American flag. However, he was not among those charged with violating the new federal statute.[35] In 1990 the Supreme Court declared the Flag Protection Act unconstitutional.[36]

Second, a constitutional decision can be overturned directly by an amendment to the U.S. Constitution. Although many such amendments have been introduced over the years, it is not easy to obtain the necessary two-thirds vote in each house of Congress to propose the amendment and then achieve ratification by three-fourths of the states. The attempt to overturn the Supreme Court's 1989 flag-burning decision by a constitutional amendment provides an excellent example of this difficulty. Although the amendment was strongly supported by President Bush, it was rejected in the Senate on October 19, 1989, by a 51–48 vote, fifteen votes short of the required two-thirds of those present and voting.[37]

In fact, only four Supreme Court decisions in the history of the Court have been overturned by constitutional amendments. The Eleventh Amendment overturned *Chisholm v. Georgia* (dealing with suits against a state in federal court); the Thirteenth Amendment overturned *Scott v. Sandford* (dealing with the legality of slavery); the Sixteenth Amendment overturned *Pollock v. Farmer's Loan and Trust Co.* (pertaining to the constitutionality of the income tax); and the Twenty-sixth Amendment overturned *Oregon v. Mitchell* (giving eighteen-year-olds the right to vote in state elections).[38]

Congressional attacks on the federal courts in general and on certain judges in particular are another method of responding to judicial decisions. Sometimes these attacks are in the form of verbal denouncements that allow a member of Congress to let off steam over a decision or series of decisions. Throughout 1997, for example, a number of Republican members of the U.S. House and Senate criticized several federal judges for their purported judicial activism. There were also threats of impeachment of sitting judges and more thorough investigations of the judicial philosophies of potential nominees to the federal bench.[39]

Federal judges may be impeached and removed from office by Congress. Although the congressional bark may be worse than its bite in the use of this weapon, it is still a part of its overall arsenal, and the impeachments of several federal judges in recent years serve as a reminder of that fact.

Finally, the confirmation process offers a chance for an attack on the courts. As a new federal judicial appointee goes through hearings in the Senate, individual senators sometimes use the opportunity to denounce individual judges or specific decisions. Without doubt, the best example was President Reagan's nomination of

Judge Robert Bork (of the D.C. Circuit Court of Appeals) to a position as an associate justice of the Supreme Court. A number of senators on the Judiciary Committee took Judge Bork to task for opinions he had written in specific cases, his writings while he served as a law professor at Yale University, and his views on several controversial Supreme Court decisions (notably *Roe v. Wade*).[40]

It should be noted, however, that Congress and the federal courts are not natural adversaries even though it occasionally may appear that way. Retaliations against the federal judiciary are fairly rare, and often the two branches work in harmony toward similar policy goals. For example, Congress played a key role in implementing the Supreme Court's school desegregation policy by enacting the Civil Rights Act of 1964, which empowered the Justice Department to initiate suits against school districts. Title VI of the act also provided a potent weapon in the desegregation struggle by threatening the denial of federal funds to schools guilty of segregation. The Department of Health, Education, and Welfare was given the authority to compile desegregation guidelines as a basis for determining whether districts were complying with the law. That department met its responsibilities under the law by assigning personnel to visit the school districts to see whether discrimination existed. If they found that it did, they tried to negotiate plans to bring about desegregation. If such a plan could not be negotiated, an administrative process culminating in loss of federal educational funds was commenced. In 1965 Congress further solidified its support for a policy of desegregated public schools by passing the Elementary and Secondary Education Act. This act gave the federal government a much larger role in financing public education and thus made the threat to cut off federal funds a most serious problem for many segregated school districts.[41] Such support from Congress was significant because the likelihood of compliance with a policy is increased when there is unity between branches of government.[42]

Executive Branch Influences on the Implementation Process

At times the president may be called upon directly to implement a judicial decision. An example is the famous Nixon tapes case.[43] The Senate committee investigation into the cover-up of the break-in at the Democratic party headquarters in the Watergate Hotel led directly to high government officials working close to the president. It was also revealed during the investigation that President Nixon had installed an automatic taping system in the Oval Office. Leon Jaworski, who had been appointed special prosecutor to investigate the Watergate affair, subpoenaed certain tapes that he felt might provide evidence needed in his prosecutions of high-ranking officials. President Nixon refused voluntarily to turn over the tapes on grounds of executive privilege and the need for confidentiality. The Supreme Court's decision—which, ironically, was announced on the day that the Judiciary Committee of the House of Representatives began holding hearings on whether to impeach Nixon—instructed the president to surrender the subpoenaed tapes to Judge John J. Sirica, who was handling the trials of the government officials. President Nixon did, of course, comply with the High Court's directive and thus a decision was implemented that led to his downfall. Within two weeks he resigned from the presidency, in August 1974.

Even when not directly involved in the enforcement of a judicial policy, the president may still be able to influence its impact. Because of the status and visibility of the position, a president, simply by words and actions, may encourage support for, or resistance to, a new judicial policy. For instance, it has been argued that President Eisenhower's lack of enthusiasm for the *Brown v. Board of Education* decision and "his unwillingness to condemn southern resistance in more than a pro forma fashion encouraged Arkansas Governor Orval Faubus to block integration of Little Rock Central High School in 1957."[44] As a consequence, Eisenhower was later forced to send federal troops to Little Rock to enforce the district court's integration order. Sending in troops, of course, made President Eisenhower's participation in the implementation process more direct.

A president can propose legislation aimed at retaliating against the courts. President Franklin D. Roosevelt, for instance, urged Congress to increase the size of the Supreme Court so he could "pack" it with justices who supported New Deal legislation. President Reagan used this tactic in another way. He was a consistently strong supporter of constitutional amendments to overturn the Supreme Court's school prayer and abortion decisions.

The appointment power also gives the president an opportunity to influence federal judicial policies. Although the White House shares the power to appoint federal judges with the Senate, evidence points to the fact that the president dominates the process at the Supreme Court and courts of appeals levels. (As we noted in Chapter 8, senatorial courtesy is a major consideration in the appointment of federal district judges.)

During his campaign for the presidency in 1968, Richard Nixon made the Supreme Court an issue by criticizing the Warren Court for its liberal decisions and activist approach. He promised that, if elected, he would appoint "strict constructionists" to the Supreme Court and lower federal courts. In his first year in office, Nixon appointed Warren Burger as chief justice and Harry Blackmun as an associate justice. Two years later, Nixon was able to appoint another pair of justices—Lewis Powell and William Rehnquist.

How successful was President Nixon in accomplishing his goal of altering the policy direction of the Supreme Court? One student of the transition from the Warren Court to the Burger Court said:

> . . . on the whole the Court's decisions demonstrated considerable withdrawal from and undercutting of Warren Court policies affecting the entire range of civil liberties policies.[45]

Thus Nixon was generally able to accomplish his goal for the Supreme Court. Also, the uncertainty and ambiguity in Court precedents brought about by the transition from the Warren to the Burger Court left the lower federal courts with more discretion. The authors of a study of the federal district courts, for example, said:

> With the advent of the Burger Court, the trial court jurists could no longer count on the Supreme Court for as clear and unambiguous legal guidelines as they had received from the Warren Court's more stable majority. With the decline of the fact-law congruence after 1968 the trial court judges became more free to take their decision-making cues from personal-partisan values rather than from guidelines set forth by the High Court. Consequently, the level of partisan voting increased markedly.[46]

Presidents have long realized that lower federal judges are important in the judicial policy-making process. For this reason, as we noted in Chapter 8, many chief executives have shown an interest in appointing lower-court judges who share their basic ideologies and values.[47]

The most careful screening of lower-court nominees in recent times was carried out by the Reagan administration.[48] The Reagan team established the Office of Legal Policy to screen potential judicial nominees for ideological compatibility with the president. Recent studies of the voting patterns of lower federal court judges show that the Reagan appointees differ significantly from those placed on the bench by Jimmy Carter or other recent presidents of either party.[49]

A president can also influence judicial policy making through the activities of the Justice Department, a part of the executive branch that we discussed briefly in Chapter 5. The attorney general and staff subordinates can emphasize specific issues according to the overall policy goals of the president. Recall, for example, that the 1964 Civil Rights Act authorized the Justice Department to file school desegregation suits. This allowed the executive branch to become more actively involved in implementing the policy goal of racial equality. The other side of the coin, however, is the fact that the Justice Department may, at its discretion, deemphasize specific policies by not pursuing them vigorously in the courts.

Another official discussed in Chapter 5 who is in a position to influence judicial policy making is the solicitor general. Historically, this official has been seen as having dual responsibility, to both the judicial and executive branches. Because of the solicitor general's close relationship with the Supreme Court, this official is sometimes referred to as the "tenth justice."[50] In other words, the solicitor general is often seen as a counselor who advises the Court about the meaning of federal statutes and the Constitution. As we noted earlier, the solicitor general also determines which of the cases involving the federal government as a party will be appealed to the Supreme Court. Furthermore, he or she may file an *amicus curiae* brief urging the Court to grant or deny another litigant's certiorari petition or supporting or opposing a particular policy being urged upon the High Court. The solicitor general thus reacts to the policy decisions of the Supreme Court.

Many judicial decisions are actually implemented by the various departments, agencies, bureaus, and commissions that abound in the executive branch. The Supreme Court decision in *Frontiero v. Richardson* called upon the U.S. Air Force to play the major implementation role.[51] The *Frontiero* case called into question congressional statutes that provided benefits for married male members of the Air Force but did not provide similar benefits for married female members. Under the laws, a married Air Force serviceman who lived off the base was entitled to an allowance for living quarters regardless of whether his wife was employed or how much she earned. Married female members of the Air Force, on the other hand, were not entitled to such an allowance unless their husbands were physically or mentally incapable of self-support and dependent on their wives for more than half their support. Lieutenant Sharron Frontiero challenged the policy on the ground that it constituted sexual discrimination in violation of the Fifth Amendment. Her suit was filed in a federal district court in Alabama on December 23, 1970. It was not until April 5, 1972, that the three-judge district court announced its decision upholding the Air Force policy. Lieutenant Frontiero appealed to the Supreme Court, which overturned the lower-court decision on May 14, 1973. The Air Force was then required to implement a policy it had fought for nearly three years.

Other Implementors

To this point we have concentrated primarily upon lower-court judges, Congress, the president, and others in the executive branch as interpreters and implementors of judicial policies. There are, of course, many other actors involved in the implementation process.[52]

Although our focus thus far has been primarily on various federal officials, it should be noted that implementation of judicial policies is often performed by state officials as well. Many of the Supreme Court's criminal due process decisions, such as *Gideon v. Wainwright* and *Miranda v. Arizona*, have been enforced by state court judges and other state officials. State and local police officers, for instance, have played a major role in implementing the *Miranda* requirement that criminal suspects must be advised of their rights. The *Gideon* ruling that an attorney must be provided at state expense for indigent defendants in felony trials has been implemented by public defenders, local bar associations, and individual court-appointed lawyers.

State legislators and executives are also frequently drawn into the implementation process, quite often as unwilling participants. A judge who determines that a wrong has been committed may use the power to issue an equitable decree as a way of remedying the wrong. The range of remedies available is broad since cases vary in the issues they raise and the types of relief sought. Among the more common affirmative remedy options from which a judge may choose are process remedies, performance standards, and specified remedial actions.[53] *Process remedies* provide for such things as advisory committees, citizen participation, educational programs, evaluation committees, dispute resolution procedures, and special masters; the remedies do not specify a particular form of action. *Performance standards* call for specific remedies—a certain number of housing units or schools or a certain level of staffing in a prison or mental health facility; the specific means of attaining these goals are left to the discretion of the officials named in the suit. Examples of *specified remedial actions* are school busing, altered school attendance zones, and changes in the size and condition of prison cells or hospital rooms. This type of remedy provides the defendant with no flexibility concerning the specific remedy or the means of attaining it.

Implementation of these remedial decrees often devolves, at least partially, to the state legislatures. An order calling for a certain number of prison cells or a certain number of guards in the prison system might require new state expenditures, which the legislature would have to fund. Similarly, an order to construct more modern mental health facilities or provide more modern equipment would mean an increase in state expenditures. Governors would also naturally be involved in carrying out these types of remedial decrees since they typically are heavily involved in state budgeting procedures. Also, they may sign or veto laws. Some even have an item veto power, which permits them to veto certain budget items while approving others.

Sometimes judges appoint certain individuals to assist in carrying out the remedial decree. Special masters are usually given some decision-making authority. Court-appointed monitors are also used in some situations, but they do not relieve the judge of decision-making responsibilities. Instead, the monitor is an information gatherer who reports on the defendant's progress in complying with the remedial decree. When there is a failure to implement orders or when barriers of one kind or another block progress in providing a remedy, a judge may name someone as a receiver. A good example occurred in the 1970s when the fights within Alabama's mental health agencies and facilities made it virtually impossible to obtain the action Judge Frank Johnson wanted. Finally, Judge Johnson ordered the governor to take over as receiver and empowered him to disregard normal organizational barriers.[54]

Space does not permit us to discuss every state and local public official in the implementation process, but one group of individuals has been so deeply involved in implementing judicial policies that we feel compelled to deal with them here, if only briefly. These implementors are the thousands of men and women who constitute school boards throughout the country.

Two major policy areas stand out as having embroiled school board members in considerable controversy as they faced the inevitable task of trying to carry out Supreme Court policy. First, when the High Court ruled in 1954 that segregation has no place in the public schools, it was school boards and school superintendents, along with federal district judges, who bore the brunt of implementing that decision.[55] Their role in this process has affected the lives of millions of schoolchildren, parents, and taxpayers all over America.

The second area that has involved school boards is the Supreme Court's policies on religion in the public schools. In *Engel v. Vitale* (1962), the Court held unconstitutional a New York requirement that a state-written prayer be recited daily in the public schools.[56] Some school districts responded to the decision by requiring instead the recitation of a Bible verse or the Lord's Prayer. Their reasoning was that since the state did not write the Lord's Prayer or the Bible, they were not violating the Court's policy. A year later, the Supreme Court struck down these new practices, pointing out that the constitutional violation lay in endorsing the religious activity and its determination did not depend on whether the state had written the prayer.[57] Some school districts continued to evade the spirit, if not the letter, of the High Court's policy by requiring a period of silent meditation during which students could pray if they wished. The Alabama silent meditation law was declared void by the Supreme Court June 4, 1985, because students were instructed that they could use the time for prayer. This action was said to unconstitutionally endorse religion as a "favored practice." The Court indicated, however, that "moment of silence" laws not endorsing prayer would pass constitutional muster.[58]

Both of these policy areas involve basically private citizens—school board officials—in implementing controversial, emotion-charged policies that they may neither clearly understand nor agree with. The lack of understanding of the Supreme Court's school prayer decisions, for example, led some school districts to take no action at all, while other school boards placed a ban on all religious activities.[59]

The Impact of Judicial Policies

Thus far, we have focused primarily on the implementation of judicial policies by various government officials. This is entirely appropriate, since court decisions are often specifically directed at other public policy makers. However, as a recent study of the Supreme Court tells us, the ultimate importance of the Court's decisions "depends primarily on their impact outside government, on American society as a whole."[60] We will explore briefly a few policies that have had significant effects on "society as a whole": the courts' role in developing a policy of racial equality, criminal due process, and abortion.

Racial Equality

One team of judicial impact scholars has said:

Perhaps the judiciary's biggest impact on modern America came in the *Brown* decision, which initiated the drive for racial equality. However, it took the active participation of Congress and the president to sustain this effort and ensure substantial implementation of such policies. The state of race relations in America might be quite different if the courts had ignored the issue, but it also might be different if Congress and the president had not joined the effort.[61]

Quite clearly, the United States could not have achieved as much as it has in the quest for racial equality had Congress and the president stayed out of the picture. However, as the preceding statement correctly points out, it was the courts that initiated the pursuit for a national policy of racial equality with the *Brown* ruling. Thus one of the most important ways the federal judiciary can influence policy is to place issues on the national political agenda.

In the beginning, the court decisions were often vague, leading to evasion of the new policy. The Supreme Court justices and many lower federal judges were persistent in decisions following *Brown,* and in this way kept the policy of racial equality on the national political agenda; their persistence paid off with passage of the 1964 Civil Rights Act, ten years after *Brown*. That act, which had the strong support of Presidents Kennedy and Johnson, squarely placed Congress and the president on record as being supportive of racial equality in America.

One other aspect of the federal judiciary's importance in the policy-making process is illustrated by *Brown* and the cases that followed it. Although the courts stood virtually alone in the quest for racial equality for several years, their decisions did not go unnoticed. It is argued that "the psychological impact of the decision far exceeded its immediate legal consequences. *Brown* stood as a symbol to blacks and whites alike that racial equality now had an institutional champion at the highest level." Spurred on by this knowledge, civil rights activists engaged in sit-ins, freedom marches, freedom rides, and other types of demonstrations and protests. Such actions "stirred up so much attention and emotion that the other branches of government could no longer avoid a major policymaking role."[62]

Although no one would argue that the United States has achieved complete racial equality, some gains have been made. The federal courts are not totally responsible for those gains, of course, but they have played a major role in their achievement.

Recently, however, many civil rights activists have argued that the new conservative majority on the Supreme Court (brought about by President Reagan's appointments of Sandra Day O'Connor, Antonin Scalia, and Anthony M. Kennedy and President Bush's appointments of David Souter and Clarence Thomas) has weakened gains made prior to the 1980s. The author of one study of the Supreme Court observed that "a continuing retreat on individual rights by the Rehnquist Court would affirm that the Warren Court was an anomaly in a long history of judicial indifference or hostility to disadvantaged minorities."[63]

Criminal Due Process

Judicial policy making in the area of criminal due process is most closely associated with the Warren Court period. Speaking of this era, a former solicitor general said, "Never has there been such a thorough-going reform of criminal procedure within so short a time."[64] The Warren Court decisions were aimed primarily at changing the procedures followed by the states in dealing with criminal defendants. By the time Warren left the Supreme Court, new policies had been established to deal with a wide range of activities. A complete list of the Court's decisions is too lengthy to discuss here; among the more far-reaching were *Mapp v. Ohio*, *Gideon v. Wainwright*, and *Miranda v. Arizona*.[65]

The *Mapp* decision extended the exclusionary rule, which had applied to the national government for a number of years, to the states. This rule simply required state courts to exclude from trials evidence that had been illegally seized by the police. Although some police departments, especially in major urban areas, have tried to establish specific guidelines for their officers to follow in obtaining evidence, such efforts have not been universal. Because of variations in police practices and differing lower-court interpretations of what constitutes a valid search and seizure, implementation of *Mapp* has not been consistent throughout the country.

Perhaps even more important in reducing the originally perceived impact of *Mapp* has been the lack of solid support for the exclusionary rule among the Supreme Court justices. The decision was not a unanimous one to begin with, and over the years some of the justices, notably former chief justice Warren Burger, have been openly critical of the exclusionary rule. Furthermore, Burger and Rehnquist Court decisions have broadened the scope of legal searches, thus limiting the applicability of the rule.[66] As we saw earlier in this chapter, ambiguity and the absence of clear guidelines from the High Court increase the discretion of lower-court judges who are asked to implement a policy.

The *Gideon v. Wainwright* decision held that indigent defendants must be provided attorneys when they go to trial in a felony case in the state courts. Many states routinely provided attorneys in such trials even before the Court's decision. The other states began to comply in a variety of ways. Public defender programs were established in many regions. In other areas, local bar associations cooperated with judges to implement some method of complying with the Supreme Court's new policy.

The impact of *Gideon* is clearer and more consistent than that of *Mapp*. One reason, no doubt, is the fact that many states had already implemented the policy called for by *Gideon*. In other words, it was simply more widely accepted than the policy established by *Mapp*. The policy announced in *Gideon* was also more sharply defined than the one in *Mapp*. Although the Court did not specify whether a public defender or a court-appointed lawyer must be provided, it is still quite clear that the indigent defendant must have the help of an attorney. It should also be noted that the Burger Court did not retreat from the Warren Court's policy of providing an attorney for indigent defendants as it did in the search and seizure area addressed by *Mapp*. All these factors add up to a more recognizable impact for the policy announced in *Gideon*.

In *Miranda v. Arizona* the Supreme Court went a step further and ruled that police officers must advise suspects taken into custody of their constitutional rights, one of which is to have an attorney present during questioning. Suspects must also be advised that they have a right to remain silent and that any statement they make may be used in court; that if they cannot afford an attorney, one will be provided at state expense; and that they have the right to stop answering questions at any time. These requirements are so clearly stated that police departments have actually copied them down on cards for officers to carry in their shirt pockets. Then, when suspects are taken into custody, the police officers simply remove the card and read the suspects their rights.

If we measure compliance simply in terms of whether police officers read the *Miranda* rights to persons they arrest, we would have to say that there has been a high level of compliance with the Supreme Court policy. Some researchers, however, have questioned the impact of *Miranda* because of the method by which suspects may be advised of their rights. It is one thing simply to read to a person from a card; it is quite another to explain what is meant by the High Court's requirements and then try to make the suspect understand them. Looked at in this manner, the impact of the policy announced in *Miranda* is not quite as clear.

The Burger Court did not show an inclination to lend its solid support to the Warren Court's *Miranda* policy. Although *Miranda* has not been overruled, its impact has been limited somewhat. In *Harris v. New York*, for example, the Burger Court ruled that statements made by an individual who had not been given the *Miranda* warning could be used to challenge the credibility of his testimony at trial.[67] More recently, the Rehnquist Court, in a five-to-four decision, ruled that police are not required to stop questioning a suspect who makes an ambiguous request to have an attorney present.[68]

In sum, we would emphasize that the impact of the Supreme Court's criminal justice policies has been rather mixed, for several reasons. In some instances ambiguity is a problem. In other cases it may be less than solid support for the policy among justices or eroding support when one Court replaces another. All these variables translate into greater discretion for the implementors.

Abortion

In *Roe v. Wade* the Supreme Court ruled (1) that a woman has an absolute right to an abortion during the first trimester of pregnancy; (2) that a state may regulate the abortion procedure during the second trimester in order to protect the mother's health; and (3) that during the third trimester, the state may regulate or even prohibit abortions, except where the life or health of the mother is endangered.[69]

The reaction to this decision was immediate, and primarily negative.[70] It came in the form of letters to individual justices, public speeches, the introduction of resolutions in Congress, and the advocacy of "right to life" amendments in Congress. As might be expected, given the controversial nature of the Court's decision, hospitals did not wholeheartedly offer to support the decision by changing their abortion policies. In fact, one study, using a national sample of hospitals, found that less than one-half changed their abortion policies following the Supreme Court's decision in *Roe*.[71]

Reaction to the Court's abortion policy was not short-lived. It has not only continued but has moved into new areas. State legislatures have enacted numerous laws aimed at regulating abortion in one way or another; some have passed constitutional muster, others have not.

Recent presidential elections have seen the two major party platforms and candidates take opposing stands on the abortion issue. Democratic platforms and nominees have expressed support for *Roe v. Wade*, whereas the Republican platforms and contenders have noted opposition to the Supreme Court's decision and called for a constitutional amendment to protect the life of unborn children.

Congress also became a hotbed of activity in response to the Supreme Court's abortion decision. Unable to secure passage of a constitutional amendment to overturn *Roe v. Wade*, antiabortion forces used another approach. For several years they successfully obtained amendments to appropriations bills preventing the expenditure of federal funds for elective abortions. In 1980 the Supreme Court, in a five-to-four vote, upheld the constitutionality of such a prohibition.[72]

With its July 3, 1989, decision in *Webster v. Reproductive Health Services*,[73] the Supreme Court reignited the controversy over abortion that had been smoldering for sixteen years. Although *Roe v. Wade* was not overturned, the Court, in a five-to-four vote, upheld several provisions of a Missouri law aimed at making abortions more difficult to obtain. Most significant perhaps was the majority's ruling that states may require doctors to determine whether a twenty-week-old fetus is viable (capable of surviving outside the womb).

Perhaps encouraged by the *Webster* decision, as well as by the increasing conservatism of the Supreme Court, several state legislatures, including Pennsylvania, Louisiana, and Utah, passed tougher regulations. As the challenge to Pennsylvania's new law made its way to the Supreme Court, those who wanted to see *Roe* overturned were encouraged by the retirements of the Court's last two staunchly liberal justices, William J. Brennan, Jr., and Thurgood Marshall, which left only Justice Harry A. Blackmun remaining from the seven-member majority in *Roe*.

When the decision in *Planned Parenthood of Southeastern Pennsylvania v. Casey*[74] was announced on June 29, 1992, however, only four justices voted to overrule *Roe*.

They were Chief Justice Rehnquist and Justices Scalia, Thomas, and White. Thus, by the narrowest of margins, the Supreme Court reaffirmed the central holding in *Roe v. Wade*—state laws may not unduly burden access to or ban abortions in the first trimester of a woman's pregnancy. Nevertheless, most of the provisions in the Pennsylvania law were upheld and "the balance on the Court had clearly shifted to allowing states to impose more conditions and restrictions on the availability of abortions."[75]

While battles over the abortion issue were being fought in the courts, political campaigns, and legislative arenas, others preferred a more direct approach, demonstrating at and blockading abortion centers. Two decisions reached by the Supreme Court in 1994 promise to have an impact on such demonstrations, however. In *Madsen v. Women's Health Center* the Court, by a six-to-three vote, upheld the use of a 36-foot buffer zone to protect an abortion clinic against disruptive protest.[76] In a second clinic protest case, the High Court unanimously ruled that abortion clinics can invoke the Racketeer-Influenced and Corrupt Organizations Act to sue violent antiabortion protest groups for damages.[77]

Conclusions

There is no doubt that some judicial policies have a greater impact on society than others. Because many reasons for this situation have been offered throughout this chapter, an extended discussion of them is not needed here. Instead, we simply offer some concluding thoughts about the ability of courts to effectuate changes in society.

Quite clearly, the judiciary plays a greater role in developing the nation's policies than the constitutional framers envisioned. However, it is well to remember that

American courts are not all-powerful institutions. They were designed with severe limitations and placed in a political system of divided powers. To ask them to produce significant social reforms is to forget their history and ignore their constraints.[78]

Within this complex framework of competing political and social demands and expectations, however, there *is* a policy-making role for the courts. Because the other two branches of government are sometimes not receptive to the demands of certain segments of society, the only alternative for those individuals or groups is to turn to the courts. Civil rights organizations, for example, made no real headway until they found the Supreme Court to be a supportive forum for their school desegregation efforts. They were then able to use *Brown* and other decisions as a springboard to attack a variety of areas of discrimination. Thus a champion at a high government level may offer hope to individuals and interest groups.

As civil rights groups attained some success in the federal courts, others were encouraged to employ litigation as a strategy. For example, several scholars tell us that women's rights supporters followed a pattern established by minority groups when they began taking their grievances to the courts.[79] What began as a more narrow pursuit for racial equality was thus broadened to a quest for equality for other disadvantaged groups in society.

Clearly, then, the courts can announce policy decisions that attract national attention and perhaps stress the fact that other policy makers have failed to act. In this way the judiciary may invite the other branches to exercise their policy-making powers. Follow-up decisions indicate the judiciary's determination to pursue a particular policy and help keep alive the invitation for other policy makers to join in the endeavor.

All things considered, the courts seem best equipped to develop and implement narrow policies that are less controversial in nature. The policy established in the *Gideon* case provides a good example. The decision that indigent defendants in state criminal trials must be provided with an attorney did not meet any strong outcries of protest. Furthermore, it was a policy that primarily required the support of judges and lawyers; action by Congress and the president was not really necessary. A policy of equality for all segments of society, on the other hand, is so broad and controversy-laden that it must move beyond the judiciary. As it does so, the courts become simply one part, albeit an important part, of the policy-making process.

Summary

We began this chapter by pointing out that judicial decisions are not self-executing. The courts depend upon a variety of individuals, both inside and outside the judicial branch, to carry out their rulings.

Lower-court judges are prominent in the implementation process. Our discussion of their role in carrying out decisions of higher courts emphasized the discretion they exercise. Factors that account for the flexibility that rests with the lower-court judge include the decentralization of the judicial system and ambiguity of higher-court rulings. We examined, as well, the strategies that balking lower-court judges may employ in resisting appellate court decisions they dislike.

Congress and the president may also be involved in the implementation process. Each of these two branches can react either positively or negatively to a court decision. The wide range of influences the president and Congress exert in enforcing a judicial decision was described in some detail.

We also noted that some policies call upon state officials to take part in the implementation process. State court judges, for example, played the major role in enforcing the Warren Court's criminal due process decisions. Local school boards have also been called upon to carry out Supreme Court policies.

We concluded the chapter with a discussion of the impact on society of several important federal court policies. Explanations were offered as to why some policies have a more obvious impact on society than others; most important, perhaps, is that if a ruling—like the Supreme Court's original decision on abortion—faces opposition, Congress and other implementors are likely to drag their feet. A final section of the chapter offered some concluding thoughts on the role of courts in bringing about changes in society. In it we noted that the judiciary can act as a kind of beacon for traditionally underrepresented groups seeking to achieve their goals.

NOTES

1. *Gideon v. Wainwright,* 372 U.S. 335 (1963).

2. For a good description of the bureaucratic theory, see Walter F. Murphy, "Chief Justice Taft and the Lower Court Bureaucracy: A Study in Judicial Administration," *Journal of Politics* 24 (1962): 453–476.

3. Richard J. Richardson and Kenneth N. Vines, *The Politics of Federal Courts* (Boston: Little, Brown, 1970), 144.

4. Lawrence Baum, "Implementation of Judicial Decisions: An Organizational Analysis," *American Politics Quarterly* 4 (1976): 91.

5. The desegregation policy was announced in *Brown v. Board of Education of Topeka,* 347 U.S. 483 (1954). For a study of the lower federal courts involved in implementing *Brown,* see Jack W. Peltason, *Fifty-Eight Lonely Men* (New York: Harcourt, Brace & World, 1961).

6. For an excellent account of the school desegregation struggle in Georgia, see Harrell R. Rodgers, Jr., and Charles S. Bullock III, *Coercion to Compliance* (Lexington, Mass.: Lexington Books, 1976).

7. *Brown v. Board of Education of Topeka II,* 349 U.S. 294 (1955).

8. *Baker v. Carr,* 369 U.S. 186 (1962).

9. Ibid., 237, 251.

10. The statement was made by Justice Potter Stewart in *Jacobellis v. Ohio,* 378 U.S. 184 (1964).

11. *Furman v. Georgia,* 408 U.S. 238 (1972). A good account of the various views held by the justices, as well as the behind-the-scenes events leading to the final decision, may be found in Bob Woodward and Scott Armstrong, *The Brethren: Inside the Supreme Court* (New York: Simon & Schuster, 1979), 205–220.

12. For a good discussion of this point with pertinent examples, see Charles A. Johnson and Bradley C. Canon, *Judicial Policies: Implementation and Impact* (Washington, D.C.: CQ Press, 1984), 55–56.

13. Ibid., 29.

14. *Schenck v. United States,* 249 U.S. 47 (1919).

15. Johnson and Canon, *Judicial Policies,* 40.

16. See John Gruhl, "The Supreme Court's Impact on the Law of Libel: Compliance by Lower Federal Courts," *Western Political Quarterly* 33 (1980): 517.

17. See Donald R. Songer and Reginald S. Sheehan, "Supreme Court Impact on Compliance and Outcomes: *Miranda* and *New York Times* in the United States Courts of Appeals," *Western Political Quarterly* 43 (1990): 307.

18. Stephen L. Wasby, *The Supreme Court in the Federal Judicial System*, 4th ed. (Chicago: Nelson-Hall, 1993), 376.

19. See G. Alan Tarr, "Civil Liberties under State Constitutions," *The Political Science Teacher* 1 (Fall 1988): 8–9.

20. Ibid., 8.

21. See Barry Latzer, "The Hidden Conservatism of the State Court Revolution," *Judicature* 74 (1991): 190–197; and Michael Esler, "State Supreme Court Commitment to State Law," *Judicature* 78 (1994): 25–32.

22. See Peltason, *Fifty-Eight Lonely Men*, and Richardson and Vines, *The Politics of Federal Courts*, 98–99.

23. *Griswold v. Connecticut*, 381 U.S. 479 (1965).

24. *Roe v. Wade*, 314 F. Supp. 1217 (1970).

25. Ronald Stidham and Robert A. Carp, "U.S. Trial Court Reactions to Changes in Civil Rights and Civil Liberties Policies," *Southeastern Political Review* 12 (1984): 7.

26. See, for example, Kathleen L. Barber, "Partisan Values in the Lower Courts: Reapportionment in Ohio and Michigan," *Case Western Reserve Law Review* 20 (1969): 406–407; Robert A. Carp and C. K. Rowland, *Policymaking and Politics in the Federal District Courts* (Knoxville: University of Tennessee Press, 1983), chap. 2; C. K. Rowland and Robert A. Carp, "A Longitudinal Study of Party Effects on Federal District Court Policy Propensities," *American Journal of Political Science* 24 (1980): 301; and Ronald Stidham, Robert A. Carp, and C. K. Rowland, "Women's Rights before the Federal District Courts, 1971–1977," *American Politics Quarterly* 11 (1983): 214.

27. See, for example, Peltason, *Fifty-Eight Lonely Men*; Kenneth N. Vines, "Federal District Judges and Race Relations Cases in the South," *Journal of Politics* 26 (1964): 338–357; Richardson and Vines, *The Politics of Federal Courts*, 93–100; and Michael W. Giles and Thomas G. Walker, "Judicial Policy-Making and Southern School Segregation," *Journal of Politics* 37 (1975): 917–936.

28. Giles and Walker, "Judicial Policy-Making and Southern School Segregation," 931.

29. For a good study of the relationship between Congress and the Supreme Court, see John R. Schmidhauser and Larry L. Berg, *The Supreme Court and Congress: Conflict and Interaction, 1945–1968* (New York: Free Press, 1972).

30. 465 U.S. 555 (1984).

31. See *Congressional Quarterly Weekly Report*, March 12, 1988, 677; and March 26, 1988, 774, for accounts of the hearings.

32. Beth M. Henschen, "Statutory Interpretations of the Supreme Court: Congressional Response," *American Politics Quarterly* 11 (1983): 441–458.

33. *Texas v. Johnson*, 491 U.S. 397 (1989).

34. *Congressional Quarterly Weekly Report*, November 4, 1989, 2952.

35. Ibid.

36. *United States v. Eichman*, 496 U.S. 310 (1990).

37. *Congressional Quarterly Weekly Report*, October 21, 1989, 2803, 2830.

38. 2 Dallas 419 (1793); 19 Howard 393 (1857); 158 U.S. 601 (1896); and 400 U.S. 112 (1970), respectively.

39. See Harvey Barkman, "Spiking Judges for Rulings," *The National Law Journal*, June 30, 1997, A1, A11.

40. See *Congressional Quarterly Weekly Report*, September 12, 1987, 2159–2177; September 26, 1987, 2301–2304, 2329–2338; and October 3, 1987, 2366–2369, 2416.

41. See James E. Anderson, David W. Brady, and Charles S. Bullock III, *Public Policy and Politics in America* (North Scituate, Mass.: Duxbury Press, 1978), 291–292; and Charles S. Bullock III, "Equal Education Opportunity," in *Implementation of Civil Rights Policy*, eds. Charles S. Bullock III and Charles M. Lamb (Monterey, Calif.: Brooks/Cole, 1984), 57–58.

42. Wasby, *The Supreme Court in the Federal Judicial System*, 256.

43. *United States v. Nixon*, 418 U.S. 683 (1974).

44. Johnson and Canon, *Judicial Policies*, 160.

45. Wasby, *The Supreme Court in the Federal Judicial System*, 16.

46. Carp and Rowland, *Policymaking and Politics in the Federal District Courts*, 43.

47. For a discussion of this point, see Ronald Stidham, Robert A. Carp, and C. K. Rowland, "Patterns of Presidential Influence on the Federal District Courts: An Analysis of the Appointment Process," *Presidential Studies Quarterly* 14 (1984): 548–560.

48. See Sheldon Goldman, "Reagan's Second Term Judicial Appointments: The Battle at Midway," *Judicature* 70 (1987): 324–339.

49. See Ronald Stidham and Robert A. Carp, "Judges, Presidents, and Policy Choices: Exploring the Linkage," *Social Science Quarterly* 68 (June 1987): 395–404; and C. K. Rowland, Donald R. Songer, and Robert A. Carp, "Presidential Effects on Criminal Justice Policy in the Lower Federal Courts: The Reagan Judges," *Law and Society Review* 22 (1988): 191–200.

50. See Lincoln Caplan, "Annals of Law: The Tenth Justice," pt. 1, *The New Yorker*, August 10, 1987, 32. Also see Caplan, *The Tenth Justice: The Solicitor General and the Rule of Law* (New York: Knopf, 1988).

51. *Frontiero v. Richardson*, 411 U.S. 677 (1973).

52. One study, for example, analyzed judicial implementation and impact from the standpoint of the roles of four populations: an interpreting population, an implementing population, a consumer population, and a secondary population. See Johnson and Canon, *Judicial Policies*.

53. Our discussion of the use of powers to provide equitable remedial decrees is largely drawn from Phillip J. Cooper, *Hard Judicial Choices* (New York: Oxford University Press, 1988), 12–14, 342, 348–349.

54. Ibid., 348–349.

55. See Rodgers and Bullock, *Coercion to Compliance*, and Giles and Walker, "Judicial Policy-Making and Southern School Segregation."

56. *Engel v. Vitale*, 370 U.S. 421 (1962).

57. See *Abington School District v. Schempp*, 374 U.S. 203 (1963).

58. *Wallace v. Jaffree*, 472 U.S. 38 (1985).

59. For good studies of the responses of school boards to the Court's school prayer decisions, see Kenneth Dolbeare and Phillip Hammond, *The School Prayer Decisions: From Court Policy to Local Practice* (Chicago: University of Chicago Press, 1971); William Muir, *Prayer in the Public Schools: Law and Attitude Change* (Chicago: University of Chicago Press, 1967); Richard Johnson, *The Dynamics of Compliance* (Evanston, Ill.: Northwestern University Press, 1967); and Robert Birkby, "The Supreme Court and the Bible Belt: Tennessee Reaction to the *Schempp* Decision," *Midwest Journal of Political Science* 10 (1966): 304–319.

60. Lawrence Baum, *The Supreme Court*, 6th ed. (Washington, D.C.: CQ Press, 1998), 261.

61. Johnson and Canon, *Judicial Policies*, 269.

62. Ibid., 257, 258.

63. David Adamany, "The Supreme Court," in *The American Courts: A Critical Assessment*, ed. John B. Gates and Charles A. Johnson (Washington, D.C.: CQ Press, 1991), 18.

64. Archibald Cox, *The Warren Court* (Cambridge, Mass.: Harvard University Press, 1968), 74.

65. *Mapp v. Ohio*, 367 U.S. 643 (1961); *Gideon v. Wainwright*, 372 U.S. 335 (1963); and *Miranda v. Arizona*, 384 U.S. 436 (1966).

66. See Mary Coombs, "The Constable Never Blunders," *Texas Lawyer*, August 5, 1991, S-10–11.

67. *Harris v. New York*, 401 U.S. 222 (1971).

68. See *Davis v. United States*, 114 S. Ct. 2350 (1994).

69. *Roe v. Wade*, 410 U.S. 113 (1973).

70. For a good case study of the impact of *Roe v. Wade*, including reactions to the decision, see Johnson and Cannon, *Judicial Policies*, 4–14. Our discussion draws largely from this study.

71. See Jon R. Bond and Charles A. Johnson, "Implementing a Permissive Policy: Hospital Abortion Services after *Roe v. Wade*," *American Journal of Political Science* 26 (1982): 1–24.

72. See *Harris v. McRae*, 448 U.S. 297 (1980).

73. 109 S. Ct. 3040 (1989).

74. 112 S. Ct. 2791 (1992).

75. David M. O'Brien, *Storm Center: The Supreme Court in American Politics*, 2d ed. (New York: W. W. Norton, 1993), 60.

76. *Madsen v. Women's Health Center*, 114 S. Ct. 2516 (1994).

77. *National Organization for Women v. Scheidler*, 114 S. Ct. 798 (1994).

78. Gerald N. Rosenberg, *Hollow Hope: Can Courts Bring About Social Change?* (Chicago: University of Chicago Press, 1991), 343.

79. See Richard C. Cortner, "Strategies and Tactics of Litigants in Constitutional Cases," *Journal of Public Law* 17 (1968): 287–307; Jo Freeman, *The Politics of Women's Liberation* (New York: David McKay, 1975); Leslie Friedman Goldstein, "Sex and the Burger Court: Recent Judicial Policy Making Toward Women," in *Race, Sex, and Policy Problems*, eds. Marian Lief Palley and Michael B. Preston (Lexington, Mass.: Lexington Books, 1979), 103–113; and Karen O'Connor, *Women's Organizations' Use of the Courts* (Lexington, Mass.: Heath, 1980).

SUGGESTED READINGS

Bullock, Charles S. III, and Charles M. Lamb, eds. *Implementation of Civil Rights Policy.* Monterey, Calif.: Brooks/Cole, 1984. A collection of articles that focus on how civil rights policies are carried out.

Cooper, Phillip J. *Hard Judicial Choices.* New York: Oxford University Press, 1988. The book focuses on the use of remedial decrees in carrying out judicial decisions.

Craig, Barbara H., and David M. O'Brien. *Abortion and American Politics.* Chatham, N.J.: Chatham House, 1993. A good study of the response to the Supreme Court's abortion decisions.

Johnson, Charles A., and Bradley C. Canon. *Judicial Policies: Implementation and Impact.* Washington, D.C.: CQ Press, 1984. A good study of the process and actors involved in carrying out and enforcing judicial decisions.

Peltason, Jack W. *Fifty-Eight Lonely Men.* New York: Harcourt, Brace and World, 1961. An excellent study of the southern federal judges who were given the task of implementing the U.S. Supreme Court's *Brown v. Board of Education* decision.

Rodgers, Harrell R., Jr., and Charles S. Bullock III. *Coercion to Compliance.* Lexington, Mass.: Lexington Books, 1976. A good study of the implementation of school desegregation policies in Georgia.

Rosenberg, Gerald N. *Hollow Hope: Can Courts Bring About Social Change?* Chicago: University of Chicago Press, 1991. The book focuses on the ability of courts to effect social change.

Wasby, Stephen L. *The Impact of the United States Supreme Court: Some Perspectives.* Homewood, Ill.: Dorsey, 1970. The author discusses the various actors involved in the process of implementing decisions of the U.S. Supreme Court.

CHAPTER 13

Policy Making by American Judges: A Synthesis

The Supreme Court is the ultimate interpreter of the U.S. Constitution, state constitutions, and national and state legislation. The decision making of these jurists is a product of both the legal and democratic subcultures.

"AN EDUCATION," THE SAYING GOES, "is what you have left after you've forgotten what you've learned." This text has presented you with many facts, theories, statistics, and examples about the federal and state court systems. But as time goes on and the myriad of facts and illustrations are largely forgotten, what *education* ought you to have about the operation and policy making of American courts? It is the purpose of this chapter to pull out of the previous twelve chapters certain key ideas and significant themes that we would like you to remember long after most factual tidbits have faded from memory.

By this time it is surely clear that the decisions of federal and state judges and justices affect the lives of all of us. Whether it be the norm enforcement rulings or the broader policy-making decisions, the output of federal and state courts permeates the warp and woof of the body politic in the United States. No one can have a full and accurate understanding of the American political system without being cognizant of the work of the men and women who wear the black robe. As we look at the matter of decision making by the judiciary, two basic questions are worthy of consideration. First, what are the conditions that cause judges to engage in policy making and to do so boldly? Second, does the literature give any clues as to the substantive direction of this policy making—that is, will it be conservative or liberal, supportive of or antagonistic toward the status quo? In seeking answers to these two basic questions, we have synthesized four sets of variables that shed some light in this area: (1) the nature of the case or issue presented to the court, (2) the values and orientations of the judges, (3) the nature of the judicial decision-making process, and (4) extraneous influences that serve to implement and sustain judicial decisions.

The Nature of the Case or Issue

One critical variable that clearly affects the degree to which (and sometimes the direction in which) American jurists influence our lives is the type of controversy that might serve as grist for the judicial mills. If it is the sort of issue that judges can resolve with room for significant maneuver, the impact of the case on public policy may be impressive. Conversely, if American jurists are forbidden to enter a certain decision-making realm or enter with only limited options, the policy impact will be nil. There are several aspects of this general proposition, as we shall indicate.

Jurisdiction

In Chapter 4 we outlined the jurisdiction of the three levels of the federal and state judiciaries. A knowledge of this is important in and of itself, but it takes on a second meaning in the context of this discussion—namely, that judges may not make policy in subject areas over which they have no legal authority. The controversy between the United States and Russia over the deployment of nuclear weapons in space is of great significance to the American people—and indeed our very lives may be dependent on its successful resolution—but our judges will not affect this matter because they have no jurisdiction over war-and-peace disputes between the United States and other nations. Conversely, the courts will have considerable policy impact in matters of racial segregation and disputes over reapportionment because such disputes fall squarely within the legal jurisdiction of the U.S. judiciary.

Although the courts do have some leeway in determining whether they have jurisdiction over a particular subject, for the most part jurisdictional boundaries are set forth in the U.S. and state constitutions and by acts of Congress and the state legislatures. In the same context, a legislative body's power to create and restrict the courts' jurisdiction can often greatly affect the *direction* of judicial decision making. For example, Congress, by virtue of the Voting Rights Act, has granted citizens the right to sue local governments in federal courts if those governments alter the contours of electoral districts so as to dilute significantly the voting strength of minorities. By giving courts jurisdiction in this area and by telling judges in effect how to decide the cases (by establishing the decision-making goals), Congress has obviously had a major impact on judicial policy making. Likewise, the current threat by some members of Congress to remove certain matters from federal court jurisdiction, such as the power to use busing as a tool of desegregation, has policy-making potential of equal magnitude.

Judicial Self-Restraint

The nature-of-the-case variable is also related to whether a controversy falls into one of those forbidden realms into which the "good judge" ought not set foot. One judge might well like to sink his judicial teeth into a particular matter that is crying for adjudication, but if the litigant has not yet exhausted all legal or administrative remedies, the jurist will have to stay his hand. Another judge might well like to overturn a particular presidential action because she thinks it "smacks of fascism," but if no specific portion of the Constitution has been violated, she will have to express her displeasure in the voting booth—not in the courtroom. The enormous emphasis that our judicial system places on respecting past precedents (that is, the doctrine of *stare decisis*) further restrains jurists from giving reign to impulsive decision making. As we have indicated, the various maxims of judicial self-restraint may come from a variety of sources, including the Constitution, tradition, and acts of Congress and state legislatures; some have been imposed by the judges themselves. But whatever their source, they serve to channel the potential areas of judicial policy making. Judges would have little success in attempting to adjudicate matters if doing so would soon bring reversal, censure, or organized opposition from those who are in a position to "correct" a judge who has strayed from the accepted pathway of judicial behavior.

Norm Enforcement Versus Policy Making

Throughout this book we have discussed judicial behavior as including both norm enforcement and significant policy making. Most cases, as we have noted, fall into the former category—particularly for the lower judiciary. That is, in the majority of cases, judges routinely cite the applicable precedents, yield to the side with the weightiest evidence, and apply the statutes that clearly control the given fact situation; discretion is at a minimum. In these routine cases, judges are not so much making policy as they are applying and enforcing *existing* norms and policy. In addition to norm enforcement, however, judges are presented with cases in which their room to maneuver—their potential to make policy—is much greater. Such opportunities exist at all levels of the judiciary, but appellate judges and justices probably have more options for significant policy making than do their colleagues on the trial court bench. Since the late 1930s, it has been Bill of Rights issues rather than labor and economic questions that have provided judges with the greatest opportunities for significant policy making.

In exploring this subject, we identified several situations (or case characteristics) that greatly enhance the judge's capacity to make policy rather than merely to enforce existing policy. One such opportunity occurs when the legal evidence is contradictory or is equally strong on both sides. It is not uncommon for judges to preside over a case for which the facts and evidence are about equally compelling for both sides or for which there is about an equal number of precedents that would sustain a finding for either party. Being pulled in several directions at once may not be an entirely comfortable position, but it does allow the jurists freer rein to strike out on their own than if prevailing facts and law impelled them toward one position.

Likewise, judicial policy making can flower when jurists are asked to resolve new types of controversies for which statutory law and past judicial precedents are virtually absent. For example, when the federal courts were asked whether artificially created life forms could be patented, there was no way they could avoid making policy. (Even the refusal to decide is a decision, as the existentialists have long argued.) Thus some cases by their very nature invite judicial policy making, whereas others carry with them no such invitation. Of course, judges differ in their perceptions of whether there is an opportunity in a given case for creative, innovative decision making. To some extent such differences are a function of the judges themselves. But our contention here is that whether a case calls for garden-variety norm enforcement or whether it invites major judicial policy making depends to a large degree on the nature of the controversy itself.

Summary

In considering whether and in what direction judges' decisions will significantly affect our lives, we can say this: the nature of the case itself is a vital component in this line of inquiry. Judges can make policy only in those areas over which the U.S. and state constitutions and the legislative branches have granted them jurisdiction and only in a manner consistent with the norms of judicial self-restraint. Also, if the controversies presented to the judges provide them with some room to maneuver—as many current civil rights and liberties issues do—there will likely be more policy making than if the cases were tightly circumscribed by clearly controlling precedents and law.

The Values and Orientations of the Judges

A second set of variables to be considered if we want to know about judicial policy making and the direction it will take concerns the judges themselves. What are their background characteristics? How were they appointed (or elected) and by whom? What are their judicial role conceptions? By learning something about the values and orientations of the men and women who are tapped for judicial service, we are better able to explain and predict what they will do on the bench. (Also recall from Chapters 5, 6, and 7 that the attitudes and values of other actors in the judicial process—for example, police officers, prosecutors, and the solicitor general—affect the content and direction of their important duties.)

We have looked at judicial background characteristics in a variety of contexts in this book. Here we shall examine several that have particular relevance vis-à-vis judicial policy making and its direction.

Judges as a Socioeconomic Elite

In Chapters 8 and 9 we made much of the fact that America's jurists come from a very narrow segment of the social and economic strata. To an overwhelming degree they are offspring of upper- and upper-middle-class parents and come from families with a tradition of political, and often judicial, service. They are the men and women to whom our system has been good, who fit in, who have "made it." The mavericks, malcontents, and ideological extremists are discreetly weeded out by the judicial recruitment process.

What does all this suggest about judicial policy making and its direction? Given the striking similarity of the jurists and the backgrounds from which they come, their overall policy making is generally going to be fairly modest, conventional, and ideologically moderate. Although many judges have a commitment to reform and will use their policy-making opportunities to this end, it is to adjust and enhance a way of life that they basically believe in. Seldom bitten is the hand of the socioeconomic system that feeds them. Although an occasional maverick may slip in or develop within the judicial ranks, most judges are basically conservative in that they hold dear the traditional institutions and rules of the game that have brought success to them and their families. America's elite has its fair share of both liberals and conservatives, but it does not have many who would use their discretionary opportunities to alter radically the basic social and political system.

Judges as Representatives of Their Political Parties

Although the nature of the judicial recruitment process gives virtually all U.S. judges a similar and fairly conventional cast, there are differences. The prior political party affiliation of jurists does alter the way they exercise their policy-making discretion when the circumstances of a case give them room to maneuver. As we have noted, judges and justices who come from the ranks of the Democratic party have been somewhat more liberal than their colleagues from Republican ranks. This has meant, for one thing, that Democrats on the bench are more likely to favor government regulation of the economy—particularly when such regulation appears to benefit the underdog or the worker in disputes with management. In criminal justice matters, Democratic jurists are more disposed toward the motions made by defendants. Finally, in questions concerning civil rights and liberties, the Democrat on the bench tends to establish policies that favor a broadening position.

In the same context, we stress the important policy link between the partisan choice made by voters in a presidential election, the judges whom the chief executive appoints, and the subsequent policy decisions of these jurists. When voters make a policy choice in electing a conservative or a liberal to the presidency, they have a discernible impact upon the judiciary as well. Despite the many participants in the judicial selection process and the variety of forces that would thwart policy-oriented presidents (and governors) from getting "their kind of people" on the bench, it is still fair to say that to an impressive degree, chief executives tend to get the type of men and women they want in the judiciary.

In a speech made just prior to the 1984 presidential election, conservative Supreme Court justice William Rehnquist discussed this phenomenon with unusual candor. Although he was speaking primarily about the Supreme Court, his remarks pertain to the entire U.S. judiciary. There is "no reason in the world," said Rehnquist, why President Reagan should not attempt to "pack" the federal courts. The institution has been constructed in such a way that the public will, in the person of the president, have something to say about the membership of the Court and thereby indirectly about its decisions. Thus, Rehnquist felt, presidents may seek to appoint people who are sympathetic to their political and philosophical principles. After calling new judicial appointments "indirect infusions of the popular will," Rehnquist added that it "should come as no surprise" that presidents attempt to pack the courts with people of similar policy values, but "like murder suspects in a detective novel, they must have motive and opportunity."[1]

Judges as Manifestations of "Localism"

Another aspect of the values and orientations of the judges themselves has an impact upon their policy-making process: the attributes and mores that the judges carry with them from the region in which they grew up or in which they hold court. We have documented a wide variety of geographic variations in the way both trial and appellate jurists view the world and react to its demands. For example, we noted that on many policy issues Northern jurists have been more liberal than their colleagues in the South.

Not only does judicial policy making vary from one region of the land to another, but studies reveal that each of the circuits tends to be unique in the way its appellate and trial court judges administer the law and make decisions. The presence of significant state-by-state differences in U.S. trial judge behavior is further evidence that judges bring with them to the bench certain local values and orientations that subsequently affect their policy-making patterns.

Judges' Conceptions of Their Judicial Roles

In our discussion we noted three basic ways in which judges conceive of their roles vis-à-vis the policy-making process. At one end of the spectrum are the "lawmakers," who take a rather broad view of the judicial role. These jurists, often referred to as "activists" or "innovators," contend that they can and sometimes must make significant public policy when they render many of their decisions. At the other end of the spectrum are the "law interpreters," who take a very narrow view of the judicial function. Sometimes called "strict constructionists," they believe that norm enforcement rather than policy making is the only proper role of the judge. In between are the "pragmatists," or "realists," who contend that judging is primarily a matter of enforcing norms but that on occasion they can and must formulate new judicial policy.

Understanding the role conception that a judge brings to the bench (or develops on the bench) will not tell us much about the substantive direction of his or her policy making: it is possible to be a conservative activist just as well as a liberal activist. One can go out on a judicial limb and give the benefit of the doubt to the economic giant or to the underdog, to the criminal defendant claiming police brutality or to the police officer urging renewed emphasis on law and order. But a knowledge of the judges' role conceptions will tell us a good deal about whether they are more inclined to defer to the norms and policies set by others or to strike out occasionally and make policy on their own.

Summary

In attempting to learn about policy making by judges and its substantive direction, we have set forth a second factor that helps channel our thinking—namely, the values and orientations that the judges bring with them to the bench. Here we have suggested four items that are particularly relevant in this regard: (1) that America's judges come from the establishment's elite, a fact that serves to discourage radical policy making; (2) that judges' policy making is reflective of their partisan orientations and that of the executive who nominated them; (3) that policy decisions manifest the local values and attitudes that judges possess when they first put on the black robe; and (4) that judges will engage in more policy making if they bring to the bench a belief that it is right and proper for judges to act in this manner.

The Nature of the Judicial Decision-Making Process

Knowing how judges think and reason, how they are influenced in their decision making, provides us with a good clue about policy making by U.S. judges. Although this factor is inexorably intertwined with the first two we have outlined here, it is distinct enough to warrant a separate discussion. In the discussion of the legal subculture in Chapter 10, we examined the nature of the legal reasoning process that is at the very heart of the system of jurisprudence in America. We noted that this is essentially a three-step process described by the doctrine of precedent as follows: (1) similarity is seen between cases, (2) the rule of law inherent in the first case is announced, and (3) the rule of law is made applicable to the second case. Adherence to past precedents, to the doctrine of *stare decisis,* is also part and parcel of the legal reasoning process. Skillfully shaping and crafting the wisdom of the past, as found in previous court rulings, and applying it to contemporary problems is what this time-honored process is all about.

Decision making by collegial courts has some dimensions not inherent in the behavior of trial judges sitting alone. In Chapter 11 we examined several approaches that judicial scholars have used to get a theoretical handle on the way appellate court judges and justices think and act. One of these is small-group dynamics, an approach that sees the output of the appellate judiciary as being strongly influenced by three general phenomena: persuasion on the merits, bargaining, and the threat of sanctions.

Persuasion lies at the heart of small-group dynamics. It means quite simply that because of their training and values, judges are receptive to arguments based on sound legal reasoning, often spiced with relevant legal precedents. Both hard and anecdotal evidence exists to indicate that judicial policies are indeed influenced in the refining furnace of the judicial conference room.

Bargaining, too, molds the content and direction of judicial policy outputs. The compromises that are made among jurists—during the decision-making conference and while an opinion is being drafted—to satisfy the majority judges are almost always the product of bargaining. It's not that judges say to one another: "If you vote for my favorite judicial policy position, I'll vote for yours." Rather, a justice might phrase a "bargaining offer"—say, in a case dealing with the right of students to appeal adverse disciplinary rulings from a state university to the federal courts—more like this: "I don't agree with your opinion as it now stands permitting students to appeal *all* adverse disciplinary decisions to the local federal district court. That's just too liberal for me, and I don't approve of interfering in university affairs to that degree. However, I could go along with a majority opinion that permitted appeals in *really serious* disciplinary matters that might result in the permanent suspension of a student." The first justice must then decide how badly the colleague's vote is needed—badly enough to water down the opinion to include only cases dealing with permanent suspension rather than all cases, as in the original opinion? Such is the grist for the bargaining mill that generates judicial policies.

The sanctions that we discussed include a variety of items in the genteel arsenal of judicial weaponry. A judge's threat to take a vote away from the majority and to dissent may cause the majority judges to alter the content of a policy decision. A judge's willingness to write a strong, biting dissent is another sanction that occasionally causes a unity-conscious majority to consider policy changes in an opinion. The threat to go public is a third tactic that judges in collegial courts use to alter the policy course of other jurists. Public exposure of an objectionable internal court practice or stance is probably the least pleasant of the sanctions. Finally, we noted that chief justices of the U.S. and state supreme courts and their counterparts at the appellate and trial court levels all have singular opportunities to guide and shape the policy decisions of the courts. The status and options that are part of their unique leadership positions provide them an opportunity for crafting court policy if they have the desire and innate ability to make the most of it.

Besides small-group dynamics, we also looked at an approach to appellate court decision making known as attitude and bloc-formation analysis. This school of thought sees judges as possessing a stable set of attitudes that guide their policy choices. Such attitudes exist on civil rights and liberties issues, social issues (matters of voting and ethnic status), and economic questions dealing with the equal distribution of wealth. Justices with similar attitudes on these questions tend to vote in a similar manner on cases and thus form voting blocs. Scholars have used the techniques of content analysis of opinions (to find and measure attitudes), scaling, and bloc analysis to test this theory. Their research has borne some impressive fruit because it has been possible to demonstrate that members of the appellate judiciary do decide cases in accordance with consistent underlying value dimensions and that voting blocs do form and behave according to predictable patterns.

Fact pattern analysis competes effectively with the small-group approach and with attitude and bloc analysis to account for appellate judge behavior. As we have seen in Chapter 11, the fact pattern approach would explain the individual behavior of appellate court judges in terms of their response to key facts inherent in the cases. Unlike traditional scholars, who postulate that judges respond only to the *legal* facts of a case, the fact pattern school argues that the jurists are alert to a wide variety of extrajudicial factors, such as the race and gender of a defendant, or whether a petitioner's attorney was court-appointed or privately retained. This approach does not assume the existence (or nonexistence) of consistent patterns in the acceptance of facts or in decisions based on facts. Finally, the fact pattern scholars have used sophisticated mathematical equations to weigh the key facts they have identified and have learned the various fact combinations that have the maximum (and minimum) effect on each justice.

What does this third general factor—the nature of the judicial decision-making process—tell us about judicial policy making and its substantive direction? We would offer two observations. First, most policy making by judges is likely to be slow and incremental. Indeed, this is exactly what one would expect from a reasoning process that relies so heavily on respecting precedents and that places such emphasis on stability and continuity. The decision-making process of American judges does not lend itself to radical and abrupt departures from precedents and past behavior. Yet change does occur and new policies are made. But legal history suggests that American jurists have often "reformed to preserve," and that is a principle often associated with conservatism.

Second, an understanding of the judicial thought process and of the small-group dynamics of collegial courts does not in itself tell us anything about the substantive direction of a court's policy making. However, knowing which judges and justices are masters at persuasion, bargaining, and the use of sanctions does give us some insight into explaining and predicting the content of judicial policy decisions. If, on a given court, it is the conservatives who have developed a mastery of these tactics, then the bettor would do well to wager a few dollars on more conservative judicial decisions.

The Impact of Extraneous Influences

At this point there should be little doubt that the making and implementation of judicial policy decisions are influenced by a variety of actors and forces quite outside the courtroom. It is not just judges and law clerks with leather-bound casebooks and arguments by silver-tongued lawyers that affect the shaping and carrying out of judicial decisions. Into the calculus must also go such unwieldy variables as the values and ability of the chief executive, the will of Congress or the legislature, the temper of public opinion, the strength and ideological orientation of key interest groups, and the attitudes and goodwill of those called on to implement judicial decisions in the "real world."

The executive input into the making and implementation of key judicial decisions is considerable. As the policy choice of the citizenry in the past election, the chief executive has the opportunity to fill the courts with men and women who share the basic political and judicial philosophies of the administration. Once on the court, judges may be encouraged or discouraged in their policy making by the words and deeds emanating from the White House or the governor's mansion. For instance, the willingness of Presidents Eisenhower and Kennedy to use federal troops to help enforce judicial integration orders must have encouraged subsequent policy decisions regarding presidents' use of armed force to achieve this goal; conversely, President Bush's vocal opposition to the use of racial or gender quotas in employers' hiring practices or in the awarding of government contracts may have caused many federal judges to think at least twice before ordering or condoning the use of such quotas. The overall role of the chief executive in implementing judicial policy decisions was examined in Chapter 12.

Congress has an impact on the creation and nurturing of judicial policy decisions, just as the legislature does at the state level. In its power to establish most of the original and appellate jurisdiction of the federal judiciary, it has the capacity to determine the subject-matter arenas where judicial policy battles are fought. In its capacity to establish the number of courts and determine the financial support they will have, Congress can show its approval or displeasure regarding the third branch of government. By accepting or rejecting presidential nominees to the courts, the Senate helps to determine who the judicial decision makers will be and hence their value orientations. Finally, the implementation of many key judicial policy decisions is absolutely dependent on legislation that Congress must pass to make the ruling a meaningful reality for those affected by it. Had not Congress passed several key bills to implement the courts' desegregation orders (discussed in Chapter 12), integration of the public schools would be little more than a nice idea for those whom the rulings were intended to benefit.

Public opinion also has a role to play in this policy-making process—not an outrageous prospect for a nation that calls itself a democracy. In rendering key policy decisions, judges can hardly be oblivious to the mood and values of the citizenry of which they themselves are a part. Indeed, in many policy areas (such as obscenity, desegregation, and legislative apportionment), judges have actually been ordered by the Supreme Court to take the local political and social climate into consideration when they tender their rulings. The support or opposition of the public is often a key variable in determining whether a judge's orders are carried out in the spirit as well as the letter of the law.

Interest-group activity is another thread in the tapestry of judicial policy making. Such organizations often provide the president (or a state governor) with the names of individuals whom they support for judicial office, and they lobby against those whose judicial values they consider suspect. They often provide the vehicle for key judicial decisions by instigating legislation, by sponsoring test cases, and by giving legal and financial aid to those litigants whose cases they favor. We have seen (in Chapter 12) how they can thwart implementation of judicial decisions or help carry them out more effectively.

The final group of extraneous forces consists of those individuals and organizations that are expected to implement the judicial policy decision on a day-by-day basis out on the street: the police officer who is asked to be *sure* that the accused understand their legal rights; the physician who must certify that a requested abortion is *really* in the mental health interests of the pregnant woman; the personnel officer at a state institution who could readily find some technicality for refusing to hire a minority applicant; or the censor on the town's movie review board who is told that nudity and obscenity are not synonymous but who doesn't want to believe it. It is the values, motivations, and actions of such individuals that we must consider if we are to understand fully the judicial policy-making process. Their good-faith support of a judicial policy decision is vital to making it work; their indifference or opposition may cause the judge's ruling to die aborning.

It has been our intention in this chapter to get some grip on the slippery handle of policy making by American judges. Although many more questions have been raised than answered, perhaps we know a little better now at least where to search for some answers. If we want to learn the conditions that allow for bold policy making, and if we want some clue as to the direction that policy making will take, here is where we must focus our attention: on the nature of the case or controversy that can properly be brought into court; on the values and orientations of the jurists who preside over these courts; on the precise nature of the decision-making process of American judges; and, finally, on a variety of extraneous actors and forces whose values and effects filter into the American judicial process from beginning to end.

NOTE

1. "Rehnquist Says It's OK for a President to Pack High Court," *Houston Chronicle,* October 19, 1984, A3.

Index